CONTEMPORARY AMERICAN PLAYS

CONTEMPORARY AMERICAN PLAYS

EDITED WITH AN INTRODUCTION UPON RECENT AMERICAN DRAMA

BY

ARTHUR HOBSON QUINN

PROFESSOR OF ENGLISH, UNIVERSITY OF PENNSYLVANIA;
EDITOR OF "REPRESENTATIVE AMERICAN PLAYS"

CHARLES SCRIBNER'S SONS

NEW YORK   CHICAGO   BOSTON

C

TO THE MEMORY OF MY FATHER
WHO TAUGHT ME TO LOVE THE THEATRE

PREFACE

The friendly reception accorded to my volume of
Representative American Plays in 1917 has encouraged me
to present in this collection five of the most significant
plays of their types that have been produced since 1917
and that are available for publication. In preparing
such a collection the difficulties are obvious—the main
purpose of the book, to make accessible American plays
to the student both in college and school and to the general reader, demands that a majority of the plays shall be
published for the first time. Yet since the study should
be comparative if it is to be valuable, the main types of
drama must be represented. It is a source of great
pleasure to the editor that the generous responses from
playwrights, publishers, and producers has made it possible for him to follow so closely his original choice of the
five plays. The reasons for this selection are to be found
in detail in the introductions to the several plays and in
the General Introduction, which first appeared as an
article in *Scribner's Magazine* for July, 1922, and is here
reprinted through the courtesy of that magazine. In
brief: *Why Marry?* represents social comedy; *The Emperor Jones*, romantic tragedy; *Nice People*, the comedy
dealing with present social conditions; *The Hero*, domestic tragedy; and *To the Ladies!* domestic comedy.

The plays in this volume are arranged in the order of
their first performance.

The Emperor Jones is the only one that has been printed
in its present form, and the editor is indebted to the

courtesy of its publishers, Messrs. Boni and Liveright, for permission to reprint it here. *Why Marry?* is here presented in the acting version, which has been prepared especially for this collection by Mr. Williams and which differs materially from the reading version issued by Charles Scribner's Sons, who have cordially consented to the use of the play in this form. *Nice People*, *The Hero*, and *To the Ladies!* are published for the first time. The editor acknowledges with pleasure the interest which Mr. Williams, Mr. O'Neill, Miss Crothers, Mr. Emery, Mr. Kaufman, and Mr. Connelly have taken in the project. Through that interest he is able to present facts in the special introductions to the different plays which add greatly to their value for purposes of study. It is hoped that the "Topics for Discussion" may be useful in stimulating and guiding analysis of the plays both in individuals and in groups. For wider reading in America drama, a list of the recent collections has been made. It has seemed to the editor unnecessary to repeat in this volume his bibliographies, published elsewhere. The main thing, after all, both for the student and the general reader, is to read those American plays that are truly representative of a national drama that is only beginning to receive its due recognition.

CONTENTS

THE SIGNIFICANCE OF RECENT AMERICAN DRAMA

In view of the interesting and important developments in our native drama during the past few years, it is depressing to the close student of that field of art to read the patronizing or superficial treatments of the subject that have recently been permitted circulation. An example may be found in an article by Melchoir Lengyel, the Hungarian author of *The Czarina*, to which travesty of history Miss Doris Keane has descended, in company with its adaptor, Mr. Edward Sheldon, from the latter's own brilliant vivification of the past in *Romance*. M. Lengyel naïvely remarks that "should any one ask me what the world has gained from the work of the American playwright, I might recall several well-written dramas and comedies and remember their titles more easily than the names of their authors." He might at least have had the tact to remember the name of the adaptor of his play, a dramatist greater than he, whose tragic illness has robbed the American stage of one of its most promising playwrights. For the creator of *Romance* has illustrated again the fact that the shots of the Concord minutemen have not been the only American products that have been "heard round the world."

It is interesting to remember that it was just a century ago that Sydney Smith uttered his famous query, "In the four quarters of the globe, who reads an American book or goes to an American play?" in blissful ignorance of the crowds that had thronged Drury Lane a year before to witness John Howard Payne's great tragedy of *Brutus*. Foreign criticism is a bit more enlightened now than in 1820, or than it was even forty years ago, when Mr. William Archer solemnly lectured Bronson Howard

NOTE.—In speaking of playwrights and actors, professional names have been used.

for vulgarity in *Saratoga*, when the lines to which he ob-
jected were not in the play at all, but had been inserted
by the British adaptor! It is, perhaps, idle to expect
an Hungarian or an English critic to know thoroughly
the work of American playwrights when our native critics
are so prone to discriminate in their judgments in favor of
exotic products, especially if these are a bit peculiar,
and if the critic's appreciation implies on his part a broad
or even deep knowledge of Continental drama.

As for popular appreciation, the condition is even more
discouraging. If one speaks about the encouragement
of American drama to that irritating personage "the
man in the street," whose apprehension should certainly
have been sharpened long ago by the complexities of
traffic, he will inquire blankly, "Why should the American
drama be encouraged?" and will return contentedly to
those matters that are not for him empty of concern.
But it does concern him, and vitally. Beside the intellectual and artistic life of a nation, its commercial and
industrial achievements are but incidents, and there is
no vehicle so powerful and so competent to carry the
meaning of America to our assimilated and our unassimi-
lated population as the drama. To provide that drama,
notwithstanding M. Lengyel's ignorance, there are more
than thirty playwrights who have produced on the professional stage in the last five years plays that are worthy
of consideration. When Winthrop Ames offered a prize
in 1913 for the best American play, seventeen hundred
manuscripts were submitted in the competition. Quan-
tity production means little, of course, but before turning
to an examination of the recent work of American playwrights, it is necessary to emphasize the often-forgotten
truth that an artist needs not only proper remuneration
but also proper appreciation if he is to do his best work.
So long as producer and audience consider it appropriate
that the name of an actor shall be blazoned in letters a
foot high, while the name of the dramatist who has provided him with his thoughts and emotions shall be either
printed in letters one-tenth the size or omitted altogether,
the playwright is not to be blamed if he writes his play
with an actress rather than high art in mind. The work-

ers are here, the themes are here, and I believe the public is here, but it must be taught to think in terms of the dramatist.

As I have said, the courageous band of those who have been struggling against odds for the right of creative expression is not a small one. Of the generation that began to write in the nineteenth century, Mr. Augustus Thomas, Mr. William Gillette, Mr. David Belasco, Mr. Langdon Mitchell, and Mr. John Luther Long are happily still with us. Mr. Thomas has written four plays within the last five years, but, with the exception of one fine scene in *The Copperhead*, he has not given us anything to match *Arizona*, *The Witching Hour*, or *As a Man Thinks*. In his last play, *The Dream Maker*, Mr. Gillette gave us only at rare intervals his significant contribution of the calm, cool man of action with whom he thrilled us in *Secret Service* or *Held by the Enemy*. Mr. Belasco has contented himself with adaptations like *Kiki*, which, brilliant as they are, lie outside our province, or with revivals of *Peter Grimm* or *The Easiest Way*. If he would only once again provide the magic mould of construction into which the rich imagination of Mr. Long could pour another *Adrea* or *Madame Butterfly!* And if Mr. Mitchell would only write another social comedy like *The New York Idea!*

There is a younger generation, speaking in terms of achievement, whose work is included within the century that has just come of age. Mr. Percy MacKaye, the apostle of community drama; Miss Rachel Crothers, talented and practical, to see one of whose dress rehearsals is a theatrical treat; Mr. Booth Tarkington, whose comedies please but do not always satisfy, for he seems constantly on the verge of the very fine thing and just misses it; Mr. James Forbes, whose progress from *The Chorus Lady* to *The Famous Mrs. Fair* is one of the most encouraging steps in our recent dramatic history; Mr. A. E. Thomas, who insists on drawing gentlemen and gentlewomen without over-encouragement; Mr. Eugene Walter, whose craftsmanship is of a high order, and who may some day select material more worthy of him and treat it more sincerely; Mr. George M. Cohan, playwright and producer, who has developed the farce to a point where he alone seems to know how to keep it; Mr. Winchell Smith, who has a definite programme of presenting clean, wholesome, and entertaining comedies that play over the surface of life with a lively humor, and who has had his overwhelming reward. This group includes playwrights who have had produced a number of plays and whose manner and method are established. Equally well established are the methods of such a dramatist as Miss Josephine Preston Peabody, who gave us one stage success in *The Piper*, and who, it is hoped, will give us more.

There is a still younger group, again speaking in terms of stage life rather than of the calendar, whose methods are not so well defined, and who, in consequence, cannot be so easily characterized. Among these are Mr. Eugene O'Neill, Miss Zoë Akins, Mr. Jesse Lynch Williams, Miss Zona Gale, Miss Susan Glaspell, Mr. Gilbert Emery, Mr. Thompson Buchanan, Mr. Porter Emerson Browne, Mr. Philip Moeller, Miss Clare Kummer, Mr. George Middleton, Mr. Edwin Milton Royle, Mr. Channing Pollock, Mr. Austin Strong, Mr. Arthur Richman, Miss Gilda Varesi, Mr. Percival Wilde, Mr. John T. McIntyre, Mr. Frank Craven, Mr. William Anthony McGuire, Mr. George S. Kaufman, Mr. Marc Connelly, Mr. Owen Davis, Mr. J. H. Benrimo, and Mr. Henry Myers.

The list might have been made longer, without difficulty, but writers of musical and sentimental comedy, of "crook" melodrama, and of "thrillers" have been omitted—verily they have their own reward! And, on the other hand, if I have assumed the rôle of prophet in a few cases, I firmly believe the authors of *The Hero*, *Ambush*, *A Young Man's Fancy*, and *The First Fifty Years* will justify me.

It will be most helpful in a study of our recent drama to treat the subject, not by an appraisal of the relative merits of the individual playwrights, but from the point of view of the motives treated, the dramatic types, and the *locale* of the plays. In this way the significance of the work of the dramatists will, it is hoped, become most apparent, and since it seems best to confine our survey to the plays of the three years 1919–22, with special emphasis upon those of the season of 1921–22, the number of plays by any one author will not be large. It would not be relatively so profitable to extend our survey farther back. War conditions made the seasons of 1917–18 and 1918–19 unrepresentative, and outside of Mr. Thomas's stirring war play, *The Copperhead*, Mr. Williams's brilliant social comedy, *Why Marry?*, Mr. Moeller's artistic historical play, *Molière*, and Mr. MacKaye's exquisite masque, *The Evergreen Tree*, it is difficult to remember any real contribution to dramatic writing, although Mr. Bacon's *Lightnin'* has its importance as the successor of *Rip Van Winkle* in motive, and as probably the most popularly successful American play on record. *Why Marry?* has been so well analyzed by its author in the special introduction to that play, that it is unnecessary to treat it further here.

An apparent paradox occurs in the relations of dramatic and theatrical history in these three years. The general failure of the season 1921–22 from the standpoint of the box-office has become such a commonplace of conversation "on the Rialto" that it is unnecessary to do more than mention it here, but the declining curve in theatrical prosperity has run in a contrary direction to that of dramatic achievement. There were twice as many plays worth discussing in the season of 1921–22 as there were in the season of 1919–20. The reason for this apparent paradox is not far to seek. While business is good, long runs are plentiful; when many plays fail, opportunities are offered for new ones which might never have been given a chance under more favorable circumstances. It is interesting to note how theatrical history repeats itself, and how, almost a century ago, when the theatrical priority passed from Philadelphia to New York, never to return, the desperate conditions of the theatres in Philadelphia gave an opportunity to the playwrights of that city which brought about one of the greatest periods in our drama, and gave Edwin Forrest *Metamora*, *The Gladiator*, and *Jack Cade*.

There must be one exception made to the topical rather than the individual treatment of our recent playwriting. For the three seasons under discussion, and especially

for the season of 1921–22, the dominating figure is that
of Mr. Eugene O'Neill. Just as the outstanding event
of the season of 1919–20 was the production of *Beyond
the Horizon*, and of the season of 1920–21 the productions
of *The Emperor Jones* and *Diff'rent*, so the most significant
events in the season of 1921–22 were the performances of
The Straw, *Anna Christie*, *The Hairy Ape*, and *The First
Man*. To have had eight plays produced in three years
with only one real failure, *Gold*, which lasted only thir-
teen days in June, 1921, is an achievement scarcely par-
alleled in dramatic history. To have achieved this result without altering his own standards to accord to
popular fancy or pseudo-critical analysis places Mr. O'Neill
in a class by himself. Previous to the production of *Beyond the Horizon* he had been known as the author of one-
act plays of the sea, and of *Chris*, a play one of whose elements reappeared in *Anna Christie*. But with *Beyond the
Horizon* he took his place as a dramatist who deals with the
fundamental motives of human life, of love between man
and woman, or of man for man, and of the preservation of
individual integrity. He has pictured with rare skill the
striving of the individual soul against the crushing adverse
forces of fate, or the insistent clutch of circumstances, or
the progress of disease and death, or the overmastering impulse of the forces of nature, personified in *Anna Christie* as
"that old davil, the sea." His audiences listen spellbound
while he violates with success the so-called laws of dramatic
technique. The unities of space and time go by the board,
even the mechanical unity of action vanishes as it did at
the touch of the great Elizabethans, but for these Mr.
O'Neill has substituted a higher unity of action, which
might perhaps better be called a unity of impression. This
unity is gained through the power of the dramatist to fuse
all the utterances and objects of the stage, by the aid of
sympathetic actors, into the expression of the motive the
dramatist wishes to convey.

In *The Emperor Jones* the motive is that of terror, and
the problem is to bring that emotion into the conscious-
ness of the negro emperor's character in such a way that
the audience identifies itself with him through the deepen-
ing stages of that terror, and, consequently, enters into

that sympathy which, if secured, means dramatic triumph.
"Sympathy" is used in its broadest sense; one may not
like the negro tyrant and grafter, who has dominated his
subjects by his cleverness and good luck, but one can truly
enter into his motives and say with the British smuggler
at the end: "'E's a better man than the lot o' you put
together." Masterly is the way in which the insurgent
negroes are kept out of sight until the last scene, and
their approach indicated only by the insistent beat of
the tom-tom. This sound, continued and intensified
throughout the entire pursuit of "the Emperor," produces
an effect upon the audience akin to the knocking of the
Scottish thanes upon the gate in *Macbeth*, and when it
is combined with the effect upon the sense of sight produced by the forest through which the negro staggers
in the hopeless circle toward his doom, the result is one
of the most impressive lessons in stage-craft the English-
speaking stage has received. For the interpretation of a
motive like this, monologue secures just the unity necessary, and all the diatribes levelled against the monologue by teachers of dramatic technique fade into that
obscurity which awaits those theories that obstruct the
progress of the original artist. Monologue has been
tabooed on account of the lack of variety, but variety is
obtained in *The Emperor Jones* through the varying
shades in the intensity of terror, and through the chal-
lenging idea of taking the negro back through the stages
of his prenatal racial life.

It is the same unity of impression which ties together
the scenes of Mr. O'Neill's latest success, *The Hairy Ape*,
produced at the Provincetown Theatre in March, 1922.
Here there is more variety of place, and monologue is
employed in only one scene. The central character here
is an individual, struggling against social and industrial
injustice—a stoker in a ship, who feels that he is a force
that drives, he "belongs"—while the passengers, including the daughter of the president of the line, are only incidents who do not "belong." The scene in the stoke-
hole, with its fiery furnaces, in which the "Yank," as he
is called, and Mildred Douglas, the neurotic *poseur*, are
brought face to face, is among the unforgetable stage

pictures of our time. With true economy, the meeting is over almost at once, but there has been time to fix in the Yank's soul her look of horror, which sends him out seeking for revenge upon her and her kind. Rejected alike by the symbolic procession on Fifth Avenue and by the I. W. W., he goes to the Zoological Gardens, to the real Hairy Ape, the gorilla, whom he frees in order that they may work out their brotherhood together. Simply and naturally the gorilla chokes him and flings him into his cage, then saunters on about his own affairs! The sympathy of the audience here goes out to the Yank because of his dim striving at first for better things—the tragedy lies in his failure to find the understanding to match his physical strength. Mr. O'Neill is no doctrinaire, and he is concerned with painting a section of life rather than teaching a lesson, but surely the significance of *The Hairy Ape* cannot escape the thinking observer. Here is the force that, properly controlled and guided, may keep the world driving on. Unguided, it is like a wheel from which the belt has slipped—it may do incalculable harm. But it is no tragedy of futility, as *Liliom* was, it is a tragedy of misguided power. Its selection for representation at the Odéon in Paris as the most significant recent American play is refreshing to those who have understood its real merit.

It is, after all, as an apostle of hope, of spiritual success attained through sacrifice, that Mr. Eugene O'Neill has the greatest significance. I am aware that this statement will be challenged, but only by those who have failed to see or understand his plays. It is unfortunate that *Beyond the Horizon* was not played as he wrote it, with the last scene on the hilltop, for there the real motive of the play was established. As played, the scene closed in the sordid farmhouse, the voice of Andy Mayo denouncing Ruth, his sister-in-law, because she had not lied in time to Robert, so that he might die believing she had loved him. It brought the strong love of the brothers to the front, the love that passed the love of either for the woman who had wrecked both their lives, and it touched that love more truly than it had been touched on our stage since Boker's *Francesca da Rimini;*

but that, after all, is not the great motive of the play. It is Robert Mayo's aspiration, his visions of the great adventure "beyond the horizon"—which he had dreamed as a boy at the window at sunset, and which he had given up at the call of Ruth's passion for him. When he knows his doom, he makes one last effort to reach the hilltop, and when Andy and Ruth find him there and struggle to contain their grief, he says, "in a voice which is suddenly ringing with the happiness of hope: 'You mustn't feel sorry for me. It's ridiculous! Don't you see I'm happy at last—because I'm making a start to the far-off places—free—free! Freed from the farm—free to wander on and on—eternally! Even the hills are powerless to shut me in now.' Then he raises himself on his elbow, his face radiant, and points to the horizon. 'Look! Isn't it beautiful beyond the hills? I can hear the old voices, calling me to come—and this time I'm going— I'm free! It isn't the end. I've won to my trip—the right of release—beyond the horizon! Oh, you ought to be glad—glad—for my sake!'"

It is this same message of hope that made the last act of *The Straw*, as played by Mr. Otto Kruger in the part of Stephen Murray and Miss Margalo Gillmore as Eileen Carmody, a memorable occasion. *The Straw* has been neatly classified as a "tuberculosis play," but those who saw it, with every part nicely adjusted by Mr. George C. Tyler to the character, realized how true is Mr. O'Neill's stage instinct. They were real people on that stage— the mere finding of Miss Lamont for the minor part of Mrs. Brennan was a managerial triumph—but, after all, it was that great last scene that showed the dramatist's power. As I watched Stephen Murray battle with all his strength for the right to hope against all odds for the happiness of the girl he has just realized he loved, and saw how that great power of his love routed both science and human doubt, I could not help remembering the words of Doctor Horace Howard Furness, speaking of *Romeo and Juliet:* "This is no tragedy. They knew they loved each other. What happened afterward is a detail." And the discussion that has raged about Mr. O'Neill's "unhappy endings" seemed more futile than ever.

Mr. O'Neill is not concerned with "making" any kind of ending. The endings form themselves in his capable hands out of the characters and the situations. Given Anna Christie as she was, with the sea calling in her blood, and Mat Burke as he was, and the ending of that play is inevitable. There has to be the saving grace of the Celt in one's constitution to conceive Mat Burke or to understand him. He is just the kind who would believe he could lift a girl like Anna Christie out of her past environment, and it is just the mixture of reverence for an ideal of womanly purity and of superlative personal conceit which meet in him that make it an even chance that he may succeed. If he does, it will be because it is out of his like, highly spiritualized, that the saints are made— if he fails, we may be sure he will throw the failure up to her!

None of Mr. O'Neill's plays, except *Diff'rent*, leaves us depressed. If there has been a tragedy, it has been worth while; if the individual has been conquered, he has won our respect for his struggles, and our feeling is that of exaltation. This fact is Eugene O'Neill's strongest claim to be considered a great playwright. I happened to see *Beyond the Horizon* and *Jane Clegg* on succeeding days, and the contrast was striking in this regard. Both recorded a marriage that was a failure, but what a difference! Careful as Mr. Ervine's workmanship is, the effect of *Jane Clegg* is depression, for there is no one on the stage about whom one really cares. Art must have a worthy object, and suffering alone cannot win respect. That is the essential flaw in *Diff'rent*, also, for there is no lift in the tragedy there. It is interesting, however, to note that *Diff'rent* was accorded a flattering reception in London when it was put on at the Everyman Repertory Theatre.

In *The First Man* the lift comes in the triumph of the mother across the dividing line of death in the person of the little child, who wins his way into his father's heart against the conspiracy of all the chattering relatives in a small New England town. *The First Man* showed Mr. Eugene O'Neill's power in a direction not hitherto very apparent, the ability to give us rapid clever conver-

sation which in itself satirizes the social values of a deca-
dent patrician class. There are curious lapses in *The First
Man*, but we leave the new Jayson content in the care of
his great-aunt, a lovable and spirited old gentlewoman,
long to be remembered.

Having violated our principle of treatment as soon as
it was established, in order to analyze the work of a remarkable and individual playwright, let us return to
that principle and consider the topics which have been
treated significantly by American playwrights in the last
three years. The theme which has appealed to by far
the largest number of dramatists is that of married life,
and this preference was especially evident in the season of
1921–22. Whether the success of *Why Marry?* has been
responsible for this frequent treatment of conjugal relations, or whether it is really true that lovers become
interesting only when they are married, there can be
no doubt that the interrelations of husband and wife
have been carefully studied and brilliantly treated on
our recent stage. The drama presupposes conflict, and
so the majority of the plays represent the struggle of
wills, passions, or desires of men and women. Sometimes
this conflict is carried through relentlessly to a tragic or
sordid end, as in Mr. Thomas's *Nemesis*, Miss Akins's
Déclassée, Mr. Richman's *Ambush*, Miss Glaspell's *The
Verge*, or Mr. Myers's *The First Fifty Years*.

In fidelity to life, *Ambush* was the best of this group.
In a small suburban New Jersey town Walter Nichols, a
clerk, tries to live an upright, decent life. His wife and
daughter do not sympathize with his ideals, and the
latter, through her love for pleasure, ruins him and breaks
his spirit, till he is forced to accept help from the man who
is degrading her. In a speech that will remain long in
the memory, Mrs. Jennison, a friend, tells Walter how the
countless little facts of life lie in ambush to prevent him
from keeping his ideals. There is little lift in *Ambush*,
although Mr. Frank Reicher's portraiture of Walter
Nichols secured our full sympathy for him, but it belongs
to that field of effort in which Ibsen and Hardy shone,
and it made us wish that the Theatre Guild would devote

its powerful energies more frequently to the production
of native drama.

In *The First Fifty Years* Mr. Myers tried an interesting
experiment. There are but two characters in the play,
Martin and Anne Wells, and we see them in seven scenes,
beginning with the home-coming after the honeymoon,
and continuing, through various anniversaries, until
the golden wedding. The marriage is a failure, being
based solely on physical attraction, and there are no children to hold them together. After a violent quarrel
they vow never to speak to each other again, and so the
fourth scene is played entirely in pantomime, until at
the end Anne gives way to her grief in one broken-hearted
cry. Miss Clare Eames and Mr. Tom Powers gave a
remarkable performance in this play, which is interesting
mainly in its technique. That a dialogue would hold the
attention of an audience for an entire evening would
have seemed hardly possible until *The Emperor Jones* had
held it by a monologue. But *The First Fifty Years*,
while there are certain curious flaws in the plot, remains
one of the recent significant plays. Its picture of marriage is a warning, however, rather than an inspira-
tion.

In another group a way out of the difficulty is indicated.
In *Beyond the Horizon* the cherished dreams have paid for
the suffering; in *The First Man* the wife's spirit lives in
her child; in Miss Akins's *Daddy's Gone a Hunting*, divorce leaves inconclusive what promised in the first
two acts to be a very fine play; in *The Famous Mrs. Fair*
the danger to their daughter brings the husband and
wife together in a natural way.

Classification is useful mainly in calling attention to
variety, and various indeed are the reasons why marriage
is represented on the stage as unsuccessful. It is interesting to notice that it is usually the wife who revolts. The
husband tries it in *Daddy's Gone a Hunting* and in *Enter
Madame*, Miss Gilda Varesi's brilliant comedy, but he
gets little sympathy, and it is interesting to note that both
these plays were written by women. The woman revolts
more frequently, of course, because feminism is in the
air, and probably because of some association of the mar-

riage service with the word "obey."   In two very interesting plays, which deserved better fates than the season of
1921-22 meted out to them, Mr. Owen Davis's *The Detour* and Miss Crothers's *Everyday*, a wife revolts for the
sake of her daughter against the father's tyranny.   Helen
Hardy, in *The Detour*, has saved for years to give her
daughter an opportunity to become a painter.   Her
husband demands that she sacrifice this hope for the sake
of his farm, and she prepares to leave him.   The daughter
has really no great talent and Helen stays on the farm,
her money going to her daughter's lover to save him from
ruin and make their marriage possible.   But Helen starts
saving again, for a possible granddaughter, and, despite
her husband's laughter, she stands, as the curtain goes
down—"her face glorified, looking out into the future,
her heart swelling with eternal hope."   Helen Hardy is
a real character.   She appeals strongly because her revolt
is not selfish—she is the protest, too, of imagination
against the deadening life she knows.   "I get so tired,"
she remarks, "of sayin' nothin' but just exactly what's
so and listenin' to folks that don't ever mean the least
mite more'n they say, or the least mite less!"   In *Every-
day* a wife who has suffered mental and moral beatings
all her life revolts for her daughter's sake, and here there
is no reconciliation—the door closes on the girl just before the curtain falls, and the wife faces her husband
unflinchingly, with only his revenge to fill her otherwise
empty life.

   To make drama there must, of course, be another
interest which interferes with the current of marital
happiness.   In *Daddy's Gone a Hunting*, *Enter Madame*,
or in the revival of *He and She*, one of Miss Crothers's
best plays, the artistic career of husband or wife is intro-
duced as the conflicting motive.   It is interesting that it
did not have popular success except in the lively comedy
of *Enter Madame*, probably because to the average audience the artistic urge seems a bit remote.   For much the
same reason the scientific interest of Curtis Jayson, in
The First Man, seemed insufficient as a cause for his
hatred of his unborn child.   Much more coherent was
Mrs. Fair's restlessness after her military career abroad.

Most obvious, of course, as the disturbing element is the presence of another passion.   But while it was present in *Beyond the Horizon, Nemesis, The First Fifty Years, The Verge, The Hero, The Famous Mrs. Fair, Daddy's Gone a Hunting, Enter Madame, The First Year, Déclassée,* and *The Bad Man,* to mention only the most interesting of the treatments, in fully half of these it was but a minor motive.   It would seem that the institution itself has become a target for attack, which ran to the last extreme in *The Verge,* a very unconvincing experiment in pathology, which even the fine acting of Miss Wycherly could not save.   The serious treatments of marriage provided some very interesting human studies, but they left the thoughtful observer with the opinion that the institution was likely to continue.   They also left him with the strange old conclusion that if two people of like tastes and mutual forbearance marry and have children, the marriage will be a success, and that under other conditions it may not be.

If the serious treatments of marriage have been on the whole a bit depressing, there have been some delightful moments in which "the frank muse of comedy laughed in free air."   *Enter Madame* has carried its message of joy across the water, and hardly needs dissection here. *The First Year,* by Mr. Frank Craven, has attracted thousands by its faithful and amusing picture of life, though why the young wife was alone endowed with her excruciating intonation while the rest of the cast were permitted to speak English, is still a puzzle to at least one of that play's many auditors.   But it remained for two of the younger dramatists, Mr. George Kaufman and Mr. Marc Connelly, to provide in *Dulcy* and *To the Ladies!* two of the brightest spots in the season's experience.   *Dulcy,* although laid at a week-end party near New York City, is not intended to be a social comedy, for there is no attempt at contrasting social values, but it is the comedy of people moving in social relations, and it dramatizes without mercy but without bitterness the havoc a stupid, well-meaning woman can make of her husband's prospects.   There is not a dull moment in it for the audience, for her dulness is made entertaining, an accom-

plishment worthy of imitation by certain contemporary
novelists and dramatists.

Even better than *Dulcy* in some ways was its companion
piece, *To the Ladies!* This play has been largely advertised for its satire upon the "public banquet," and that
scene is indeed extremely well done. But what makes
the play much more significant is its representation,
simply and with sincerity, of the love of a clever young
wife for her conceited but not very able husband. The
playwrights have seized upon the great fact that the most
precious things in life are our illusions, especially those
we begin to suspect ourselves, and young Elsie Beebe
has to keep up her own faith in her husband as well as
save him from the awkward situations into which accident or his own incompetency has brought him. It is
not too much to say that in the climax of the play, when
Elsie rises at the dinner-table and makes the speech that
saves her husband's career, it was the picture of the
glorified love that impelled and sustained her that swept
the audience with the thrill that comes rarely in these
sophisticated days. Part of the thrill was for the remarkable acting of Miss Helen Hayes, but, after all, the
part was there. And lines like "nearly all the great
men have been married; it cannot be merely a coincidence"
make us hope that Mr. Kaufman and Mr. Connelly will
not write too much and too fast, for the stage needs them.
A play like *To the Ladies!* treating marriage without malice, without bitterness, with reticence and with sympathy,
is worth a dozen morbid analyses of mismated couples,
for it is nearer truth and it creates beauty, and therefore
it is better art.

Closely allied to the theme of marriage is that of the
relations of parents and children; in fact, as in *The Detour*, *Everyday*, *Ambush*, and *The Famous Mrs. Fair*, the
themes are so interwoven that separate discussion is
unnecessary. Usually the play concerns the revolt of a
daughter, this theme receiving its most striking treatment in *Anna Christie*. The sons are evidently not expected to revolt, except for comedy, and in *Clarence* and
Thank You they provide some agreeable moments. It
was extremely interesting to compare these plays with

Miss Grace George's sympathetic adaptation of Paul
Geraldy's *Les Noces d'Argent*, under the title of *The Nest*.
The theme of filial indifference as compared to filial re-
volt was treated here with quiet distinction.

The feminine revolt has not been limited to those res-
tive under the yoke of wedlock.   In Miss Gale's *Miss
Lulu Bett*, Mr. Tarkington's *Intimate Strangers*, and Mr.
A. E. Thomas's *Only 38*, the spinster or the widow has
asserted her rights and routed those who stood in her
way.   *Miss Lulu Bett* had the greatest power of charac-
terization, but there was a charm about *Only 38* in the
beginning which made us sorry when the appearance of
the college glee-club in the third act turned it into bur-
lesque.   Mr. Pollock's performance of Mr. Sanborn, who
"has been among 'em," repaid one, however, for the rest
of the play, and raised the perennial question as to the
reason why the minor characters should so often be better than the major ones.   These plays might also be classified as love-stories of maturity, and, indeed, the love-
story of youth seems to be remarkably absent from our
stage.   Perhaps that is why *Kempy*, the success of the
late season, met with so sympathetic a response.   This
play by Mr. J. C. Nugent and Mr. Elliott Nugent, despite
its evident imitation of *The First Year*, had a certain
charm in the boy and girl love-making.   Perhaps, also,
that is why Miss Clare Kummer printed the legend, "A
Love Story," on the programme of her *Mountain Man*, but
it is not the love-story that makes that play significant.
It is the sympathetic study of the North Carolina mountaineer, whose father had left his own family in disgust
at their intolerance and had brought up his boy on the
mountain.   Mr. Sidney Blackmer's interpretation of the
character of Aaron Winterfield, from his crude to his finished state after he returns from France, was masterly.
Miss Kummer had created in *Good Gracious, Annabelle!* a
comedy new to our stage, at least in recent times, one
somewhat akin to the French "vaudeville," but in *The
Mountain Man* she showed promise of doing something
much more important.   The plot of the play is weak,
but the conversation had her usual cleverness.   The quick
passage of time is illustrated again by the fact that the

motive of the "returned soldier" in this play seems already old-fashioned. The most significant studies of oversea service upon man or woman were *The Famous Mrs. Fair* and Mr. Gilbert Emery's *The Hero.* The failure of *The Hero* to run through the season was discouraging, for it is easily one of the best plays of recent years. It is a comparative study of two brothers, types of moral and physical heroism, and of their influence upon the wife of the older brother. This older brother, Andrew Lane, has sacrificed himself quietly to cover his brother's defalcations, while the younger, Oswald, returning with a heroic record from the war, shows himself to be entirely unchanged in his moral weakness. Mr. Emery's skill is shown clearly in the last act, when, after Oswald has absconded again with his brother's trust funds, he responds to the one call he knows, that of physical courage, and saves from death the little nephew he loves, at the cost of his own life. As Andrew sits with his child safe in his arms, prepared to face again the debt Oswald's theft has brought upon him, his wife, in an agony of remorse for the unfaithfulness that was in her heart, sobs out her belated appreciation of him. But he puts the praise aside. "Me? I'm just old Andy, I am—but Os—Os was a hero!" So many plays have started well, only to fade away into the obvious or the conventional in the last act, that *The Hero* remains a fit study in technique as well as a true picture of the unreconstruction of man.

It was twenty years after the Civil War before Mr. Gillette put the first successful war play on the stage in *Held by the Enemy.* Perhaps the Great War will have to wait that long until it becomes an established dramatic motive. But the disturbed social relations and conditions that have come in its train are a fit subject for drama, and playwrights have already begun to use them. Probably the most successful was Miss Crothers's *Nice People,* which draws unflinchingly a picture of the young man and woman who spend their lives in a mad search for pleasure. It may remain an open question whether the heroine of the drinking, dancing set of the first act could become the healthy, normal, outdoor girl of the last act, even through the influence of the clean-cut hero, but the dramatist may plead the even chance. *Nice People* suggests a comparison at once with *The National Anthem*, a later play by Mr. J. Hartley Manners. The English playwright laid the scene of his play in New York and in Paris, and brought his dissipated characters to tragedy. *The National Anthem* had the advantage of a remarkable presentation of the leading part by Miss Laurette Taylor, but Miss Crothers's play was more sincerely written, and she had a much keener sense of the limit of drunkenness as a source of intelligent interest on the stage.

Beside these presentations of the dissipated idle rich, *Ambush*, the picture of the poor girl's determined pursuit of pleasure, was more grim and stark in its tragic note. But the sympathy of the audience was not with her, as it was with the heroines of *Nice People* and *The National Anthem*, and in any case her material tragedy was to come. As a picture of a real situation in the domestic life of America, *Ambush* was a great achievement, and it is a pity it could not go on tour throughout the United States. For criticism of the mad rush for amusement at any cost is vitally needed, and even when it comes in the form of wild farce, like the season's most conspicuous popular success, *Six Cylinder Love*, it has its own place. It is a pity Mr. McGuire gave his farce-comedy that impossible title, for there were moments in the play when the hero, driven into dishonesty and ruin by the automobile and its accompaniments, spoke words of sincerity by which modern society might profit.

Description of our modern life on the stage has not been limited in its *locale*, though it has certain favorites. When a large city is the scene it becomes New York automatically, in such different plays as *Nemesis, Enter Madame, Nice People, Daddy's Gone a Hunting*, and *The First Fifty Years*, which was laid in Harlem. When a suburban town is needed, it is also likely to be near New York City, but whether the life is depicted seriously, as in *The Hero* and *Ambush*, or for the purpose of comedy, as in *Dulcy, To the Ladies! Kempy*, or *The Dream Maker*, it is still only background and does not really enter into the play. But when we come to those plays in which the setting forms an integral portion of the plot, we find them moving away from the metropolis. *The Detour* and *Beyond the Horizon* are laid in rural New York, and the motive of the play begins with the limitations of that life. There is a significance, too, in the laying of the scene of *Diff'rent* in a seafaring town of New England, and it was the powerful satire on the small New England patrician family that made *The First Man* so significant. Not so powerful, but very human and amusing, was the satire of the New England character in *Thank You*. The narrowness of vision and the petty tyranny of the board of trustees of a village church in that play are characteristic of hundreds of similar oligarchies, not limited to New England. The natives of a small New England village were well done in *The Wren* also, but the rest of that play of Mr. Tarkington's was too slight—or too subtle—to carry it long.

Even more characteristic, and meant to be, were the satiric treatments of the small town of the Middle West, such as *Miss Lulu Bett*, *The First Year*, *Everyday*, and the stage version of *Main Street*. Here the *locale* was very important, but it was to the credit of Miss Gale, Miss Crothers and Mr. Craven that they did not let it submerge the human interest of their characters. *Main Street* was even worse than the book, as might have been expected, for the story is essentially undramatic and all the adaptors did was to emphasize some of the most banal or tawdry features of the original. It is cheering, at least, to those hopeful of the American stage that the play did not succeed as well as the novel. Laid in the same territory and yet different from any of this group, *The Deluge* was an interesting treatment of a Middle Western town by a Swedish dramatist, Henning Berger, who gathered his experience of American life from 1892 to 1899, and wrote his play of *Syndafloden* after his return to Sweden. It has been played in Paris, Stockholm, Rome, Berlin, Moscow, and Budapesth, always retaining the American atmosphere, and was first produced here by Mr. Arthur Hopkins for a brief period in 1917. *The Deluge* is a study of the reaction of a group of human beings in a saloon, under the fear of death by drowning, when the better qualities of each come out against the background of their past loves or hatreds. Then when the danger is over the counter-reaction leaves them pretty much as they had been. It is a powerful play and took courage to produce.

As the playwrights went still farther afield for material, the characteristic note deepened. Just as Miss Kummer caught the right aspect of the North Carolina mountaineer in *The Mountain Man*, so Mr. A. E. Thomas's representation of the Virginia family with a long tradition of culture was the refreshing note in *Just Suppose*. And finally we reach the climax in the union of background and character portrayal in the West Indian forest of *The Emperor Jones*.

It is, of course, quite natural that our recent drama should be more limited in time than in space. Nearly all the plays are concerned with contemporary life, but at least four attempted with success to catch the flavor of the past. Mr. Arthur Richman gave us a charming love-story, laid in the seventies, in *Not So Long Ago*, and Miss Lilian Sabine's dramatization of *The Rise of Silas Lapham* for the Theatre Guild, recently produced in London, was a pure delight. Here the seventies came to life again upon the stage, and Silas Lapham met and faced his moral crisis as only an American of his type would have met it, the very greatness of his success as a man of business providing him with a substitute for the *noblesse oblige* of other days. The reticent and tender love-story of Tom Corey and Penelope Lapham and what the union of their two family stocks implied, provided quite a number of suggestive speculations upon the future of the republic.

The First Fifty Years portrays periods of considerable extent, since the play began in the seventies, but there was not the same brilliant effect that was present in one of the most interesting efforts of Miss Zoë Akins, *The Varying Shore*. Here is a play which truly "proceeds backward." Julie Venable is shown in a prologue through her effect upon others, especially upon Lawrence Sturgis, who has been faithful to her all his life. Then we see her in three stages of her career—first, in Paris in 1870, as

the mistress of Garreth Treadway, with her son's love-
story forcing her to face her past and its present compli-
cations; next, in New York in 1859, as the mistress of Joe
Leland, who is beginning to love another woman; third,
in Richmond in 1846, when as a girl of sixteen she has
had a love-affair with John Garrison, the father of the
boy who has appeared in the first act. In each situation
she runs true to type—reckless of consequences, she takes
what she wants and just as recklessly faces the consequences with courage and generosity. It is most interesting that, owing to some misguided criticism, the play
was changed so as to follow the chronological order, and
then happily replaced as the playwright wrote it. For
the order of sympathy proceeds here inversely to the order
of time. The audience likes Julie much more as the girl
of sixteen, refusing to be forced upon an unwilling husband, and declining to take advantage of Lawrence
Sturgis's chivalric offer, than it does as the sophisticated
woman of forty. Julie was triumphantly played by Miss
Elsie Ferguson, who surmounted the technical difficulties
caused by the necessity of playing with a partially new
set of characters, and therefore new actors, in each act.
But Miss Akins could take chances with technical difficulties, for she had a central motive, that of the moral
contrast, which rarely misses its aim. The generous,
lovable wanton and the generous, lovable drunkard have
appealed to the popular heart long before *Rip Van Winkle*
started on its century run, and will continue to appeal
when *Déclassée*, *The Varying Shore*, and *Lightnin'* are
only a memory. It is not only the theme, however, that
carried *The Varying Shore*. It is because that play appeals to the ever-present love of romance, and the playwright who can furnish romance has now his opportunity.
It is a pity Mr. Tyler did not select this last season instead of that of 1919–20 to produce Mr. McIntyre's *A
Young Man's Fancy*, one of the most exquisite dream
plays our stage has seen. Cannot the writers and producers of plays take a lesson from musical comedy, as
musical comedy takes lessons from them? *Marjolaine*,
for example, is a great success, and it deserves to be.
The lyrics of Brian Hooker, the book by Mrs. Cushing,

the music by Hugo Felix, all based on Mr. Parker's *Pomander Walk*, make a combination that is simply joy and youth and love and sunshine, and, moreover, is good art. We could not live, artistically speaking, on Marjo-laines; sorrow is needed on the stage as well as joy, but above and beyond everything else is sympathy. Human beings are just as willing to listen to a tragedy as to a comedy, and the tragedies have always outlasted the comedies of their day. Mr. Howells once gave the reason in *April Hopes* when he said:

It has been the experience of every one to have some alien concern come into his life and torment him with more anxiety than any affair of his own. This is, perhaps, a hint from the infinite sympathy which feels for us all that none of us can hope to free himself from the troubles of others, that we are each bound to each by ties, which for the most part we cannot per-ceive, but which, at the moment their stress comes, we cannot break.

Sympathy, however, usually goes out to the significant and to that only. The suffering and the joy on the stage must both be worth while. And, on the whole, the stu-dent of the American drama is hopeful, for much that is worth while is being accomplished. The very existence of the plays I have mentioned is encouraging, and only the professional plays have been touched. Outside of New York, in practically every college, in hundreds of schools, in many communities, the drama is being studied, plays are being produced, and plays are being written. Such an impulse as that started by Professor Koch in North Dakota, and now carried to North Carolina, where the folk-play is made and produced in its own birthplace, is of great significance. But all that is another story, and simply confirms the statement that the dramatic impulse is in the air we breathe. The best example of sustained interest in American playwrighting has suc-ceeded even against the competition of the "commercial theatre." Starting eight years ago with a group of ama-teurs and semi-professionals, The Provincetown Players, under the leadership of Mr. Eugene O'Neill, Miss Susan Glaspell, Mr. George Cram Cook, and Miss M. Eleanor Fitzgerald, have pursued the consistent policy of producing only American plays. They do not always hit the popular fancy and sometimes their selection is open to question, as in the case of *The Verge*, or not open at all, as in that of *The Hand of the Potter*, but their general purpose is as sincere as their success has been marked. And if they had done nothing but provide for Mr. Eugene O'Neill his opportunity, the movement would have been justified.

I am not one of those who condemn the "commercial theatre." It is a business as well as an art. But that it is inhospitable to the American playwright is not a fact. According to statistics given in the New York *Times* in June, 1922, there were, exclusive of musical comedies and revivals, one hundred and thirty-seven plays produced in New York City during the theatrical year. Of these, seventeen were English and nineteen French, and after allowing for the few other Continental plays, the vast majority remain to the credit of the native playwright. Mr. Hopkins, Mr. Tyler, Mr. Duncan, Mr. Belasco, Mr. Golden, Mr. Brady, Mr. Harris, Mr. Selwyn, and Mr. Cohan have all shown themselves willing to produce native plays, even by unknown writers. There is no lack of playwrights, of actors, or of producers—it is for the American public to decide whether its national drama is to fail or to succeed.

WHY MARRY?

A PLAY IN THREE ACTS

BY

JESSE LYNCH WILLIAMS

"Those who love each other truly, don't need anything to bring them together. The difficulty is to keep them apart."—*Act Second.*

Why Marry? is reprinted by special permission of the author. Applications for permission to perform this play should be addressed to the author in care of Charles Scribner's Sons.

WHY MARRY?

Jesse Lynch Williams, the author of *Why Marry?*, was born in Stirling, Illinois, August 17, 1871. He graduated from Princeton University in 1892, and his first book was his well-known volume of *Princeton Stories*, 1895. He has published about a dozen books. His best-known short story is *The Stolen Story* (1899), his best-known novel, *The Married Life of the Frederick Carrolls* (1910). Mr. Williams's first play was his dramatization of *The Stolen Story*, which opened in Providence, Rhode Island, in the spring of 1906 and was played two hundred times. After writing and producing two short plays, Mr. Williams began *Why Marry?* as fiction, but it soon became evident to him that it was better fitted for dramatic treatment. In view of the success, artistically and commercially, of *Why Marry?* it is interesting to read in the author's own words the accounts of its early history, taken from a personal letter to the editor, which he has received Mr. Williams's permission to publish.

It took me a long time, about three years, to make the kind of play out of it I wanted it to be. And then, when it was finished, it took an even longer time to make the managers see what kind of a play it was. I think it was submitted to about all of them and all of them refused to touch it. Nothing could have been luckier for me and for the play. It was written ahead of its time—*i. e.*, ahead of the public's time for such treatment of such ideas. Of course, if I had treated marriage sentimentally or salaciously, my play might have arrived earlier. But I dealt with the matter socially and satirically, and that was still rather shocking to the public and puzzling to the producer.

It might never have been produced at all—professionally—if it had not first been put on by amateurs. I had published the play in 1914 (under the original title, *And So They Were Married*, though a subsequent edition is called *Why Marry?*).* Some one in Mr. Sargent's American Academy of Dramatic Art

* The actual acting version, however, as revised and abridged for production, is here published for the first time.—ED.

2

asked permission to use it for the annual public production of the graduating class. I was very glad to grant the permission because I now saw a chance at last to prove the acting possibilities of the piece. So I gave up all other work and helped rehearse it. At first some of them seemed to think that it was a polemic against marriage. (The professionals thought so, too, until they saw it acted.) But gradually the comic light dawned, and the young people gave a very creditable performance. Before the final curtain rang down, three well-known managers opened negotiations with a view to the play's professional production. All three had refused it in manuscript. Of course I had seen to it that professional managers were dragged into the theatre. That was one reason why I had worked so hard over the amateur rehearsals, though Mr. Charles Jehlinger, who directed it with rare skill, and Mr. Diestal, who had selected this play (with—ahem—rare intelligence!), deserve all possible credit.

Professionally the play had its first production in Columbus, Ohio, November 1, 1917. Its New York opening was on Christmas evening of that year. After the "Metropolitan run" it went out to the Pacific coast and toured the Northern States. It was booked for a third year throughout the South, but soon after Nat Goodwin died the play followed his example—for a curious reason. Ernest Lawford, who had played the part of "Theodore," the human clergyman, and understudied Goodwin as "Uncle Everett," inherited Goodwin's part and really gave a better performance than his more famous predecessor; but, most unfortunately, the management had allowed the impression to go forth that this play had been written for and about the most-married man in the United States! Of course there is nothing even remotely analogous in the play to Goodwin's marital career, but to paragraphers all over the country Nat Goodwin in a play called *Why Marry?* was irresistible. The result of all this publicity was that when poor old Nat died the Southern theatres all began cancelling the bookings! An interesting example of a boomerang in advertising. Possibly the management deserved it, but the author did not.

Since then the piece has appeared in stock houses in various parts of the country, and is now taken up occasionally by amateur dramatic clubs, though I have no doubt it rather shocks some of them, even in these dissolute days. For so few people see—so few of the critics saw—that my young people, products of the scientific age, were not "destroying" marriage, but defining it. They were merely scraping the slush of sentimentality and the scum of hypocrisy from our most ancient and necessary institution; really doing it a pretty good turn. Inci-

dentally, the joke was on them, and that was part of the comedy.
Also on me, for though the play received even more praise than
the well-known vanity of authors could demand, this one was
accused, by certain critics who ought to have seen and known
better, of surrendering to our happy-ending fetich. I always
resented that.

Miss Maxine Elliot wanted her sister Gertrude to produce
Why Marry? in England. So, the English rights now having
reverted to me, I sent a copy of the manuscript to London,
telling Lady Forbes-Robertson that she could have a four
months' option, as I was leaving for a trip in the Orient.

Now you will see why I periodically swear off writing plays.

While I was gone, some one else, who had no more right to
my play than I have to your watch, caused it to be produced
by a London manager, without my knowledge or consent.
This, despite the fact that I had taken the precaution to "protect" the copyright by every device known to the Authors
League of America and the New York bar. That was over
two years ago, and to this day I have not succeeded in collecting a cent of royalties or damages, although I have employed
two able lawyers for the purpose. The chances of another
London production of this play are nil, and if I ever send another play to London my reputation will be a severe handicap.
For the piece was ruined, and the English critics were quite as
unanimous in condemning my play as the American critics
were in commending it.

Despite all this, despite my intention to stick to fiction, I
have now been led into temptation again. In 1916 I published
a novelette called *Remating Time*, which nobody read except Mr.
Howells, who said things about it in *Harper's Magazine* which I
want graven on my tombstone. (I had always believed that he
was the best judge of literature in America—now I was sure of
it.) Two years ago Oliver Herford told me I ought to make a
play of it—and the worst of it was I thought so too. That was
all that was necessary to make me fall.

It is a charming idyl of divorce in three acts. Last year I
gave it a try-out with the Amateur Comedy Club of New York.
As a result of what I learned by watching it and the audience,
I have been rewriting it ever since, and it is now scheduled for
production by the Equity Players at the Forty-eighth Street
Theatre, New York, on Christmas evening, the anniversary of
the New York opening of *Why Marry?* I have called it *Why Not?*

Why Marry? was awarded the Pulitzer Prize for the
best American play produced during the year 1917. It

was the first play to be so honored. It was published first by Charles Scribner's Sons in 1914 under the title of *And So They Were Married,* though a subsequent edition bears the title used in the play. It is republished here through the courtesy of the author and the publishers.

CAST

ASTOR THEATRE, NEW YORK, DECEMBER 25, 1917

In the order of their first appearance

JEAN, *the host's younger sister (who has been brought up to be married and nothing else)*...Lotus Robb.

REX, *an unmarried neighbor (who has been brought up not to be anything but rich)*......Harold West.

LUCY, *the hostess (trying to be an old-fashioned wife in a new-fashioned home)*..........Beatrice Beckley.

UNCLE EVERETT, *a judge who understands all of them (and who believes in divorce)*...Nat C. Goodwin.

JOHN, *who owns the house, and almost every one in it (and who does not believe in divorce)* Edmund Breese.

COUSIN THEODORE, *a clergyman (who believes in everything—except divorce)*.........Ernest Lawford.

HELEN, *the host's other sister (whom every one wants to marry and who doesn't want to marry any one)*.....................Estelle Winwood.

ERNEST, *a scientist (who believes neither in divorce nor marriage, but makes a great discovery)*
Shelley Hull.

THE BUTLER......................Richard Pitman.

THE FOOTMAN.....................Walter Goodson.

TIME: *A September week-end, not long ago.*
PLACE: *A country house, not far away.*

ACT I.   The sun-parlor.   Saturday afternoon.
ACT II. The sun-parlor.   Sunday morning.
ACT III. The sun-parlor.   Sunday evening.

WHY MARRY?*

ACT I

SCENE: *The sun-parlor of* JOHN'S *country place.*
*The house is on the right side, showing through the open
doors the library. The large latticed double doors up
centre show the veranda with a rambler rose-bush growing over it. At the left, columns, set at about four-feet
intervals down to the tormentor, show beyond a formal
garden, with hedges, trees, and shrubs. All indicates
comfort and luxury. Between the doors, right, an outdoor fireplace. Before the fireplace there is a large
upholstered sofa; at right centre a tea-table with three
chairs around it. At left centre there is a smaller couch
with a wicker armchair just below it.*
It is a bright sunny summer afternoon.
When the curtain is fully up, JEAN, *an attractive girl of
twenty-five, comes running in through the centre door,
hotly pursued by* REX, *a good-looking young man, a
year or two older. It is clear that she is the calmer of
the two and knows just what she is doing, while he is
impetuous, ardent, and thoughtless. Both of them laughing as they run on.*

REX [*as* JEAN *seeks refuge below the sofa on the left*].
Take that back, I tell you.
JEAN. I won't.
REX. I'll make you. [*Starts for her.*]
JEAN. You can't. [*Runs across stage to the right of the
tea-table.*]
REX [*almost catches her, but she dodges behind the table.
She turns and faces him defiantly across the table. Both are
panting from the race. Both laugh*]. Think I'll let you
say that to me?

7

JEAN. Think I'm afraid of you?

REX. I'll show you. [*Makes a start for her.*]

JEAN. Booh! No you don't. [*Runs to centre, pulling chair out from behind the table and getting behind it.*]

[*He feints, turns suddenly and catches her. A girlish gasp, "Oh!" He has her hands, but she draws back, her face averted from him toward the audience, who can see her watching him out of the corner of her eye.*]

REX [*triumphant, dragging her to centre*]. Now! you would, would you?

JEAN [*struggling*]. Let me go.

[*He catches her about the waist.*]

REX. I couldn't think of it.

JEAN [*tries, not very hard, to free herself*]. You're so strong—it isn't fair.

REX [*kisses her lightly*]. You're so sweet—it isn't fair.

JEAN. No, Rex.

REX. Yes, Jean.

JEAN. You mustn't.

REX. I will!

[*She struggles. Therefore, REX draws her close, kisses her again, passionately—without laughter.*]

JEAN. Don't! Oh, please! Somebody will come.

REX [*with the intoxication of such moments*]. I don't care who comes—I love you!

JEAN [*grasps his hands to release herself*]. Let me go.

REX [*laughing with the joy of his strength and her weakness*]. Not till you kiss me, Jean.

JEAN [*hesitates, kisses him shyly on the cheek*]. There! [*She draws back with pretty modesty. She knows that it is pretty.*]

REX [*keeping her imprisoned*]. Not till you tell me you love me, Jean.

[*She nods, her eyes downcast.*]

No! Say it!

JEAN [*low voice, but watching him all the same*]. I—er—do.

REX. Do *what?* . . . *Say* it!

[*She hesitates. He swings her about, brings face close to his.*]

You've got to say it, Jean.

JEAN. I love you, Rex—are you sure you love me?

REX. Am I sure! You irresistible little . . .

JEAN [*holding him off*]. And want to marry me, Rex?

REX [*startled, had not thought of that. They search each other's eyes*]. Why—er—of course. [*Drops his eyes, sobered. His honor is touched now, so he squares his shoulders.*] Why, what kind of a man do you take me for? [*He holds out his arms again.*]

JEAN [*giving herself to him, head sinking upon his shoulder*]. Then, oh, Rex, love me and be nice to me and—and take me away from all this! [*She covers her face with her hands and sobs. He pats her tenderly, a manly look on his face.*]

> [LUCY *enters from the garden. She is dressed in white, with a garden hat, and carries a few cut garden flowers in her hand. She is* JOHN'S *wife, the mistress of the house, sister-in-law to* JEAN. *She is conspicuously a "sweet" woman—affectedly so—a contrast with* JEAN'S *more modern, less delicate charm.* JEAN *is frank and honest, or wants to be;* LUCY *indirect and timid; pretty but fading, forty, but fighting it. The lovers, startled, break away from each other.*]

[*A second's pause of embarrassed silence.*]

JEAN [*the calmer of the two. Laughing*]. It's all right, Lucy—we're engaged!

LUCY [*in a flutter*]. Well, I should hope so! [*Shoots a glance at* JEAN.] "Ah?"

REX [*recovering himself, gallantly to* LUCY]. I have often tried to thank you and good old John for letting me come over here so much, but now! how can I *ever* thank you—see't I mean?

LUCY. I'll tell you how. By being a good boy—after you are married to John's little sister.

JEAN [*mock-tragic manner, crosses to him*]. Rex, have you had a "fearful past"? How fascinating.

REX. I'm going to have a glorious future, all right.

JEAN [*attractively bossy*]. Not unless you do as I tell you. Going to obey me, Rex?

REX [*amused*]. You bet I am.

JEAN. Then begin now. Go! . . . Get out!

REX [*laughing and protesting as* JEAN *pushes him*]. I *will* not.

JEAN. But I want to tell Lucy how nice you are! [*Pushes him up to the centre door,* REX *still lingering.*] Oh, run along over to the club-house, and by and by if you *are* good, you can take me out in your new car.

REX. Fine. [*Kisses his hand to* JEAN *and leaves, laughing.*]

JEAN [*goes to* LUCY]. If it hadn't been for you I could never have got him. My dear, he has five cars! Thank you so much.

[*Alone, they throw off the mask worn before men.*]

LUCY [*embracing* JEAN]. Jean, you've done well. [*They kiss.*] How delighted John will be . . . Now, dearie, tell me all about it. How did you work it?

JEAN. Oh, I simply followed your advice.

LUCY [*smiles*]. Picked a quarrel with him?

JEAN [*laughing and nodding gaily*]. Pretended to believe in economic independence!

LUCY. Good! They always hate that. And then you ran away.

JEAN. Of course.
LUCY. And he after you?
JEAN. Of course.   } (*Quickly*)
LUCY. And you let him catch you?

JEAN. Of course—well . . . he *caught* me.

LUCY [*both laughing*]. Oh, I can guess the rest.

JEAN. Why, it didn't take five minutes.

LUCY [*sentimentally*]. And now it's to last through all eternity— Isn't love wonderful!

JEAN [*casually*]. Um-hum.

LUCY [*looks up*]. But you do love him, don't you, dear?

JEAN. I do not.

LUCY. What? Why, what do you mean?

JEAN. I did then, for a minute—I don't now. I hate him now.

LUCY. Oh. The Bakers are one of the wealthiest families in the country—you can *learn* to love him.

[JEAN *shrugs and turns away.*]

Now, now, no worrying. It brings wrinkles.

JEAN. Lucy, what is the use of bluffing each other?

Lucy. Jean, you're growing cynical. You must stop thinking about that boy at the law school. Do you understand?

Jean. Don't—don't.

Lucy. Ah, you poor child. John would kill me if he heard me say this, but I'm sorry for you. Why couldn't you wait, dear?

Jean. He never asked me to.

Lucy. Perhaps he would if you let him.

Jean. But it wouldn't be fair. It takes so long to get started—everything costs so much. Why, nowadays, men in the professions—unless they have private means— they can't marry until nearly forty. Helen told me that. [*Pause.*] When Bob's forty, I'll be forty.

Lucy. I know, I know.

Jean. Oh, Bob and I'll get over it, I suppose—people do. [*Sighs.*] Some day he'll smile and say: "Just think, once I loved that fat old thing." [*Suddenly changes to sobbing.*] Oh, Lucy, when Rex caught me and kissed me just now, I shut my eyes and tried to think it was Bob.

Lucy. But you can't keep on thinking so, dear.

Jean. And that isn't the worst. When he held me close and I couldn't get away, I began to forget Bob— to forget everything—ugh! [*Breaks off, overcome with shame.*] But not now, not now. It's not the same thing at all.

Lucy. Poor little Jean.

Jean [*buries her head on* Lucy's *breast and sobs it out*]. Oh, I feel like the devil, dear. He doesn't want to marry me any more than I want to marry him—I trapped him into it. I trapped him.

> [*The* Butler *and the second man enter and place tea-service on the table and the tea-wagon behind and to the right of the table.*]

> [Rex *enters from centre as the men depart.*]

Rex. Ready, Jean? Car's outside. [*To* Lucy.] Oh, say, John's here. [*Indicating terrace.*]

Lucy. Oh, and I wasn't there to meet him. [*Going.*] He'll take my head off.

Rex. Just a minute; your cousin Theodore and the

Judge came out from town with him. Here for the
week-end?

Lucy [*starts to go*].   Yes.

Rex.   I wouldn't go out there if I were you.   John
and Theodore are having a fine old-fashioned family
fight with the Judge.

Lucy.   With Uncle Everett?   What about?

Rex.   They shut up when they saw me.   All I heard
was the parson—"Marriage is a social institution."
Grand old row though. [*Catching sight of servants.*]
Looks as if they were coming in here.   Come on, Jean.
Let's go this way and duck the family. [*Starts up to
the left.*]

    [Jean *starts to follow* Rex, *but* Lucy *stops her.*]

Lucy.   Jean, what are *you* going to do?

Jean.   What am *I* going to do?   Why, I'm going to
follow—the only profession I have been allowed to learn.

Rex.   What's this?   *What* profession?

Jean [*runs across and kisses him lightly*].   It is called
marriage, my dear. [*She gives him a teasing caress and
they run off laughing.*]

Lucy.   Yes, that's what it is called.

    [*Enter from garden* John, *the* Judge, *who is* Uncle
    Everett, *and* Cousin Theodore.]

    [John, *the masterful type of successful American busi-
    ness man; well set up, close-cropped mustache,
    inclined to baldness; keen eye, vibrant voice, quick
    movements, quick temper; well satisfied with him-
    self and the world. He has plenty of ability but
    very little perception; doesn't know much—not even
    this fact—but he is as generous with his own money
    as he is intolerant of other people's opinions. Just
    now he is rather excited.* Uncle Everett *is a
    genial satirist—not only of human nature but of
    human institutions.* Cousin Theodore, *a care-
    worn rector, who though he buttons his collar behind
    likes those who don't; a noble soul, self-sacrificing
    and sanctified, who does not obtrude his profession
    upon others—never talks shop unless asked to do so,
    and prides himself upon not being a bigot.* John
    and Judge *are smoking cigars. As these characters*

enter they are continuing an earnest discussion with the intimate manner of friendly concern. UNCLE EVERETT *is humorous and amused. As they enter,* LUCY *goes behind the table and sits, busying herself with the tea-things.*]

THEODORE. But, Uncle Everett, I can't believe it.

JOHN. Well, I never heard of such a thing.

THEODORE. But, Uncle Everett, hasn't Aunt Julia always been a good wife to you?

JUDGE. Quite so, Theodore, quite so; a good wife, a good wife.

JOHN. And a *devoted* mother to your children?

JUDGE. Devoted, John, devoted.

JOHN. Hasn't she always obeyed you, Uncle Everett?

JUDGE. Yes, John—a true old-fashioned woman.

THEODORE. She has been a great help in the parish work, Uncle Everett.

JUDGE. An earnest worker in the vineyard, Theodore—in fact, I might say, a model female.

JOHN. Then why, *why* do you want a divorce?

JUDGE [*calmly*]. Because, damn it, I don't like her!

LUCY [*in surprised whisper*]. Divorce?

JOHN. How about Aunt Julia?

JUDGE. She doesn't like *me*.

[JOHN *crosses to the right.*]

THEODORE. Ah, yes, fault on both sides. [*Crosses to sofa and sits down.*]

JUDGE. No fault on *either* side . . . both patterns of Christian fortitude, to the end!—we still are. Just listen to this telegram. [*Reaches in his pocket—brings out the telegram.*]

LUCY [*seated behind table, puzzled*]. From Aunt Julia?

JUDGE [*unfolding telegram*]. Yes, from Aunt Julia in Reno. Not used to travelling without me; knew I'd worry. [*Puts on glasses.*] A night-letter. Your aunt Julia was always a frugal wife, John—except with words. She never could keep within ten words. [*Reads.*] "Arrived safely. Charming rooms with plenty of air and sunlight. Our case docketed for March 15th. Wish you were here to see the women in Divorcée Row—overdressed and underbred." [*Looks up.*] Rather neat, eh?

"Overdressed and underbred." [*Resumes reading.*] "I should love to hear *your* comments on the various types." Now isn't that sweet of her? Well, you know, I always could make her laugh—except when I made her cry. [*Resumes reading.*] "Write soon. With love, Julia." Now [*folds up telegram*] isn't that a nice message to receive from a wife suing for divorce? Bet you happily married people couldn't beat that. [*Pats telegram and puts it in pocket.*]

JOHN [*like a practical business man—breaking in*]. But if there's no other woman, no other man—what's it all about?

JUDGE. She likes her beefsteak well done; I like mine underdone. She likes one window open so much [*indicates four inches*]; I like all the windows open wide. She likes to stay at home; I like to travel. She loves the opera and hates the theatre; I love the theatre and hate the opera. She . . . .

THEODORE. Aren't you willing to make a few little sacrifices for each other?

JUDGE. A few? Done nothing but make sacrifices for a quarter of a century, Theodore. Why, I remember the first dinner we had together after we were pronounced man and wife, with a full choral service and a great many expensive flowers—quite a smart wedding, Lucy, for those simple days. "Darling," I asked my blushing bride, "do you like tutti-frutti?" "I adore it, dearest," she murmured. I hated it, but nobly sacrificed myself, gave her tutti-frutti and gained character every evening of our honeymoon. Then when we got back and began our "new life" together in our "little home," my darling gave *me* tutti-frutti and indigestion three times a week until I nearly died.

LUCY. But why didn't you tell her?

JUDGE. I did finally. By the time we celebrated our wooden wedding, I got chronic dyspepsia and struck. "*You* may like this stuff—darling," I said, "but I hate it." What do you think she said? "Dearest, I hate it, too." "Then why in thunder have you had it all these years, sweetheart?" "Because I thought you liked it, beloved." That tells the story of our whole married life.

We have nothing in common but a love of divorce and a mutual hatred of tutti-frutti.

JOHN. Bah! All a cloak to hide the true story, and you know it.

JUDGE. I know it. [*Looks guilty.*] Do you want to know the truth? [*Glances about and with a hushed voice.*] John, Lucy, Theodore, your aunt Julia has broken her marriage vow.

THEODORE. Not Aunt Julia!

JUDGE. Yes, Aunt Julia. Twenty-five years ago last June she solemnly vowed before God and some of the nicest people in town to love me until death. But she has broken her marriage vow, she doesn't love me any more than I love her, not in the least.

THEODORE. Oh, come, the promise to love doesn't mean that.

JUDGE. Then what does it mean?

THEODORE. It means—well, it means you must try to love.

JUDGE. Try. Good Lord, for twenty-five years, a quarter of a century, we have been trying our damnedest.

JOHN. Bah! A man of your age, your common sense, a distinguished member of the bar—to break up his home for that? Rot! [*Brings chair to the table and sits down.*]

JUDGE. Right again, John, that is not why I am breaking up my home. I prefer my club. What does the modern home amount to, anyway? Merely a place to leave your wife.

LUCY. How could you neglect Aunt Julia?

JUDGE. But I *didn't* neglect her. I *sacrificed* myself, stayed at home, listened to her prattle about clothes and people, people and clothes—and got bored to death every night like a good husband.

LUCY. That's the way men always talk. It never occurs to you that business, business, business, is just as much of a bore to us.

JUDGE. Wrong again, Lucy. It did occur to me. I knew I bored her—she told me so; she knew she bored me, I told her so. Just like tutti-frutti.

JOHN. Well, couldn't you do something?

JUDGE. We are doing it now. Getting a divorce. What more could we do?

JOHN. You ought to be ashamed. Every man should love his home.

JUDGE. Certainly, every man should love his wife, too. But a promise can't make you love. It only makes you lie.

THEODORE. I love *my* home.

JOHN. So do I. [*He glances sternly at* LUCY.]

LUCY [*nervously*]. So do I.

JUDGE. All right, stick to it, if you love it!—only don't claim credit for doing what you *enjoy*. Now, I detest domesticity myself, yet I stuck to it all the same—for a quarter of a century, and at last—I'm free to tell the truth about it. Just think of it, Lucy, free to utter those things about marriage we all know but don't dare say! Free to be honest, John. No longer a hypocrite, Theodore, a soul set free—two souls, in fact. Two souls with but a single thought—two hearts that beat as one.

THEODORE [*rises and comes to centre*]. Seriously, Uncle Everett, "whom God hath joined together"!

LUCY. Yes, Uncle Everett, marriages are made in heaven.

JUDGE [*seeing through her bluff*]. I see, Lucy, I see, but your aunt Julia and I were joined together by a pink parasol made in Paris.

LUCY. Pink parasol!

JOHN [*exasperated*]. Oh, stop your fooling and speak the truth, man!

JUDGE. The truth? Just what I'm doing, John, but nobody wants or expects the truth about marriage— that's why you think I'm fooling. A very pretty parasol —but it wasn't made in heaven, Lucy. You see God made poor dear Julia *pale*, but on that fatal day twenty-five years ago the pink parasol, not God, made her rosy and irresistible. I did the rest—with the aid of a clergyman, whom I tipped even more liberally than the waiter who served us tutti-frutti. Blame *me* for it—*blame her*, blame the parasol, blame the parson—but do not, my dear Theodore, blame God for our own mistakes. It's so blasphemous.

[*They are all seated at the tea-table.*]

LUCY. We've forgotten all about the tea. [*She hands a cup of tea to the* JUDGE.]

JUDGE. Ah! yes—and I love tea—your aunt Julia hates it. [*To* THEODORE.] That's another thing.

LUCY. And to think we invited Uncle Everett here—of all people! To-day of all days! [*To* JOHN.] We mustn't let Rex know—the Bakers don't believe in divorce.

JOHN [*leaning forward excited*]. What's this—you don't mean Jean is engaged at last? Why didn't you tell me! [*To others, loud, excited, crossing to the centre.*] Jean has landed him! We're marrying into the Baker family! Why, Jean'll have more money than any of us!—Well, well! [*Laughs.*] We'll *all* have to stand around before little *Jean* now! My! [*Kisses* LUCY.] Lucy, you're a wonder— Those pearls—I'll buy them, they're yours?

LUCY. Now, if we could only get Helen to give up her unwomanly ambitions for a scientific career.

JOHN. Yes, to give up this absurd fad for scientific research, and be safely married to some nice man.

THEODORE. What's the matter with her scientist, Ernest Hamilton?

JOHN. I said some nice man.

JUDGE [*sipping tea*]. Meaning one having money?

THEODORE. The Hamiltons are an older family than the Bakers, older than our own.

JUDGE. Meaning they *once* had money.

JOHN. Waste a beauty on a bacteriologist?—A crime!

THEODORE. See here, John, Ernest Hamilton is the finest fellow in the world, and if you expect me—why did you ask me here?

JUDGE. Far as I can see, we're here to help one of the girls marry a man she doesn't love, and prevent the other from marrying the man she does.

THEODORE [*as* LUCY *hands him a cup of tea*]. John, Doctor Carmen, the head of the Institute, told me the other day that Hamilton has the biggest future of all those brilliant fellows down there. Why, he has already been called one of the most *useful* men in America.

JOHN. But he gets just two thousand dollars a year. Lucy, send for Helen. This is a practical world, Theodore.

[LUCY *goes obediently.*]

JUDGE. Well, you're one of the trustees of the Baker Institute. Why not give the young man a raise?

JOHN [*standing, legs apart, hands in pockets, jingling coins*]. Oh, that's not a bad salary for scientists, college professors, and that sort of thing. Why, even Doctor Carmen, the *head* of the Institute, gets less than the superintendent of my mills. [*To* THEODORE.] No future in science. Got to look at these things *practically*, Theodore.

JUDGE. Yes, you've got to look at these things practically, Theodore; the superintendent of John's mills saves the company thousands of dollars. This bacteriologist merely saves the nation thousands of babies. All our laws, written and unwritten, value private property above human life—I'm a distinguished jurist and I always render my decisions accordingly—I'd be reversed by the United States Supreme Court if I didn't! We're all rewarded in inverse ratio to our usefulness to society, Theodore. That's what business men call "practical."

JOHN [*good-naturedly*]. Muck-raker!

JUDGE. It's all on a sliding scale, John. For keeping up the cost of living, you and old man Baker get—oh, so much. [*Stretches arms out full length.*] For saving the Constitution, I get, well, I get a good deal myself. [*Rises, hands three feet apart.*] For saving in wages and operating expenses, your superintendent gets—so much. [*Hands two feet apart.*] For saving human life, Ernest Hamilton gets—so much. [*Hands six inches apart.*] For saving immortal souls, Theodore gets—so much. [*Holds up two forefingers an inch apart.*] Now if any one came along and saved the world— [*To* JOHN.]

THEODORE [*interrupts*]. They crucified Him.

JOHN [*re-enter* LUCY*;* JOHN *rises and turns to her*]. Where's Helen?

[THEODORE *places cup on table.*]

LUCY [*comes to table timidly*]. Tried my best, John, but Helen says she prefers to talk with you alone some time.

JOHN [*furious*]. She prefers? Am I master in my own house or not!

JUDGE. Of course you are, John; that's why your sister left it.

THEODORE. John, you can't stop Helen marrying Ernest, if she wants to—he's head over heels in love with her.

[*Others show surprise.*]

LUCY. What! Are you sure?

JOHN [*to* LUCY]. You told me he was a woman-hater. You told me he was in love with his work.

LUCY. But, John, dear, I thought he was. He's always so brusque with her, so different from nice men.

THEODORE. All a bluff, Lucy—thinks there's no hope for him, poor boy.

LUCY [*to* JOHN]. And she is mad about him! What'll we do?

JOHN [*to* LUCY]. And he is on the way out here now! What *can* we do?

JUDGE. What's this, coming here? Before she even gets her trunk unpacked?

THEODORE. What did I tell you? Head over heels.

JOHN. Oh, he doesn't know she got back this morning —thinks she's still in Paris.

JUDGE. Then why is he coming?

JOHN [*goes up stage*]. Because I invited him, damn it.

THEODORE. You *invited* him? [*He and* JUDGE *laugh at* JOHN.]

LUCY. But when we invited him we thought Helen would not be back till next week. We wanted to have a frank talk with him first.

JOHN. That's why we invited you fellows.

JUDGE [*to* THEODORE]. Oh, we're to do the dirty work. As usual.

JOHN [*to* JUDGE]. But *we* don't know how to talk to highbrows, and you do. And Theodore, here—well, Hamilton's a Harvard man, so's Theodore.

THEODORE. You want us to talk to him about the love microbe?

JOHN. I want you to put it up to him as a gentleman to quit compromising *my sister*.

JUDGE. Has he got the habit?

JOHN [*with his "Do be serious" manner*]. But you

know perfectly well what happened a month ago, before she sailed.

LUCY. Everybody knows.

JUDGE. Yes, the newspapers were full of it.

[JOHN *and* LUCY, *startled and perplexed.*] You mean his discovery of the Hamilton antitoxin. [*He knows they mean nothing of the sort.*]

JOHN. I mean *our* discovery that he kept her working with him *all night* in his laboratory.

LUCY. Without a chaperon.

JUDGE. Oh, shocking, Lucy, shocking.

JOHN. Come. You see. Something's got to be done at once and done delicately.

JUDGE [*bursts out laughing*]. Well, you've done it— all right. These lovers haven't met for a month and *to-night there's a moon.*

THEODORE [*also laughing*]. You may as well give in, John—the simplest solution.

LUCY [*timidly*]. John, perhaps, after all, they are right. Think how she treats all the *nice* men.

JOHN [*to* LUCY]. Who's doing this? You go tell Helen—that her *Uncle Everett* wants to see her! That'll fetch her. [JOHN *goes up to the door at centre.*]

[LUCY *shrugs, starts reluctantly, then lingers listening at the door on the right.*]

THEODORE. Now, uncle, you have more influence over Helen than any of us—don't let her know about—Aunt Julia.

JUDGE. Of course not. Never let the rising generation suspect the truth about marriage—if you want 'em to marry.

THEODORE [*modestly, charmingly, not preachy*]. There are other truths than unpleasant truths, Uncle Everett, other marriages than unhappy marriages.

JUDGE [*seriously*]. Want me to tell her the *truth* about your marriage?

[THEODORE *rises slowly.*]

LUCY [*surprised*]. Why, uncle! Even you must admit that Theodore and poor dear Mary are happy.

JUDGE [*from the sofa*]. Happy? What's that got to do with marriage? Selfish to be happy. Theodore told me so. A social institution. When a boy kisses a girl she must first inquire: "Are you doing this for the benefit of society?" And if he really loves her he will answer: "Yes, a sacrifice to gain character." Then, but not till then, "Darling," she will murmur, "do your duty," and he'll do it.

LUCY [*brightly*]. Well, Theodore has certainly done *his* duty to society—six children!

JUDGE. Then society hasn't done it's duty by Theodore—one salary.

JOHN [*coming back to centre*]. The more credit to him! He and Mary have sacrificed everything to their children, and the church—even health and success.

THEODORE [*at the door*]. We don't need your pity. We don't want your *praise*. We love each other through it all! Poverty, suffering, even separation, have only drawn us closer. Why, in her last letter from the sanitarium she said, she said . . . [*Suddenly overcome with emotion, turns abruptly.*] Excuse me, Lucy . . . [*He breaks down and goes into the house.*]

JUDGE [*rises—facing* THEODORE'S *exit—with a touch of tenderness*]. They don't need your praise or pity. They need something more substantial—and, by George, I'll raise it for them! [*Turns to* JOHN, *who interrupts.*]

JOHN [*reprovingly*]. See the example *he* sets to society. Character! Courage!

JUDGE. Character and courage can't restore Mary's radiant health, Theodore's brilliant youth.

LUCY. Ah, but they have their children. Think how they *adore* those beautiful children.

JUDGE. Think how they *rear* those beautiful children—in the streets. One boy gone to the devil already from things picked up in the streets. [*To* LUCY *as he crosses to the table.*] If you really want the *truth* . . . why, a marriage like mine is worth a dozen like Theodore's—to society. Look at *my* well-launched children. Look at my successful *career*, as a jackal to big business, look at my now *perfectly contented* spouse.

LUCY [*blinking,* JOHN *scowling*]. Yes, look at her?—getting a divorce.

JUDGE. Is the object of marriage merely to stay married? Holy matrimony a vulgar endurance contest? Shocking, Lucy, shocking!

JOHN [*reprovingly sharp*]. Then, what *is* the object of marriage?

JUDGE [*coming down behind table—in same manner*]. Something you two have never attained, John—children!

[JOHN *and* LUCY *turn their backs.*]

But it takes more than character and courage to raise kids, it takes cash. [*Takes check-book from* JOHN's *pocket and fountain-pen from his own. Offering them.*] I supply the ink, you supply the check. Fifty-fifty.

JOHN [*snatches away check-book*]. Why should I pay for the other people's children?

JUDGE. Why should other people's children pay for you?

JOHN. For me!

JUDGE [*rapidly*]. If none of us had any more children than you, who'd work your mills, consume your products, increase your dividends?

LUCY. Please, John, I'll give up those pearls.

JUDGE [*rapidly*]. We're in the world for two social purposes, John, production and reproduction. Theodore and Mary are underpaid for the one, and not paid at all for the other, so they are failing at both. But simply because they never complain, simply because, God bless 'em, they love each other through it all, you call it a "successful marriage"—hand them out praise and pity. Humph! that's cheap. [*Sits behind table, hands pen to* JOHN, *spreads out check-book.*] Go on, pay your honest debts.

JOHN [*seated at left of the table, he writes a check*]. You make me tired with all your talk. [*Looking up, he stops writing.*] But they're both so confoundedly proud.

JUDGE. Leave that to me. You sign that check! [*While* JOHN *writes.*] And now they've got to sacrifice even their pride, the one thing left to sacrifice.

JOHN. Well, you get this to them somehow. [*Hands check to* JUDGE, *who takes it eagerly.*]

JUDGE. Five thousand? Generous John!

JOHN [*impatiently*]. Never mind about me. *That* problem is all settled— Lucy, I thought I told you to find Helen.

[LUCY, *in a guilty hurry, goes out.*]

JUDGE. Charity never settles problems, John; it perpetuates them. We can't cure social defects by individual treatment.

JOHN [*seated at the table—more impatiently*]. Does talk settle anything?

JUDGE. Everything! Just got this out of you [*waving check*] by talk. We may even settle the marriage problem if we talk *honestly*—only, you won't.

[LUCY *and* THEODORE *enter*.]

LUCY. She'll be down in a moment.

THEODORE. Now remember, uncle, not a word about your divorce. [*Crosses up behind table.*]

JUDGE. Oh, I'm not divorced *yet*. So I'll lie like a married man.

JOHN. Ha! I have it. I know how to work this thing.

JUDGE. What're you going to do, John?

JOHN. You'll see. As long as she wouldn't stay abroad, I'm going to make her give up her job. That'll put a stop to this gossip—that'll keep them apart.

THEODORE. John, these two *love* each other.

JUDGE. Yes, young people still fall in love. They *will* do it. Only, if you church people had any imagination, you'd change your tactics. If we ever expect to reform marriage, instead of making it harder to get apart, we've got to make it easier *to stay together*.

LUCY [*sits back of table*]. Ssh, here she comes.

THEODORE [*to the* JUDGE]. Please, please, don't say such things before *her*.

JUDGE. I won't tell the truth! Can't you believe me?

[*Enter* HELEN.]

HELEN [*greeting* THEODORE *and the* JUDGE *affectionately*]. Hello, uncle—hello, Theodore—I'm *so* sorry to hear about dear Mary. [*As* THEODORE *turns away, she speaks to the* JUDGE.] But why didn't Aunt Julia come? [*Slight panic in the family group.*] Is she ill, too?

JUDGE. Yes, needed a complete change. Gone to Re-Re-Rio Janeiro— Lie number one. [*To* JOHN.]

[JUDGE *crosses the stage and sits on the couch. Another silence.* JUDGE *wags head.* LUCY *makes tea for* HELEN. JOHN *has seated himself in a chair on the left.* THEODORE *sits to the right of the table.* HELEN *looks at each and smiles.*]

HELEN [*taking cup from* LUCY]. Well, go on!

THEODORE. Go on with what?

HELEN [*stirring tea*]. Whatever it was I interrupted.

JUDGE [*with great gravity*]. We were just discussing holy matrimony.

HELEN [*smiles and nods*]. I might have guessed it. [*All look consciously at one another.*] Everybody's talking about marriage nowadays.

THEODORE. My dear, marriage is woman's only true career.

HELEN [*sipping her tea*]. So Lucy tells me, Cousin Theodore. But a woman cannot pursue her career. Her career must pursue her, otherwise she is unwomanly.

JUDGE [*on sofa*]. Ahem! As we passed the garden a while ago, I think I saw your little sister being pursued by her career.

HELEN [*laughing. She and the* JUDGE *understand each other*]. Yes, uncle, but Jean is a *true* woman. I'm only a *new* woman.

JUDGE. All the same, you'll be an old woman some day—if you don't watch out.

HELEN. Ah, yes, my life's a failure. I haven't trapped a man into a contract to support me.

LUCY. You ought to be ashamed—making marriage so mercenary. Haven't you new women any sentiment?

HELEN [*returning cup*]. Enough sentiment not to make a mercenary marriage, Lucy, dear.

LUCY. Some more tea?

HELEN. Not any, thank you, Lucy.

JUDGE. Ahem! And what kind of a marriage *will* you make?

HELEN. Not any, thank you, uncle. I don't believe in marriage.

[JUDGE *amused,* LUCY *shocked,* THEODORE *distressed,* JOHN *pleased.*]

JUDGE [*with assumed gravity*]. What! You don't believe in holy matrimony?

HELEN. Only as a last extremity, uncle, like—UN-HOLY DIVORCE.

JUDGE [*in alarm*]. What do *you* know about that?

HELEN. I know all about it!

[*All arise in alarm.*]

I have been reading up on the subject.

[*All sit with relief.*]

THEODORE. Come now, simply because many young people rush into marriage without thinking . . .

LUCY [*interrupts*]. Simply because these new women . . .

JOHN. Simply because one marriage in a thousand ends in divorce!

HELEN [*interrupting*]. One in a thousand! Dear me. In America there's one divorce to every eleven marriages, John.

JOHN [*turning with others to* JUDGE *incredulously*]. One in eleven? Is that true?

JUDGE. It is not.

JOHN. There!

JUDGE [*to* HELEN]. Such inaccuracy! And you a scientist.

[JOHN *goes behind sofa and down to the left.*]

HELEN. According to last year's census reports, one divorce to every eleven marriages.

JUDGE. But don't you know that according to *this* year's census reports there is one divorce to every *ten* marriages?

[JOHN *exasperated at the* JUDGE'S *defection.*]

LUCY. Well, I may be old-fashioned, but it seems to *me* that *nice* girls shouldn't *think* of such things . . . their husbands will tell them all they ought to know about marriage—after they're married.

HELEN [*comedy*]. I see. In other words, nice girls must not rush in without thinking, but they mustn't think until after they rush in. You make it all so simple for us.

JUDGE. Right! The way to cure all evil is for "nice people" to close their minds and mouths to it. "Unpleasant" for the mind—"leaves a bad taste in the mouth." [*Goes up stage and sits.*]

JOHN [*to* HELEN]. See here, everybody down-town wonders why a sister of mine works for a living. You get just nine hundred a year at the Institute——

HELEN [*to the others, blaspheming* JOHN's *gods with her smiling flippancy*]. Oh, but John's so rich now, his credit can stand having a working girl in the family.

LUCY. But, my dear, it's so hard to explain you to one's friends.

HELEN [*dryly*]. Then you have the wrong kind of friends, my dear. It's quite smart nowadays for women to have a job.

LUCY. But, Helen, going down-town every day! working with those horrible highbrows? It seems so, well, so unwomanly.

HELEN. But when I first came back from college, didn't I try my best to be "womanly"? Instead of going down-town and working with highbrows, I stayed up-town and played with lowbrows until I was bored to death.

LUCY [*secretly envies* HELEN, *but must play up to* JOHN's *"ideals"*]. Well . . . I'm just an old-fashioned wife. Woman's sphere is the home— My husband says so.

HELEN [*smiling*]. But suppose you haven't any husband! What can a poor spinster do in the home?

LUCY [*vexed but not ill-natured*]. She can *stay* in it— till she gets one. That's what the *old-fashioned* spinster used to do.

HELEN. But the old-fashioned spinster used to—SPIN.

LUCY [*becoming nettled, for the very reason that she envies* HELEN]. At any rate, even the new-fashioned spinster needn't stay *out* of her home all *night!* And get herself *compromised!* Talked about! Sent *abroad* by her family! [*Still higher.*] Or if she does, she ought to know enough to *remain* abroad until the *gossip* blows over, and it hasn't blown over. Helen, every one is still talking about that night.

HELEN [*mock-romantically*]. Ah, that wonderful night!

[JOHN *jumps up from his chair.*]

[*All start, shocked, excepting* JUDGE.]

The night he discovered the Hamilton antitoxin! The night that made the Baker Institute famous! And just think, I had a hand in it, Lucy, a hand in the *unwomanly work* of saving children's lives! [*Drops that note and burlesques maidenly coyness.*] But of course an old-fashioned spinster would have blushed and said: "Excuse me, Doctor Hamilton, but now we must let a whole year's work go to waste because you are a man and I am a woman, and it's dark outdoors!"

LUCY. You think we can't see through all this? Science—fiddlesticks! The good-looking young *scientist*—that's why you couldn't stay abroad. Came back in a month. We see it—John sees it . . .

JOHN. You're right, Lucy. See here, young lady, I offered to pay all your expenses abroad for a year. As Lucy says, you came back in a month. You didn't seem to appreciate it—well, the trustees of the Institute are now to give *Doctor Hamilton* a year abroad. How do you like that?

[*All turn to see how she likes it.* JOHN *has air of triumph.*]

HELEN. Splendid! [*Pause, others show surprise.*] Just what he needs! Doctor Metchnikoff told me in Paris that America always kills its big men with routine. When do we start, John?

JOHN. "We"! Think *you* are going?

HELEN. Of course! I'm his assistant—quite indispensable to him. [*To all.*] Oh, well, if you don't believe *me*—ask *him.*

JOHN. Paris! Alone! With a man! Good Lord! What next! Here's where I call a halt!

HELEN. But if my job calls me, I really don't see what you have to say about it, John.

JOHN [*smiling—not snarling. He loves and admires her*]. Better not defy me, Helen!

HELEN [*quite good-naturedly*]. Better not bully me, John!

JOHN. I am your brother!

HELEN. But not my—owner.

JOHN [*a gesture sweeping all that aside*]. That's all right in theory, but this is a practical world. You give up this wild idea or give up your job.

HELEN. What if I refuse to give up either, John?

JOHN [*loud*]. Then, as a trustee of the Baker Institute of Medical Experiment, I ask for your resignation—right here and now! [*Turns away—all settled.*] I guess that will hold her a while!

HELEN [*rises*]. On the contrary, I *must* go to Paris now. Nothing else to *do*.

JOHN [*turns back—triumphant smile*]. You will, eh? Who'll pay your expenses this time?

HELEN [*calmly matter-of-fact*]. Doctor Hamilton.

JOHN [*all scandalized except* JUDGE]. What!

THEODORE [*rises*]. Helen—please!

LUCY. You oughtn't to say such things, my dear, even in joke.

HELEN. He'll be delighted to take me—as his private secretary, if I ask him. [*Pause.*] I'll telephone him at once. [*Going to right to* THEODORE, *who stops her.*]

JUDGE. John, she's got you—might as well quit. [*Seated up stage.*]

JOHN [*confidently*]. Nonsense, I have just begun.

THEODORE [*detaining* HELEN]. If you're so independent, my dear, why don't you marry your scientist and be done with it.

HELEN. You want to know why? . . . Can you keep a secret? [*She comes in front of table—all gather about her.*] He has never asked me!

[*All smile.*]

LUCY [*match-making ardor*]. No wonder, dear; he has never *seen* you except in that awful apron. Now in one of these stunning frocks John bought you in Paris, or in one of the evening gowns, you are quite irresistible.

JUDGE [*apart to* JOHN]. Irresistible? Pink parasol— same old game.

HELEN [*suppressing mirth and amusement at* LUCY]. Thanks for your advice, Lucy, but, you see, I don't *want* him to ask me.

LUCY. What! You don't want him!

HELEN. Why, I've had all I could do to keep him from it.

[*All dumfounded.*]

LUCY. But suppose he did ask you, dear?

HELEN [*she's not going to take them into her confidence— too sacred*]. Why, I'd simply refer the matter to John. If John said, "Love him"—I'd love him; if John said "Don't love him"—I don't love him. I'd turn it off like electric light.

LUCY [*insinuating*]. Oh, you can't deceive us—*we* know how much you admire him.

HELEN [*warmly. The truth is the surest way to deceive them*]. Oh, no, you don't.

[*They all look surprised again.*]

Not even *he* does. Did you ever hear how he risked his life in battle? Why, to me he's a perfect hero of romance!

JOHN [*sneers*]. Never even saw a battle—mollycoddle germ-killer.

HELEN. The battle against yellow fever, John, down in Cuba. No drums to make him brave, no correspondents to make him famous—merely rolled up his sleeve and let an innocent-looking mosquito bite him, and then took notes on his symptoms till he became delirious. He happened to be among those who recovered. Four of the others died. [*She is betrayed into showing considerable feeling, after all.*]

THEODORE [*after a pause*]. Old-fashioned maidens used to marry their heroes, Helen.

HELEN [*bracing up, getting herself together. With a glance at* JOHN—*smiling*]. But this new-fashioned hero gets only two thousand a year, Theodore.

JOHN. She's got some sense left.

THEODORE [*rises and goes down stage a little, disappointed*]. Helen! You selfish, too? Why, Mary and I married on half that, didn't we, John? and see how successful our marriage has been. [*He looks around, but all drop eyes.*]

JUDGE. Couldn't you live on that, Helen?

HELEN [*quietly*]. Live? Yes, but Doctor Hamilton needs every cent of that enormous salary for his work—books, travel, scientific conferences—all the advantages he simply must have if he's to do his best for the world. Why, nowadays the most selfish thing a girl can do is to marry a poor man. Besides, I don't believe in marriage, I tell you—not at any price. [*Shrug.*]

THEODORE. All the same, deep down under it all you have a true woman's yearning for a home to care for and a mate to love. [*He finds that she is in tears.*] Why, my dear child, what's the matter?

HELEN [*to all of them, strong. She has reached her limit.*

Can't stand any more]. Oh, why can't you let me *alone!*
You make what ought to be the holiest and most beautiful thing in life the most horrible and dishonest. I hate
marriage—I hate it.

THEODORE [*going down to* HELEN]. Oh, just you wait
till the right one comes along.

BUTLER [*entering—to* LUCY]. Doctor Hamilton has
come, ma'am.

HELEN [*with old-fashioned gasp*]. Good gracious!
What's he doing here? [*No answer.*] What does this
mean? [*Looks from one to other, but no one answers.*]

LUCY [*calmly to* BUTLER]. Show Doctor Hamilton
out here.

[*The* BUTLER *takes off the tea-wagon.*]

HELEN [*with increasing perturbation*]. Does he know
I'm here? [*No answer.*] Surely you didn't invite him?

JOHN. Why, er . . .

JUDGE. Why not?

HELEN [*to* JUDGE]. But they never invite *him*. They
don't "approve" of him.

JUDGE. Oh, John will learn to love him.

JOHN. Why, er . . .

JUDGE. John issued the invitation himself.

HELEN [*stops*]. Then I understand! [*Excited but
smilingly.*] You think it's my last chance to marry. A
plot to *entrap* him.

JOHN. Nothing of the sort.

HELEN [*going*]. Oh, I understand now. Ugh! these
horrible relatives! But it's no use! I'm going out and
I'm going to stay out until he's gone! [*She goes into the
garden.*]

JUDGE. Fighting hard, poor child!

THEODORE [*to* LUCY]. But what'll we do?

JUDGE. Don't worry—she can't stay away—the sweet
thing!

JOHN [*with something up his sleeve*]. Now we must
all jolly him up, make a fuss over him.

JUDGE. Going to surrender, John?

JOHN [*knowingly*]. What I'm going to do requires
finesse. . . . Now that SHE's home I'll get HIM sent
abroad for a year . . . he'll jump at the chance. That'll

keep them apart. Now, then, follow my lead. Jolly him up, I tell you.

LUCY [*rises. In a flutter, seeing* HAMILTON *approach*]. Oh, dear! How does one talk to highbrows? [*To* JUDGE.]

JUDGE. Talk to him about himself—highbrows, low-brows—ALL men love it.

[*The* BUTLER *announces* DOCTOR HAMILTON.]

[*Enter* ERNEST HAMILTON, *about thirty-five years old; although a highbrow, he looks like a pretty good fellow, and he is not in the least shy or embarrassed, being "well born and well bred." He talks very rapidly; does not take the trouble to despise conventions; merely views them with frank, scientific curiosity, tinged with amused contempt. He is startlingly honest.*]

JOHN [*crosses and greets the distinguished guest at entrance*]. Ah, Doctor Hamilton! Delighted to see you on my little farm at last. Out here I'm just a plain old-fashioned farmer. [*Shakes hands effusively.* ERNEST *glances about at the magnificence, raises his eyebrows, and smiles quietly to himself. Says nothing at first to these greetings; merely bows urbanely, complete master of self and situation.*]

LUCY [*comes down in front of the table and, after greeting him, returns to her seat with an affected manner before a stranger*]. Doctor Hamilton! So good of you to come.

THEODORE [*an old friend*]. How are you, Ernest? Glad to see you. [*Shakes hands.*]

LUCY. I don't think you've met Judge Grey.

JUDGE [*rising. Humorously adopting their manner, across table*]. Charmed! I've heard so much about you —from—ahem—my niece . . . [*Sits again.*]

LUCY [*hastily coming to* ERNEST'S *rescue*]. A cup of tea, Doctor Hamilton?

ERNEST [*not disturbed by mention of* HELEN]. Thanks. [*Sits at the table. As the jolly proceeds, he catches on and has fun with them*].

JOHN [*standing right of table, while* LUCY *makes tea, trustee manner.*] I have often desired to express my admiration of your heroism in the war against yellow fever in er— ah . . .

JUDGE. Cuba . . .

JOHN. *Cuba,* when you let an innocent-looking mosquito bite you, and, and . . . [*Looks around for help.*]

LUCY [*coming to* JOHN'S *rescue, nodding and poising the tongs*]. And then took notes on your symptoms till you became delirious!

ERNEST [*to* LUCY]. No sugar, thanks.

JUDGE. No drums to make you famous—no correspondents to make you brave.

[JOHN *nudges* JUDGE *to call his attention to his blunder. To* JOHN.]
I got that wrong, didn't I? I mean the other way round!

ERNEST [*to* LUCY *poising cream-pitcher*]. No cream, please.

JOHN [*straight now*]. Senator Root says this one triumph alone saves *twenty million dollars a year* to the business interests of the United States. I call that patriotism.

ERNEST [*with a whimsical nod, to* LUCY]. Lemon.

THEODORE. General Wood says it saves more *human lives* a year than were lost in the whole Spanish War! I call it service.

JUDGE. General Goethals says the Panama Canal could not have been built if it had not been for you fellows.

JOHN. In fact, scientists might well be called philanthropists!

ERNEST [*receiving cup from* LUCY]. Thanks. Better let it go at heroes and patriots. Philanthropists give dollars. [*Stirring tea.*] Never give a cent to charity myself.

JOHN [*to others*]. I happen to know that Doctor Hamilton gave up a lucrative private practice to join the staff of the Baker Institute.

ERNEST [*getting rather bored*]. Private practice didn't interest me. [*Drinks.*] The ones who deserve your praise are the ones who died to prove that theory. But I don't suppose you ever even heard of 'em.

JOHN [*standing right of table*]. Why, Doctor Hamilton! Of course we've heard of them. The fame of those four men is immortal.

ERNEST. I see— One of the "four men" happened to be a woman.

[*Silence . . .* JOHN *looks at* THEODORE, *who looks at*
LUCY, *who looks at* JUDGE. *All uncomfortable.*]
By the by, of course you all know their immortal *names?*
    [JOHN *looks at* THEODORE, *who looks at* LUCY, *who
looks at* JUDGE. *Same business.*]
Then, if you don't mind, cut out [*good-natured sneer*]
"philanthropists" and make it *scientists.* Everybody
knows the names of philanthropists.
    [JUDGE *coughs.*]
Delicious tea.

JUDGE. He's right. Philanthropists don't give their
lives. They give their names.

THEODORE [*standing*]. Ah, but that is what makes the
sacrifices of scientists so beautiful—they don't work for
fame, they don't work for money, they work for humanity.

ERNEST [*with his quiet smile*]. I see . . . that's what
Congress told us when we suggested a pension for one of
the widows. [*Finishes his tea.*]

THEODORE [*to* ERNEST]. Do you mean to say Congress
refused to grant the pension?

ERNEST. Not at all. They granted the pension.

JOHN. How much?

ERNEST [*to* JOHN]. Seventeen dollars a month for the
widow. Two dollars a month for each of the children.

JOHN. Is that all?

ERNEST [*returning cup, answers* LUCY'S *business of
offering to fill it*]. No more, thanks—charming little farm
you have out here. [*Rises and crosses to* THEODORE.]

JOHN [*to* JUDGE]. Watch me.

JUDGE. Oh! I'm watching you *all the time.*

JOHN [*crosses to* ERNEST. *Approaching with a "Now
watch me" manner*]. Doctor Hamilton—America kills
its big scientists with routine, you are too valuable to
the nation to lose—the trustees think you need a year
abroad!

ERNEST. Funny! I was going to suggest that very
thing. Somebody's been rooting for me over in Paris—
just had a letter from Metchnikoff himself—invites me
to come and work a year in the Pasteur Institute. You
didn't have to jolly me up to consent to that!

    [THEODORE *lights his pipe here.*]

JOHN [*pacing up to terrace arm in arm with* ERNEST].
By the by, my *sister* is rather keen on science.

ERNEST [*businesslike. Turns back down centre*].   Best
assistant I ever had.   She's over there already, so we can
go right to work.

JOHN [*coming down*].   Well—er—she'll be back before
you start.

ERNEST [*stops short*].   I didn't know that.   [*Looking
from one to the other.   A keen observer, he knows that* JOHN *is
trying to do something, and is both amused and annoyed.
To* THEODORE.   *The others all watching.*]   Oh, hell, what's
it all about?

THEODORE [*seated on the bench*].   Don't you see, old
chap, under the circumstances it would hardly do for her
to go back to Paris with you?

ERNEST.   Why not?

LUCY.   You're a man.

ERNEST [*smiles*].   You mean I'm dangerous.

LUCY.   But she's a woman.

JUDGE.   They mean *she's* dangerous!

JOHN.   My dear fellow, we are going to ask you very
frankly to decline to take her.

ERNEST [*looks about at the circle of anxious faces*].   So
that's it, eh?   But she needs it more than I do.   She's
had so little chance to do original work.

JOHN.   But she's a woman.

ERNEST [*impatiently*].   What of it?

JOHN.   Doctor Hamilton, we have the highest opinion
of you, but one must respect the opinions of the world,
you know.

ERNEST [*thinks it over*].   That's right, one must.   I
forgot to think of that.   When you *work* with women of
ability you learn to respect them so much that you quite
lose the habit of insulting them.

JUDGE.   Too bad how new conditions spoil fine old cus-
toms.

ERNEST.   Suppose we let *her* go, and *I'll* stay.

JOHN.   But I fear that would offend our generous bene-
factor.   Mr. Baker has set his heart upon your going abroad
for a year—[*winks at others*] meeting the big men over
there, getting fresh ideas for our great humanitarian work.

[*The family exchange glances as* JOHN *lies on.*]

Besides, my sister would only go to accommodate you. She particularly desires to stay with us this winter.

ERNEST [*believes it*]. I didn't know that. I thought she didn't like you.

JOHN. Why else should she be returning so soon?

ERNEST. Oh, I see. Well, I'm sure I have no desire to *drag* her over with me. I thought . . . but that's all right; if she doesn't care to go with me, that settles it.

JOHN. You agree to go alone?

ERNEST. Yes, alone.

JOHN. And we have your word on it?

ERNEST. Certainly.

JOHN. How soon could you start?

ERNEST. Soon as I get some one to run my department.

JOHN. Could my sister run it?

ERNEST. Could she RUN it? It can't run without her! She's a born executive. I hate that side of it.

JOHN [*with a look at the others*]. Then that's all fixed. Could you arrange to start on Monday's steamer?

ERNEST [*hesitating*]. By leaving here at once I could.

JOHN [*with a triumphant glance at others, takes* ERNEST's *arm and rushes him toward the door*]. Then come, we'll telephone for your passage. The next train leaves directly after dinner.

ERNEST [*protesting*]. But—er—don't you see——

JOHN. Of course I hate to cut short your week-end, but I take great interest in scientific careers . . . [JOHN *rushes* ERNEST *off.*]

THEODORE. Well, John certainly did finesse it.

LUCY. Can't you see, you stupid MEN, Doctor Hamilton's crazy about her, but thinks there's no hope.

JUDGE [*sitting down*]. When she finds he's leaving Monday for a year, her views about marriage may undergo a sudden change.

THEODORE. They were made for each other. They need a woman's helping hand. Come, Lucy, now . . .

LUCY [*still seated behind table*]. Oh, *I* could manage it. See how I landed Rex, but John would kill me.

JUDGE. John needn't know anything about it until too late. Just bring the two together and let Nature take its course.

LUCY. All right, we'll get Helen and Doctor Hamilton together in some way, and after a decent interval we'll excuse ourselves, leave them alone . . .

JUDGE. And let Nature take its course.

ERNEST [*as he re-enters*]. Well, I'm sorry to have to run away like this after dinner . . .

JUDGE. Oh, er—where's John? [*Rising and going to* ERNEST.]

ERNEST. Waiting in his den for the long-distance telephone.

JUDGE. Ahem! We were just discussing the marriage danger—I mean the marriage problem.

ERNEST. Go right on, don't mind me.

THEODORE [*old-friend manner*]. See here. When are *you* ever going to get married?

ERNEST. When am I ever going to get more than two thousand a year? [*Pulling chair down stage and sitting at head of sofa.*]

THEODORE. Bah! What has money got to do with it?

ERNEST. Nothing—I don't believe in marriage.

JUDGE. I've heard that before.

THEODORE. Just you wait till the right one comes along.

ERNEST [*smiling*]. How do you know "the right one" hasn't come already?

[HELEN *comes from the garden. She stands and looks at him, unseen by* ERNEST. THEODORE *sees her and smiles. She signals* THEODORE, *finger on lips, and tiptoes toward house.*]

THEODORE [*with a chuckle*]. Then don't let her go by.

ERNEST. Oh, I couldn't stop her, if I wanted to.

[HELEN *is so interested that she stops.*]

THEODORE. Looks to me as if you could.

ERNEST. And what do YOU know about it?

[THEODORE *laughs.*]
What's the joke?

THEODORE [*still laughing*]. Ever try?

ERNEST. To marry her? Lord, no. Even if I did believe in marriage, I wouldn't marry *that* girl.

[HELEN *is amazed and indignant.*]

THEODORE. Why not?

ERNEST. She hasn't any money.

Lucy [*surprised*]. Well, really!

Judge [*astonished*]. Good Lord!

[Helen *is surprised*.]

Theodore [*straight*]. Money! I didn't suppose *you* would marry for money!

Ernest. You don't suppose I'd marry a girl *without* money? Most selfish thing a poor man can do.

[Helen *pantomimes applause, makes a moue at* Theodore, *pantomimes "just what I said."*]

Theodore [*wagging his pipe at* Helen]. Oh, you modern young people!

[Judge *and* Lucy *see* Helen.]

Ernest. Make her nothing but a superior servant in an inferior home. Not *that* girl.

[Helen *gives silent applause*.]

Theodore [*to* Ernest]. Feministic nonsense! [*To* Helen.] The old-fashioned womanly woman . . .

Ernest [*interrupts*]. Sentimental twaddle. Why more "womanly" to do menial work *for* men than intellectual wotk *with* them? Twaddle, Theodore, twaddle!

[Helen *gives silent applause, now enthusiastic*.]

Theodore. All the same, if you really cared for a woman enough to marry her . . .

Ernest. But I don't.

Theodore. Then why run away to Paris just as she returns?

Ernest. Well, if you must know, you silly old idealist, I don't believe in marriage, but, Theodore, she *does*.

Helen [*coming down behind* Ernest]. I do not.

[*All laugh*.]

Ernest [*jumps up and retreats*]. My heavens! Where did you drop from?

Helen. I dropped from Paris. Don't be afraid, I agree with you perfectly.

Ernest [*going up to* Helen *and shaking her hand*]. I'm awfully glad to see you.

Helen. And I'm awfully glad to see you.

Ernest. Do you know, I thought *you believed* in marriage.

Judge. Wronged her. Apologize.

Helen. And all this time I thought you did.

JUDGE. Wronged him. Both apologize.

HELEN [*with humor*]. Think of the *discussions* we might have had.

JUDGE. Not too late yet. Your aunt Julia and I had discussions for twenty-five years.

HELEN [*crossing to the right with* ERNEST, *humorously provoked with him*]. Why didn't you ever tell me?

ERNEST. Why didn't you ever tell me?

JUDGE. Each understands the other now . . . everything is lovely!

HELEN [*indicating the others*]. Please don't think *I* had any hand in this. [*Laughs.*]

ERNEST. In what?

HELEN [*mock-tragic whispers*]. Can't you see? . . . A plot to entrap us in marriage! They want to *throw* me at your head. [HELEN *crosses to the tea-table, and busies herself with the tea things.*] Come! Sit there! We'll have some fun with them. [*Indicating chair to the right of the table, in which* ERNEST *sits.*]

THEODORE [*to* JUDGE *and* LUCY—*in a whisper*]. Shall we go now?

LUCY. No, no! too obvious!

HELEN [*leans toward* ERNEST]. Come, you must be attentive to me; tell me all about anterior poliomyelitis.

[THEODORE, LUCY, JUDGE—*all have their heads together.*]

THEODORE. The strangest courtship *I* ever saw.

LUCY. They ought to be spanked.

JUDGE. Old Mother Nature will attend to that. [*With hand to his ear tries to hear what* ERNEST *and* HELEN *are saying.*]

[ERNEST *and* HELEN *have heads together.*]
I can't hear a damn word.

THEODORE. They're getting on famously.

LUCY [*rises and crosses to* ERNEST]. If you'll excuse me, Doctor Hamilton, I always take forty winks before dressing. We dine at eight. [*Going.*]

[ERNEST *and* HELEN *exchange glances and smile.*]

THEODORE [*whispers to* JUDGE]. Come on, Uncle Everett.

JUDGE. Excuse me, Theodore—I want to be in at the death.

THEODORE. If you'll excuse me, Ernest, I think I'll have a look at the evening papers. [*He follows* LUCY.]

HELEN [*seated behind table*]. Seriously, you oughtn't to have dropped the polio experiments.

ERNEST [*seated right of table*]. You oughtn't to have dropped *me* . . . right in the *midst* of the experiments. Those agar plates you were incubating all dried up and spoiled. You played the very devil with my data.

JUDGE [*on couch*]. God bless my soul, what are we coming to?

HELEN. Oh, it's perfectly proper for your little ears, uncle, only you can't understand a word of it. . . . Won't *any* one play billiards with you? [*And turns at once to* ERNEST.]

JUDGE. But I'm fascinated. It's so idyllic. Makes me feel young again. [*Rises and goes up centre.*]

HELEN [*seated behind table. To* ERNEST]. Oh, you have plenty of men assistants who can estimate anti-toxin units.

JUDGE. Estimate *what?*

ERNEST [*shakes his head. To* HELEN]. Men assistants lose interest. They are all so confoundedly ambitious to do original work. Why is it women can stand monotonous details better than men? "The female of the species is more *faithful* than the male."

HELEN. Because men have always made them tend the home!

JUDGE [*coming behind the table and getting between the two*]. Ah, nothing like a good old-fashioned love-scene— in the scientific *spirit*.

HELEN [*to* JUDGE *after pause*]. Uncle, dear! Haven't you any tact? *Can't* you see that he is paying me wonderful compliments? Go and play Canfield in the library.

JUDGE. Very well, I'll leave you to your own devices— [*Keeps lingering up stage.*] But don't forget the scientific spirit.

HELEN [*with animation and camaraderie—she thinks they are alone at last. Transition*]. Now I must tell you what Metchnikoff said about you and your great future. He said that if you will only let nothing interfere with your career—absolutely nothing— [*Significance.*]

[ERNEST *pantomimes that* JUDGE *is listening—she proceeds, brisk and loud.*]
He advises you to confine your original research to proving the absence of toxicity and antiphylaxis following the absorption of albumnosis and protiosis from the anteric mucosa.

JUDGE.   Help! Help! [*Running off.*] May God, your God, have mercy on your scientific souls.

ERNEST [*different note, now they are alone*].   I wonder why they all take for granted that I want to make love to you?

HELEN [*avoids his eye*].   Well, you took for granted that I wanted you to.   You are about the most conceited man I ever knew, and that's saying a good deal.

ERNEST.   How can I help it when you admire me so?

HELEN [*aroused*].   I? Admire you?

ERNEST.   You're always telling me what great things I'm going to do, stimulating me, pushing me along.   Why, if it hadn't been for you, the so-called "Hamilton Antitoxin" would never have been discovered.   And, after you left, everything went slump.   Tell me, why did you leave me?   Was I rude to you?   Did I hurt your feelings?

HELEN [*looks away*].   On the contrary, it was entirely out of respect for your feelings.

ERNEST.   My feelings?   Oh, I see.   You got it into your head that I wanted to marry you.   Well, well. What an idea!

HELEN.   Men sometimes do.

ERNEST [*looks at her. She is adorable. What of it?*].   I suppose they do.

HELEN.   It's been known to happen.

ERNEST [*looks away*].   I suppose it has. . . . Well, you needn't be afraid.   *I'll* never ask you to marry me.

HELEN.   You can't imagine what a weight this takes off my mind.

ERNEST.   Yes.   I feel as if a veil between us had been lifted.

HELEN [*slightly nervous*].   What were you saying— about those agar plates?

ERNEST.   What agar plates?   Oh, yes, yes, the polio

experiments. Look, look, there's a new moon. [*Looking off to the left.*]

HELEN [*seriously*]. You promise never to mention the absurd subject again?

ERNEST. What subject?

HELEN. Marriage.

ERNEST [*with undue force*]. Oh, that. Certainly, I promise. [*He keeps eyes averted.*]

HELEN [*turning to him with sudden change to girlish delight*]. Good! Then—I'll go to Paris with you!

[ERNEST *recoils suddenly. She misunderstands.*]
Why, Doctor Metchnikoff—he *promised* me he'd invite you!

ERNEST. Yes, but . . . you—*you* can't go.

HELEN. If you need me, I can. And you just said . . .

ERNEST. But *you* mustn't go to Paris with me.

HELEN. Don't you want me with you?

ERNEST. I thought you would like to stay at home and run the department for me!

HELEN [*hurt*]. Don't you *want* me?

ERNEST [*with heart in voice*]. Do I *want* you! But . . . [*Stops.*] I am a man—you *are* a woman.

HELEN. What of it? [*Contemptuously.*] Are you one of those small men who care what people say? No. That's not your reason. What is it? Tell me.

ERNEST [*hesitates*]. It's only for your sake.

HELEN. Then I'm to be left behind like a child because you don't care to be embarrassed with me.

ERNEST. It's so unfair. I simply can't take you now.

HELEN. Oh. Very well, that's settled then. [*Rises and goes down below the table.*] Go on to your wonderful career and leave me behind. Only I can't understand it. It's not what I'd do, that's all.

ERNEST [*rises*]. Oh. Please, please.

HELEN. Oh. I hate men. I hate you.

ERNEST. And I love you.

HELEN [*to self more than to him*]. Oh. This spoils everything.

ERNEST. No! It glorifies everything! [*He takes a step forward and breaks loose.*] I have loved you from the first day you came to my dreary old workroom. I didn't want you there. I didn't want any woman there. I tried to tire you out with overwork but couldn't. I tried to drive you out, by rudeness, but you stayed. And that only made me love you more. Oh, I love you! I love you!

HELEN [*breaks in*]. Do you? Oh, don't love me—ah, say it just once more.

ERNEST. I love you! I love you! I love you! I love everything about you—those wonderful brave eyes that face the naked facts of life and are not ashamed; these beautiful hands that have worked so hard, so long, so close to mine, and not afraid, not afraid.

HELEN. Oh, don't! don't! I *am* afraid now. I made you say this. [*She smiles—though near to tears.*] I have always wanted to make you say it—I have always sworn you *shouldn't*.

ERNEST. Because you can't care enough?

HELEN. Enough? Too much!

ERNEST [*overwhelmed*]. *You—love—me*. [*He takes her in his arms. He laughs—then she laughs—both are embarrassed.*]

HELEN. It is because I loved you that I didn't want you to say it—only I did. It is because I loved you that I went abroad—to stay, only I couldn't. I couldn't stay away! Oh, do you know how much I love you? No!—you're only a *man!*

ERNEST. You darling—do you know how much I love you? Every day there in the laboratory, when you in your apron, the apron I stole from your locker after you left—when you asked me for orders, did you never guess that I wanted to say "Love me!" Every day when you took up your work, did you never feel how I wanted to take you up in my arms?

HELEN [*eyes shut—nods*]. Why didn't you?

ERNEST. Why didn't I? How could I dare to hope that all this trembling loveliness could be just for me? I never dreamed there could be women like you. I always thought women were merely something to be wanted and worshipped, petted, patronized, soft little things to be wooed and won, married and owned. But you . . .

[HELEN *looks front. Moves away to left a step.*]
Helen, what's wrong?

HELEN.   Married, Ernest; *we* can't marry.

ERNEST.   Can't marry—why *can't* we marry— Oh! You mean your career——

HELEN.   My career—what does that matter? No, I mean yours . . .

ERNEST [*with a snap of his fingers*].   That for my *career*—you love me. You have been in my arms once—you and I can never forget that now. There's no turning back. It's all or nothing. Come to me!

[*She darts toward him, then stops.*]

HELEN.   But, Ernest! We *can't* marry. Think of all we've said.

ERNEST [*seizing her in man-fashion—he holds her fast*].   All we've said?—all we've said is nonsense. I love you.

CURTAIN

ACT II

SCENE: *Same as Act I. The next morning, Sunday.*
ERNEST *and* THEODORE *are discovered at breakfast, at table down right centre.* ERNEST *doesn't seem hungry and forgets to eat.* THEODORE, *enjoying his breakfast heartily, watches* ERNEST *out of the corner of his eye and smiles knowingly.*

THEODORE. What's the matter, old top? No appetite this morning?
[ERNEST *is gazing at the door at right, and doesn't hear. He is smoking a cigar.*]
Expecting something, eh? Why, of course, you were longing for codfish balls. [*Removes cover from plate and helps himself.* ERNEST *refuses the offered fish-ball, abstractedly shakes his head, and returns his gaze to the door.*] Oh, I know what you want. You want to go to church with me.
[ERNEST *doesn't hear.*]
Their rector is ill. So I agreed to take the service this morning. [*No answer.*] Always the way when off for a rest. [*No answer.*] Isn't it? [*No answer.* THEODORE *rises and walks around behind table and shouts in* ERNEST'S *ear.*] Isn't it?
ERNEST [*startled, jumps up*]. I beg your pardon.
THEODORE [*laughing*]. Oh. You're hopeless. [*Crossing to centre.*] I can't stand people who talk so much at breakfast.
ERNEST [*suddenly waking up*]. Wait a minute. Sit down. Have a cigarette. [*Offers cigarettes which are in a silver box on the table.*] Let's talk about God.
[THEODORE, *about to take cigarette, drops his hand.*]
But I mean it.
[THEODORE *takes cigarette.*]
I'd like to have a religion myself.
THEODORE. My dear boy, I never talk shop at the table.

44

ERNEST [*laughs*]. You never talk shop at all, unless one wants it. That's what I like about you, Theodore; you button your collar behind, but you believe in those who button theirs in front.

THEODORE. I had an idea you took no stock in religion. [*Sits left of table and lights cigarette.*]

ERNEST. Just what I thought—until—well, I've made a discovery, old friend. [*Sits at right of table.*]

THEODORE. Oh. Another discovery! [*Smiling.*] A scientific discovery?

ERNEST [*not sentimentally*]. It makes all science look like a . . . mere machine.

THEODORE. Well, if you feel so strongly about it—better come to church, after all!

ERNEST. I'm not talking about the church—I'm talking about religion.

THEODORE [*after surprise*]. You're not talking about religion; you're talking about love——

ERNEST. Same thing, isn't it?

THEODORE [*amused*]. Well, I'd hardly go *that* far!

ERNEST [*quietly*]. The divine fire that glorifies life and perpetuates it—the one eternal thing we mortals share with God— If *that* isn't religion, what is?

[THEODORE *smiles indulgently.*]

Tell me, Theodore—you know, my father never allowed me to go to church when young, and since then I've always *worked* on the holy Sabbath day [*smiles*]—like yourself—does the church still let innocent human beings think there's something carnal and wrong about sex?

[THEODORE *drops his eyes.* ERNEST *amused.*]

I see "nice" people should drop their eyes even at the mention of the word.

THEODORE [*uncomfortably*]. Sex is a necessary evil, I admit, but . . .

ERNEST. Evil! The God-given impulse which accounts for you sitting there, for me sitting here? The very heart and soul of life evil! Really, Theodore, I don't know much about *religion*, but that strikes me as blasphemy against the *Creator!*

THEODORE. My dear boy, unlike the modern young person of eighteen, I haven't the relish for such subjects.

I still feel outrageously reticent—a quaint heirloom from
the Victorian age.   But I think I may say that the church
believed in marriage before science was born.

ERNEST.   But why does the church keep on making
women promise to "serve and obey"?   Why marry them
with a ring?   It's merely a link of the ancient chain
[*smiles*]—in the days of physical force, made of iron, in
the days of financial force, made of gold.   But still a
chain, Theodore, still a chain.

THEODORE.   Symbols, my dear fellow, not to be taken
in a literal sense; time-honored and beautiful symbols.

ERNEST.   But why insult a woman you love even
symbolically?

THEODORE [*with a laugh*].   Oh, you scientists!   Have
you no idealism in your views?

ERNEST.   I haven't any *views*.   Science merely tries to
find the truth, and the church—the church tries to hide it.

THEODORE [*teasingly*].   Well, I know two young *scientists* who tried to hide the truth from each other and
from themselves.   And if I'm not mistaken, the church
helped to find it for them.   [*Leans across the table.*]   You
may as well know, my boy, the whole family are on to you.
Last evening after dinner when you took Helen for a walk
in the moonlight, instead of taking the train for town,
John threw fits all over his "little farm."   By the way,
how late did you two stay up?   I was in the library writing
my sermon until half after one.   You and Helen were still
out here telling each other—well, about ANTERIOR POLIO-
MYELITIS!

ERNEST [*has scarcely heard* THEODORE].   Theodore,
there's one belief you and I have in common, one faith
I'll never doubt again—I believe in heaven now.

THEODORE.   Why?

ERNEST.   Because I've been there.

[*Enter* JOHN *scowling.*]

Good morning.

[JOHN *grumpily rings bell, for breakfast.*]

Could you spare me five minutes?

JOHN.   Haven't had breakfast yet.   [*Picks newspaper
from couch, sits down and reads paper.   ERNEST looks at
THEODORE and smiles—then rises and follows JOHN to
centre.*]

ERNEST. Oh, all right, after breakfast.

JOHN. I've an appointment.

ERNEST [*smiles*]. I'll wait *my* turn.

JOHN. Going to be pretty busy to-day—you, too, I suppose, if you're sailing to-morrow.

[*Enter* THOMAS.]

Breakfast, Thomas!

[THOMAS *signals the second man, who brings on table, set for breakfast. He places it in centre, then picks up other table and leaves.* THOMAS *arranges chairs and brings couch down stage a little before he goes.*]

ERNEST [*still agreeable*]. I can postpone sailing till next week.

JOHN. Mustn't let *anything interfere* with your scientific career.

LUCY [*as she enters*]. Good morning.

ERNEST [*ignores* JOHN, *eagerly to* LUCY]. Could you tell me when she'll be down?

JOHN [*overriding* LUCY]. My sister is ill and won't be down at all, until *after* you leave.

[LUCY *shows discomfort.* THEODORE *tactfully turns to go.* LUCY *sits behind breakfast-table.*]

ERNEST [*crosses back to* JOHN. *Aroused at this snub, but controls himself and smiles*]. I don't believe you quite understand. It's merely as a conventional courtesy to you that I suggest and *advise* an interview.

JOHN. Don't inconvenience yourself on my account. When I want your advice I'll ask it.

ERNEST [*shrugs shoulders*]. Oh, very well, do as you please. [*To* THEODORE, *who has picked up hat and Bible.*] Wait, Theodore. [*Crosses up centre for his hat, which is on a small table, and looks at his watch.*] I think I'll go to church after all—until my train leaves.

THEODORE [*smoothing it over as he leaves*]. Come along . . . I'm going to preach about marriage!

ERNEST [*going, turns to* LUCY, *and bows urbanely*]. Thanks for all your kindness . . . may I trouble you to have the valet pack my things? I'll call for them on the way to the station. [*Starts off, then stops and turns to* JOHN.] I have no favors to ask of you. You don't own your sister—she owns herself. You might remember that. [*The scientist goes to church.*]

JOHN [*looks after* ERNEST. *Then sits at the table, with a loud laugh to show he doesn't care—and turns to* LUCY]. Rather impertinent for a two-thousand-dollar man. [*Throws newspaper on table, turns to his grapefruit—*LUCY *says nothing—she pours his coffee daintily, hands it to him solicitously. With growing resentment.*] Got his nerve! Seems to forget that I'm a trustee of the Baker Institute.

[LUCY *says nothing.* JOHN *tastes coffee, puts down cup violently and glares at* LUCY.]

Cold again! [*Eats grapefruit during following.*] Helen got her own way about going to college, going to work, going to live in her own apartment, but if she thinks she can marry *that* fellow . . .

[LUCY *cringes in dutiful silence as* JOHN *glares at her.*]

Humph! I've got more influence with old man Baker than all the rest of the Board combined. I could get Hamilton fired, too, if I tried.

[LUCY *pretends to be proud of her wonderful husband, like a true old-fashioned wife.*]

Well, why don't you say something?

LUCY [*startled*]. Why—why—I thought you did not like me to talk at breakfast, dear. [*She is frightened now—a worm that has never turned.*]

JOHN. Think I like you to sit there like a mummy?

[LUCY *hurt, but hiding it, smiles at her husband's witticism, makes no reply.*]

Doesn't it ever occur to you that I'd like my wife to be interesting? [*No reply.* JOHN *starts to open and glance at letters during following.*] Not often—just once in a while —for a *change*.

LUCY. Nothing I say seems to interest you any more, dear.

JOHN. Well, is that my fault?

LUCY. You don't like me to discuss your business affairs, John.

JOHN. What do you know about business affairs?

LUCY. What do you ever tell me?

JOHN. Why should I tell you? Suppose I want *my wife* to bother about money-making? Your business is to spend it. Woman's place is in the home.

LUCY. But, John, you're never interested in what I do in the home— Oh, not that I blame you, but . . .

JOHN. Well, why should I be? How many roses were transplanted Monday; what Cousin Margaret told you about the baby's new tooth Tuesday. Humph!

LUCY. When I try to take an interest in anything outside the home . . .

JOHN. Bah! Fads! Fads! One unwomanly female is enough for any family.

LUCY. Then, whatever you like, John, I'll try!

JOHN [*opens second letter*]. I'd like you to be just an old-fashioned wife, like my mother.

LUCY [*the tragedy of her life is in this line, but both the suppressed yearning and the reproach should be conveyed, if at all, quietly*]. But I'm not a mother.

JOHN [*angered. It's clearly an old sore subject. Crushes letter in his hand*]. If I've told you once, I've told you a hundred times! You're not to throw that up in my face. Haven't I given you everything else to make up for it? And what do I get? In season and out, when you speak and when you're silent, when you look at me and when you look away—it's reproach, reproach, reproach, all my married life. . . . For the last time, *cut that subject* out! [*He turns to his mail, opens the letter containing check.*]

LUCY. I'm sorry, John. It's only that—well, one finds it rather difficult to be an old-fashioned wife in a new-fashioned home.

JOHN [*does not reply. Tense over a letter. Sudden change in manner*]. Have you a dressmaker named Charcot?

LUCY. Yes, John, this is one of Charcot's— [*Indicating the dress she wears.*] Do you like it, dear?

JOHN [*holding letter*]. Did you have it charged in my name?

LUCY. Why, John! You *know* you never let me pay cash for anything. Every shoe-string is charged to you.

JOHN [*significantly now*]. Do they ever overcharge me?

LUCY [*suddenly terrified, but controlling it*]. I suppose we all make mistakes at times.

JOHN. Yes, Thomas made a mistake this time. He put this letter among mine. It's addressed to you.

Lucy [*panting*].   Then give it to me.   [*Reaches for letter.*]

John [*keeping it out of her reach*].   No! I'll read it to *you* first.   [*Reads.*]   "Dear Madam, enclosed please find check to your order for twenty-five dollars, being balance due from bill paid August 1st."

[Lucy's *eyes down, she is twisting her napkin.*]
You said nothing about their overcharging me when we went over the bills last month.

Lucy.   I never *can* understand business affairs.

John.   But the bill was paid by my secretary at my office.   This check—[*holding it up*] is sent to my wife at my home.   Why?

[Lucy *makes no reply.*]
Lucy, how long has this been going on?

Lucy [*after a pause*].   The first time I ever tried it— and of course I'm caught.

John [*growing wrath*].   So!   My own wife deliberately enters into a conspiracy with a vulgar little dressmaker to overcharge her husband so that she may obtain a rebate in cash!   Oh, Lucy, Lucy!   And all for twenty-five dollars.

[Lucy *weeps.*]
Who taught you this woman's trick?

Lucy.   It was not a woman.

John.   What's this?   A man, eh?   [*Half rises.*]   Oho! [*Jealousy surging up.*]   Who is he?

[Lucy *cowers in silence, leaning across table.*]
Are you going to tell me?

Lucy [*leaning back, nods*].   As soon as I get my courage up.

John [*rising*].   Quick!   His name.   I'll kill him.

Lucy [*surprisingly bold—sneers*].   Oh, no you won't!

John.   The damned sneak—   [*Goes down stage a step or two, then turns back.*]   Who taught you this contemptible trick?   Answer me.

Lucy.   You did.

John.   I?   What are you talking about?

Lucy.   Weren't you indicted and fined for entering into a conspiracy to take rebates from the railroads?

John.   Lucy!   How dare you?

LUCY. Well, that's how I got the idea.

JOHN [*crosses down right*]. How like a woman! That was business. Why, at that time the biggest men in the country were indicted.

LUCY. Precisely. You told me at the time it was all right to do such things.

JOHN. Of course it was, everybody did it. But to cheat your own husband.

LUCY. But it's all right to cheat your own country.

JOHN. Bah! At that time those fellows at Washington—they understood the country's needs about as well as you do.

LUCY. And what do *you* know about *my* needs?

JOHN. Your needs! That's the limit! Why, I give you everything! [*Crosses back to table.*] You don't have to raise a finger, you don't even have to *think* for yourself. What more do you want? [*To himself.*] Twenty-five dollars.

LUCY. Yes, twenty-five dollars. I wanted a little ready cash . . . something I could call my own—spend as I pleased without first wheedling it out of you and then having you scowl over the bills. Oh, if men only knew how we loathe this begging and wheedling!

JOHN. But don't I give you everything money can buy?

LUCY. But you never give me money to buy anything.

JOHN. What did you want money for?

LUCY. A taxicab.

JOHN [*amazed, perplexed, sits again*]. A taxicab? Haven't we cars enough?

LUCY. I can't always take one of our cars when I go into town to shop—it's too far. The day I bought this frock, Jean paid for the taxicab from the station— That's why I asked her to go with me. You give her a regular allowance—you never give me a cent, if you can help it. Marjorie Hendricks paid for my luncheon. Why, I didn't even have a twenty-five-cent piece to tip the porter on the train or the girl in the restaurant cloakroom; and oh, it's so humiliating always to let one's friends pay for everything.

JOHN [*a pause*]. Say, do you suppose Marjorie Hendricks and the others talk this over with their husbands?

LUCY. I don't know; I don't care!

JOHN. Well, I do. See here, Lucy, I'm going to forgive you [*tears up check*]; I'm going to tell my secretary to send you a regular monthly allowance like Jean's and you can spend it as you damn please. Nobody shall say *I'm* a tightwad with my wife. [*Rises, crosses to right.*]

LUCY. I don't want an allowance.

JOHN [*crossing back to table again*]. You don't want an allowance! Then what *do* you want?

LUCY [*after a slight pause*]. I want to go.

JOHN. Go where? When? How long?

LUCY. Now—any place—always.

JOHN [*sits again. Picks up newspaper and starts to read*]. Oh, I guess not. This is just a sudden feminine whim.

LUCY. It's been my constant thought ever since I married you. But—I never dared tell you till now.

JOHN. So you'd like to leave me, would you? Divorce?

[LUCY *nods yes.*]
You have no grounds for divorce, my dear.

LUCY. But *you* will have, after I leave you.

JOHN. You've got no lover to leave with.

LUCY [*fastidiously*]. But couldn't I just *desert* you—without anything horrid?

JOHN. No money to desert with— [*Smiles.*] You don't expect me to grant you that allowance on *such* terms?

LUCY. I'll earn my own living.

JOHN. You, you've never been trained to earn money, only to spend it. Think of all the young women looking for work who *are* trained for it. You, you aren't even young!

LUCY. You won't let me escape decently when I tell you I don't care to stay? When I tell you I can't stand being under the same roof with you? When I tell you that I am sick [*rises*] in my soul of this life!

JOHN. But, you see, I *can* stand it. I want you to stay. I am not sick of it.

[LUCY *turns to him in disgust.*]
In fact, when you look that way, you interest me. [*Throws newspaper over on couch. Rises and crosses to* LUCY.]

LUCY [*shrinking from him*]. Don't come near me!

Every time you touch me I have to nerve myself to stand it.

JOHN. Why, what's suddenly got into you?

LUCY. Suddenly! Since the first.

JOHN. Good Lord, if I only gave you something to worry about; if I ran after other women like old man Baker . . .

LUCY. If you only would! Then you would let *me* alone.

JOHN. Oh, I'll buy you those pearls. [*Crosses in anger over to the right.*]

LUCY [*indignant and infuriated by his lack of imagination*]. Pearls! Ugh! I'm not your mistress to be bought with pearls!

JOHN [*shocked*]. Why, Lucy, you ought to be ashamed. [*Coming back to her.*] You are my wife.

LUCY. Yes, that's the difference. If I were your mistress, I could get away.

JOHN. I forbid your saying such things. I forbid your even thinking such things!

LUCY. By what right?

JOHN. The right given me by law and religion. I am your lawful husband. [*Takes her in his arms.*]

LUCY. Yes, this is lawful but—oh, what laws you men have made for women.

JOHN [*making free with her*]. I love you—despite everything. I want you and you belong to me. I'll never let you go.

LUCY. But you don't respect me, and I—I hate you; oh, how I hate you.

JOHN [*releasing* LUCY, *whispers*]. Now brace up; what's the use of letting others know? Play the game. You must.

LUCY. Oh, I suppose so. I always do. What else can I do? But day after day—day after day—ugh!

[*Enter the* JUDGE, *telegram in hand.* LUCY *and* JOHN *separate.*]

JUDGE [*enters in a very unhappy frame of mind*]. I never felt so blue in my life. [*Almost to himself.*]

JOHN [*turning from* LUCY]. Another telegram from Aunt Julia? Get them every day?

JUDGE [*proudly*]. Yes, John, fresh every hour. What do you think's happened? [*Shows the telegram.*] She went to the theatre last night and caught cold.

JOHN [*smiling*]. But why telegraph *you* about *that?*

JUDGE. Got the habit of telling me her troubles—can't break it, even in Reno.

JOHN [*signalling* LUCY *to play up*]. But you said she hated the theatre.

JUDGE. She does, she does, but I'm fond of it. Went for my sake—got the habit of sacrificing herself for my sake. Just as hard to break good habits as bad, John, just as hard.

JOHN [*with a significant glance at* LUCY]. True women enjoy sacrificing themselves.

[LUCY *crosses up to centre.*]

JUDGE. Yes, that's what we tell 'em. Well, we ought to know, John, we make 'em do it. [*Brings out fountain pen and sits abruptly on the couch.*] That's what I'll tell *her*. I can hear her laugh. Say, John— [JOHN *looks.*] You remember her laugh?

LUCY. A telegraph blank?

JUDGE [*with a humorous expression he brings a whole pad of telegraph blanks out of another pocket*]. No, thanks, carry them with me nowadays. [*Begins to write.*] Wish I hadn't sold my Western Union stock, John.

JOHN. I don't think you want that divorce very much.

JUDGE [*reprovingly as he begins to write*]. Doesn't matter what *I* want—what she wants is the point. You should give the woman you marry tutti-frutti, divorces—everything . . . Good heavens! I believe I've got the habit myself—and God knows *I* don't enjoy sacrifice. I'm a man! . . . The superior sex. . . .

JOHN. I don't believe you appreciate that wife of yours.

JUDGE [*between the words he's writing*]. Don't I? It isn't every wife—that'd travel away out to Reno—you know how she hates travelling—and go to a theatre—and catch a cold—and get a divorce—all for the sake of an uncongenial husband. I'm proud of that woman. [*Suddenly getting an idea, strikes stand.*] *I* know what gave her a cold. She raised all the windows in her bedroom—

for *my* sake. I'll give her the very devil for that—
[*Writing*.] "How dare you leave the windows open in
your bedroom when I'm not there." [*Pause—sentimentally*.] Poor little thing! She doesn't know how to take
care of herself without me. [*Musing*.] I wonder if she
ever will.

JOHN [*as a servant enters*]. Thomas, send that telegram.

JUDGE. Wait till I sign it. [*Writes*.] "Ducky."

[BUTLER *takes telegram and goes*.]

JOHN. Uncle Everett, I want your advice.

JUDGE [*as if shocked*]. Oh, John, you want a divorce?

JOHN. No, we are not that sort—are we, Lucy? [*No
answer*.] Are we, dear?

LUCY [*after a pause*]. No. We are not that sort.
[*She turns away*.]

JOHN. We believe in the sanctity of the home, the
holiness of marriage.

LUCY. The holiness of marriage. [*Turns away, shuddering and goes into house*.]

[JUDGE *replaces small stand*.]

JOHN [*goes up stage and sees* JEAN *and* REX *on the terrace*]. Oh. Here come Jean and Rex. Let's give them
a clear field. Love's young dream, Uncle Everett.

[JUDGE *rises and goes toward the door with* JOHN.]

JUDGE. Hum. So you've given that young scalawag
your consent. You didn't bring up that little chorus-girl matter?

JOHN. Oh. That's all fixed. No scandal, no black-mail. The old man fixed it.

JUDGE. Old man Baker? Well, that old reprobate
ought to know how.

[*As* JOHN *and* JUDGE *go out,* JEAN *and* REX *enter*.]

JEAN [*coming down as if to go out*]. Good-by, Rex,
I'll see you at dinner.

REX [*coming to centre, stopping* JEAN *before she can
leave*]. But, what's the matter, Jean? You've hardly
said a word all through our ride.

JEAN. Rex, you weren't in love with me yesterday—
you aren't now. You would get out of it if you could;
but you can't, honorably. You're a good sport and I
admire you for that.

Rex. Do you? I can't say I admire myself very much, after what happened yesterday. I've felt like a brute ever since. Of course you tried your best to prevent it—see what I mean? you ran away from me.

Jean. Don't you know why I ran away? to make you follow. I made you catch me. I made you kiss me. Then you realized that we had been thrown together constantly, purposely together, if you care to know it.

Rex. Why, I never thought a woman could be capable of such honesty. Say, you aren't like the rest that have been shoved at me. Why, I can respect you.

Jean. Could you respect me if you knew that I let you propose to me yesterday, when I cared for some one else?

Rex. What's that, Jean, some one else? . . .

Jean. That's not fair to you—to me—to him.

Rex. Who is he? why didn't you tell me?

Jean. I am telling you now. What have you ever told me about yourself?

Rex [angry, loud]. You had no right to play fast and loose with me.

Jean [agreeing, low]. I'm making the only amends I can. You are free, I tell you.

Rex [with sudden desire, high]. But I don't want to be free. He can't have you. You are mine. If you think you can make me stop loving you . . .

Jean [interrupting, low]. You don't love me, Rex. You're jealous. You've never been in love with me. Let's at least be honest about it. You merely want me now because you can't have me.

Rex [frantic to possess what he cannot have]. You're thinking of that other chap. You're engaged to me and you stay engaged to me. I usually get what I want, and I want you now as I never wanted anything in my life! I'll win you from him yet.

[Enter Helen from the house.]

Helen. Oh, I beg your pardon. Lucy said John was out here.

Jean. I'll call him. [She goes into the garden, running, glad to escape from Rex.] John! John!

[Helen sits down.]

Rex. I'll call him. [*He runs into the garden after* Jean.] Jean! Wait, Jean!

    [John *enters. He looks after* Rex *and then comes down. He and* Helen *take each other's measure in smiling silence.*]

John [*pleasantly, but with gravity*]. You and I aren't going to quarrel, are we, Little Sister?

Helen. Depends on you, Big Brother.

John [*insisting on seriousness*]. Helen, dear, you are about to make the most momentous decision of your whole life.

Helen [*lightly*]. I've already made it. And now I'll tell you a-all about it.

John [*stopping her*]. Just a minute. . . . I'm afraid that we'll have to look at this little romance of yours practically, my dear. I know it all sounds very pretty in a story-book—"willing to sacrifice her career for love" and all that. But how about the man you love? Want to sacrifice his career too?

Helen. But I have no intention of sacrificing what you are pleased to call my career. And so he won't have to sacrifice his. All you have to do is to give me back my job.

John [*taken aback*]. What's that?

Helen. I am absolutely indispensable to him. He is going to demand of the Board that I be reinstated. [*She looks determined.* John *does too, but temporizes.*]

John. Is Hamilton that sort? Would he want the woman he loves to work?

    [*She understands* John's *views, and smiles.*]

Helen. He says the woman he loves is too good to loaf. Wasn't it nice of him? I think it's one of the nicest things he ever said to me.

    [*He cannot comprehend her views, and scowls.*]

John [*sitting on sofa with* Helen]. That's all very well in theory, but who'll take care of your home when you're at work and who'll take care of your work when you're at home? Combine the two and you'll fail at both.

Helen. But suppose I stop working with him.

John. But you couldn't both live on his salary. What

was it you said yesterday . . . "needs every cent of his two thousand for books, travel, scientific conferences" . . .

HELEN.   Then what do you want?

JOHN [*with force*].   I want you to show that you meant what you said.   Invent some excuse to send him off to Paris at once.   For the lives of little children, for the whole future of the race, sacrifice yourself!   Refuse to marry Ernest Hamilton.

HELEN.   You needn't shout so, John.   [*Places hand over* JOHN's *mouth, then rises.*]   I've done it already.

JOHN [*rises and follows her*].   What!   You have refused to marry him?

HELEN [*calmly*].   That's what I came to tell you.

JOHN.   You give him up?   He'll go to Paris alone?

HELEN [*directly, forcefully, but still amused*].   Give him up?   Never!   We'll give up marriage but we won't give up each other.   We're sailing for Paris in the morning.

JOHN [*springing back, almost screams*].   Without a marriage ceremony?

HELEN [*quietly*].   Of course.   We never believed in it, anyway.

JOHN.   What!   And this is my own sister!   Think what you're saying.

HELEN.   I've thought all night, John.   You've shown me how to say it.   I agree with all you said.   Marriage *would* destroy his usefulness, *but* so would separation. "Your great humanitarian work"—he needs *me* for that work—more than he needs a home.

JOHN [*interrupting*].   But—but . . .

HELEN.   As you said: "Who would take care of my home when I'm at work—who would take care of my work when I'm at home."   It's all true, too true.   We cannot have a home . . .

JOHN [*interrupting*].   But—I . . .

HELEN.   But didn't you say "For the lives of little children—for the whole future of the race, I must sacrifice myself—refuse to marry Ernest Hamilton"?   Well, John, I have followed your advice already.

JOHN [*still gasping*].   But—but—why, I'm not even shocked.   Do you notice?   I'm not even shocked.   Because everything you have said, everything you have done—it all *proves* that you are a good woman.

HELEN. If I were a bad woman I'd inveigle him into *marriage*.

JOHN. Inveigle? Into marriage? Are you joking?

HELEN [*as if saying "calm yourself"*]. John, weren't you serious when you begged me not to marry him?

JOHN. But this . . . did you for one moment dream that I would consent to this sort of thing?

HELEN. Not for one moment. I'm not asking your consent—I'm just telling you.

JOHN [*looks at her. She returns his gaze. She is not defiant, just determined and sweet*]. Bah! All pose and poppycock! [*Crosses and touches push-button on doorframe.*] I'll soon put a stop to this nonsense. [*Muttering.*] Most ridiculous thing I ever heard of.

HELEN. John, I haven't told you half my reasons—only those you can understand, but nothing you can say, nothing you can do, will stop me now.

JOHN. We'll see about that.

[*Enter BUTLER.*]

Ask the others to step out here at once—all except Miss Jean and Mr. Baker. I don't want them.

[*BUTLER bows and starts off.*]

Is Doctor Hamilton about?

BUTLER. No, sir, he's gone to church. [*He goes out.*]

JOHN. To church! My God!

[*HELEN pays no attention, looks straight out in front, head high, eyes clear and wide open.*]

First of all, I'm going to ask them to look you in the *face*. Then you can make this statement to them if you wish, and . . . look *them* in the face.

HELEN [*dignity—force—conviction*]. John, if I were being forced into such a marriage as poor little Jean's—if I led such a life as Lucy's—I'd be ashamed to look any one in the face; but in the eyes of God who made *love*—no matter how I may appear in the eyes of man, who made *marriage*—I *know* that I am doing right.

[*Enter LUCY followed by the JUDGE.*]

JOHN [*not seeing them*]. Say that to Uncle Everett and Cousin Theodore, say that to my wife, stand up and say that to the world if you dare!

HELEN. Certainly, I'll say it now. [*To others, simply, quite cheerfully.* JOHN *turns and sees* LUCY *and* JUDGE.]

John has convinced me *practically* of what I already believed *theoretically* about marriage, and I have made up my mind not to marry Doctor Hamilton.

LUCY *and* JUDGE. What! [*Turn to each other.*]

JOHN [*takes* HELEN *by the hand and brings her over a little*]. Wait, Uncle Everett! Lucy! Look this girl in the eye.

[*They do so.*]
Go on, Helen.

HELEN [*looking back at them*]. But as we need each other—in our work and in our life—why, we simply are going to have each other—always, until life is ended and our work is done, and that's all there is to it.

JOHN. That's all there is to it!

JUDGE. That's all there is to it!

JOHN [*laughing*]. Without a marriage ceremony! Can you beat it?

LUCY. Helen! No! [LUCY *almost faints and sits on sofa.*]

JOHN. Don't you see through all this? A bluff to gain my consent—a trick to get his salary raised.

HELEN [*simply*]. No amount of money can induce me to marry Ernest Hamilton. I have too much self-respect.

LUCY [*gasping*]. Too much!

JOHN. Why, the whole thing is utterly absurd on the face of it. If she really meant to run away with this highbrow, would she stand up here and announce it in cold blood to her own family?

[*All turn and look at* HELEN.]
[*Enter* THEODORE *from the left.*]

HELEN [*with quiet scorn*]. Do you suppose I'd run away *without* announcing it to my own family?

THEODORE [*coming down to* HELEN—*beaming*]. Announcing it? Aha! And what are you announcing, my dear?

[*All in a panic.* JOHN *gets behind the sofa.*]

LUCY. Her engagement, Theodore, her engagement.

JUDGE [*crossing to centre*]. Exactly. John has suddenly seen a new light.

JOHN [*louder*]. Helen has gained my full consent to marry Doctor Hamilton. I think most highly of him.

JUDGE [*apart*]. Yes, I thought you would.

THEODORE [*delighted*]. And withal he has a deep religious nature. Congratulations, my dear; he'll make an ideal husband.

[*Takes Helen's hands, about to kiss her.*]

HELEN [*can't help smiling*]. Thank you, Theodore, but I don't want a husband and I'm not engaged to be married.

THEODORE [*looks from one to the other*]. A lovers' quarrel?—already!

JUDGE [*enjoying it*]. No, Theodore, these lovers are in perfect accord; they both have conscientious scruples against marriage.

JOHN. Conscientious!

JUDGE. So they are simply going to set up housekeeping without the mere formality of a wedding ceremony.

[THEODORE *drops* HELEN'S *hands.*]

HELEN [*crosses to* JUDGE]. We are not going to do anything of the sort.

THEODORE. Shame, Uncle Everett, shame.

HELEN. We are not going to set up housekeeping at all. In Paris I'll go back to that same nice little pension near the Luxembourg Gardens, and he'll live near the Pasteur. We'll work together and we'll play together and we'll take wonderful trips together. When we come back to America, he will keep his present quarters and I mine. But we won't have that daily binding, grinding prosaicness of married life together.

JUDGE. There are worse things, Helen, even than marriage.

HELEN. I thought so too at first, but I know what marriage will do for this man. I haven't played with him, I've worked with him, and I know.

THEODORE. But if you love him, my dear, marriage brings together those who love each other truly.

HELEN. But those who love each other truly, don't need anything to bring them together. The difficulty is to keep them apart.

JOHN. Oh, that's all romantic rot. Every one feels that way when they are first married.

HELEN. First? Then the object of marriage is not to bring together those who love each other, but to keep together those who do not. What a horrible thing marriage must be.

JUDGE [*puzzled*]. Let me get that, will you? [*Then understanding.*] Oh, you wish to be free to separate. Now I have it.

HELEN. To separate? What a dreadful idea. Free to keep together. Marriage always puts people asunder.

JUDGE. God bless my soul! [*Apart to others.*] Always goes me one better.

HELEN [*correcting herself*]. Oh, not all people, uncle. [*She fondles* JUDGE.] I admit that *you* and dear Aunt Julia are happy together—you have so many tastes in common.

JUDGE [*apart*]. Tutti-frutti!

HELEN [*takes* THEODORE'S *arm and* JUDGE'S]. But look at *most* modern marriages. He goes down-town and works, she stays up-town and plays. He belongs to the laboring class, she to the leisure class. They think different thoughts, talk different languages, care for different things; legally it's union, but socially it's a mesalliance, and in the eyes of God it must be something worse. [*To* JUDGE.] No wonder there's one divorce to every ten marriages, uncle.

JUDGE. Be logical, my dear, married first and divorced later. Be chronological, at least.

HELEN. But you see *I* don't want to be divorced—or married either.

JOHN [*behind the sofa*]. Do you want to be disgraced?
  [*During this bit of conversation* THEODORE *goes up and around behind sofa with* JOHN.]

LUCY. Do you want to be ostracized?

HELEN [*crosses to* LUCY]. Of course none of those costly well-kept *wives* on your visiting-list will call upon me. But so much the better! Instead of *one* day at home like a lady, instead of making a tired husband work for me, I'll have all my days free to work *with* him, like the true old-fashioned woman you all admire.

JOHN [*bursts out*]. Oh, this is all nonsense. I tell you,

whether you like it or not, you've simply *got* to marry this fellow.

LUCY. Why, certainly.

THEODORE. You've got to.

HELEN. I can't marry Ernest, I love him.

[THEODORE *is astonished, the others throw up their hands, the* BUTLER *appears.*]

BUTLER. Doctor Hamilton is outside in a taxicab, sir.

JOHN. Ha! Show him here at once.

BUTLER. He says he does not care to come in, sir, unless you are ready to talk to him.

JOHN. Well, of all the nerve! You bet I'm ready.

[*Starts off;* LUCY *comes down restraining* JOHN.]

JUDGE [*rising and coming to centre*]. Now, wait a minute, wait a minute. [*Restraining* JOHN. *Calmly to servant.*] Ask Doctor Hamilton kindly to wait in the library.

[*The* BUTLER *goes.*]

Now, we're *all* a bit overwrought. [*Soothes* HELEN, *pats her hand, puts arm about her.*] I still believe in you, Helen. I still believe in him. [*To all.*] They both want to do right, but love has made them blind—blind to *their own interests.* He's so absorbed in his great work for mankind that he doesn't realize what he has asked Helen to do.

HELEN [*can't help smiling as she puts in quietly*]. So I told him—when he asked me to marry him.

JOHN. What?

LUCY. He asked you?

THEODORE [*coming down to right centre*]. To marry him?

HELEN. Of course! So absorbed—not in mankind, uncle, but in me, that he—"didn't realize what he was asking me to do."

LUCY [*utterly amazed*]. And you refused him? The man who loves you honorably?

HELEN. Of course!

[*All amazed, look at one another.*]

You don't suppose I'd take advantage of the poor fellow's weakness.

JOHN. And then he proposed this wicked substitute!

Poisoned her innocent mind—the bounder! [*Going.*]
I'll . . .

HELEN [*interrupts, unexcitedly*].   But he did nothing of
the sort.

JOHN [*turning*].   Oh, your own idea, was it?

HELEN.   Of course!

[*All exchange looks.*]

In justice to Ernest, I must tell you that in his heart he
quite agrees with me about marriage, but he has a quaint
mannish notion that I must be "protected"!

JOHN [*to others*].   But he's willing to take advantage of
the poor child's ignorance—the cad! [*To* THEODORE.]
"Deep religious nature"—eh?

THEODORE.   I can't believe it of Ernest.

HELEN.   He knows nothing about it yet.

JOHN [*stops*].   What?

HELEN.   Why, I haven't even seen him since I refused
to marry him.   [*Sensation.*]

[*The* BUTLER *returns.*]

BUTLER.   Doctor Hamilton asks to see Miss Helen
while waiting.

[HELEN *crosses to the right.*   JOHN *stops her.*]

JOHN.   Just a minute, Helen—please. [*To* LUCY.]
Hold her! [JOHN *crosses to centre as* HELEN *goes up to the
sofa with* LUCY.   *Apart to* JUDGE *and* THEODORE.]   We've
got to get him off to Paris at once.

JUDGE [*apart to* JOHN].   But you can't stop her following.   John, she's on the edge of the precipice—don't
shove her over! [*Calmly to* BUTLER, *overriding* JOHN.]
Tell Doctor Hamilton that Miss Helen will see him here.

[*The* BUTLER *leaves.*]

JOHN.   Are you crazy?   We've got to keep 'em apart
—our one chance to save her!

JUDGE.   No, bring them together.   *That* is our one
chance!

JOHN.   All the same, I'm going round in front and keep
an eye on that taxi.   [*Starting up stage.*]

JUDGE.   What for?

JOHN [*excitedly*].   Because I know they are going to
elope in it.

JUDGE.   They're not going to elope.

JOHN.   How do you know?

JUDGE.   If they were going to elope they'd elope first, and write you all about it later.

[*Exit all except* HELEN *and* LUCY, *who lingers.*]

LUCY [*has turned back to* HELEN, *as the others leave*]. Helen . . . do you really mean to offer yourself on such terms to the man who loves you honorably?

HELEN.   Under the circumstances no other terms would be honorable—yes, Lucy, I'm going to do it now.

LUCY.   Then if you do he'll never look at you again. [*Exit* LUCY.]

[ERNEST *enters from the house and rushes down to* HELEN *eagerly.* HELEN *is seated on the sofa. She rises as* ERNEST *enters.*]

HELEN.   Ernest!

ERNEST.   At last! [*He takes her in his arms, she clings to him and gazes into his eyes, a long embrace.*] Tell me that you're all right again.

HELEN [*smiling with love and trust*].   Except that you deserted me, dear, just when I needed you most.

ERNEST.   Deserted you? Your brother said you were ill.

HELEN.   Ah, I see [*shrugs*] . . . he was mistaken.

ERNEST.   But, never mind now, I've got you at last, and I'll never, never let you go. You've got to sail with me to-morrow. Together! Oh, think! Together! [*Another embrace. He is jubilant and boyish.*]

HELEN.   Are you *sure* you love me?

ERNEST [*laughs from joy of her nearness*].   Am I sure? Ten million times more to-day than yesterday.

HELEN.   All the same, it can never be as I love you.

ERNEST [*gaily, her hands in his*].   Then you can apologize.

HELEN.   Apologize, for what?

ERNEST.   For saying, years and years ago—in other words, last night—that you didn't think you'd marry me after all.

[*She starts.   Sits on sofa.*]

Why, what's the matter? You *are* ill.

HELEN.   No, oh, no.

ERNEST [*sitting with* HELEN *on sofa*].   Then let's get good old Theodore to marry us to-day.

[HELEN *gazes at him.*]

Still a few lingering doubts? I had hoped a good night's rest would put those little prejudices to sleep.

HELEN. Sleep? [*Just gazes at him.*]

ERNEST. So you couldn't sleep? Neither could I, I was too happy to sleep. I was afraid I'd miss some wondrous throbbing thought of your loveliness. [*Takes her passive hand, puts a kiss in it, and closes it reverently, while she looks on without moving.*] Do you know— [*smiling sigh*] I'm disappointed in love. I always thought it meant soft sighs and pretty speeches. It means agony, an agony of longing, delicious agony, but oh, terrific.

[*She says nothing but gazes at him.*]

HELEN. Ernest. [*Rises.* ERNEST *also rises.*] It isn't easy for me to say this, but— I cannot marry you, dear.

ERNEST [*takes her in his arms*]. You've got to. You are in my arms. You are helpless. So am I— In the clutch of forces more potent than our little selves—forces that *brought* us into the world. Forces that have *made* the world. Whether you will or no, this beautiful thing is sweeping you and me together. And you must yield.

HELEN. Ah, my dear, could anything make it more beautiful than it is now?

ERNEST. It is perfect. The one divine thing we share with God. The church is right in that respect. I used to look upon it as a mere contract. It's a religious sacrament.

HELEN. Do the words repeated by a clergyman make it sacred?

ERNEST [*laughs*]. That mediæval incantation? No, love given by God—not the artificial *form* made by man.

HELEN [*jubilant*]. Just what I said! I knew you'd agree. [*Steps back and offers her hand.*] Yes, I'll go with you.

ERNEST [*about to take her in his arms again*]. You darling!

HELEN [*stops him*]. But not as your wife.

ERNEST [*stops—perplexed*]. You mean . . . [*a long pause*] without marriage?

HELEN. I mean without marriage.

[*They look into each other's eyes; neither blinks.*]

ERNEST [*solemnly*]. A moment ago I thought I loved you as much as man could love woman. I was mistaken in you—I was mistaken in myself. I love you as man never loved before. [*With adoration.*] You wonderful woman!

HELEN [*holds out her hand to be shaken, not to be caressed*]. Then you agree?

ERNEST [*takes her hand*]. Why, of course not! You blessed girl, don't you suppose I understand? It's all for my sake. Therefore, for your sake—no. Do you think I'd let you do anything for anybody's sake you're sure later to regret?

HELEN. Then don't ask me to marry you, Ernest. We'd both regret that later. It would destroy the two best things in life, the things that have brought us together, love and work.

ERNEST. Nonsense. Nothing could do that, not even marriage! And, besides—think of our poor horrified families! Think of the world's view.

HELEN. Do you fear the world's views?

ERNEST [*enfolding her*]. With you in my arms, I want nothing from heaven. I fear nothing from hell, but my dear . . . [*shrugs and comes down to earth, with a smile, releasing her*] consider the price.

HELEN. I am willing to pay it.

ERNEST. I am not willing to let you.

HELEN [*getting away from him*]. You'll have to be. I shall go with you on my terms or not at all.

ERNEST [*steps back. Emphatic*]. You will come with me as my wife or stay at home!

HELEN [*gasping*]. Now? After all I've said, all I've done? Ernest! I've told the family! I took for granted . . . why, Ernest! You wouldn't, you couldn't leave me behind now.

ERNEST. Thanks to you and what you've made of me, I must and will!

HELEN. Ernest! . . . Ernest! [*She puts arms around his neck.*]

ERNEST. If you love me enough for that—[*taking her arms away*] I love you enough for this. Come when you're ready to marry me.

HELEN [*breaks out angry and injured*]. Do you think I'll offer myself again on any terms? Never!

ERNEST [*low*]. You must marry me, and you will!

HELEN.   You don't know me.   I will not!

ERNEST [*after a struggle*].   Then—I go alone.

HELEN [*broken-hearted*].   No!

ERNEST.   Good-by!   [ERNEST *goes out.   She waits motionless until she hears the automobile carrying him away. Immediately she turns from stone to tears, with a low wail. In utter despair, hands outstretched, she sinks down, and buries her face in her hands.*]

> [LUCY, THEODORE, JUDGE, *and* JOHN *hurry back all excited.*]

THEODORE [*enters first*].   Did you see the horrified look on Ernest's face?   [*Going down.*]

LUCY.   Revolted—running away from her.

JOHN [*to* HELEN].   What did I tell you?

LUCY.   You've thrown away the love of an honorable man.

THEODORE.   Trampled on the finest feelings of a deep nature.

JOHN.   You've lost your chance to marry, you've lost your chance to work—and now, by George, you'll cut out independence, and stay at home where women belong—and live down this disgrace, if you can.

LUCY.   With one excuse or another—he'll stay away, he'll never come back.

HELEN.   He will, he will.   He can't stay away.

> [ERNEST *enters rapidly, stops and takes in scene.   No one sees him.*]

JOHN.   He'll never look at you again, and I don't blame him.   I'm a man and I know.   We don't respect women who sell out so cheap.

ERNEST.   You lie!   [*Coming down.   All turn amazed.*] Helen!

HELEN.   Ernest!   [*He takes her in his arms.*]   I knew you'd come back.   You *will* accept my terms.

ERNEST.   We'll discuss that later.

HELEN.   Then why did you come back?

ERNEST.   Because, just as I started, I saw in a flash all this.   I knew what they'd think.   I knew what they'd say.   I knew *they* could not understand.

JOHN.   Understand what?   If you respected this girl why did you run away?

ERNEST [*turning to* JOHN].   To protect her from myself.

JOHN.   Then why come back?

ERNEST.   To protect her from you.   Cowards, hypocrites, pharisees.

JOHN [*advancing menacingly*].   By what right do you come into my home?   By what right do you take my sister in your arms?

JUDGE [*gravely, judicially*].   Careful, John, careful.

ERNEST.   By a right more ancient than man-made law. I have come to the cry of my mate.   I'm here to fight for the woman I love.   [*Turning to* JOHN, *defying the world.*] My trip to Paris is postponed.   One week from to-day gather all your family here, and we'll make our declaration to the world.

JUDGE [*stepping down to* JOHN].   Play for time, John.

JOHN [*to* ERNEST].   Do you mean to marry her or not?   Speak my language.

ERNEST.   She decides.   Not you.   [*He steps back and* HELEN *crosses to* JOHN.]

HELEN.   No.   No.   No.

JOHN [*to* HELEN].   Then you'll go with this damned fanatic, only over my dead body.   [JOHN *advances toward* HELEN *in rage.*   THEODORE *and* JUDGE *cross between* JOHN *and* HELEN, *restraining him.*]

HELEN [*high*].   And that will only tell the world the thing you wish to hide.

ERNEST [*higher*].   There are laws to prevent marrying in some cases, but none to enforce it on women—unless they will it.

[JEAN *enters from centre.   Stops on hearing the following.*]

JOHN.   Enforce?   Do you think I will ever allow a sister of mine to marry a libertine?

JEAN.   But I'm not going to marry Rex.   I've just told him.   My engagement is broken.

[*General consternation.*   JEAN *runs into the house sobbing.*]

JOHN [*to* LUCY].   Great heavens.   What next?   Don't let the Bakers get wind of this, or we'll never patch it up. [*Turning to* ERNEST.]   As for you, you get right out of here.

[JUDGE *goes up stage and sits, and remains there to the curtain, trying to think of some way out of the difficulty.*]

ERNEST [*stepping back a little*]. Oh, very well, this is your property.

HELEN [*starts up. To* JOHN]. But I am not your property. I go, too.

THEODORE. Helen, don't commit this sin.

JOHN. Let her go. A woman who will give herself to a man without marriage is no sister of mine.

HELEN. Give? But if I sold myself as you are forcing poor little Jean to do—to a man she does not love, a libertine, who does not really love her—that is not sin. That is respectability. To entrap a man into marriage by playing the shameless tricks of the prostitute, that is "holy matrimony." But to give yourself of your own free will to the man you love—and trust—and can help— oh, if this is sin—then I will live and die a sinner. [*She turns to* ERNEST, *then bursts into tears on his shoulder, and, with his arms around her protectingly, they go out.*]

JOHN [*in an awed tone*]. I didn't suppose she had the nerve.

JUDGE [*strong*]. You fool! You drove her to this yourself.

LUCY. But what'll we do, what'll we do?

JUDGE [*to* LUCY]. Order your fastest car, your best chauffeur. [*Looks at watch.*] Quick! Their train leaves in five minutes.

[LUCY *rushes out.*]

If I miss the train I'll have to chase them all the way to town by motor. [*Buttons up coat to go.*]

JOHN. What's the idea?

JUDGE. Idea? They don't want to do wrong—they want to do right. [*Going.*] I'm going to patch up with common sense and sympathy what you bungled with bullying and browbeating. Leave it to your uncle Everett. I'M GOING TO GET 'EM MARRIED.

CURTAIN

ACT III

SCENE: *Same as Act II.*

It is early evening of the same busy day of rest. The draperies at right are down, shutting out the night.

It is dark outside. The bracket-lamps over the mantel and the piano-lamp are lighted.

THEODORE *is pacing up and down, shaking his head, glancing toward the door down right, when* LUCY *enters, also worried. He crosses to her eagerly, inquiringly.*

THEODORE. Hasn't Uncle Everett telephoned from town yet?

LUCY. No, and he must have reached town long ago.

THEODORE. If Uncle Everett only hadn't missed their train.

LUCY. If John only hadn't lost his head, Uncle Everett might have brought them to their senses before they left. Oh, what will people say, what will people say?

THEODORE. Calm yourself, Lucy, calm yourself. Has John come back?

LUCY. No, John is still hunting for Rex. Rex disappeared as soon as Jean broke with him this morning, and no one has seen him since.

THEODORE. I wonder if he has looked for Rex on the links? Shall I telephone over to the club?

LUCY. I'll be so grateful to you if you would.

[THEODORE *goes out.*]

[JOHN *enters hurriedly from centre and goes down to* LUCY.]

JOHN [*breathless and excited*]. Well, I found Rex. Over at the golf club. Terribly cut up, but listen, not a drink, not one.

[LUCY *turns away from* JOHN.]

Oh, Lord, what's the matter now? Can't you forget what happened this morning?

LUCY. Forget?

JOHN. Well, what good does it do to keep on talking about it?

LUCY. Have I talked about it?

JOHN. To keep on thinking about it, then.

LUCY. It's hard not to think.

JOHN. But this is no time to think about yourself. What do your little troubles amount to? Play the game.

LUCY. Haven't I played the game all day? I will play it to the end. I have no alternative.

JOHN. We've got to stick together now. The reputation of the whole family is at stake. We've got to patch it up between Rex and Jean and we've got to do it quick. Any news from Uncle Everett?

[THEODORE *enters on hearing* JOHN's *voice*.]

LUCY. No, and when the Bakers hear about Helen! They'll never let Rex marry into our family! Never! We're disgraced, John, disgraced!

JOHN. They're not *going* to hear about Helen. No one knows, and no one *will*.

LUCY. But, John! John, don't you recall, just before they ran off, Doctor Hamilton threatened to announce it to the whole family next week?

JOHN. Uncle Everett will attend to them. *He'll* make them keep it dark. They'll do *that* much for the family.

THEODORE. But if he doesn't catch them?

JOHN. Don't be an ass! I attended to *that*. When Uncle Everett missed their train this morning, I telephoned a detective to meet their train and follow them— to report to Uncle Everett when he arrived by motor. All fixed.

THEODORE. It's bound to leak out in time. Why, if they both sail on the same steamer to-morrow——

JOHN [*interrupts*]. Before the story can get back from Paris, Jean is going to be married to Rex—and then we're safe. See? The Bakers will *have* to stand for us *then*. Everything now hangs on little *Jean*—our position in the world, my business relations with the old man— everything. [*To* LUCY.] Tell her I've got to see her at once. . . . Hurry! *Rex* is coming to see her later. He's gone to get his father's approval.

[LUCY *stops*.]

LUCY. But will he give it?

JOHN. Go on—I fixed the old man long ago.

LUCY. All right, I'll get Jean. [LUCY *goes out.*]

THEODORE [*crosses as if to follow* LUCY, *but stops and calls to* JOHN]. John, you're not going to put it up to Jean to go in for that sort of a marriage. You're too good a fellow.

JOHN. Haven't I done everything in the world to please my sisters? Can't they even marry to please me?

THEODORE. But not Rex, not if I can prevent it.

JOHN [*harassed*]. But you can't. You have nothing to do with it—except to perform the ceremony and get a big fat fee.

THEODORE. I—marry Jean and Rex?

JOHN [*pacing and thinking about* JEAN]. Oh, you think you won't, but you will. [JOHN *goes up to door.*]

[JEAN *enters from the house. She looks frightened, runs to* THEODORE *for protection.* THEODORE *puts arm about her, pats shoulder.*]

THEODORE. There, there, my dear, don't cry any more. I'm on your side.

[JEAN *cries on* THEODORE'S *shoulder.*]

Now, now, now! John's got a rough outside, but the kindest heart in the world. I've found that out for myself.

JOHN [*gently*]. Jean, we mustn't detain Theodore. He has an important business letter to write.

THEODORE [*to* JOHN]. No, I haven't.

JOHN. Yes, you have.

[THEODORE *turns to* JOHN *in surprise.*]

Your wife's sanitarium bills——

[JEAN *turns away.*]

Better settle up before they dun you again.

THEODORE. Oh, that's the idea; with *your* money? [*Takes* JOHN'S *check out of pocket, about to tear it.*]

JOHN [*catching* THEODORE'S *hand*]. Want to kill your wife? Then take her out of the sanitarium. Want to ruin your children? Then take them out of school. Cash that check, I tell you, and pay your debts.

[THEODORE *glances at* JEAN, *at check—a struggle. At bay, he finally pockets the check and goes out.*]

JEAN [*turns to* JOHN, *with crumpled handkerchief in hand*]. Well? You can't force me to marry Rex. So what are you going to do about it? Cut off my allowance or merely bully me to death?

JOHN [*kindly*]. Oh, come! You've filled your romantic little head full of novels. I never force *anybody* to do *anything*.

> [JEAN *looks at him in surprise.* JOHN *suddenly breaks out.*]

My heavens! What's the matter with this family anyway? Lord! I guess I have some rights, even if I have got money!

JEAN. Rex has money, too. Should that give him the right to women? I, too, have some rights—even though I *am* a woman.

JOHN. Well, if you expect to find a saint, you'll never get married at all.

JEAN. And if I never married at all? Then what?

JOHN. Yes! *Then* what?

JEAN. Oh, it's so unfair—you wouldn't allow me to go to college—you wouldn't allow me to learn a profession—oh! I wish I could earn my own living. I envy Helen so.

JOHN. Helen? bah! You don't know what you're saying. If you don't marry Rex now, you'll never have a chance to marry anybody. Now think before it's too late. Think what it means to be a dependent old maid.

JEAN. It isn't fair to train girls only for this. To live on the charity of a disapproving brother, or a man I can't love. What choice have I?

JOHN. There you are.

> [REX *enters.* JOHN *sees him and goes up to him.*]

> [*As* JEAN *crosses the stage, not seeing* REX, *but sobbing with her face in her hands,* JOHN *pantomimes and whispers to* REX.]

It's all right. [JOHN *goes out.* REX *steals down upon* JEAN *unawares, and taking her in his arms, kisses her.*]

JEAN [*indignant, struggles, frees herself and rubs her cheek*]. Ugh! How could you!

REX. Because I love you.

JEAN. Love! It isn't even respect now.

REX. Has that chap at Harvard ever kissed you?

JEAN [*shuddering*]. I have begged you never to refer to him again.

REX [*becoming more jealous*]. He has! He has held you in his arms. He has kissed your lips.

JEAN. How many women have you held in your arms? Have I ever tried to find out?

REX. Ah! You don't deny it, you can't.

JEAN. I can! *He* respects me. [*Turns away.*] I don't deserve it, but he *does*.

REX. Thank heavens. You don't know how this has tormented me, little Jean. The thought of any other man's coming near you——

JEAN [*biting lips—then deliberatly whirls around to him*]. Well, then, other men *have* come near me—other men *have* kissed me.

REX [*getting wild again*]. What! When? Where?

JEAN [*laughing cynically*]. Oh, conservatories in town —John's camp in the North Woods, motor rides in the country—once or twice out here on this very spot when I felt sentimental in the moonlight.

REX. Oh, Jean! I never supposed *you* were that sort!

JEAN [*with distaste*]. Oh, I don't make a habit of it! I'm not *that* sort. I've merely been handled, not hurt. Slightly shop-worn, but as good as new.

REX. Oh, stop! If you're not going to marry me, say so.

JEAN. But I am! I am *not* going to be dependent on my *brother* all my life.

[REX, *nonplussed, only gazes at her.*]
But first, I want you to know exactly what you're getting for your money. That seems only businesslike.

REX [*recoils*]. Would you marry me only for that?

JEAN. I told you I loved another man. Do you still want me?

REX [*with jealousy returning*]. Do I *want* you! [*Seizes her passionately.*] I'll make you love *me!* [*Kisses her triumphantly.*] I'll bring a different light into those cold eyes of yours. Wait until you're married! I'll make you forget that man, all other men. You are mine, all mine.

[JEAN *remains passive.*]

Can't you love me a little? Haven't you any sentiment in your cynical little soul?

JEAN. In my soul? Yes, but must I sell my soul too?

REX. Look out, here comes the parson.

[THEODORE *re-enters from the house.* REX *retreats.*]

JEAN [*cynical, rapid, gay, reckless, with abandon*]. Oh, Theodore! Rex and I have come to an understanding. Will you solemnize our blessed union?

THEODORE [*surprised and grieved. Stern*]. No, not unless you truly love each other. Marriage is sacred.

JEAN [*rapidly*]. A large church wedding—that will make it sacred. A full choral service—many expensive flowers—all the smartest people invited—that always makes the union of two souls sacred.

THEODORE. My dear child, when two people love each other, their friends should witness the solemn rites . . .

JEAN [*interrupts—to* REX]. And my wedding-gown will be white satin with a point-lace veil caught up with orange-blossoms, and a diamond tiara—"the gift of the groom." That will make it solemn.

THEODORE. The white veil is the symbol of purity, Jean.

JEAN. Of purity, Rex, do you hear? Whenever you see a bride in the white symbol of purity she is pure—that proves it. That makes it all so sacred. So holy! [*As she goes to the door.*] Holy! Holy!

THEODORE [*stopping* REX *as he follows her*]. Stop! I command you to stop.

[JOHN *enters.*]

You shall not marry that woman.

JOHN. That's all right, Rex, I'll take care of him.

[REX *crosses* THEODORE *and leaves.*]

THEODORE [*to* JOHN]. I warn you—I'll prevent this marriage! I'll tell every clergyman in the diocese. I'll inform the bishop himself. Such a marriage would be sacrilege.

JOHN [*voice trembling with rage*]. You *dare* threaten me! After all I've done for you?

THEODORE [*excited*]. Your five thousand was a loan—not a bribe—every cent of it will be returned.

JOHN. You can't return it, I wouldn't let you if you

could. [*Calms down.*] Come, it's all in the family. We've all got to stand together now.

[THEODORE *shakes his head.*]

Say, you know the Gothic chapel old man Baker is building on his estate—he likes you, Theodore; I'll tell him you're just the man he's looking for.

THEODORE. But I'm *not*. He told me this morning after service that he was looking for a "safe and sane" man. . . .

JOHN. Oh, he needn't know anything about those radical views of yours.

THEODORE. But I'd know—that I was preaching one thing while believing another; praising the easy generosity of the rich when I know the awful sufferings of the poor—advocating charity while I long to fight for justice.

JOHN. Oh, there are plenty of other things to preach about. Come, don't be an idiot. I can land that job for you.

THEODORE. Don't trouble yourself. Mr. Baker offered it to me this morning.

JOHN. What! You didn't refuse a chance like that?

THEODORE. Do you think I want to live on that old hypocrite's money?

JOHN [*losing all patience with him*]. Then how *do* you expect to live? On your relatives?

THEODORE [*insulted*]. I never asked *your* aid.

JOHN. But you took it?

THEODORE. I never shall again. . . . Yes, I did refuse the offer this morning, but just now, out here, when you showed me what it meant to be in debt to you, I reconsidered. I telephoned Mr. Baker . . . John, I've landed "the job."

[JOHN *rises and goes to* THEODORE *and smiles at him cynically.*]

JOHN. I thought you didn't want to live on that old hypocrite's money?

THEODORE. Want to? Do you think I'm doing this for myself! I'm doing it to keep my wife alive. To keep my children out of the streets. To keep myself out of deeper debt to you. That's why many a man sells his soul to the devil. If I had only myself to consider—why, John, to me a little thing like death would be a blessed luxury. [*Pause.*] But I cannot afford—even to die. I must compromise and live—live for those dependent on me.

JOHN. But you're going to marry Jean and Rex all the same.

THEODORE. You are mistaken. Your money can dictate to me no longer.

JOHN. Theodore, *money* talks in this world—louder than the church. Refuse to marry Baker's son and how long will you keep Baker's Chapel?— Think it over, Theodore, you'll be fixed for life.

THEODORE [*staggered*]. John—you're right— Yes! I'll be fixed for life. Fixed for life.

JUDGE [*off stage*]. John! Where's John? [*The* JUDGE *suddenly enters in motor clothes covered with dust, followed excitedly by* LUCY. *The* JUDGE *is panting and running.*]

LUCY. But Uncle Everett! Uncle Everett! Couldn't you find them?

JOHN. Will they keep it dark?

LUCY. Where did they go—quick!

JUDGE [*panting*]. Just give me time to get my breath. [*Fans himself with hat, pants, and mops his brow.*]

JOHN. My detective—didn't he meet their train?

[JUDGE *nods yes.*]

LUCY. But they saw him first?

[JUDGE *shakes head no.*]

JOHN. Didn't he follow them?

[JUDGE *nods yes.*]

LUCY. Where are they *now?*

JOHN. Speak, man, speak!

JUDGE [*raises his hands, holding his hat and handkerchief*]. Now, just give me a chance and I'll tell the whole story. . . . The detective was waiting at the station. He saw them step out of the train—watched them get into a taxi—jumped into another himself—and followed them— Even now they don't know they were watched—or— [*pauses, shakes head*] they might have taken another course.

LUCY. Quick, tell us the worst.

JUDGE [*hesitates*]. Well . . . they drove straight to Helen's apartment.

JOHN [*all horrified—heads shaking*]. To Helen's apartment! Oh!

LUCY. And you were too late! [*To* THEODORE.] What did I tell you?

JOHN. But my detective?

JUDGE. He followed and reported to me when I reached town.

LUCY. Reported what? Tell us all.

JUDGE. First he saw Ernest help Helen out of the taxi —very tenderly, like this. [*Pantomimes helping a lady out of a cab with exaggerated manner.*] By the way, they never dreamed how every detail was to be reported to you.

JOHN [*impatient*]. Go on! Go on!

JUDGE. Then the detective saw Ernest deliberately . . .

LUCY [*interjecting*]. Yes, go on.

JUDGE. Deliberately lift his hat . . . [*removes hat*] like that, say good afternoon, and drive on to his own apartment a mile away. [*Turns up stage—removes coat and hat—places them on sofa. There is a sudden silence, the others waiting.*]

LUCY. Oh, is *that* all?

> [*They exchange glances.* LUCY *seems somehow disappointed.*]

JOHN [*exasperated by* JUDGE's *fooling*]. But where are they now?

> [JUDGE *drops his eyes, business of hating to tell.*]

Quick, man, speak.

LUCY. They met later!

> [JUDGE *nods.*]

I knew it.

JUDGE. They are alone together at this very moment!

ALL [*excited*]. Where? Where?

JUDGE [*pointing to the house*]. There. [*Takes out cigarcase and smiles—and sits on sofa.*]

ALL [*amazed*]. What?

JOHN [*amazed*]. What are they doing here?

JUDGE [*clipping cigar*]. Waiting to receive your blessing.

JOHN. My *blessing?*
LUCY. *Married?* } [*Almost simultaneously*]
THEODORE [*down left*]. Already!

JOHN. Hurray! [JOHN *slaps* JUDGE *on the back with joyous relief, knocking cigar out of his hand. During following* JUDGE *tries to speak but they give him no chance.*]

JOHN. Cold feet—he saw it wouldn't pay. } [*Together*]
LUCY. The disgrace—she couldn't face it. }

THEODORE. A deep religious nature— I said so all along. [*Then turning to* JUDGE *again.*]

JOHN. How'd you work it? } *Rapidly, laughingly,*
LUCY. Tell us all about it. } *almost simultaneously*
THEODORE. Who married them?

JUDGE [*having a chance at last*]. Married . . . If you only wouldn't interrupt— They aren't *dreaming* of marriage!

ALL. What!

JUDGE. Helen has a worse opinion of holy matrimony now than ever. . . .

[*All three in despair again.* THEODORE *groans*, LUCY *throws up her hands*, JOHN *starts indignantly toward terrace—then stops bewildered.*]

JOHN. But, see here! If they're not married—how on earth did you get 'em back?

JUDGE [*seated on sofa smoking calmly*]. Oh, perfectly simple! Promised Helen you'd apologize to Ernest, promised Ernest you'd apologize to Helen. Theodore, go tell them John's ready.

JOHN. Apologize— I?

JUDGE. Of course you will—and I promised both we'd arrange a nice little family party for them.

JOHN. A family party?

LUCY. For *them?*

THEODORE. Why?

JUDGE. To spread the glad tidings that they're not going to marry—merely going to Paris.

JOHN [*higher*]. See here. Are *you* crazy? Are *they* crazy? Do you think *I'm* crazy?

JUDGE. Well, don't jump on *me*. You did your best to make them crazy, but they indignantly decline to run away together until after they make a formal announcement to the whole damn family. Theodore, Helen's got a million new arguments against marriage, and if you don't hurry, she'll tell them to you.

LUCY. You expect us to invite the family here for that?

JOHN. We'll do nothing of the sort!

JUDGE. You don't have to. *I* have invited them already. They're coming for dinner this evening.

LUCY. This evening!

JOHN. You invited the family!

JUDGE [*nodding*]. I had your detective send out an S. O. S. call by telephone.

JOHN [*crosses down left*]. You think you're very funny, don't you? But that's *my own sister* in there planning to be that fellow's mistress—right here in my own home— anything funny about that?

JUDGE [*flicks cigar-ashes*]. Oh, well, if you don't like your sister to be that fellow's mistress, as you call it, why don't you put a stop to it?

JOHN [*turns*]. You bet I will!

JUDGE [*stopping* JOHN *with voice*]. How are you going to stop it, John?

[JOHN *hesitates*.]

Kick them *out* of your home again? [*Stopping* JOHN *again*.] Think they'll come back again?

[JOHN *comes down quickly, alarmed*.]

John, you're up against it. I know it pains you to think, but sometimes it's necessary. Women like Helen are a new proposition to men like you. Maybe you can force *Jean* into marriage—with a man she doesn't love. She is the old-fashioned girl. But Helen—you can't force Helen into marriage, even with the man she does love. She's the New Woman. We're at the dawn of a new era, John; women are going to do what they believe is right, not what we men *tell* 'em to believe is right. What are you going to do about it?

[JOHN *is silent*.]

Nothing. I thought so. Call 'em bad and let it go at that. Blame it all on human nature, made by God, and leave unchanged all human institutions, made by man. But I tell you right now, unless we change the rules and regulations of the game, marriage is doomed.

JOHN [*has shown signs of growing impatience, and now breaks out*]. All right, all right, but we can't alter marriage overnight, just to suit Helen—what are *you* going to do about it?

JUDGE. There's only one thing to do now. They didn't have to come back, if they didn't want to, did they?
   [*All assent.*]
You don't deserve it, if you ask me. Why, they're the kindest, truest, noblest pair of lovers I ever knew.

THEODORE. Uncle Everett, would you call immorality noble, exactly?

JUDGE. Have they done anything immoral?

THEODORE. Not yet, but . . .

JUDGE. Well, they won't either, if we work it right.

JOHN. What are you going to do?

JUDGE. Will you back me up in everything I do, anything I say?

JOHN. Everything. Anything.

JUDGE. Then tell them they don't have to marry!

THEODORE. What's that?

JOHN. Don't have to *marry!*

THEODORE. You don't expect us to countenance their wicked *substitute* for marriage?

JUDGE. No, but I expect you to pretend to do so.
   [*All draw around him.*]

THEODORE. How do you mean?

JOHN. What's the idea?

JUDGE. If we pretend we don't want them to marry, then they'll want to marry. John, when you want your dog to come in out of the rain and be happy, how does he invariably behave when you try to *drag* him in by the collar? Balks, doesn't he? Just let him alone and he will trot right in of his own accord and wag his tail.
   [*The others nod understandingly.*]
We've been fighting these young idealists, so naturally they fought back. Just let them alone and they'll come to their senses. They're not fools. And they've done a lot of thinking since you saw them last. Now just follow my lead and you'll see. Keep your eye on your uncle Everett. [*Goes up and calls off to the right.*] Oh, Helen! Ernest!

Lucy [*to* John *and* Theodore].   Now, we must be nice to them.

Theodore.   After all, they've done nothing wrong. We misjudged them.

[Helen *enters first, then* Ernest.]

Lucy [*in a low voice, and quickly*].   Now, John, be nice.

Helen.   Well, John?

[John *opens his arms magnanimously*.]

John.   My sister! All is forgiven!

Helen [*stops short, her lips curl*].   *You* forgive *me?*

Ernest [*faces* John].   You forgive her? For what?

John.   Didn't my sister run away with you? Under the circumstances wasn't it natural for us to think that—that——

Ernest [*to* John].   You evil-minded married people! How dare you judge us by yourselves! [*Turns to* Helen.]

John [*apart, gasping*].   Well, I'll be damned!

Judge [*whispers*].   Stand for it, John . . . he's right.

Theodore.   But, Ernest, I'm bound to say when two people run away together——

Ernest [*pityingly disgusted*].   Oh, Theodore, not you, too! Are all married people alike?

Theodore.   But, Ernest . . .

Ernest.   Did we *want* to "run away," as you call it? [*To all.*] Didn't I distinctly state that we'd wait a full week to give this question calm consideration? That at the end of that week our final decision would first have to be announced *before the whole family?* Could language have been clearer? [*Turns to* John *and sneers*.] But this absurd person—what did *he* do? Ordered us off his property like poachers. What could *we* do? Sit down in the road and wait a *week?* Bah! You suspicious married people. You hypocritical, *unspeakable* married people!

[John *starts in anger toward* Ernest. Judge *stops him and crosses to* Ernest *at right centre*.]

Judge.   Oh, now, wait a minute—don't be hard on them, Ernest. John wants to apologize to you.

[Ernest *turns to* Helen, *and* Judge *forces* John *over to* Ernest *to apologize*.]

John [*to* Ernest, *angrily*].   I apologize! [*He then goes up centre*.]

Lucy [*after* Judge *has urged her*]. So do I.

Theodore. We all do, Ernest, we all do. [*Crosses to* Ernest *and then joins* John *and* Lucy *up stage*.]

Ernest [*to* John, Theodore, *and* Lucy]. Not to me . . . to her. It doesn't matter about me, but . . .

Judge. Do it all over again, if he wants you to. [*Pushing* Theodore *over to* Helen, *who is still standing*.]

Theodore [*coming down to* Helen]. Why, certainly, Helen, I apologize most humbly.

Lucy [*kissing* Helen]. My dear! Of course . . . [*Passes* Helen *over to* John *and crosses to* Theodore.]

John. [Judge *forces* John *down to* Helen.] My sister, forgive me. [*Crosses to* Lucy *and* Theodore.]

Judge [*to* Ernest *over L*]. There—I told you they would.

Ernest [*coming to L C*]. Then I'm going. That's all I came back for. Now, then, one week from to-day gather all your family here and we'll announce our decision.

[Helen *crosses and joins* Ernest. *They start up.* Judge *stops them.*]

Judge [*coming between* Helen *and* Ernest]. Oh, wait a minute, wait. I've got some good news for you. [*To both.*] I've talked the whole thing over with John and Lucy and Theodore and I find they agree with all you say about marriage. Your arguments are unanswerable— we all advise you to try this conscientious experiment.

Helen. What?

Ernest. What's this?

[*Lovers exchange glances during following.*]

Judge. Why, we wouldn't let a little thing like matrimony come between them for the world, would we, Theodore?

Theodore. Those who love each other truly don't need anything to bring them together.

Judge. John, how do *you* feel?

John. How do I feel— [*Pounces on* Judge, *who retreats a step.*]

Judge. Don't raise your voice. I'm nervous.

John [*recovers, swallows*]. "Marriage always puts people asunder." [*Goes up to mantel.*]

Judge [*to* Lucy]. You agree, don't you, Lucy?

LUCY [*to* HELEN]. You can't marry Doctor Hamilton. You love him.

JUDGE. Exactly. Too much self-respect.

HELEN [*laughs and turns to* JUDGE]. I don't know what you are up to, you dear old fraud, but we don't believe a word of it.

JUDGE. You wait and see.

HELEN [*to* LUCY, JOHN, *and* THEODORE]. Very well, then, if you really mean it, you will invite the whole family here a week from to-day.

ERNEST. That was our stipulation—a week from to-day.

LUCY. They'll be here in half an hour.

HELEN [*taken aback, recoils*]. In half an hour.

ERNEST. But we said in a week.

JUDGE. A little surprise-party.

JOHN. Why wait? Begin your new life together this evening.

JUDGE. Isn't it all lovely?

HELEN. But—but—that's so sudden.

ERNEST. We . . . we aren't ready.

THEODORE. You're just as ready as you'll ever be.

JUDGE. And the family dinner this evening, your—in a manner of speaking—wedding-party. [*Waving aside all the lovers' objections.*] Now it's all fixed, let's go and dress for the—as it were—ceremony.

[LUCY, JOHN, THEODORE, *and* JUDGE *start to go out.*
JUDGE *leads the way, speaking apart to the others.*]

When it comes to the scratch, you'll see. [*Almost off.*]

ERNEST. Wait! Judge Grey!

[*All stop, turn, exchange glances.*]

Did I ever say I would not marry Helen?

JUDGE. What did I tell you? [*To* JOHN, LUCY, *and* THEODORE.]

JOHN. Ah! so you'd like to marry my sister after all?

ERNEST [*turning to* JOHN]. What have I been doing for the past twenty-four hours? *Begging* her to marry me. What have you been doing? Preventing it. Why did I postpone sailing for a week? Why did I insist upon a family gathering? Oh, you're *such* an ass.

JUDGE [*coming behind* JOHN *and holding him as he starts*

for ERNEST]. Stand for it—he's right. Tell him you love him, like a brother . . . *in-law.* [JUDGE *sits on the sofa.*]

JOHN [*controls self—to* ERNEST]. Well, I—I—you have my consent.

ERNEST. Your consent? What's that got to do with it?

[JOHN *starts for him again.*]

Now wait! This morning you tried bullying. Did that work? And now bluffing. Think that will work? You can't frighten this glorious girl into marriage. I've tried that myself. If you want *this* woman to marry, prove the morality of *marriage*.

THEODORE. The morality of marriage! What next?

ERNEST [*to* THEODORE]. That's what I said—the morality of marriage. [*To all.*] This woman is not on trial before you. Marriage is on trial before her, and thus far you've made out a rotten case for it. Simply *justify* Helen's marrying me, and—[*to* THEODORE] I give you my word, you can perform the ceremony this very evening. No license is required in this State, you know.

JUDGE [*rises*]. Now, what could be fairer than that! [*To* HELEN.] You agree, Helen? [*Rises and goes down stage a little.*]

HELEN. Ernest and I agree in everything. But why should I contract by law for what is better done by love? What's the sense?

THEODORE. Perfectly simple—I will leave out the promise to obey.

HELEN. But the promise to love.

THEODORE. Well, no, we can hardly leave that out, my dear.

HELEN. But what right has Ernest in his present state of emotional irresponsibility to promise to go on loving me? Look at him!

JOHN. Yes, look at him! The idiot!

[JUDGE *goes back to sofa and sits.*]

THEODORE. My dear Helen, are you so cold, so scientific, so unsexed as not to trust the man you love?

HELEN. Trust? Contracts are not for those who trust. They're for those who don't. Why, if I couldn't

trust Ernest—[*she turns to him*] I'd be terribly tempted
to marry you, dearest.

JOHN [*impatient to settle the matter*].   But the plain,
every-day, practical question is—if you don't marry him,
how long would he keep his job in the Institute?   Old
man Baker's views happen to be old-fashioned.

ERNEST.   Baker?   Every one knows Baker's public
views and private practices.   Even the church knows and
pretends not to, like his wife.

HELEN.   The church, like his wife, needs his support.

THEODORE [*weakly*].   At least, Mr. Baker does not
parade his sin in public.

ERNEST [*more sarcastic*].   Oh, now we have it; a sin to
be honest, but moral to be a hypocrite.

HELEN.   Why, Theodore!   You defend Mr. Baker!
What has got into you?

ERNEST [*to* HELEN, *half-seriously*].   I'm beginning to believe you're right, after all!   If I learn much more about
morality—I'll withdraw my offer of marriage and ask your
pardon for making it.

JOHN [*can't stand it*].   And then I'll withdraw my offer
of a year abroad and ask for your resignation.

JUDGE [*rises*].   There he goes— My God!   [*Throws
up hands in despair.*]

ERNEST [*angered, to* JOHN].   You can have it now!   I
don't need the support of church pillars.

JOHN.   Then how'll you get your bread and butter?
Private practice?   No respectable home will let you inside the door!

ERNEST [*more angry*].   I've seen quite enough of "respectable homes."   [*Takes a cablegram from pocket.*]   This
morning I came to ask for your sister's hand in marriage.
Your manners were very bad.   So I cabled over to
Metchnikoff.   [*Hands cablegram to* JOHN.]   Here's the answer.   Positions await us both at the Pasteur Institute
in Paris.

[JOHN *glances at cablegram and returns it to* ERNEST.]

JOHN [*excited, rapidly but beaten*].   Doctor Hamilton,
you're a man of the world.   You know what this means;
she doesn't.   She is in your power.   For God's sake, go
to Paris without her.

ERNEST. What! Leave her here in *your* power? No! You've forced her out of her job. You'd force her into legalized prostitution, if you could, like her innocent little sister. No, married or not, she sails with me in the morning. That's final. Come, Helen!

[*The lovers start up hand in hand.*]

THEODORE [*stopping them*]. Ernest! This dear child loves you better than herself! You cannot, must not, *will* not let her sin.

ERNEST [*angered, turns on* THEODORE]. Sin! Who dares accuse this woman of sin? I've had enough of this ridiculous cant about sin.

[ERNEST *and* HELEN *continue up stage to the centre door.*]

JUDGE [*up at centre door, stops* HELEN *and* ERNEST. *He is the only calm one*]. Where are you going?

HELEN. To ask Julie to pack my things.

ERNEST. To telephone for a taxi.

JUDGE [*detaining lovers*]. You are determined to go to Paris together without being married?

HELEN. Yes.

JUDGE. Nothing can alter your decision?

HELEN. Nothing.

ERNEST. Absolutely nothing.

[JOHN *desperate but helpless*, LUCY *distracted but futile*, THEODORE *grieved but silent*, JUDGE *the only calm one*.]

JUDGE. Just a minute. [*Comes down a few steps, then turns to* HELEN.] Well, at least you won't start until the family arrive.

JOHN [*interrupting, crossing over to* HELEN *and* ERNEST]. In ten minutes—they're on the way here now.

HELEN. Of course not.

JOHN [*to* ERNEST *now, not* HELEN]. We have your word on that? You promise not to leave this house until after you meet the family?

ERNEST [*about to say* "You ass," *but instead*—]. Didn't we ask to meet the family?

[HELEN *and* ERNEST *turn to go.*]

JOHN. Wait. Helen, do you actually mean to acknowledge before the bishop and all your relatives that when you leave this house to-night you leave as this man's mistress?

HELEN [*returning a step—to* JOHN]. Oh, do you still think that we are entering upon a sordid *liaison*? Can't you see that in the sight of God I am to be his wife, he is to be my husband?

JOHN. Oh, that sounds all right, but when it comes to the scratch she won't dare. [*This is to* LUCY *and* THEODORE.]

ERNEST. Won't she? You don't know her—oh, you're *such* an ass!

[HELEN *and* ERNEST *go out.*]

JUDGE. Well, you bungled it. I knew you would.

[*Enter* BUTLER *from the right.*]

BUTLER. Mr. and Mrs. Willoughby and the bishop have come.

LUCY. Good gracious! Already?

JOHN. Ask them to wait in the drawing-room.

[*The* BUTLER *goes out.*]

LUCY. Oh, save us, Uncle Everett, save the family.

JUDGE. How do you expect me to save the family? If John could only keep his mouth shut . . . [*To* JOHN.] Finesse! You can't do anything but make money.

JOHN. Ah! Why didn't I think of it! Money. We've given 'em nothing but scares and sermons—we've got to give 'em some real *inducement* to marry.

THEODORE. John, that won't work.

JOHN [*with a significant smile*]. Every man has his price, Theodore.

[THEODORE *turns away.* JUDGE *comes down and sits on the arm of the sofa.*]

Listen. First, I'll announce Jean's engagement. Then I'll offer Hamilton and Helen a big raise in salary and——

LUCY. And announce *their* engagement.

JOHN. Yes, and with Theodore right here on the job, why, we'll get 'em safely married before they leave the house.

JUDGE [*rising and coming to centre*]. And if that doesn't work, I have a plan that will—if I can only manage it.

JOHN [*turns to* JUDGE]. What is it—quick!

[BUTLER *enters with a telegram on tray.*]

JUDGE. It's desperate, it's high-handed, it's one chance in a million, but it's our last hope. If I can only work it, only work it!

BUTLER. Telegram, sir. [BUTLER *hands telegram to* JUDGE.]

JUDGE. Hello! Another? [*Opens telegram.*]

BUTLER [*after crossing back to door on the right*]. Shall I announce dinner as soon as all the family arrive?

THEODORE. What shall we do with them?

LUCY. We're not even dressed.

JOHN. All right, all right, Thomas.

[BUTLER *goes out.*]

JUDGE [*jumping up and waving the telegram*]. Your aunt Julia's coming back to me! She's coming back, I tell you. [*Hands telegram to* JOHN.]

JOHN. Think—man—think. Rex is dining here, too. If Hamilton gets up and announces to the whole table that he is taking Helen to Paris as his mistress— [JOHN *hands it to* LUCY.]

JUDGE [*to* LUCY]. Read it, read it!

LUCY [*handing telegram unread to* THEODORE]. Jean's engagement will be broken . . .

JUDGE [*to* THEODORE]. She's coming back, I tell you. Theodore, read it.

THEODORE [*handing telegram unread to* LUCY, *who returns it to* JOHN]. And my chapel's gone . . .

JOHN [*handing telegram, still unread, back to* JUDGE]. My business with the old man is gone; everything is gone.

JUDGE. What do I care about all that! What do I care about Jean's engagement—my wife's coming home! [*Starts to dance, crosses and grasps* LUCY *about the waist and begins to dance with her. He sings.*]

"Your aunt Julia's coming home,
    Coming home, coming home;
Your aunt Julia's coming home,
    Coming home from Reno."

[*After finishing he goes up centre.*]

JOHN. Oh, won't you keep quiet?

JUDGE. Why should I keep quiet? My wife's coming home.

JOHN [to JUDGE]. Aunt Susan and the bishop will hear you. [Goes down and joins THEODORE and LUCY.]

JUDGE. What do I care—I want 'em to hear. [Shouts.] My wife's coming home! [Comes down to left of JOHN.] Just hear this . . .

[JOHN, LUCY, and THEODORE confer apart excitedly.] JUDGE [reads telegram]. "Dear Boy: I can't stand this separation another day. Come to me or I'll go to you." [He sits on the sofa. Kisses telegram—brings out from his pocket his sheaf of blanks—and during the triologue below —singing between sentences:]

> "My bonnie is coming from Reno—
> My bonnie will not be divorced—
> My bonnie is coming from Reno—
> Oh, bring back my bonnie to . . ."

[Stops and makes correction in his writing.]

JOHN [to LUCY and THEODORE—speaks through the JUDGE's singing]. First I'll propose a toast to Rex and Jean; then I'll say: "Another toast, and another engagement."

LUCY [nodding]. They won't deny that they're engaged.

THEODORE [nodding]. Yes, sweep them off their feet, conquer them by kindness, and then play for time.

JUDGE [stops writing, thinking they are all interested]. You know, we thought we believed in trial marriage. Nothing of the sort. Trial separation. What marriage put asunder divorce has joined together! Good! [Ducks down to write.] She'll love that. [Rises and crosses to JOHN, as if granting them a favor.] I'm going to let you hear my telegram. [Reads.] "Come home immediately, darling. Can't live without you. Wire me at Ogden— also at Cheyenne, Omaha, and Chicago, and Pittsburg. Sweetheart."

JOHN [to JUDGE, over shoulder]. Oh, won't you please shut up? [To others again.]

JUDGE [too happy to notice JOHN's rebuke, sorting out received telegrams]. You know, John, this morning when she telegraphed me about catching cold for my sake, I wired back a question. [Picks out one of the many telegrams.] Want to see her reply, John?

JOHN [*turning from others to* JUDGE]. I do not. [*Turns to others.*]

JUDGE [*insists*]. Only one word. I had asked her: "Are you getting a divorce for my sake, too?" Here is what she says—the sweetest word in the English language, John; read it.

[JOHN, *irritated and angry, snatches telegram and reads it.*]

JOHN. "Tutti-frutti"—Bah! [JOHN *crosses to left and throws down telegram.* JUDGE *at once picks it up and smooths it out, kisses it, places with the others in his pocket, and goes up centre, where he meets* HELEN *and* ERNEST.]

[*The* BUTLER *enters.*]

BUTLER. Mr. and Mrs. Spencer and Doctor Hawksbee are in the drawing-room. All the guests have arrived and dinner is served.

[HELEN *and* ERNEST *enter.*]

LUCY. What'll we do? Oh! what a day, what a day!

JOHN [*to* BUTLER, *waving him off*]. In a moment, in a moment.

ERNEST. Thomas, let me know when my taxi comes.

BUTLER. It's coming up the drive now, sir.

HELEN [*coming down centre*]. Thomas, have my trunk brought down.

[THOMAS *goes out.*]

JOHN. Helen, for the last time, the whole family are in there. Rex is dining here, too. In a minute we are going to announce Jean's engagement——

[JEAN *enters and joins* LUCY.]

If you announce that you and he— [*Sees* JEAN.] If you announce your plan, you will ruin the whole family and your whole future.

HELEN. Jean, you are not going to marry Rex?

JEAN. I *am* going to marry him. You can earn your own living; I can't.

HELEN. Jean, are you going to live on a man you don't really love?

JEAN. Haven't I got to live on some man?

ERNEST [*who has come down to left of* HELEN. *To* HELEN]. The morality of marriage.

JOHN [*turning to* ERNEST]. How dare you talk of morality? By what right do you sneer at my sister's marriage?

REX [*entering*]. Oh, I beg your pardon, I'm afraid I'm butting in.

JOHN [*nervously*]. Oh, no. We've just been having a pleasant little family talk. You see—you see our two distinguished scientists here have hesitated to marry, and for the best reason in the world. But it's all right now, Helen, it's all right! [*Joyously.*] Beginning to-morrow, his salary is doubled. [*To* HELEN.] You are reinstated, your salary is doubled; you are both to have a year abroad at full pay. And when Doctor Carmen retires, Doctor Hamilton is to be head of the whole Institute at ten thousand a year!

ERNEST. That is very kind, but——

HELEN. But you can't *bribe* us to marry. [*She crosses in front of* ERNEST *to* JOHN.]

[*The* BUTLER *enters.*]

BUTLER. The bishop begs to know if he has made a mistake in the date. What shall I tell him, sir?

JOHN. Tell him just a moment more.

HELEN. What are we waiting for?

ERNEST. Come, we'll tell them now.

JOHN [*pleading*]. No! Please! Go to Paris if you must, but go now, go that way. [*Points off left.*] But don't let the family know.

ERNEST. But the family *must* know.

HELEN. Why, of course.

JEAN. Know what?

REX. What it's all about.

JUDGE [*rising and coming down centre*]. Oh, it's perfectly simple. You see these two—[*smiles at lovers*] thought they did not believe in the promise of love, but I—heard them take it—[*smiling teasingly at lovers*] in the car coming out. They thought it was nobody's business, but none the less, they consulted the church—[*points to* THEODORE] the law—[*indicates self*] the next of kin— [*points to* JOHN]. Why, from the first to last they have been not only honorable but really quite old-fashioned. And now I am sure—[*mellow, wheedling, lovable, he turns to lovers*] that just to please an old man who loves and sympathizes with you and has rebelled for a *quarter of a cen-*

tury against the tyranny of marriage, only to acknowledge its triumph in the end—that you will not disrupt the peace of a happy united family, but do the good old-fashioned thing in the good old-fashioned way.

[*All gather about and plead.*]

THEODORE. Yes, just to please us.

LUCY. To please the whole family.

JUDGE. Come, my children, it can do you no harm.

[ERNEST *looks questioningly to* HELEN.]

HELEN. Surrender after all. No.

JUDGE. Not surrender—sacrifice. You've proved your courage, now prove your kindness. [*Goes up stage a little and listens to the scene.*]

LUCY. And we'll have a beautiful double wedding next month, in the new chapel.

JOHN. Jean and Rex will be married on the fifteenth, but Helen and Ernest now— Now, Theodore. [*Beckons to* THEODORE.]

THEODORE [*coming to centre and opening his prayer-book, which he takes from vest pocket*]. "Dearly beloved, we are gathered together here in the sight . . ."

[JEAN *sobs and turns to* LUCY.]

HELEN. Wait, Theodore, are you going to marry Jean and Rex next month? Are you going to give the sanction of the church to that marriage?

[THEODORE *turns away.*]

JOHN. Of course, he's Mr. Baker's chaplain.

ERNEST. Are you going to stand up and tell the world that God has joined these two together—God?

HELEN. Then you will be blaspheming love and God who made it. No, you shall not marry us.

ERNEST. You're right—we'll not be married at all. Some things are too sacred to be profaned. Come, Helen. [*Starts off with* HELEN.]

THEODORE [*to* ERNEST]. Profaned, by the church?

ERNEST. Come, Helen, the car's waiting.

[*They start up.* JOHN *pantomimes* JUDGE *to stop them.*]

JUDGE [*up centre, stopping* HELEN *and* ERNEST. *He produces an impressive silence, then:*] Which of us has a purer ideal of love, a higher sense of duty? Have you, Rex, Lucy, Theodore, Jean, John, have you?

[*Each in turn characteristically declines to answer.*]

You funny little cowards! You're afraid of life, afraid of truth, afraid of love. You worship lies and call it God.

THEODORE. But such as they will destroy marriage.

JUDGE [*loud, fast, with feeling*]. Such as they will save it! There never was, there never can be, a finer tribute to the divine spirit of true marriage than from this fearless pair you now accuse of seeking to destroy it. [*To* HELEN *and* ERNEST, *who are hand in hand.*] Helen, you know, because you've said it, that in the sight of God you are taking this man to be your husband——

HELEN. Why, of course. In the sight of God—I take Ernest to be my husband, but——

JUDGE. And you, Ernest?

ERNEST. Why, of course, in the sight of God—but——

JUDGE [*hand raised—august—authoritative*]. Then, since you, Helen, and you, Ernest, have made this solemn declaration before God, and in the presence of witnesses, I by the authority vested in me by the laws of this state do now pronounce you man and wife.

[MR. *and* MRS. HAMILTON *turn and gaze at each other in bewilderment; then, as if horrified, they recoil from each other,* ERNEST *raving up stage to centre door and back again.* HELEN *rushes over to left, where* JOHN *attempts to congratulate her. General babble.* JUDGE *comes down in triumph to the others over right. Great excitement all through this scene.*]

ERNEST [*after the noise has quieted down. To* JUDGE]. How dare you make this woman my wife!

[JUDGE *attempts to shake his hand and* ERNEST *dashes up stage again.*]

HELEN. You *knew* I didn't want a husband!

JUDGE. You'll live to thank me for it.

JOHN [*grabs* HELEN *and rushes her over to the others*]. Saved, saved. Respectable at last.

[*The family gather around* HELEN *and all kiss her. General babble.*]

ERNEST [*coming down the stage and pointing at* HELEN *now being kissed by the family*]. Look! look! A moment ago she was a bad woman. Now she is a good woman. Marriage is a hypocritical farce.

JUDGE [*to* ERNEST. *Raising his hand. All are silent*]. All you've said of marriage is true. There is only one thing worse—and that is what you tried to do. But bad as marriage is, until we reform it, it is the best we have to offer you. What are you going to do about it? [*Loud and laughing.*] Separate and get divorced?

ERNEST. Separate?

HELEN. Divorced?

ERNEST [*rushing to* HELEN, *laughing*]. Never. ⎱ [*Spoken*
HELEN [*rushing to* ERNEST, *laughing*]. Never. ⎰ *together*]

JUDGE [*coming between* HELEN *and* ERNEST]. Just a minute— Dinner.

ERNEST [*offering arm with bow*]. Mrs. Hamilton.

JUDGE [*interrupts and takes* HELEN *himself*]. Take your own wife in to dinner? Shocking, Ernest, shocking. [*Crosses with* HELEN *toward door right, following the family, who are going into the house.*]

ERNEST [*tagging along behind*]. Didn't we tell you? Marriage always puts people asunder.

CURTAIN

THE EMPEROR JONES

BY

EUGENE O'NEILL

"'E's a better man than the lot o' you put together."—*Scene Eight.*

The Emperor Jones is reprinted by special permission of the author and publishers, Boni and Liveright. Applications for permission to perform this play should be addressed to the author in care of Boni and Liveright, New York.

THE EMPEROR JONES

Eugene O'Neill was born October 16, 1888. His childhood was spent in the atmosphere of the theatre since his father, the late James O'Neill, was touring the United States in his romantic play *Monte Cristo* and repertoire. After six years of boarding-school life in Catholic schools and four years' preparation for college at the Betts Academy at Stamford, Connecticut, he entered Princeton University with the class of 1910, but stayed only one year. After some business experience, the latent romanticism of Mr. O'Neill began to assert itself and he went to Spanish Honduras with a mining engineer on a prospecting expedition. At the end of eight months he was sent home on account of malarial fever, and had, to quote his own biographical account, sent at the request of the editor, "much hardship, little romance, and no gold" to show for his trip. Returning to the United States, he became assistant manager of the "White Sister" Company, and toured with them from St. Louis back to Boston. Having read Conrad's *Nigger of the Narcissus* and the works of Jack London, the urge for the sea came over him, and he sailed from Boston for Buenos Aires on a Norwegian bark, being out of sight of land for sixty-five days. During 1910–11 he remained in Buenos Aires with the Westinghouse Electric Company and other firms until an opportunity came to make a voyage on a cattle-boat to Durban, South Africa. On his return to Buenos Aires, he was "'on the beach' for a considerable period—having no job, and eating and a place to sleep were intermittent." Finally, returning home as an ordinary seaman on a British tramp steamer to New York, he became, after a time, an able seaman in the American Line, on the steamers *New York* and *Philadelphia*. This was his last experience as a sailor, but he had already acquired the first-hand knowledge of sailor's life which has been reflected in his plays. After touring the Orpheum Circuit in the Far West as a member of his father's company in *Monte Cristo*, he acted as a reporter on a morning paper in New London, Connecticut, for six months. His health became poor, and, being threatened with pulmonary tuberculosis, he spent six months in a sanitarium.

After he was released in the latter part of 1913 he started to write for the first time. In the winter of 1913–14 he completed eight one-act plays and two longer ones, only one, *Bound East for Cardiff*, being, in his judgment, worth preserving. During the year 1914–15 he attended Professor George P. Baker's course in playwriting at Harvard University. After a winter in Greenwich Village he joined the Provincetown Players and acted in his own plays, *Thirst* and *Bound East for Cardiff*, at their theatre in Provincetown, Massachusetts. When they opened their first season in New York in 1916, *Bound East for Cardiff* was on the opening bill. The Provincetown Players have produced all but one of Mr. O'Neill's one-act plays, and he has remained one of the moving forces of that significant organization, which has devoted itself exclusively to the production of American plays. His striking one-act play *In the Zone* was the first play to be produced elsewhere, being put on at the Comedy Theatre by the Washington Square Players, November 1, 1918. Mr. O'Neill's first play to be performed by a strictly professional company was *Beyond the Horizon*, produced at the Morosco Theatre, New York, February 2, 1920, at a special matinée, Mr. Richard Bennett playing Robert Mayo. It had a successful run in New York but was not well received in Chicago in the fall of 1920, so closed there. It received the Pulitzer Prize for that year.

The Emperor Jones began at the Provincetown Theatre in Macdougall Street on November 1, 1920, and created such instant interest that it was moved first to the Selwyn and then to the Princess Theatre in January, 1921. After the New York season it went on tour for thirty-five weeks, playing as far west as St. Louis and as far south as Norfolk. It is planned to send the company to the Far West during the season of 1922–23, and to take the play to London along with *Anna Christie* and *The Hairy Ape* during the following year. The central character, Brutus Jones, had a masterly interpretation at the hands of Mr. Charles S. Gilpin, a negro actor. It is interesting to note, however, that when *The Emperor Jones* was produced at the Little Theatre in Indianapolis and at the Howard University in Washington, D. C., the success was immediate, which indicates that the effect of the play is not dependent upon an individual actor.

Diff'rent, a two-act play laid in a seaport village in New England in 1890 and in 1920, and concerned with the change in a woman's character during the interval of thirty years, was first produced at the Provincetown Theatre on December 27, 1920, and was taken to the Princess Theatre on January 29, 1921.

Gold, an expansion of an earlier one-act play, is a study of the effect of the discovery of supposed treasure on a desert island upon the men who found it and an account of the trail of murder and madness that came in the wake of the discovery. It was produced at the Frazee Theatre, New York, June 1, 1921, but was not successful.

Anna Christie, a powerful study of the redeeming influence of the sea and of a great love upon a woman's nature, which received the Pulitzer Prize for the best play of 1921–22, opened at the Vanderbilt Theatre, November 2, 1921, and after a successful run in a very bad theatrical season, went to Chicago on April 9. Miss Pauline Lord's presentation of the leading character was one of the finest pieces of work done in many years.

The Straw, in which Mr. O'Neill used his experiences in the sanitarium for tuberculosis, had a short run at the Greenwich Village Theatre beginning November 10, 1921, neither the remarkable qualities of the play nor those of the cast being able to withstand the poor theatrical conditions.

The First Man, a play bringing into dramatic conflict the love for his science and the love for his wife on the part of Curtis Jayson, an anthropologist, was first played at the Neighborhood Playhouse March 4, 1922, as part of the season's repertoire.

The Hairy Ape, which began its triumphant career on March 9 at the Provincetown Theatre, was taken to the Plymouth Theatre on April 17, and after a successful season was sent on tour in the fall of 1922.

Mr. O'Neill's work has already attracted attention abroad. Mr. Norman MacDermott has produced at his Everyman Repertory Theatre in London *In the Zone* (June 15, 1921), *Diff'rent* (October 4, 1921), and *Ile*, a one-act play (April 17, 1922). *The Hairy Ape* was selected in 1922 as the most significant American play for production at the Odéon in Paris.

Mr. O'Neill's plays have been published as follows. By Boni and Liveright, New York: *The Moon of the Caribbees and six other plays of the Sea* (1919). *Beyond the Horizon* (1920). *Gold* (1920). *The Emperor Jones, Diff'rent, The Straw* (in one volume, 1921). *Anna Christie, The Hairy Ape, The First Man* (in one volume, 1922). By the Gorham Press: *Thirst* and other one-act plays, Boston, 1914. *The Emperor Jones* is here reprinted through the courtesy of the author and of Messrs. Boni and Liveright.

For an analysis of the plays, see General Introduction.

CAST OF CHARACTERS

PROVINCETOWN THEATRE, NOVEMBER 1, 1920

In order of their first appearance

AN OLD NATIVE WOMAN............Christine Ell.
HARRY SMITHERS, *white trader*.......Jasper Deeter.
BRUTUS JONES, *Emperor*............Charles S. Gilpin.
LEM, *a native chief*..................Charles Ellis.

THE SOLDIERS..................... {
S. I. Thompson.
Laurence Vail.
Leo Richman.
James Martin.
Owen White.

THE LITTLE FORMLESS FEARS; JEFF; THE NEGRO CONVICTS; THE PRISON GUARD; THE PLANTERS; THE AUCTIONEER; THE SLAVES; THE CONGO WITCH-DOCTOR; THE CROCODILE GOD.

The action of the play takes place on a West Indian island not yet self-determined by white marines. The form of government is, for the moment, an empire.

THE EMPEROR JONES*

SCENE I

SCENE: *The audience chamber in the palace of the Emperor —a spacious, high-ceilinged room with bare, white-washed walls. The floor is of white tiles. In the rear, to the left of centre, a wide archway giving out on a portico with white pillars. The palace is evidently situated on high ground, for beyond the portico nothing can be seen but a vista of distant hills, their summits crowned with thick groves of palm-trees. In the right wall, centre, a smaller arched doorway leading to the living quarters of the palace. The room is bare of furniture with the exception of one huge chair made of uncut wood which stands at centre, its back to rear. This is very apparently the Emperor's throne. It is painted a dazzling, eye-smiting scarlet. There is a brilliant orange cushion on the seat and another smaller one is placed on the floor to serve as a footstool. Strips of matting, dyed scarlet, lead from the foot of the throne to the two entrances.*

It is late afternoon but the sunlight still blazes yellowly beyond the portico and there is an oppressive burden of exhausting heat in the air.

As the curtain rises, a native negro woman sneaks in cautiously from the entrance on the right. She is very old, dressed in cheap calico, barefooted, a red bandanna handkerchief covering all but a few stray wisps of white hair. A bundle bound in colored cloth is carried over her shoulder on the end of a stick. She hesitates beside the doorway, peering back as if in extreme dread of being discovered. Then she begins to glide noiselessly, a step at a time, toward the doorway in the rear. At this moment SMITHERS *appears beneath the portico.*

SMITHERS *is a tall, stoop-shouldered man about forty. His bald head, perched on a long neck with an enormous Adam's apple, looks like an egg. The tropics have tanned his naturally pasty face with its small, sharp features to a sickly yellow, and native rum has painted his pointed nose to a startling red. His little, washy-blue eyes are red-rimmed and dart about him like a ferret's. His expression is one of unscrupulous meanness, cowardly and dangerous. He is dressed in a worn riding-suit of dirty white drill, puttees, spurs, and wears a white cork helmet. A cartridge-belt with an automatic revolver is around his waist. He carries a riding-whip in his hand. He sees the* WOMAN *and stops to watch her suspiciously. Then, making up his mind, he steps quickly on tiptoe into the room. The* WOMAN *looking back over her shoulder continually, does not see him until it is too late. When she does,* SMITHERS *springs forward and grabs her firmly by the shoulder. She struggles to get away, fiercely but silently.*

SMITHERS [*tightening his grasp—roughly*]. Easy! None o' that, me birdie. You can't wriggle out now. I got me 'ooks on yer.

WOMAN [*seeing the uselessness of struggling, gives way to frantic terror, and sinks to the ground, embracing his knees supplicatingly*]. No tell him! No tell him, Mister!

SMITHERS [*with great curiosity*]. Tell 'im? [*Then scornfully.*] Oh, you mean 'is bloomin' Majesty. What's the gaime, any'ow? What are you sneakin' away for? Been stealin' a bit, I s'pose. [*He taps her bundle with his riding-whip significantly.*]

WOMAN [*shaking her head vehemently*]. No, me no steal.

SMITHERS. Bloody liar! But tell me what's up. There's somethin' funny goin' on. I smelled it in the air first thing I got up this mornin'. You blacks are up to some devilment. This palace of 'is is like a bleedin' tomb. Where's all the 'ands?

[*The* WOMAN *keeps sullenly silent.* SMITHERS *raises his whip threateningly.*]

Ow, yer won't, won't yer? I'll show yer what's what.

WOMAN [*coweringly*]. I tell, Mister. You no hit.

They go—all go. [*She makes a sweeping gesture toward the hills in the distance.*]

SMITHERS. Run away—to the 'ills?

WOMAN. Yes, Mister. Him Emperor—Great Father. [*She touches her forehead to the floor with a quick mechanical jerk.*] Him sleep after eat. Then they go—all go. Me old woman. Me left only. Now me go too.

SMITHERS [*his astonishment giving way to an immense, mean satisfaction*]. Ow! So that's the ticket! Well, I know bloody well wot's in the air—when they runs orf to the 'ills. The tom-tom'll be thumpin' out there bloomin' soon. [*With extreme vindictiveness.*] And I'm bloody glad of it, for one! Serve 'im right! Puttin' on airs, the stinkin' nigger! 'Is Majesty! Gawd blimey! I only 'opes I'm there when they takes 'im out to shoot 'im. [*Suddenly.*] 'E's still 'ere all right, ain't 'e?

WOMAN. Yes. Him sleep.

SMITHERS. 'E's bound to find out soon as 'e wakes up. 'E's cunnin' enough to know when 'is time's come. [*He goes to the doorway on right and whistles shrilly with his fingers in his mouth. The old WOMAN springs to her feet and runs out of the doorway, rear. SMITHERS goes after her, reaching for his revolver.*] Stop or I'll shoot! [*Then stopping—indifferently.*] Pop orf then, if yer like, yer black cow. [*He stands in the doorway, looking after her.*]

[JONES *enters from the right. He is a tall, powerfully built, full-blooded negro of middle age. His features are typically negroid, yet there is something decidedly distinctive about his face—an underlying strength of will, a hardy, self-reliant confidence in himself that inspires respect. His eyes are alive with a keen, cunning intelligence. In manner he is shrewd, suspicious, evasive. He wears a light-blue uniform coat, sprayed with brass buttons, heavy gold chevrons on his shoulders, gold braid on the collar, cuffs, etc. His pants are bright red with a light-blue stripe down the side. Patent-leather laced boots with brass spurs, and a belt with a long-barrelled, pearl-handled revolver in a holster complete his make-up. Yet there is something not altogether ridiculous about his grandeur. He has a way of carrying it off.*]

JONES [*not seeing any one—greatly irritated and blinking sleepily—shouts*]. Who dare whistle dat way in my palace? Who dare wake up de Emperor? I'll git de hide frayled off some o' you niggers sho'!

SMITHERS [*showing himself—in a manner half afraid and half defiant*]. It was me whistled to yer. [*As* JONES *frowns angrily.*] I got news for yer.

JONES [*putting on his suavest manner, which fails to cover up his contempt for the white man*]. Oh, it's you, Mister Smithers. [*He sits down on his throne with easy dignity.*] What news you got to tell me?

SMITHERS [*coming close to enjoy his discomfiture*]. Don't yer notice nothin' funny to-day?

JONES [*coldly*]. Funny? No, I ain't perceived nothin' of de kind!

SMITHERS. Then yer ain't so foxy as I thought yer was. Where's all your court? [*sarcastically*] the Generals and the Cabinet Ministers and all?

JONES [*imperturbably*]. Where dey mostly runs to minute I closes my eyes—drinkin' rum and talkin' big down in de town. [*Sarcastically.*] How come you don't know dat? Ain't you sousin' with 'em most every day?

SMITHERS [*stung but pretending indifference—with a wink*]. That's part of the day's work. I got ter—ain't I—in my business?

JONES [*contemptuously*]. Yo' business!

SMITHERS [*imprudently enraged*]. Gawd blimey, you was glad enough for me ter take yer in on it when you landed here first. You didn' 'ave no 'igh and mighty airs in them days!

JONES [*his hand going to his revolver like a flash—menacingly*]. Talk polite, white man! Talk polite, you heah me! I'm boss heah now, is you fergettin'?

[*The Cockney seems about to challenge this last statement with the facts but something in the other's eyes holds and cows him.*]

SMITHERS [*in a cowardly whine*]. No 'arm meant, old top.

JONES [*condescendingly*]. I accepts yo' apology. [*Lets his hand fall from his revolver.*] No use'n you rakin' up ole times. What I was den is one thing. What I is now's another. You didn't let me in on yo' crooked work out o' no kind feelin's dat time. I done de dirty work fo' you —and most o' de brain-work, too, fo' dat matter—and I was wu'th money to you, dat's de reason.

SMITHERS. Well, blimey, I give yer a start, didn't I— when no one else would. I wasn't afraid to 'ire yer like the rest was—'count of the story about your breakin' jail back in the States.

JONES. No, you didn't have no s'cuse to look down on me fo' dat. You been in jail you'self more'n once.

SMITHERS [*furiously*]. It's a lie! [*Then trying to pass it off by an attempt at scorn.*] Garn! Who told yer that fairy-tale?

JONES. Dey's some tings I ain't got to be tole. I kin see 'em in folk's eyes. [*Then after a pause—meditatively.*] Yes, you sho' give me a start. And it didn't take long from dat time to git dese fool, woods' niggers right where I wanted dem. [*With pride.*] From stowaway to Emperor in two years! Dat's goin' some!

SMITHERS [*with curiosity*]. And I bet you got yer pile o' money 'id safe some place.

JONES [*with satisfaction*]. I sho' has! And it's in a foreign bank where no pusson don't ever git it out but me no matter what come. You didn't s'pose I was holdin' down dis Emperor job for de glory in it, did you? Sho'! De fuss and glory part of it, dat's only to turn de heads o' de low-flung, bush niggers dat's here. Dey wants de big circus show for deir money. I gives it to 'em an' I gits de money. [*With a grin.*] De long green, dat's me every time! [*Then rebukingly.*] But you ain't got no kick agin me, Smithers. I'se paid you back all you done for me many times. Ain't I pertected you and winked at all de crooked tradin' you been doin' right out in de broad day. Sho' I has—and me makin' laws to stop it at de same time! [*He chuckles.*]

SMITHERS [*grinning*]. But, meanin' no 'arm, you been grabbin' right and left yourself, ain't yer? Look at the taxes you've put on 'em! Blimey! You've squeezed 'em dry!

JONES [*chuckling*]. No, dey ain't *all* dry yet. I'se still heah, ain't I?

SMITHERS [*smiling at his secret thought*]. They're dry right now, you'll find out. [*Changing the subject abruptly.*] And as for me breakin' laws, you've broke 'em all yerself just as fast as yer made 'em.

JONES. Ain't I de Emperor? De laws don't go for him. [*Judicially.*] You heah what I tells you, Smithers. Dere's little stealin' like you does, and dere's big stealin' like I does. For de little stealin' dey gits you in jail soon or late. For de big stealin' dey makes you Emperor and puts you in de Hall o' Fame when you croaks. [*Reminiscently.*] If dey's one thing I learns in ten years on de Pullman ca's listenin' to de white quality talk, it's dat same fact. And when I gits a chance to use it I winds up Emperor in two years.

SMITHERS [*unable to repress the genuine admiration of the small fry for the large*]. Yes, yer turned the bleedin' trick, all right. Blimey, I never seen a bloke 'as 'ad the bloomin' luck you 'as.

JONES [*severely*]. Luck? What you mean—luck?

SMITHERS. I suppose you'll say as that swank about the silver bullet ain't luck—and that was what first got the fool blacks on yer side the time of the revolution, wasn't it?

JONES [*with a laugh*]. Oh, dat silver bullet! Sho' was luck! But I makes dat luck, you heah? I loads de dice! Yessuh! When dat murderin' nigger ole Lem hired to kill me takes aim ten feet away and his gun misses fire and I shoots him dead, what you heah me say?

SMITHERS. You said yer'd got a charm so's no lead bullet'd kill yer. You was so strong only a silver bullet could kill yer, you told 'em. Blimey, wasn't that swank for yer—and plain, fat-'eaded luck?

JONES [*proudly*]. I got brains and I uses 'em quick. Dat ain't luck.

SMITHERS. Yer know they wasn't 'ardly liable to get no silver bullets. And it was luck 'e didn't 'it you that time.

JONES [*laughing*]. And dere all dem fool, bush niggers was kneelin' down and bumpin' deir heads on de ground like I was a miracle out o' de Bible. Oh, Lawd, from dat time on I has dem all eatin' out of my hand. I cracks de whip and dey jumps through.

SMITHERS [*with a sniff*]. Yankee bluff done it.

JONES. Ain't a man's talkin' big what makes him big —long as he makes folks believe it? Sho', I talks large when I ain't got nothin' to back it up, but I ain't talkin' wild just de same. I knows I kin fool 'em—I *knows* it— and dat's backin' enough fo' my game. And ain't I got to learn deir lingo and teach some of dem English befo' I kin talk to 'em? Ain't dat wuk? You ain't never learned ary word er it, Smithers, in de ten years you been heah, dough you knows it's money in yo' pocket tradin' wid 'em if you does. But you'se too shiftless to take de trouble.

SMITHERS [*flushing*]. Never mind about me. What's this I've 'eard about yer really 'avin' a silver bullet moulded for yourself?

JONES. It's playin' out my bluff. I has de silver bullet moulded and I tells 'em when de time comes I kills myself wid it. I tells 'em dat's 'cause I'm de on'y man in de world big enuff to git me. No use'n deir tryin'. And dey falls down and bumps deir heads. [*He laughs.*] I does dat so's I kin take a walk in peace widout no jealous nigger gunnin' at me from behind de trees.

SMITHERS [*astonished*]. Then you 'ad it made—'onest?

JONES. Sho' did. Heah she be. [*He takes out his revolver, breaks it, and takes the silver bullet out of one chamber.*] Five lead an' dis silver baby at de last. Don't she shine pretty? [*He holds it in his hand, looking at it admiringly, as if strangely fascinated.*]

SMITHERS. Let me see. [*Reaches out his hand for it.*]

JONES [*harshly*]. Keep yo' hands whar dey b'long, white man. [*He replaces it in the chamber and puts the revolver back on his hip.*]

SMITHERS [*snarling*]. Gawd blimey! Think I'm a bleedin' thief, you would.

JONES. No, 'tain't dat. I knows you'se scared to steal from me. On'y I ain't 'lowin' nary body to touch dis baby. She's my rabbit's foot.

SMITHERS [*sneering*]. A bloomin' charm, wot? [*Venomously.*] Well, you'll need all the bloody charms you 'as before long, s' 'elp me!

JONES [*judicially*]. Oh, I'se good for six months yit

'fore dey gits sick o' my game. Den, when I sees trouble comin', I makes my getaway.

SMITHERS. Ho! You got it all planned, ain't yer?

JONES. I ain't no fool. I knows dis Emperor's time is sho't. Dat why I make hay when de sun shine. Was you thinkin' I'se aimin' to hold down dis job for life? No, suh! What good is gittin' money if you stays back in dis raggedy country? I wants action when I spends. And when I sees dese niggers gittin' up deir nerve to tu'n me out, and I'se got all de money in sight, I resigns on de spot and beats it quick.

SMITHERS. Where to?

JONES. None o' yo' business.

SMITHERS. Not back to the bloody States, I'll lay my oath.

JONES [suspiciously]. Why don't I? [Then with an easy laugh.] You mean 'count of dat story 'bout me breakin' from jail back dere? Dat's all talk.

SMITHERS [sceptically]. Ho, yes!

JONES [sharply]. You ain't 'sinuatin' I'se a liar, is you?

SMITHERS [hastily]. No, Gawd strike me! I was only thinkin' o' the bloody lies you told the blacks 'ere about killin' white men in the States.

JONES [angered]. How come dey're lies?

SMITHERS. You'd 'ave been in jail, if you 'ad, wouldn't yer then? [With venom.] And from what I've 'eard, it ain't 'ealthy for a black to kill a white man in the States. They burns 'em in oil, don't they?

JONES [with cool deadliness]. You mean lynchin' 'd scare me? Well, I tells you, Smithers, maybe I does kill one white man back dere. Maybe I does. And maybe I kills another right heah 'fore long if he don't look out.

SMITHERS [trying to force a laugh]. I was on'y spoofin' yer. Can't yer take a joke? And you was just sayin' you'd never been in jail.

JONES [in the same tone—slightly boastful]. Maybe I goes to jail dere for gettin' in an argument wid razors ovah a crap game. Maybe I gits twenty years when dat colored man die. Maybe I gits in 'nother argument wid de prison guard was overseer ovah us when we're wukin' de roads. Maybe he hits me wid a whip and I splits his

head wid a shovel and runs away and files de chain off
my leg and gits away safe. Maybe I does all dat an'
maybe I don't. It's a story I tells you so's you knows
I'se de kind of man dat if you evah repeats one word of
it, I ends yo' stealin' on dis yearth mighty damn quick!

SMITHERS [*terrified*]. Think I'd peach on yer? Not
me! Ain't I always been yer friend?

JONES [*suddenly relaxing*]. Sho' you has—and you'd
better be.

SMITHERS [*recovering his composure—and with it his
malice*]. And just to show yer I'm yer friend, I'll tell yer
that bit o' news I was goin' to.

JONES. Go ahead! Shoot de piece. Must be bad
news from de happy way you look.

SMITHERS [*warningly*]. Maybe it's gettin' time for you
to resign—with that bloomin' silver bullet, wot? [*He
finishes with a mocking grin.*]

JONES [*puzzled*]. What's dat you say? Talk plain.

SMITHERS. Ain't noticed any of the guards or servants
about the place to-day, I 'aven't.

JONES [*carelessly*]. Dey're all out in de garden sleepin'
under de trees. When I sleeps, dey sneaks a sleep, too,
and I pretends I never suspicions it. All I got to do is to
ring de bell and dey come flyin', makin' a bluff dey was
wukin' all de time.

SMITHERS [*in the same mocking tone*]. Ring the bell
now an' you'll bloody well see what I means.

JONES [*startled to alertness, but preserving the same careless tone*]. Sho' I rings. [*He reaches below the throne and
pulls out a big, common dinner-bell which is painted the
same vivid scarlet as the throne. He rings this vigorously
—then stops to listen. Then he goes to both doors, rings
again, and looks out.*]

SMITHERS [*watching him with malicious satisfaction, after
a pause—mockingly*]. The bloody ship is sinkin' an' the
bleedin' rats 'as slung their 'ooks.

JONES [*in a sudden fit of anger flings the bell clattering
into a corner*]. Low-flung, woods' niggers! [*Then catching* SMITHERS'S *eye on him, he controls himself and suddenly
bursts into a low, chuckling laugh.*] Reckon I overplays
my hand dis once! A man can't take de pot on a bob-

tailed flush all de time.   Was I sayin' I'd sit in six months
mo'?   Well, I'se changed my mind den.   I cashes in and
resigns de job of Emperor right dis minute.

SMITHERS [*with real admiration*].   Blimey, but you're a
cool bird, and no mistake.

JONES.   No use'n fussin'.   When I knows de game's
up I kisses it good-by widout no long waits.   Dey've all
run off to de hills, ain't dey?

SMITHERS.   Yes—every bleedin' man jack of 'em.

JONES.   Den de revolution is at de post.   And de Emperor better git his feet smokin' up de trail.   [*He starts
for the door in rear.*]

SMITHERS.   Goin' out to look for your 'orse?   Yer
won't find any.   They steals the 'orses first thing.   Mine
was gone when I went for 'im this mornin'.   That's wot
first give me a suspicion of wot was up.

JONES [*alarmed for a second, scratches his head, then
philosophically*].   Well, den I hoofs it.   Feet, do yo' duty!
[*He pulls out a gold watch and looks at it.*]   Three-thuty.
Sundown's at six-thuty or dereabouts.   [*Puts his watch
back—with cool confidence.*]   I got plenty o' time to make
it easy.

SMITHERS.   Don't be so bloomin' sure of it.   They'll
be after you 'ot and 'eavy.   Ole Lem is at the bottom o'
this business an' 'e 'ates you like 'ell.   'E'd rather do for
you than eat 'is dinner, 'e would!

JONES [*scornfully*].   Dat fool no-count nigger!   Does
you think I'se scared o' him?   I stands him on his thick
head more'n once befo' dis, and I does it again if he come
in my way—   [*Fiercely.*]   And dis time I leave him a
dead nigger fo' sho'!

SMITHERS.   You'll 'ave to cut through the big forest—
an' these blacks 'ere can sniff and follow a trail in the
dark like 'ounds.   You'd 'ave to 'ustle to get through that
forest in twelve hours even if you knew all the bloomin'
trails like a native.

JONES [*with indignant scorn*].   Look-a-heah, white man!
Does you think I'se a natural bo'n fool?   Give me credit
fo' havin' some sense, fo' Lawd's sake!   Don't you s'pose
I'se looked ahead and made sho' of all de chances?   I'se
gone out in dat big forest, pretendin' to hunt, so many

times dat I knows it high an' low like a book. I could go through on dem trails wid my eyes shut. [*With great contempt.*] Think dese ignerent bush niggers dat ain't got brains enuff to know deir own names even can catch Brutus Jones? Huh, I s'pects not! Not on yo' life! Why, man, de white men went after me wid bloodhounds where I come from an' I jes' laughs at 'em. It's a shame to fool dese black trash around heah, dey're so easy. You watch me, man! I'll make dem look sick, I will. I'll be 'cross de plain to de edge of de forest by time dark comes. Once in de woods in de night, dey got a swell chance o' findin' dis baby! Dawn to-morrow I'll be out at de oder side and on de coast whar dat French gunboat is stayin'. She picks me up, takes me to the Martinique when she go dar, and dere I is safe wid a mighty big bank-roll in my jeans. It's easy as rollin' off a log.

SMITHERS [*maliciously*]. But s'posin' somethin' 'appens wrong an' they do nab yer?

JONES [*decisively*]. Dey don't—dat's de answer.

SMITHERS. But, just for argyment's sake—what'd you do?

JONES [*frowning*]. I'se got five lead bullets in dis gun good enuff fo' common bush niggers—and after dat I got de silver bullet left to cheat 'em out o' gittin' me.

SMITHERS [*jeeringly*]. Ho, I was fergettin' that silver bullet. You'll bump yourself orf in style, won't yer? Blimey!

JONES [*gloomily*]. You kin bet yo' whole roll on one thing, white man. Dis baby plays out his string to de end, and when he quits, he quits wid a bang de way he ought. Silver bullet ain't none too good for him when he go, dat's a fac'! [*Then shaking off his nervousness—with a confident laugh.*] Sho'! What is I talkin' about? Ain't come to dat yit and I never will—not wid trash niggers like dese yere. [*Boastfully.*] Silver bullet bring me luck anyway. I kin outguess, outrun, outfight, an' outplay de whole lot o' dem all ovah de board any time o' de day er night! You watch me!

    [*From the distant hills comes the faint, steady thump of a tom-tom, low and vibrating. It starts at a rate exactly corresponding to normal pulse beat—72 to the*

*minute—and continues at a gradually accelerating
rate from this point uninterruptedly to the very end
of the play.*]

[JONES *starts at the sound. A strange look of apprehension creeps into his face for a moment as he listens. Then he asks, with an attempt to regain his
most casual manner.*]

What's dat drum beatin' fo'?

SMITHERS [*with a mean grin*]. For you. That means
the bleedin' ceremony 'as started. I've 'eard it before
and I knows.

JONES. Cer'mony? What cer'mony?

SMITHERS. The blacks is 'oldin' a bloody meetin', 'avin'
a war-dance, gettin' their courage worked up b'fore they
starts after you.

JONES. Let dem! Dey'll sho' need it!

SMITHERS. And they're there 'oldin' their 'eathen religious service—makin' no end of devil spells and charms
to 'elp 'em against your silver bullet. [*He guffaws loudly.*]
Blimey, but they're balmy as 'ell!

JONES [*a tiny bit awed and shaken in spite of himself*].
Huh! Takes more'n dat to scare dis chicken!

SMITHERS [*scenting the other's feeling—maliciously*].
Ter-night when it's pitch black in the forest, they'll 'ave
their pet devils and ghosts 'oundin' after you. You'll
find yer bloody 'air'll be standin' on end before ter-morrow
mornin'. [*Seriously.*] It's a bleedin' queer place, that
stinkin' forest, even in daylight. Yer don't know what
might 'appen in there, it's that rotten still. Always sends
the cold shivers down my back minute I gets in it.

JONES [*with a contemptuous sniff*]. I ain't no chicken-
liver like you is. Trees an' me, we'se friends, and dar's
a full moon comin' bring me light. And let dem po' niggers make all de fool spells dey'se a min' to. Does yo'
s'pect I'se silly enuff to b'lieve in ghosts an' ha'nts an' all
dat ole woman's talk? G'long, white man! You ain't
talkin' to me. [*With a chuckle.*] Doesn't you know dey's
got to do wid a man was member in good standin' o' de
Baptist Church? Sho' I was dat when I was porter on
de Pullmans, befo' I gits into my little trouble. Let dem
try deir heathen tricks. De Baptist Church done pertect
me and land dem all in hell. [*Then with more confident*

satisfaction.] And I'se got little silver bullet o' my own, don't forgit.

SMITHERS. Ho! You 'aven't give much 'eed to your Baptist Church since you been down 'ere. I've 'eard myself you 'ad turned yer coat an' was takin' up with their blarsted witch-doctors, or whatever the 'ell yer calls the swine.

JONES [*vehemently*]. I pretends to! Sho' I pretends! Dat's part o' my game from de fust. If I finds out dem niggers believes dat black is white, den I yells it out louder 'n deir loudest. It don't git me nothin' to do missionary work for de Baptist Church. I'se after de coin, an' I lays my Jesus on de shelf for de time bein'. [*Stops abruptly to look at his watch—alertly.*] But I ain't got de time to waste no more fool talk wid you. I'se gwine away from heah dis secon'. [*He reaches in under the throne and pulls out an expensive Panama hat with a bright multicolored band and sets it jauntily on his head.*] So long, white man! [*With a grin.*] See you in jail some time, maybe!

SMITHERS. Not me, you won't. Well, I wouldn't be in yer bloody boots for no bloomin' money, but 'ere's wishin' yer luck just the same.

JONES [*contemptuously*]. You're de frightenedest man evah I see! I tells you I'se safe's 'f I was in New York City. It takes dem niggers from now to dark to git up de nerve to start somethin'. By dat time, I'se got a head start dey never kotch up wid.

SMITHERS [*maliciously*]. Give my regards to any ghosts yer meets up with.

JONES [*grinning*]. If dat ghost got money, I'll tell him never ha'nt you less'n he wants to lose it.

SMITHERS [*flattered*]. Garn! [*Then curiously.*] Ain't yer takin' no luggage with yer?

JONES. I travels light when I wants to move fast. And I got tinned grub buried on de edge o' de forest. [*Boastfully.*] Now say dat I don't look ahead an' use my brains! [*With a wide, liberal gesture.*] I will all dat's left in de palace to you—and you better grab all you kin sneak away wid befo' dey gits here.

SMITHERS [*gratefully*]. Righto—and thanks ter yer.

[*As* JONES *walks toward the door in rear—cautioningly.*] Say! Look 'ere, you ain't goin' out that way, are yer?

JONES. Does you think I'd slink out de back door like a common nigger? I'se Emperor yit, ain't I? And de Emperor Jones leaves de way he comes, and dat black trash don't dare stop him—not yit, leastways. [*He stops for a moment in the doorway, listening to the far-off but insistent beat of the tom-tom.*] Listen to dat roll-call, will you? Must be mighty big drum carry dat far. [*Then with a laugh.*] Well, if dey ain't no whole brass band to see me off, I sho' got de drum part of it. So long, white man. [*He puts his hands in his pockets and with studied carelessness, whistling a tune, he saunters out of the doorway and off to the left.*]

SMITHERS [*looks after him with a puzzled admiration*]. 'E's got 'is bloomin' nerve with 'im, s'elp me! [*Then angrily.*] Ho—the bleedin' nigger—puttin' on 'is bloody airs! I 'opes they nabs 'im an' gives 'im what's what! [*Then putting business before the pleasure of this thought, looking around him with cupidity.*] A bloke ought to find a 'ole lot in this palace that'd go for a bit of cash. Let's take a look, 'Arry, me lad. [*He starts for the doorway on the right as*

THE CURTAIN FALLS

SCENE II: NIGHTFALL

SCENE: *The end of the plain where the Great Forest begins. The foreground is sandy, level ground dotted by a few stones and clumps of stunted bushes cowering close against the earth to escape the buffeting of the trade-wind. In the rear the forest is a wall of darkness dividing the world. Only when the eye becomes accustomed to the gloom can the outlines of separate trunks of the nearest trees be made out, enormous pillars of deeper blackness. A sombre monotone of wind lost in the leaves moans in the air. Yet this sound serves but to intensify the impression of the forest's relentless immobility, to form a background throwing into relief its brooding, implacable silence.*

[JONES *enters from the left, walking rapidly. He stops as he nears the edge of the forest, looks around him quickly, peer-*

ing into the dark as if searching for some familiar landmark. Then, apparently satisfied that he is where he ought to be, he throws himself on the ground, dog-tired.] Well, heah I is. In de nick o' time, too! Little mo' an' it'd be blacker'n de ace of spades heahabouts. *[He pulls a bandanna hand-kerchief from his hip pocket and mops off his perspiring face.]* Sho'! Gimme air! I'se tuckered out sho' 'nuff. Dat soft Emperor job ain't no trainin' fo' a long hike ovah dat plain in de brilin' sun. *[Then with a chuckle.]* Cheah up, nigger, de worst is yet to come. *[He lifts his head and stares at the forest. His chuckle peters out abruptly. In a tone of awe.]* My goodness, look at dem woods, will you? Dat no-count Smithers said dey'd be black an' he sho' called de turn. *[Turning away from them quickly and looking down at his feet, he snatches at a chance to change the subject—solicitously.]* Feet, you is holdin' up yo' end fine an' I sutinly hopes you ain't blisterin' none. It's time you git a rest. *[He takes off his shoes, his eyes studiously avoiding the forest. He feels of the soles of his feet gingerly.]* You is still in de pink—on'y a mite feverish. Cool yo'selfs. Remember you done got a long journey yit befo' you. *[He sits in a weary attitude, listening to the rhythmic beating of the tom-tom. He grumbles in a loud tone to cover up a growing uneasiness.]* Bush niggers! Wonder dey wouldn' git sick o' beatin' dat drum. Sound louder, seem like. I wonder if dey's startin' after me? *[He scrambles to his feet, looking back across the plain.]* Couldn't see dem now, nohow, if dey was hundred feet away. *[Then shaking himself like a wet dog to get rid of these depressing thoughts.]* Sho', dey's miles an' miles behind. What you gittin' fidgety about? *[But he sits down and begins to lace up his shoes in great haste, all the time muttering reassuringly.]* You know what? Yo' belly is empty, dat's what's de matter wid you. Come time to eat! Wid nothin' but wind on yo' stumach, o' course you feels jiggedy. Well, we eats right heah an' now soon's I gits dese pesky shoes laced up. *[He finishes lacing up his shoes.]* Dere! Now le's see! *[Gets on his hands and knees and searches the ground around him with his eyes.]* White stone, white stone, where is you? *[He sees the first white stone and crawls to it—with satisfaction.]* Heah

you is! I knowed dis was de right place. Box of grub,
come to me. [*He turns over the stone and feels in under it—
in a tone of dismay.*] Ain't heah! Gorry, is I in de right
place or isn't I? Dere's 'nother stone. Guess dat's it.
[*He scrambles to the next stone and turns it over.*] Ain't
heah, neither! Grub, whar is you? Ain't heah. Gorry,
has I got to go hungry into dem woods—all de night?
[*While he is talking he scrambles from one stone to another,
turning them over in frantic haste. Finally, he jumps to
his feet excitedly.*] Is I lost de place? Must have! But
how dat happen when I was followin' de trail across de
plain in broad daylight? [*Almost plaintively.*] I'se hungry, I is! I gotta git my feed. Whar's my strength
gonna come from if I doesn't? Gorry, I gotta find dat
grub high an' low somehow! Why it come dark so quick
like dat? Can't see nothin'. [*He scratches a match on
his trousers and peers about him. The rate of the beat of
the far-off tom-tom increases perceptibly as he does so. He
mutters in a bewildered voice.*] How come all dese white
stones come heah when I only remembers one? [*Suddenly, with a frightened gasp, he flings the match on the
ground and stamps on it.*] Nigger, is you gone crazy mad?
Is you lightin' matches to show dem whar you is? Fo'
Lawd's sake, use yo' haid. Gorry, I'se got to be careful!
[*He stares at the plain behind him apprehensively, his hand
on his revolver.*] But how come all dese white stones?
And whar's dat tin box o' grub I hid all wrapped up in
oilcloth?

> [*While his back is turned, the* LITTLE FORMLESS
> FEARS *creep out from the deeper blackness of the
> forest. They are black, shapeless, only their glit-
> tering little eyes can be seen. If they have any de-
> scribable form at all it is that of a grubworm about the
> size of a creeping child. They move noiselessly, but
> with deliberate, painful effort, striving to raise them-
> selves on end, failing and sinking prone again.*
> JONES *turns about to face the forest. He stares up at
> the tops of the trees, seeking vainly to discover his
> whereabouts by their conformation.*]

Can't tell nothin' from dem trees! Gorry, nothin'
'round heah look like I evah seed it befo'. I'se done lost

de place sho' 'nuff! [*With mournful foreboding.*] It's mighty queer! It's mighty queer! [*With sudden forced defiance—in an angry tone.*] Woods, is you tryin' to put somethin' ovah on me?

> [*From the formless creatures on the ground in front of him comes a tiny gale of low mocking laughter like a rustling of leaves. They squirm upward toward him in twisted attitudes.* JONES *looks down, leaps backward with a yell of terror, yanking out his revolver as he does so—in a quavering voice.*]

What's dat? Who's dar? What is you? Git away from me befo' I shoots you up! You don't?——

> [*He fires. There is a flash, a loud report, then silence broken only by the far-off, quickened throb of the tom-tom. The formless creatures have scurried back into the forest.* JONES *remains fixed in his position, listening intently. The sound of the shot, the reassuring feel of the revolver in his hand, have somewhat restored his shaken nerve. He addresses himself with renewed confidence.*]

Dey're gone. Dat shot fix 'em. Dey was only little animals—little wild pigs, I reckon. Dey've maybe rooted out yo' grub an' eat it. Sho', you fool nigger, what you think dey is—ha'nts? [*Excitedly.*] Gorry, you give de game away when you fire dat shot. Dem niggers heah dat fo' su'tin! Time you beat it in de woods widout no long waits. [*He starts for the forest—hesitates before the plunge—then urging himself in with manful resolution.*] Git in, nigger! What you skeered at? Ain't nothin' dere but de trees! Git in! [*He plunges boldly into the forest.*]

SCENE III

SCENE: *Nine o'clock. In the forest. The moon has just risen. Its beams, drifting through the canopy of leaves, make a barely perceptible, suffused, eerie glow. A dense low wall of underbrush and creepers is in the nearer foreground, fencing in a small triangular clearing. Beyond this is the massed blackness of the forest like an encompassing barrier. A path is dimly discerned leading down to the clearing from left, rear, and winding away from it again toward the right. As the scene opens nothing can be distinctly made out. Except for the beating of the tom-tom, which is a trifle louder and quicker than in the previous scene, there is silence, broken every few seconds by a queer, clicking sound. Then gradually the figure of the negro* JEFF *can be discerned crouching on his haunches at the rear of the triangle. He is middle-aged, thin, brown in color, is dressed in a Pullman porter's uniform, cap, etc. He is throwing a pair of dice on the ground before him, picking them up, shaking them, casting them out with the regular, rigid, mechanical movements of an automaton. The heavy, plodding footsteps of some one approaching along the trail from the left are heard and* JONES'S *voice, pitched in a slightly higher key and strained in a cheering effort to overcome its own tremors.*

De moon's rizen. Does you heah dat, nigger? You gits more light from dis out. No mo' buttin' yo' fool head agin' de trunks an' scratchin' de hide off yo' legs in de bushes. Now you sees whar yo'se gwine. So cheer up! From now on you has a snap. [*He steps just to the rear of the triangular clearing and mops off his face on his sleeve. He has lost his Panama hat. His face is scratched, his brilliant uniform shows several large rents.*] What time's it gittin' to be, I wonder? I dassent light no match to find out. Phoo'. It's wa'm an' dat's a fac'! [*Wearily.*] How long I been makin' tracks in dese woods? Must be hours an' hours. Seems like fo'evah! Yit can't be, when de moon's jes' riz. Dis am a long night fo' yo', yo'

Majesty! [*With a mournful chuckle.*] Majesty! Der ain't much majesty 'bout dis baby now. [*With attempted cheerfulness.*] Never min'. It's all part o' de game. Dis night come to an end like everything else. And when you gits dar safe and has dat bank-roll in yo' hands you laughs at all dis. [*He starts to whistle but checks himself abruptly.*] What yo' whistlin' for, you po' dope! Want all de worl' to heah you? [*He stops talking to listen.*] Heah dat ole drum! Sho' gits nearer from de sound. Dey're packin' it along wid 'em. Time fo' me to move. [*He takes a step forward, then stops—worriedly.*] What's dat odder queer clicketty sound I heah? Dere it is! Sound close! Sound like—sound like— Fo' God sake, sound like some nigger was shootin' crap! [*Frightenedly.*] I better beat it quick when I gits dem notions. [*He walks quickly into the clear space—then stands transfixed as he sees* JEFF—*in a terrified gasp.*] Who dar? Who dat? Is dat you, Jeff? [*Starting toward the other, forgetful for a moment of his surroundings and really believing it is a living man that he sees—in a tone of happy relief.*] Jeff! I'se sho' mighty glad to see you! Dey tol' me you done died from dat razor cut I gives you. [*Stopping suddenly, bewilderedly.*] But how you come to be heah, nigger? [*He stares fascinatedly at the other, who continues his mechanical play with the dice.* JONES's *eyes begin to roll wildly. He stutters.*] Ain't you gwine—look up—can't you speak to me? Is you—is you—a ha'nt? [*He jerks out his revolver in a frenzy of terrified rage.*] Nigger, I kills you dead once. Has I got to kill you agin? You take it den. [*He fires. When the smoke clears away* JEFF *has disappeared.* JONES *stands trembling—then with a certain reassurance.*] He's gone, anyway. Ha'nt or no ha'nt, dat shot fix him. [*The beat of the far-off tom-tom is perceptibly louder and more rapid.* JONES *becomes conscious of it— with a start, looking back over his shoulder.*] Dey's gittin' near! Dey's comin' fast! And heah I is shootin' shots to let 'em know jes' whar I is. Oh, Gorry, I'se got to run. [*Forgetting the path, he plunges wildly into the underbrush in the rear and disappears in the shadow.*]

SCENE IV

SCENE: *Eleven o'clock. In the forest. A wide dirt road*
runs diagonally from right, front, to left, rear. Rising
sheer on both sides the forest walls it in. The moon is
now up. Under its light the road glimmers ghastly
and unreal. It is as if the forest had stood aside momen-
tarily to let the road pass through and accomplish its
veiled purpose. This done, the forest will fold in upon
itself again and the road will be no more. JONES
stumbles in from the forest on the right. His uniform
is ragged and torn. He looks about him with numbed
surprise when he sees the road, his eyes blinking in the
bright moonlight. He flops down exhaustedly and
pants heavily for a while. Then with sudden anger.

I'm meltin' wid heat! Runnin' an' runnin' an' runnin'!
Damn dis heah coat! Like a strait-jacket! [*He tears*
off his coat and flings it away from him, revealing himself
stripped to the waist.] Dere! Dat's better! Now I kin
breathe! [*Looking down at his feet, the spurs catch his eye.*]
And to hell wid dese high-fangled spurs. Dey're
what's been a-trippin' me up an' breakin' my neck. [*He*
unstraps them and flings them away disgustedly.] Dere!
I gits rid o' dem frippety Emperor trappin's an' I travels
lighter. Lawd! I'se tired! [*After a pause, listening to*
the insistent beat of the tom-tom in the distance.] I must 'a'
put some distance between myself an' dem—runnin' like
dat—and yit—dat damn drum sound jes' de same—
nearer, even. Well, I guess I a'most holds my lead anyhow. Dey won't never catch up. [*With a sigh.*] If on'y
my fool legs stands up. Oh, I'se sorry I evah went in for
dis. Dat Emperor job is sho' hard to shake. [*He looks*
around him suspiciously.] How'd dis road evah git heah?
Good level road, too. I never remembers seein' it befo'.
[*Shaking his head apprehensively.*] Dese woods is sho'
full o' de queerest things at night. [*With a sudden terror.*]
Lawd God, don't let me see no more o' dem ha'nts!
Dey gits my goat! [*Then trying to talk himself into confi-*
dence.] Ha'nts! You fool nigger, dey ain't no such

things! Don't de Baptist parson tell you dat many time?
Is you civilized, or is you like dese ign'rent black niggers
heah? Sho'! Dat was all in yo' own head. Wasn't
nothin' dere. Wasn't no Jeff! Know what? You jus'
get seein' dem things 'cause yo' belly's empty and you's
sick wid hunger inside. Hunger 'fects yo' head and yo'
eyes. Any fool know dat. [*Then pleading fervently.*]
But bless God, I don't come across no more o' dem, whatever dey is! [*Then cautiously.*] Rest! Don't talk!
Rest! You needs it. Den you gits on yo' way again.
[*Looking at the moon.*] Night's half gone a'most. You
hits de coast in de mawning! Den you'se all safe.

> [*From the right forward a small gang of negroes enter.
> They are dressed in striped convict suits, their heads
> are shaven, one leg drags limpingly, shackled to a
> heavy ball and chain. Some carry picks, the others
> shovels. They are followed by a white man dressed
> in the uniform of a prison guard. A Winchester
> rifle is slung across his shoulders and he carries a
> heavy whip. At a signal from the* GUARD *they stop on
> the road opposite where* JONES *is sitting.* JONES, *who
> has been staring up at the sky, unmindful of their
> noiseless approach, suddenly looks down and sees
> them. His eyes pop out, he tries to get to his feet and
> fly, but sinks back, too numbed by fright to move.
> His voice catches in a choking prayer.*]

Lawd Jesus!

> [*The* PRISON GUARD *cracks his whip—noiselessly—
> and at that signal all the convicts start to work on
> the road. They swing their picks, they shovel, but
> not a sound comes from their labor. Their movements,
> like those of* JEFF *in the preceding scene, are those of
> automatons—rigid, slow, and mechanical. The*
> PRISON GUARD *points sternly at* JONES *with his whip,
> motions him to take his place among the other shovel-
> lers.* JONES *gets to his feet in a hypnotized stupor.
> He mumbles subserviently.*]

Yes, suh! Yes, suh! I'se comin'.

> [*As he shuffles, dragging one foot, over to his place, he
> curses under his breath with rage and hatred.*]

God damn yo' soul, I gits even wid you yit, some time.

[*As if there were a shovel in his hands he goes through weary, mechanical gestures of digging up dirt and throwing it to the roadside. Suddenly the* GUARD *approaches him angrily, threateningly. He raises his whip and lashes* JONES *viciously across the shoulders with it.* JONES *winces with pain and cowers abjectly. The* GUARD *turns his back on him and walks away contemptuously. Instantly* JONES *straightens up. With arms upraised as if his shovel were a club in his hands he springs murderously at the unsuspecting* GUARD. *In the act of crashing down his shovel on the white man's skull,* JONES *suddenly becomes aware that his hands are empty. He cries despairingly.*]

Whar's my shovel? Gimme my shovel till I splits his damn head! [*Appealing to his fellow convicts.*] Gimme a shovel, one o' you, fo' God's sake!

[*They stand fixed in motionless attitudes, their eyes on the ground. The* GUARD *seems to wait expectantly, his back turned to the attacker.* JONES *bellows with baffled, terrified rage, tugging frantically at his revolver.*]

I kills you, you white debil, if it's de last thing I evah does! Ghost or debil, I kill you agin!

[*He frees the revolver and fires pointblank at the* GUARD's *back. Instantly the walls of the forest close in from both sides, the road and the figures of the convict gang are blotted out in an enshrouding darkness. The only sounds are a crashing in the underbrush as* JONES *leaps away in mad flight and the throbbing of the tom-tom, still far distant, but increased in volume of sound and rapidity of beat.*]

SCENE V

SCENE: *One o'clock. A large circular clearing, enclosed by the serried ranks of gigantic trunks of tall trees whose tops are lost to view. In the centre is a big dead stump worn by time into a curious resemblance to an auction-block. The moon floods the clearing with a clear light.* JONES *forces his way in through the forest on the left. He looks wildly about the clearing with hunted, fearful glances. His pants are in tatters, his shoes cut and misshapen, flapping about his feet. He slinks cautiously to the stump in the centre and sits down in a tense position, ready for instant flight. Then he holds his head in his hands and rocks back and forth, moaning to himself miserably.*

Oh, Lawd, Lawd! Oh, Lawd, Lawd! [*Suddenly he throws himself on his knees and raises his clasped hands to the sky—in a voice of agonized pleading.*] Lawd Jesus, heah my prayer! I'se a po' sinner, a po' sinner! I knows I done wrong, I knows it! When I cotches Jeff cheatin' wid loaded dice my anger overcomes me and I kills him dead! Lawd, I done wrong! When dat guard hits me wid de whip, my anger overcomes me, and I kills him dead. Lawd, I done wrong! And down heah whar dese fool bush niggers raises me up to the seat o' de mighty, I steals all I could grab. Lawd, I done wrong! I knows it! I'se sorry! Forgive me, Lawd! Forgive dis po' sinner! [*Then beseeching terrifiedly.*] And keep dem away, Lawd! Keep dem away from me! And stop dat drum soundin' in my ears! Dat begin to sound ha'nted, too. [*He gets to his feet, evidently slightly reassured by his prayer—with attempted confidence.*] De Lawd'll preserve me from dem ha'nts after dis. [*Sits down on the stump again.*] I ain't skeered o' real men. Let dem come. But dem odders— [*He shudders—then looks down at his feet, working his toes inside the shoes—with a groan.*] Oh, my po' feet! Dem shoes ain't no use no more 'ceptin' to hurt. I'se better off widout dem. [*He unlaces them and pulls them off—holds the wrecks of the shoes in his hands and*

regards them mournfully.] You was real, A-one patin'
leather, too. Look at you now. Emperor, you'se gittin'
mighty low!

> [*He sighs dejectedly and remains with bowed shoulders,
> staring down at the shoes in his hands as if reluctant
> to throw them away. While his attention is thus
> occupied, a crowd of figures silently enter the clearing
> from all sides. All are dressed in Southern costumes
> of the period of the fifties of the last century. There
> are middle-aged men who are evidently well-to-do
> planters. There is one spruce, authoritative indi-
> vidual—the* AUCTIONEER. *There are a crowd of
> curious spectators, chiefly young belles and dandies
> who have come to the slave-market for diversion. All
> exchange courtly greetings in dumb show and chat
> silently together. There is something stiff, rigid,
> unreal, marionettish about their movements. They
> group themselves about the stump. Finally a batch
> of slaves are led in from the left by an attendant—
> three men of different ages, two women, one with a
> baby in her arms, nursing. They are placed to the
> left of the stump, beside* JONES.]

> [*The white planters look them over appraisingly as if
> they were cattle, and exchange judgments on each.
> The dandies point with their fingers and make witty
> remarks. The belles titter bewitchingly. All this
> in silence save for the ominous throb of the tom-tom.
> The* AUCTIONEER *holds up his hand, taking his place
> at the stump. The groups strain forward attentively.
> He touches* JONES *on the shoulder peremptorily,
> motioning for him to stand on the stump—the auction-
> block.*]

> [JONES *looks up, sees the figures on all sides, looks wildly
> for some opening to escape, sees none, screams, and
> leaps madly to the top of the stump to get as far
> away from them as possible. He stands there, cower-
> ing, paralyzed with horror. The* AUCTIONEER *be-
> gins his silent spiel. He points to* JONES, *appeals
> to the* PLANTERS *to see for themselves. Here is a good
> field hand, sound in wind and limb as they can see.
> Very strong still in spite of his being middle-aged.*

Look at that back. Look at those shoulders. Look at the muscles in his arms and his sturdy legs. Capable of any amount of hard labor. Moreover, of a good disposition, intelligent, and tractable. Will any gentleman start the bidding? The PLANTERS *raise their fingers, make their bids. They are apparently all eager to possess* JONES. *The bidding is lively, the crowd interested. While this has been going on,* JONES *has been seized by the courage of desperation. He dares to look down and around him. Over his face abject terror gives way to mystification, to gradual realization—stutteringly.*]

What you all doin', white folks? What's all dis? What you all lookin' at me fo'? What you doin' wid me, anyhow? [*Suddenly convulsed with raging hatred and fear.*] Is dis a auction? Is you sellin' me like dey uster befo' de war? [*Jerking out his revolver just as the* AUCTIONEER *knocks him down to one of the planters—glaring from him to the purchaser.*] And *you* sells me? And *you* buys me? I shows you I'se a free nigger, damn yo' souls! [*He fires at the* AUCTIONEER *and at the* PLANTER *with such rapidity that the two shots are almost simultaneous. As if this were a signal the walls of the forest fold in. Only blackness remains and silence broken by* JONES *as he rushes off, crying with fear—and by the quickened, ever-louder beat of the tom-tom.*]

SCENE VI

SCENE: *Three o'clock. A cleared space in the forest. The limbs of the trees meet over it, forming a low ceiling about five feet from the ground. The interlocked ropes of creepers reaching upward to entwine the tree-trunks give an arched appearance to the sides. The space thus enclosed is like the dark, noisome hold of some ancient vessel. The moonlight is almost completely shut out and only a vague, wan light filters through. There is the noise of some one approaching from the left, stumbling and crawling through the undergrowth.* JONES'S *voice is heard between chattering moans.*

Oh, Lawd, what I gwine do now? Ain't got no bullet left on'y de silver one. If mo' o' dem ha'nts come after me, how I gwine skeer dem away? Oh, Lawd, on'y de silver one left—an' I gotta save dat fo' luck. If I shoots dat one I'm a goner sho'! Lawd, it's black heah! Whar's de moon? Oh, Lawd, don't dis night evah come to an end? [*By the sounds, he is feeling his way cautiously forward.*] Dere! Dis feels like a clear space. I gotta lie down an' rest. I don't care if dem niggers does cotch me. I gotta rest.

[*He is well forward now where his figure can be dimly made out. His pants have been so torn away that what is left of them is no better than a breech-cloth. He flings himself full length, face downward, on the ground, panting with exhaustion. Gradually it seems to grow lighter in the enclosed space and two rows of seated figures can be seen behind* JONES. *They are sitting in crumpled, despairing attitudes, hunched, facing one another with their backs touching the forest walls as if they were shackled to them. All are negroes, naked save for loin-cloths. At first they are silent and motionless. Then they begin to sway slowly forward toward each other and back again in unison, as if they were laxly letting themselves follow the long roll of a ship at sea. At the same time, a low, melancholy murmur rises among them, increasing gradually by rhythmic degrees which seem to be directed and controlled by the throb of the tom-tom in the distance, to a long, tremulous wail of despair that reaches a certain pitch, unbearably acute, then falls by slow gradations of tone into silence and is taken up again.* JONES *starts, looks up, sees the figures, and throws himself down again to shut out the sight. A shudder of terror shakes his whole body as the wail rises up about him again. But the next time, his voice, as if under some uncanny compulsion, starts with the others. As their chorus lifts he rises to a sitting posture similar to the others, swaying back and forth. His voice reaches the highest pitch of sorrow, of desolation. The light fades out, the other voices cease, and only darkness is left.* JONES *can be heard scrambling to his feet and running off, his voice sinking down the scale and receding as he moves farther and farther away in the forest. The tom-tom beats louder, quicker, with a more insistent, triumphant pulsation.*]

SCENE VII

SCENE: *Five o'clock. The foot of a gigantic tree by the edge of a great river. A rough structure of boulders, like an altar, is by the tree. The raised river-bank is in the nearer background. Beyond this the surface of the river spreads out, brilliant and unruffled in the moonlight, blotted out and merged into a veil of bluish mist in the distance.* JONES'S *voice is heard from the left rising and falling in the long, despairing wail of the chained slaves, to the rhythmic beat of the tom-tom. As his voice sinks into silence, he enters the open space. The expression of his face is fixed and stony, his eyes have an obsessed glare, he moves with a strange deliberation like a sleep-walker or one in a trance. He looks around at the tree, the rough stone altar, the moonlit surface of the river beyond, and passes his hand over his head with a vague gesture of puzzled bewilderment. Then, as if in obedience to some obscure impulse, he sinks into a kneeling, devotional posture before the altar. Then he seems to come to himself partly, to have an uncertain realization of what he is doing, for he straightens up and stares about him horrifiedly—in an incoherent mumble.*

What—what is I doin'? What is—dis place? Seems like—seems like I know dat tree—an' dem stones—an' de river. I remember—seems like I been heah befo'. [*Tremblingly.*] Oh, Gorry, I'se skeered in dis place! I'se skeered! Oh, Lawd, pertect dis sinner!

[*Crawling away from the altar, he cowers close to the ground, his face hidden, his shoulders heaving with sobs of hysterical fright. From behind the trunk of the tree, as if he had sprung out of it, the figure of the* CONGO WITCH-DOCTOR *appears. He is wizened* and old, naked except for the fur of some small animal tied about his waist, its bushy tail hanging down in front. His body is stained all over a bright red. Antelope horns are on each side of his head, branching upward. In one hand he carries a bone rattle, in the other a charm stick with a bunch of white cockatoo feathers tied to the end. A great number of glass beads and bone ornaments are about his neck, ears, wrists, and ankles. He struts noiselessly with a queer prancing step to a position in the clear ground between JONES and the altar. Then with a preliminary, summoning stamp of his foot on the earth, he begins to dance and to chant. As if in response to his summons the beating of the tom-tom grows to a fierce, exultant boom whose throbs seem to fill the air with vibrating rhythm. JONES looks up, starts to spring to his feet, reaches a half-kneeling, half-squatting position, and remains rigidly fixed there, paralyzed with awed fascination by this new apparition. The WITCH-DOCTOR sways, stamping with his foot, his bone rattle clicking the time. His voice rises and falls in a weird, monotonous croon, without articulate word divisions. Gradually his dance becomes clearly one of a narrative in panto-mime, his croon is an incantation, a charm to allay the fierceness of some implacable deity demanding sacrifice. He flees, he is pursued by devils, he hides, he flees again. Ever wilder and wilder becomes his flight, nearer and nearer draws the pursuing evil, more and more the spirit of terror gains possession of him. His croon, rising to intensity, is punctuated by shrill cries. JONES has become completely hyp-notized. His voice joins in the incantation, in the cries, he beats time with his hands and sways his body to and fro from the waist. The whole spirit and meaning of the dance has entered into him, has become his spirit. Finally the theme of the panto-mime halts on a howl of despair, and is taken up again in a note of savage hope. There is a salva-tion. The forces of evil demand sacrifice. They must be appeased. The WITCH-DOCTOR points with

*his wand to the sacred tree, to the river beyond, to the
altar, and finally to* JONES *with a ferocious command.* JONES *seems to sense the meaning of this.
It is he who must offer himself for sacrifice. He
beats his forehead abjectly to the ground, moaning
hysterically.*]

Mercy, oh, Lawd! Mercy! Mercy on dis po' sinner.

[*The* WITCH-DOCTOR *springs to the river-bank. He
stretches out his arms and calls to some God within
its depths. Then he starts backward slowly, his arms
remaining out. A huge head of a crocodile appears
over the bank and its eyes, glittering greenly, fasten
upon* JONES. *He stares into them fascinatedly. The*
WITCH-DOCTOR *prances up to him, touches him
with his wand, motions with hideous command toward
the waiting monster.* JONES *squirms on his belly
nearer and nearer, moaning continually.*]

Mercy, Lawd! Mercy!

[*The crocodile heaves more of his enormous hulk onto
the land.* JONES *squirms toward him. The* WITCH-
DOCTOR'S *voice shrills out in furious exultation, the
tom-tom beats madly.* JONES *cries out in a fierce,
exhausted spasm of anguished pleading.*]

Lawd, save me! Lawd Jesus, heah my prayer!

[*Immediately, in answer to his prayer, comes the thought
of the one bullet left him. He snatches at his hip,
shouting defiantly.*]

De silver bullet! You don't git me yit!

[*He fires at the green eyes in front of him. The head
of the crocodile sinks back behind the river-bank, the*
WITCH-DOCTOR *springs behind the sacred tree and
disappears.* JONES *lies with his face to the ground,
his arms outstretched, whimpering with fear as the
throb of the tom-tom fills the silence about him with a
sombre pulsation, a baffled but revengeful power.*]

SCENE VIII

SCENE: *Dawn. Same as Scene II, the dividing line of
　　forest and plain. The nearest tree-trunks are dimly
　　revealed, but the forest behind them is still a mass of
　　glooming shadow. The tom-tom seems on the very spot,
　　so loud and continuously vibrating are its beats. LEM
　　enters from the left, followed by a small squad of his
　　soldiers and by the Cockney trader, SMITHERS. LEM
　　is a heavy-set, ape-faced old savage of the extreme Afri-
　　can type, dressed only in a loin-cloth. A revolver and
　　cartridge-belt are about his waist. His soldiers are in
　　different degrees of rag-concealed nakedness. All wear
　　broad palm-leaf hats. Each one carries a rifle. SMITH-
　　ERS is the same as in Scene I. One of the soldiers, evi-
　　dently a tracker, is peering about keenly on the ground.
　　He grunts and points to the spot where JONES entered
　　the forest. LEM and SMITHERS come to look.*

SMITHERS [*after a glance, turns away in disgust*]. That's
where 'e went in right enough. Much good it'll do yer.
'E's miles orf by this an' safe to the coast, damn 's 'ide !
I tole yer yer'd lose 'im, didn't I ?—wastin' the 'ole
bloomin' night beatin' yer bloody drum and castin' yer
silly spells ! Gawd blimey, wot a pack !

LEM [*gutturally*]. We cotch him. You see. [*He makes
a motion to his soldiers, who squat down on their haunches
in a semicircle.*]

SMITHERS [*exasperatedly*]. Well, ain't yer goin' in an'
'unt 'im in the woods? What the 'ell's the good of
waitin' ?

LEM [*imperturbably—squatting down himself*]. We cotch
him.

SMITHERS [*turning away from him contemptuously*]. Aw !
Garn ! 'E's a better man than the lot o' you put together.
I 'ates the sight o' 'im but I'll say that for 'im.

　　[*A sound of snapping twigs comes from the forest. The
　　　soldiers jump to their feet, cocking their rifles alertly.
　　　LEM remains sitting with an imperturbable expres-
　　　sion, but listening intently. The sound from the*

woods is repeated. LEM *makes a quick signal with his hand. His followers creep quickly but noiselessly into the forest, scattering so that each enters at a different spot.*]

SMITHERS [*in the silence that follows—in a contemptuous whisper*]. You ain't thinkin' that would be 'im, I 'ope?

LEM [*calmly*]. We cotch him.

SMITHERS. Blarsted fat 'eads! [*Then after a second's thought—wonderingly.*] Still an' all, it might 'appen. If 'e lost 'is bloody way in these stinkin' woods 'e'd likely turn in a circle without 'is knowin' it. They all does.

LEM [*peremptorily*]. Sssh!

[*The reports of several rifles sound from the forest, followed a second later by savage, exultant yells. The beating of the tom-tom abruptly ceases.* LEM *looks up at the white man with a grin of satisfaction.*]
We cotch him. Him dead.

SMITHERS [*with a snarl*]. 'Ow d'yer know it's 'im an' 'ow d'yer know 'e's dead?

LEM. My mens dey got 'um silver bullets. Dey kill him shore.

SMITHERS [*astonished*]. They got silver bullets?

LEM. Lead bullet no kill him. He got um strong charm. I cook um money, make um silver bullet, make um strong charm, too.

SMITHERS [*light breaking upon him*]. So that's wot you was up to all night, wot? You was scared to put after 'im till you'd moulded silver bullets, eh?

LEM [*simply stating a fact*]. Yes. Him got strong charm. Lead no good.

SMITHERS [*slapping his thigh and guffawing*]. Haw-haw! If yer don't beat all 'ell! [*Then recovering himself—scornfully.*] I'll bet yer it ain't 'im they shot at all, yer bleedin' looney!

LEM [*calmly*]. Dey come bring him now.

[*The soldiers come out of the forest, carrying* JONES'S *limp body. There is a little reddish-purple hole under his left breast. He is dead. They carry him to* LEM, *who examines his body with great satisfaction.* SMITHERS *leans over his shoulder—in a tone of frightened awe.*]

SMITHERS. Well, they did for yer right enough, Jonesey, me lad! Dead as a 'erring! [*Mockingly.*] Where's yer 'igh an' mighty airs now, yer bloomin' Majesty? [*Then with a grin.*] Silver bullets! Gawd blimey, but yer died in the 'eighth o' style, any'ow!

    [LEM *makes a motion to the soldiers to carry the body out left.* SMITHERS *speaks to him sneeringly.*]

And I s'pose you think it's yer bleedin' charms and yer silly beatin' the drum that made 'im run in a circle when 'e'd lost 'imself, don't yer?

    [*But* LEM *makes no reply, does not seem to hear the question, walks out left after his men.* SMITHERS *looks after him with contemptuous scorn.*]

Stupid as 'ogs, the lot of 'em! Blarsted niggers!

THE CURTAIN FALLS

NICE PEOPLE

BY

RACHEL CROTHERS

"The vital things of character don't belong to anybody's day—they're eternal and fundamental."—*Act First.*

NICE PEOPLE

Miss Rachel Crothers was born in Bloomington, Illinois, and after graduation from the State Normal School studied dramatic art in Boston and New York. Three years of practical stage experience came next and then she began her career as a professional playwright with a one-act sketch, *The Rector*, played at the Madison Square Theatre, New York, in 1902. Her plays since then have been *The Three of Us* (1906); *The Coming of Mrs. Patrick* (1907); *Myself Bettina* (1908); *A Man's World* (1910); *He and She* (1912), revived (1920); *Ourselves* (1913); *Young Wisdom* (1914); *The Heart of Paddy Whack* (1914); *Old Lady 31* (1916); *Once Upon a Time* (1917); *A Little Journey* (1918); *39 East* (1919); *Nice People* (1921); and *Everyday* (1921).

Miss Crothers has been the most consistent exponent in modern American drama of the claims of woman's nature for its proper fulfilment. In *A Man's World* she criticised the "double standard" of morality tolerated by the world, and in *Ourselves* she showed the responsibility of good women for the existence of such a standard. In *He and She* she drew a powerful contrast between the conflicting demands made upon a woman by her artistic career and by her responsibilities as a wife and mother. *Everyday* dealt with the revolt of a daughter against the crushing influence of a father's tyranny and the stultifying effects of a small-town life.

In *Nice People* Miss Crothers has drawn an incisive picture of a certain kind of social life in America which has developed since the war. In the heroine Teddy Gloucester she has created a girl better than her background but still of it, and apparently willing to marry another representative of it in Scottie Wilbur. As a contrast to him, Billy Wade, a clean-cut young man from a different world, shows Teddy the way out.

Nice People was first put on at the Klaw Theatre, March 2, 1921, and remained until October in New York

City. It was then taken to Chicago, where it remained
at the Cort Theatre until March, 1922, when it went on
tour through Milwaukee, Cleveland, Pittsburg, Washington, and other places, and returned to New York in
May. An Eastern tour, including Philadelphia and
Boston, was arranged for the season of 1922–23 with the
cast headed by Miss Larrimore, and the play ran until
December, 1922, while another company played on the
Western circuit.

The Rector, *Young Wisdom*, and *The Three of Us* have
been published by Samuel French and *A Man's World*
by Richard Badger. *He and She* was included in *Representative American Plays*, by the present editor. *Nice
People* was printed in abstract in *The Ten Best Plays of*
1920–21, edited by Burns Mantle. It is now published
in complete form for the first time, through the courtesy
of Miss Crothers, who also furnished the information on
which this introduction is based.

CAST OF CHARACTERS

KLAW THEATRE, NEW YORK, MARCH 2, 1921

In the order in which they appear

HALLIE LIVINGSTON...............Tallulah Bankhead.
EILEEN BAXTER-JONES.............Katharine Cornell.
TREVOR LEEDS....................Edwin Hensley.
THEODORA GLOUCESTER............Francine Larrimore.
OLIVER COMSTOCK.................Guy Milham.
SCOTTIE WILBUR..................Hugh Huntley.
MARGARET RAINSFORD.............Merle Maddern.
HUBERT GLOUCESTER..............Frederick Perry.
BILLY WADE.....................Robert Ames.
MR. HEYFER.....................Frederick Maynard.

ACT   I.   The Gloucester apartment, Park Avenue, New
           York.   An evening in spring.
ACT II.   The Gloucester cottage in the country.
           Scene I.—The evening of the following day.
           Scene II.—Daylight—the following morning.
           Scene III.—The next day.
ACT III.   Outside of the Gloucester cottage.   Afternoon,
           three months later.

NICE PEOPLE*

ACT I

SCENE: *The Gloucester apartment in Park Avenue, New York, at half after eleven o'clock on an evening in May. The walls of the room are hung in a very old silk of a soft greenish gray in tone. At the centre back is a fireplace of cream marble—very simple in design. To the left of this fireplace is a single door opening into the hall. In the left wall are two long windows hung with velvet curtains which melt into the walls in color. At the right are double doors standing open and showing a grand piano in the room beyond. A large armchair is at the left of fireplace and turned toward it. To the right of the fireplace and well away from it toward the centre of the room is a large sofa; behind this sofa, at upper end, stands a floor-lamp of old iron with antique lace shade. A small low table in front of the sofa at the lower end holds a decanter of whiskey and siphon. The lighting gives a general luminous quality and soft brilliancy to the room. The furniture is upholstered in an old brocade of ashes of roses, which makes a charming background for the delicate orchid tints of* HALLIE'S *gown, the rose velvet of* EILEEN'S, *and the white transparent tissue of* TEDDY'S.

At lower centre of the stage is a low seat without back; at right centre a round table holding a telephone with a screen about it; above this table to the left is a large armchair, below it a single chair facing the table.

As the curtain rises, EILEEN, HALLIE, *and* TREVOR *are in the room, singing gaily and carelessly to the music which* OLIVER *is playing in the room beyond.*

EILEEN BAXTER-JONES, *about twenty-one, is dark and piquant, frankly impertinent and very wholesomely*

*lovable. She is sitting on the low seat at centre, with
her legs crossed, unconcernedly, displaying a very
pretty pair of legs and ankles.*

HALLIE LIVINGSTON, *perhaps twenty-three, beautiful in a
large and brilliantly blonde way, half reclining on the
couch, is sipping her Scotch with a slow and self-
centred enjoyment, indicative of her general psychology. The girls are exquisite in their youth and
freshness, the finely bred product of care and health and
money—dressed with daring emphasis of the prevailing
fashion, startling in their delicate and sensuous charm.*

THEODORA *is twenty, slender and vibrating, pretty, intelligent, and high-keyed, alertly and intensely interested
in herself and the art of extracting from life all which
she considers her due. She has a very radiant charm
and vivid responsiveness.*

TREVOR. You look like an orchid, Hallie, absolutely.

HALLIE. You say it as if you'd made a great discovery.
That's what I'm supposed to look like—darling.

EILEEN. You're slow getting that, Trevor. Did you
say we were going some place to dance, Ted?

TEDDY [*from off stage, to the right*]. Yes, don't you want
to?

EILEEN. Crazy about it.

TEDDY. I thought we'd wait just a few minutes for
Scottie.

TREVOR. Well, why the devil doesn't he come? He's
got a nerve.

HALLIE. But there's no other man in the world for
Teddy. Of course she'll make us wait for him.

[TEDDY *and* OLIVER *enter from the other room.*]

TEDDY. No, no, it can't be done, Oliver; you need
another drink.

OLIVER. Thanks.

TEDDY. Eileen?

EILEEN. No, thanks, I know when I've had enough.

OLIVER. You mean you think you do. You're never
so enticing as when you have a nice little bun, Eileen.

[TREVOR LEEDS, *who is tall and extremely good-looking
in rather an effete way, rises from chair very lan-*

guidly to light EILEEN'S *cigarette. There is about them all the carelessness and indifference of very intimate friendship and a keen alertness to each others' foibles and idiosyncrasies.* OLIVER *takes the bottle of Scotch from a small table near the couch and, after a gesture of general invitation, pours some in* HALLIE'S *glass and his own.*]

THEODORA. What time is it, Trevor?

TREVOR [*looking at his watch*]. Ten forty-seven, to be exact.

EILEEN. Time Scottie was turning up, I should say, if he ever is going to.

TEDDY. I'm not at all sure that he will. I know of nothing in life so uncertain as the uncertainty of Scottie Wilbur.

HALLIE. How you can allow him to be so rude to you, Teddy, is absolutely beyond my comprehension.

TEDDY. There are so many things beyond your comprehension, Hallie—dearest. Scottie isn't rude to me in the least. On the contrary, he's perfect.

HALLIE. Not according to my ideas of taste and sensibilities. I call it horribly rude to phone you at the last minute he couldn't come to dinner.

EILEEN. Sweetly adding he forgot he was booked for some place else.

OLIVER. At least he might have had the decency to lie a little.

TEDDY. But it was adorable of him not to lie. How can he help it if he forgot? I think it was wonderful of him to go there when of course he wanted to be here. Rena Maxwell actually needed him. Rena's so intellectual, her dinners are deadly. And there's nothing to drink there now—not a drop. She's taken prohibition seriously.

EILEEN. She's taken it as an excuse, you mean. She always was too stingy to give a fellow a real drink.

TEDDY. Rena believes in drinking only with thine eyes.

TREVOR. Yes; Rena's a fish.

[TEDDY *sings a snatch of* "*Drink to Me Only with Thine Eyes*" *to* TREVOR. *The others join in.*]

HALLIE. It's so awfully middle-class to make one's education as evident as she makes hers, isn't it?

EILEEN. Is that why you conceal yours so carefully?

HALLIE. I was beautifully educated in Paris, of course.

TEDDY. But not in much of anything else.

[*They laugh.*]

HALLIE. Mother was clever enough to have me taught just enough to appreciate everything in the world—but not to go far enough to be—you know. They said I might have been a great musician. But that would have been too stupid.

TREVOR. Of course appreciation is our vocation—appreciation of other people's work.

EILEEN. I don't know. Sometimes I think I'd like to be able to do some one thing awfully well. To dance, for instance. I'd like to dance on the stage.

HALLIE. Horrors!

EILEEN. I would, really.

TEDDY. Why don't you, then?

EILEEN. They wouldn't let me.

TEDDY. Piffle! Do it, anyway. What are you afraid of? I think the most vulgar, second-rate thing in the world is to be afraid. Anything can be made chic and frightfully individual—if one just does, you know.

TREVOR. Of course, if one has the individuality to get away with it.

OLIVER. Ted, I think you come as near getting away with anything you want to as anybody I know.

HALLIE. I do, too. If I did half the things you do, Ted, I'd be horribly talked about.

TEDDY. Well, of course, because you're always trying to hide things. Do everything right before everybody's eyes—and dare them to talk.

[*They laugh. The telephone rings.*]

There's Scott now. Take it, Trevor. If he's downstairs, tell him to come up and have a drink before we go.

TREVOR [*taking the receiver and imitating* TEDDY'S *voice*]. Hello! Oh! [*Drawing away.*] You'd better come, Ted. Right you are. Where the devil are you, Scottie? He's yelling for you. [*Holding the receiver out to* TEDDY.]

NICE PEOPLE

HALLIE [*as* TEDDY *goes to the phone*]. Tell him to meet us some place. Why should we wait?

TEDDY [*taking the receiver*]. Where are you? Well, hurry. Yes—we will, if you're here in five minutes. Ten's the limit. Is it a very dry party? Well, this isn't. Hurry or there won't be anything left in the house. [*Putting up the receiver.*]

EILEEN. Is he headed this way at last?

TEDDY. Well, golly, let's go. You must be having a hell of a time here.

HALLIE. Oh, we don't mind *waiting*. But it's so killing to see you hold your breath till he gets here. Of course everybody's chasing Scottie Wilbur. Ethel Montague is at it hard. *She's* the one who says Scottie wants to marry *you* for your money, Ted. Silly of her to say that, isn't it?

TEDDY. I always notice when you have anything particularly disagreeable to say *yourself*, you pretend somebody else has said it.

EILEEN. Hallie, you're always nasty when you've had too long a drink.

TEDDY. Yes, but it's the only time she's honest. Give her another one, Oliver. What's biting you? Go on—get it out of your system.

HALLIE. Heavens—don't take it seriously. You must be used to that by this time. Any girl who has as much money as you have, Ted, must expect somebody to say that every man who looks at her wants her money.

TEDDY. I don't know that I have so much more than *you* have, for instance.

HALLIE [*rising*]. Well—but you look as though you had, honey. You have so many cars and things, you know. Three of your own, isn't it? And your pearls are marvellous—simply marvellous. No wonder Scottie wants you.

[HALLIE *walks slowly and a trifle uncertainly into the room at right and sits at the piano. She plays softly. A pause—*TREVOR *goes out after her.* OLIVER *goes to* TEDDY, *about to speak, but follows* TREVOR *out.*]

EILEEN [*going to* TEDDY]. To put it delicately—Hallie is tight.

TEDDY. Oh, no, she isn't. What did she mean?

EILEEN. Yes, she is, too. She's getting entirely too fond of booze lately and it's disgusting—absolutely disgusting.

TEDDY. What did she mean? *Do* people say Scott only wants to marry me for my money?

EILEEN. Why, you know she's mad about him herself, and she's always been jealous of you. Why pay any attention to it? I like Hallie, but she is a damned cat and she simply can't help scratching *you.*

TEDDY. Scott doesn't care anything more about money than anybody does. And he *does* care for me.

EILEEN. Of course he does. That's why Hallie is so vicious.

HALLIE [*coming back into the room*]. Hasn't Scott come yet? If I don't dance soon I shall expire.

TEDDY. Oh, come on, Hallie—be a sport. Pretend you like me just for to-night. It's better for the party.

HALLIE. Well, I like your gown.

TEDDY. Can you dance in that one?

HALLIE. Of course. Just throw it over my arm. [*Throwing the sash train over her arm.*]

TEDDY. Oh, I didn't mean that. The back—where's a man going to put his hand?

HALLIE. Where he always does, of course. What's the matter with my back? [*Turning her back to the girls.*]

TEDDY. Nothing at all. It's doing very well this evening, so far as I can see—which is quite far.

EILEEN. That's the most economical kind of costume going, because you *can* wash your back; but when a man puts his old wet hand on this velvet I nearly die. It simply ruins it.

HALLIE. Did you see Rena Maxwell's gown last night?

TEDDY. I did. It looked as if she were advertising her virtue.

EILEEN. And the Lord knows she doesn't need to do that.

TEDDY. I don't see why Rena doesn't stay at home altogether.

HALLIE. I don't, either. Nobody dances with her. Scottie was stuck with her last night and nobody would cut in. He whistled and made signs to them till he was black in the face, but he had to go through the whole dance with her.

TEDDY. Of course no man wants to dance with her if she *will* wear corsets.

EILEEN. Old Ironsides, they call her.

TEDDY. Rena doesn't go in for much personal contact when she dances.

HALLIE. No; this is the way she stands. [*Rising and standing very straight in an old-fashioned way.*] You know, if her head were only turned round the other way she wouldn't have such a bad figure. [*Slumping, to show how* RENA *ought to stand.*] Oh! I'm dying to dance with Scottie. Don't you think he's the best dancer in town, Ted?

TEDDY. Oh, I don't know. He thinks I am—so of course I like dancing with him.

HALLIE. I adore the way he holds me. Just as though he were going to crush me.

TEDDY. But he never does.

HALLIE. Not while we're dancing. I adore a man who is absolutely mad about me and yet who controls himself in that perfectly marvellous way.

TEDDY. Oh, I don't know. I'm not so keen about so much self-control.

HALLIE. Oh, I am. I think it's much more subtle.

EILEEN. Well, I must say I like sort of a frank flash of passion once in a while—so you sort of know where you're at. Elemental stuff, you know.

TEDDY. You like to be in danger sometimes, uh?

HALLIE. Oh, I hate horrible obvious emotion. It doesn't interest me in the least.

EILEEN. You're trying to make us think you're subtly and insidiously wicked, Hallie.

TEDDY. Like Trevor. Psychologically he's a devil—and physiologically he's as tame as your grandmother. Did Trevor ever kiss you?

EILEEN. Don't remember.

HALLIE. Well—really. I don't tell.

TEDDY. That's just it. There'd be nothing to tell if he ever did.

HALLIE. Your pearls *are* large—aren't they?

TEDDY. They're just the way I want them.

HALLIE. Some one was saying the other day they're *just* like Mrs. Allister's and wondered if your father got them both at the same time.

TEDDY [*after a pause*]. I have to hand it to you, Hallie. You can say the most putrid things in the sweetest way of anybody I know.

TREVOR [*coming back with* OLIVER]. Hasn't Scott come yet?

HALLIE. Oh, no; we're still waiting. [*Going back into the other room,* HALLIE *plays again.*]

TEDDY. We'll only give him three minutes more.

TREVOR [*beginning to dance with* EILEEN]. You don't mind so long as you have me, do you, love?

EILEEN. I don't mind anything as long as I'm in your arms. We've just been saying how dangerous you are, Trevor.

TREVOR [*dancing out of the room with her*]. I might fool you some of these days.

[OLIVER *comes to* TEDDY. *She mechanically puts her arm across his shoulder as they dance.*]

OLIVER [*with lips close to* TEDDY'S *ear*]. Don't you want to go without Scottie?

TEDDY. Of course.

OLIVER. No, you don't. You care an awful lot, don't you?

[*She shakes her head.*]

Yes, you do. He'll never love you as much as I do. [*Holding her closer.*] I've always been crazy about you, Teddy. You did care, didn't you? Don't you a bit any more?

TEDDY [*tightening her arm about his neck*]. Yes, I do. Of course I do. You're a dear.

OLIVER. Oh, I know—*pal* stuff—but I don't want that.

TEDDY. But I'm awfully fond of you. Really, dear, I am.

OLIVER. Then kiss me.

TEDDY. No.

OLIVER. Please.

[*They're still dancing.*]

TEDDY. No.

OLIVER. Not even a sisterly one?

[TEDDY *kisses his cheek. He stops dancing and kisses her lips.*]

TEDDY. Don't please. No. I don't like it. Go on. You do dance divinely, old man. You're the only man I can dance with.

OLIVER. Will you give the others the slip after a while and go some place else to dance with me?

TEDDY. I'll—se-see.

OLIVER. Promise.

TEDDY. I'll——

SCOTTIE. Hello!

[SCOTTIE WILBUR *dashes in from the hall, excited and smiling. His handsome face, with its irresistible charm, is radiant. He smiles at both* TEDDY *and* OLIVER *with equal eagerness.*]

TEDDY. Hello, Scottie. [*Stopping dancing and giving her hand to* SCOTTIE.]

SCOTTIE. How are you, old man? Terribly sorry, Teddy. I beat it as soon as I could. Wasn't it the limit? Don't know how I ever did such a thing. But I knew you'd understand. You always do.

TEDDY [*beaming at* SCOTTIE]. We're going some place to dance. Get them started, Oliver, will you?

OLIVER. Hello! [OLIVER, *looking not too graciously from one to the other, goes into the other room.*]

SCOTTIE. You're a peach not to care.

[*She lets him take her in his arms and kiss her.*]
You're the——

TEDDY [*drawing away*]. Careful!

SCOTTIE. Who's here?

TEDDY. Eileen and Hallie. Let's get off. Was the dinner awful?

SCOTTIE. Not so bad. Only, of course, I wanted to be here.

TEDDY. It really doesn't make the slightest difference to you where you are, Scottie. Does it? So long as the food is good and the fire burns.

SCOTTIE. It wouldn't if you were along.

TEDDY. Every girl you know thinks you mean that.

SCOTTIE.   And you *know* I do.

TEDDY.   I know you *don't*.   That's why you—that's why it's all right with us.

SCOTTIE.   It *is* all right, isn't it?

[*They dance.*]

TEDDY.   You're wonderful.   You're the only man I can dance with.

SCOTTIE.   I adore *you*.

[MARGARET RAINSFORD *opens the hall door and hesitatingly comes into the room.   She is forty-five, tall, distinguished; a little tired, a little pale, with a critical intelligence in her face which makes her a trifle cold, but a frank simplicity of manner which makes her extremely appealing.   She is wearing a black evening gown which is at once modish but conservative.*]

TEDDY [*after a pause—they stop dancing*].   Aunt Margaret, this is Scottie Wilbur.   My aunt, Mrs. Rainsford.

SCOTTIE [*going to* MRS. RAINSFORD *as she puts out her hand*].   How do you do?

MRS. RAINSFORD.   How do you do?   Are you Arthur Wilbur's son—the Philadelphia Wilburs?

SCOTTIE.   No, I'm afraid not.   We aren't anything in particular—just New York.

[MRS. RAINSFORD *laughs agreeably and* SCOTTIE *laughs with her.*]

MRS. RAINSFORD.   You see, I've been away a long time, and I keep trying to catch hold of threads I used to know.   Rather foolish, I suppose.

SCOTTIE.   Rather hopeless, I expect.   Threads break awfully fast—don't they?—and awfully short.

MRS. RAINSFORD [*laughing, and with him again*].   They seem to.

TEDDY.   Aunt Margaret was my mother's sister, you know, Scottie.

SCOTTIE.   Oh, really?

MRS. RAINSFORD.   Did you know my sister?

SCOTTIE.   No—no, I didn't, I—no—I didn't.

TEDDY.   Oh, no—I've only known Scottie long enough to still like him.   Oh, dad, may we take your car?

[*As* HUBERT GLOUCESTER *comes in from the hall.*]
You aren't going to use it to-night, are you?

SCOTTIE. I've got mine here.

TEDDY. But yours is open. We don't want that. May we, dad?

GLOUCESTER. Certainly.

TEDDY. You're an angel. 'Phone for both of them, will you? There's a dear. And tell them to hurry. Your man's awfully slow, dad. I wouldn't have him.

GLOUCESTER. I didn't engage him to keep up with you, you know.

> [GLOUCESTER *is fifty, of medium height, slightly inclined to portliness. His hair, which grows with an attractive wave, is quite white. He has a tolerant air of well-being and entire satisfaction with life in general.*]

SCOTTIE [*to* MRS. RAINSFORD]. Aren't you coming with us?

MRS. RAINSFORD. Do you need me? Haven't you a chaperon?

TEDDY. Chaperon? Heavens, Aunt Margaret, we're not babies.

MRS. RAINSFORD. You don't mean to say you're going without one?

TEDDY. Why, I haven't been any place with a chaperon for a million years.

MRS. RAINSFORD. You're twenty, I believe.

TEDDY. I believe I am; something like that.

MRS. RAINSFORD. You surely don't consider that old enough to go about alone?

TEDDY. I won't be alone. We'll all be together. Everybody does it. It would be too foolish. I'd feel as if I had a nurse.

> [*As the four other young people come in from the other room and* GLOUCESTER *comes back from the hall, every one talks at once for a moment. Gradually scraps of conversation are distinguished.*]

OLIVER [*to* TREVOR]. I'll bet you anything you like.— Good evening, Mr. Gloucester.—She stands up against anything.

TREVOR. I don't agree with you. I'll put my car up against anything.

OLIVER. You're hipped on that little wagon of yours, Trevor.

SCOTTIE. It hasn't got a look-in with a real car.

HALLIE [*coming back from the other room*]. Oh, hello, Scottie. Did you condescend to come, after all?

SCOTTIE. I broke my neck to get here. [*As he pours himself a drink at table, down right.*]

HALLIE. I wouldn't forgive you if I were Teddy. Don't ever break a date with me.

SCOTTIE. I never did—did I?

HALLIE. Do you want to come to dinner to-morrow night?

SCOTTIE. Love to.

HALLIE. Nobody else—just me. Like it?

SCOTTIE. Crazy about it. If I haven't anything on——

HALLIE. Break it, whatever it is. I want to talk to you. We haven't had a real talk for such a——

TEDDY. Let's go. Did you get the cars, dad?

GLOUCESTER. They'll be here in a very few minutes. Won't you young men have something more before you go? In the dining-room. Help yourselves.

THE MEN [*very indefinitely through the other voices*]. Thanks.

> [*Very slowly they move toward the hall door, all talking at once.* MRS. RAINSFORD *sits on the couch, watching them.*]

TREVOR [*stopping* TEDDY *at the door*]. Will you dance with me first?

TEDDY. Of course; you're the only man I can dance with.

> [*He goes out.*]

Oh, dad, let me have your key. I can't find mine.

GLOUCESTER [*slipping a key off the ring*]. That's about the third one I've given you this week, young lady. Mind you give that back.

TEDDY. Thanks a lot. Good night, Aunt Margaret. Good night, dad. Oh, Lordy, I forgot. [*Coming back to her father.*] I haven't a cent and this is my party.

GLOUCESTER [*putting his hand in his pocket*]. I don't think I can do much for you.

TEDDY [*counting as he unfolds some bills*]. Twenty—forty. Oh, come on, dad. You must have more than—try again.

[GLOUCESTER *takes out more bills.*]

Forty—eighty. That's all?

GLOUCESTER. Absolutely.

TEDDY. "For this relief, much thanks." If anybody telephones—tell them we're—no—I don't know where we'll be. I'll be home by morning. Good night. [*She flutters out through the hall.*]

[GLOUCESTER *goes to stand before the fire, lighting a cigar.*]

MARGARET [*after a pause, watching* GLOUCESTER *with a critical smile*]. The guests didn't even say good night. It isn't done, I suppose.

GLOUCESTER [*with an amused chuckle*]. Nothing is done that's too much trouble—you can count on that.

MARGARET. You think bad manners are amusing, then?

GLOUCESTER. Not especially—no—just prevalent.

MARGARET. It's appalling—simply appalling!

GLOUCESTER. What?

MARGARET. All of it—everything.

GLOUCESTER. Oh, you take it too seriously entirely, Margaret.

MARGARET. You mean, you think it's all right . . . all of it?

GLOUCESTER. It's the way things are. The manners of yesterday have nothing to do with the case. This is to-day.

MARGARET. If my sister could see her daughter now—I only hope to Heaven she can't.

GLOUCESTER. Bosh! If Lucille had lived she would have come right along with the tide.

MARGARET. No!

GLOUCESTER. Yes!

MARGARET. Never!

GLOUCESTER. Yes! She was too much a woman of the world not to.

MARGARET. A woman of the world—but a gentle-woman.

GLOUCESTER. See here, Margaret, do you mean you think I'm not keeping Teddy up to what Lucille would have made her?

MARGARET. Well, do you think you are?

GLOUCESTER. Why, these are the nicest kind of young people. Smart families—every one of them.

MARGARET. That's just it! That's what makes it so horrible. If they were common little upstarts and parvenus it would be easy enough to understand, but *nice people!* What are their parents thinking? Can't they see what this is going to do to the future generations?

GLOUCESTER. Why, Margaret—there never was a generation that grew up that didn't think the next one coming on was going to the dogs. They're free—yes—because they *are* younger. But, by Jove, I actually believe they're safer than the bottled-up age I went through—when we had to sneak about all the deviltry we did. They're perfectly open and aboveboard about it. You have to admit that. And they're going to work out their own salvation in their own way and come out all right.

MARGARET. Oh, there's something far more serious in it than merely the difference between two generations.

GLOUCESTER. Oh, you exaggerate. Frankly, I think you're awfully priggish. If you judge everything from your own conservative ideas of good form, of course, these youngsters seem a little raw. But this is their day—not ours—and we can't . . .

MARGARET. Oh—their day! I'm not talking about superficial fashions and manners. The vital things of character don't belong to anybody's day—they're eternal and fundamental, and I see Lucille's daughter without them.

GLOUCESTER [*throwing his cigar into the fire and taking a step toward* MARGARET]. That's pretty plain talk.

MARGARET. I mean to be plain. Why not? I know that what I am feeling now *she* would feel. I know that what I find in her house since I have come back would have——

GLOUCESTER. And what have you found? I'm able to do more for Teddy than I did for Lucille. That's the only bad thing about it—that she isn't here to have it.

MARGARET. She would have hated it. She wouldn't have let you give that child eighty dollars to throw away in an evening.

GLOUCESTER. Eighty dollars! Well, that won't get them more than a sandwich or two apiece.

MARGARET. She wouldn't have let her go about half naked and wearing pearls no young girl should ever wear.

GLOUCESTER. Nonsense. You're old-fashioned. What in the name of Heaven is the matter with Teddy? What's the matter with her? She's a charming girl and a great success and her friends are as nice as anybody in New York.

MARGARET. The emptiness—the soullessness of it all.

GLOUCESTER. What?

MARGARET. I've been here three days and I haven't heard her or any of her friends say a single word or express a thought about anything on earth but their clothes, their motors, and themselves. They all talk alike, think alike, dress alike, sound alike. And the drinking—your house is a bar. It pours out—at all hours.

GLOUCESTER. That's prohibition. It only amuses them to have it about when they can't get it at other places.

MARGARET. Is that all you see in it?

GLOUCESTER. That's all there is in it.

MARGARET. And the smoking. Those delicate young girls are as dependent upon their cigarettes to quiet their nerves as any—oh, it's too horrible. [*She covers her eyes with her hands.*]

GLOUCESTER. I *have* rowed with Ted about the cigarettes. That is bad, I admit. But what are you going to do? It's not her fault. They all do it.

MARGARET. Who are those boys who are making love to her—running about with her alone? Are you willing that she should marry them?

GLOUCESTER. I don't know that she wants to.

MARGARET. Do you never advise her?

GLOUCESTER. I'm doing all I can to make her happy. She's all right. She's a nice girl, and she's perfectly capable of taking care of herself.

MARGARET. She isn't. She isn't. She is only a child.

She's surrounded by everything that hurts her and nothing that can help her. It's all chaos and waste and degeneracy. And my boy lying out there in France! And this is all it was for. He went so gladly. He gave himself for something greater than himself—to save civilization. Oh, the farce of it! The hideous, horrible, useless sacrifice! [*She leans back on the pillows, shaken with sobs.*]

GLOUCESTER. Don't think I don't know how you feel. Of course you're cut up. But, Margaret—if you'll allow me to say so, you're allowing your own personal sorrow to color everything. You're letting it make you bitter and —well, I don't see what all this has to do with Theodora.

MARGARET. It has everything to do with her. She's the most poignant part of it all. I came back so eager to see her because she meant part of Lucille; I was so thankful she was alive even if John . . . [*She breaks.*]

GLOUCESTER. Margaret——

MARGARET. I said I'll try to put my selfish grief aside. I'll try to mean something to her—something of what she's lost in her mother. I could scarcely wait to get here. She was going to be so wonderful—and——

GLOUCESTER. Well?

MARGARET. And instead of that——

GLOUCESTER. Well—what?

MARGARET. Oh, my God, Hubert, she's been killed and thrown away just as absolutely as John. She's the very essence of this thing that's in the air. America's infinitely worse than Europe. There's some excuse for it over there, perhaps—as the inevitable reaction, that is dinned into one's ears all the time, but why in Heaven's name are sane, decent people over here allowing themselves and their children to wallow in food and clothes and pleasure at the expense of their breeding—their culture— and their inheritance of wholesome American common sense? Why have you let it kill Theodora?

GLOUCESTER. I don't admit what you say—I don't admit that she's doing or having anything that isn't the custom of any nice girl with——

[THEODORA *throws the hall door open and comes in quickly followed by* SCOTTIE. *She hesitates slightly, a little surprised at finding* MARGARET *and her father still in the room.*]

TEDDY [*after a pause*]. I . . . You two still up?

GLOUCESTER. I thought you'd gone to dance.

TEDDY. We changed our minds. We're going some place else.

GLOUCESTER. Where?

TEDDY. Why—some place—farther up—out—everything's so frightfully crowded, you know it's really no fun.

GLOUCESTER. What place? Where are you going?

TEDDY. A place Oliver knows. Where is it, Scottie?

SCOTTIE. I'm not dead sure. I've been there. Awfully nice. But Oliver will have to direct us. We're all going together, you know.

GLOUCESTER [*looking at his watch*]. Everything closes at one. You wouldn't more than get there till you'd have to come back.

TEDDY. We can try. It will be fun to drive up, anyway. I'm going to get a heavier coat. That's what I came back for.

GLOUCESTER. I don't want you to go.

TEDDY. What?

GLOUCESTER. I don't want you to go.

TEDDY [*in amused amazement*]. Why, dad! What do you mean?

GLOUCESTER. Just that. It's too late. You've done enough to-night.

TEDDY. You're frightfully amusing. Why this sudden sternness? Of course I'm going. I promised; the others are waiting.

GLOUCESTER. You can't go.

TEDDY. Why—dad!

GLOUCESTER. Say good night to Mr. Wilbur.

TEDDY. Really, you're funny. I'll do nothing of the kind. I'm not going to disappoint those people. [*She starts to the door.*]

GLOUCESTER. You'll not go.

TEDDY. You can't speak that way to me. I'm not a baby.

GLOUCESTER. I'm sorry, but——

TEDDY.   I'm sorry too—but I'm going.

GLOUCESTER.   You're not!

TEDDY.   Dad! You're extremely disagreeable. You can't make me break a positive engagement and treat people——

GLOUCESTER.   We won't say anything more about that. You're not going. That will do.

TEDDY [*looks at him a moment, goes quickly to desk, tears a small piece of paper, writes on it, folds it and gives it to* SCOTTIE].   There's the telephone number I promised you. Good night, Scott. Please apologize to the others for me and tell them how extremely sorry I am that such a ridiculously embarrassing thing has happened.

SCOTTIE.   Good night, good night, good night. [*He goes out.*]

TEDDY.   What on earth do you mean, dad?   How dare you treat me like that?

GLOUCESTER.   You shouldn't have made it necessary. If you don't know by this time that a young girl can't go motoring out to dance-halls at this time of night, it's high time you did.

TEDDY.   You've never questioned my good taste before about where I go and what I do. Why this sudden . . .

GLOUCESTER.   I hope that you've never done anything before that needed questioning.

TEDDY.   Do you think we've never done this before? We do it all the time and then we come down-town and have breakfast at Childs—and it's lots of fun and I intend to keep on doing it—or anything else I want to do. I suppose I can thank you, Aunt Margaret, for this sudden interest in my affairs.

GLOUCESTER.   Teddy——

TEDDY.   I've never been so humiliated in my life.

GLOUCESTER.   Teddy!

TEDDY.   Father's always had the decency and common sense to believe that whatever I did was all right. This is the absolutely first time he's ever behaved in this absurd manner and I know you put it into his head.

GLOUCESTER.   Be careful.

TEDDY.   Well—isn't it true?

GLOUCESTER. I . . . I simply didn't know you were doing such things. It isn't necessary. There are plenty of other things to do for amusement.

TEDDY. I think I must be the judge of what I find amusing. I like this.

GLOUCESTER. Then your judgment is not to be trusted.

TEDDY. Trusted? I don't know that yours is, father. You do a great many things that perhaps I don't think altogether good taste.

GLOUCESTER. Teddy!

TEDDY. A great many things. Mrs. Allister, for instance, is far from what I call good taste, and yet you seem to find her extremely amusing.

GLOUCESTER [helpless and much embarrassed]. You go to bed.

TEDDY. I don't want to go to bed.

GLOUCESTER. Well, you ought to want to.

TEDDY. Are you going to decide when I go to bed, too? You'd better put me on a leash, father. It will make it easier for you.

GLOUCESTER. You don't treat me with any respect.

TEDDY. I didn't know you wanted me to.

GLOUCESTER. You . . . [Trying to be dignified and stern, he goes out helplessly.]

[THEODORA turns to MARGARET. A pause, as they look steadily at each other.]

MARGARET. Oh, my dear girl, understand this. It all happened because I care for you very much.

TEDDY. Please don't let your interest make father lose his head and behave like this again.

MARGARET. Don't, Theodora! Listen to me just a moment—please. You're so young, dear.

TEDDY. Oh!

MARGARET. I'm saying things your mother would say to you if she were here.

TEDDY. Just what's wrong with what we were going to do to-night? Just what's wrong, pray? Don't you think we're to be trusted alone? Don't you think we're decent enough to behave without being watched every minute?

MARGARET. I think you're young and impetuous and

human, and that you're getting your pleasure in the very way that the fastest, commonest sort of people get it, and it all leads to a looseness and laxness that can't possibly have anything but harm in it.

TEDDY. I don't agree with you at all. I believe in freedom. I think it makes us strong and independent. Nothing is so dangerous as narrow evil-mindedness—and nothing is so safe as frankness.

MARGARET. That's the song the world is riding to the devil on just now. That's what we're fooling ourselves with.

TEDDY. If you're going to judge me and what I do by yourself and what you think is right, I dare say everything I do and say and think is wrong. We aren't getting any-where—let's drop it. Say good— [*She starts toward the door.*]

MARGARET. Theodora—wait, please. You surely know it's very hard to say these disagreeable things to you.

TEDDY. Then why on earth do you say them?

MARGARET. Because you're in danger—because I want to help you.

TEDDY. What a joke!

MARGARET. The very dress you have on is indecent.

TEDDY. What?

MARGARET. Positively indecent.

TEDDY. Well, really.

MARGARET. These boys—the promiscuous love-mak-ing I see going on here all the time—the familiarity—the freedom, as you call it—the kissing—it's all wrong—as wrong as can be.

TEDDY. Kissing? How stupid, there are kisses and kisses. Kissing doesn't mean any more than shaking hands did—I suppose—when you were a girl——

MARGARET. Don't you know that you're wasting the most precious years of your life without—without doing one ounce of good to anybody—or thinking one thought about anything but yourself and your body. You're spending too much money—wasting it here and there, when there never was a time that greater good could be done with it. Don't you know you're being criticised for it?

TEDDY.   You've said quite enough, Aunt Margaret.

MARGARET [*going to her*].   I've hurt you—and I wanted to help you.

TEDDY.   But I don't need your help.

MARGARET.   My dear little girl—try to see that I'm only— Won't you kiss me good night, dear?

> [THEODORA *doesn't move.* MARGARET *goes to the door.*]

You will see when you aren't angry! [MARGARET *goes out. Slow tears come into* THEODORA's *eyes—she fights them away—hesitates a moment—closes the hall door—goes quickly to the telephone—takes down the receiver.*]

TEDDY.   Hello, there's a young man waiting downstairs. Ask him to come to the telephone. Hello, Scottie, I'll change my dress and be down in fifteen minutes. Phone the others and tell them where to meet us. I know of a peach of a place to go for breakfast. What? Yes, of course—he nearly choked. Stuff—I hope you don't think I'm afraid of dad. He was only showing off before Aunt Margaret—trying to make a noise like a father.

THE CURTAIN FALLS

ACT II

SCENE I

It is seven o'clock in the evening of the following day, at the
    Gloucester cottage in the country.
As the curtain rises, the stage is almost dark—a little light
    coming through the windows.
After a moment SCOTTIE *and* TEDDY *are seen outside the*
    window.

SCOTTIE.   The window's locked.   What do I do now?
TEDDY.   Break it.   Break the pane near the catch.
Let me do it.   It's one of those little funny ones.   Take
my slipper off.
    [SCOTTIE *takes one of* TEDDY'S *slippers off and she*
        breaks a pane of glass near the catch at side, puts her
        hand in, slips the catch, and pushes the window up.]
Pretty spiffy!   Now give me a boost.
    [SCOTTIE *helps her and she climbs in at the window.*]
Come on.   Don't stand on ceremony.   [*As* SCOTTIE
climbs in, she hops down the stage on one foot and puts her
slipper on.]   Take the stuff off the table and those chairs.
SCOTTIE.   Oh, is it all done up in moth-balls?   [*Seeing*
the coverings on the furniture as he goes toward the table
at right centre.]
TEDDY.   Dad and I only use it for week-ends once in a
while.   It's really a peachy little place.   Mother loved
it.   Now where's the key?   I know.   Here!   [*Getting the*
key which hangs at the side of the door and unlocking the
door.]   Oh, pull.   It sticks.
    [*They get the outer door open.*]
Oh, isn't it pretty out there!   Isn't it going to be divine
going home!   These little crossroads are too heavenly in
the moonlight.
SCOTTIE.   This is immense!   [*He gets the thermos bottle*
and packages of sandwiches from the door-step outside.]

See if we can start a fire. [*Going to the fireplace.*]
There's just a speck of stuff here.

TEDDY. The wood-house is straight through the dining-room beyond the kitchen. [*Pointing to the door at the left.*] Keep going till you bump your head against a funny little door.

SCOTTIE [*as he goes out*]. If I fall dead, come and get me.

TEDDY [*opens the sandwiches and unscrews the two cups which are on the top of the thermos bottle—taking out the cork and looking at her watch*]. It's just a little after seven now. The others are all dressing for dinner and wondering where we are and cussing us out for giving them the slip. And father is pacing up and down foaming at the mouth. Oh, fine! Put some on.

[*As* SCOTTIE *comes back with an armful of wood and puts some on the fire.*]

SCOTTIE. Will he raise the devil?

TEDDY. Of course. It will do him good. This will show him the stern-parent idea is extinct.

SCOTTIE. He's pretty fine, you know.

TEDDY. Dad's really a peach. I was awfully disappointed in him kicking up such a row last night. I thought I had him too well trained for that. Shut the door. It's not exactly balmy in here, is it?

SCOTTIE [*closing the door*]. It's always balmy for me where you are, dear.

TEDDY. It's always tropical for me—where you are, precious.

SCOTTIE. Angel! [*He starts to kiss her.*]

TEDDY. Let's eat! Um! I never was so hungry in my life!

[*They sit in the two chairs above table.*]
Oh, the coffee's boiling hot.

SCOTTIE. Gosh!

TEDDY. What?

SCOTTIE. I forgot. I had a date with Hallie to-night.

TEDDY. Oh, I thought it was something important. Gosh!

SCOTTIE. Promised I'd go to dinner with her.

TEDDY. Well, you've escaped that. She won't do a thing to me for keeping you away from her. I bet she's telephoned dad every fifteen minutes all day just to keep him stirred up. And by *this* time I bet she's got him thinking I've been out two nights.

Scottie. You can't expect him to be exactly calm about it, you know, old girl. This is going some, even for you.

Teddy. Well, I want to make an impression—so he won't misbehave again. We can get back by ten. That will be a *very* chaste hour to stroll in and say I've had a *sweet* quiet day in the country.

Scottie. Having left home last night about midnight——

Teddy. Danced all night at three different joints——

Scottie. Four!

Teddy. Had breakfast at a very queer road-house and then, with a few deft lies, given the others the slip.

Scottie. Motored with me all day—and here we are!

Teddy. Alone at last with night coming on apace. Don't you love it? I'm crazy about it.

Scottie. You're a peach. I adore you! See here, honey, there couldn't be a better time and place to tell me you'll marry me.

[*Lighting their cigarettes.*]

Teddy. Why do you want to marry me—Scottie?

Scottie. I like that!

Teddy. I mean—how do you know you do?

Scottie. How do I know anything?

Teddy. But you've been in love with so many girls.

Scottie. But I never wanted to marry so many.

Teddy. Am I the *great* passion of your life?

Scottie. You are! [*He starts to kiss her. The door blows open.*]

Teddy. Oh, shut it tight! Heavens, is it raining?

Scottie. [*looking out*]. Don't think so. [*Closes the door with a bang.*] Are you cold, dear?

Teddy. N-o, but I'm not exactly roasting.

Scottie. This will make you all right. [*Taking a flask from his pocket.*]

Teddy. Goodness, is there any left?

Scottie [*pouring some whiskey into the cups*]. I got it filled at the last place. [*Giving her a cup.*]

TEDDY. Yes, *you* got filled in the last place too. [*Taking a sip.*] Oh, I hate it this way—without water.

SCOTTIE. But there isn't any water—so don't be so fastidious. Drink it all, dearest. You must. I wouldn't have you take cold for anything. Come and sit over here by the fire. [*Drawing the armchair nearer the fire.*]

TEDDY. We must go in a minute. Aren't there any candles there to light?

SCOTTIE. What's the use? I love it this way.
   [*She sits in the chair, he sits on the arm.*]
I adore being alone with you, sweetheart. Way off like this! It makes me feel you really do care. Tell me, how much? [*Putting his head against hers.*]

TEDDY. I don't know.

SCOTTIE. Don't say that, Ted. You make me miserable. Tell me this—has there ever been anybody else you *cared* for *more?* Be honest.

TEDDY. N-O. Unless, perhaps, no—there really hasn't.

SCOTTIE. Was Oliver *the* one? [*Putting some whiskey in his own cup.*]

TEDDY. Dear old Ollie! I always *will* love him.

SCOTTIE. Don't.

TEDDY. Not *this* way—silly. He's just a perfectly adorable, old darling.

SCOTTIE. Yes, with money to burn and I haven't a cent—that's why I'm jealous of him.

TEDDY. Don't be stupid! Dad's got enough. I'm glad you *haven't* any. Scott—so if I do marry you I'll know it's for yourself alone, see?

SCOTTIE. Don't say *if*. You aren't just flirting with me, are you, Ted?

TEDDY. Of course not. I'm making up my mind.

SCOTTIE. Well, how's your mind getting along? Where are we now?

TEDDY. I'll tell you *one* thing—pos-i-tively—I feel very much more as if I *might* marry you than I ever did anybody else.

SCOTTIE. That's wonderful!

TEDDY. I thought you'd appreciate it. I believe I like you because you haven't any character, Scott.

SCOTTIE. Thanks.

TEDDY.　See that queer light in the fire.　Pretty!
Isn't it weird and nice—shut up here with the whole
world outside?　I *want* to believe in love.　I'd like to.
It *ought* to be the most wonderful thing in the world.

SCOTTIE.　It is!　[*He puts more whiskey in his cup.*]

TEDDY.　See here, you don't need all that to keep from
being chilly.

SCOTTIE [*putting his arm about her and speaking with
his lips on her cheek*].　I'm mad about you.　I don't
give a rap about anybody else in the world.

TEDDY.　Not even Hallie?

SCOTTIE.　Hallie—stuff!

TEDDY.　She's mad about you.

SCOTTIE.　*Are* you jealous of Hallie, sweetheart?

TEDDY.　Not a bit—I think she's a pill!

SCOTTIE.　Kiss me!　[*He snatches her in his arms and
kisses her lips.*]　Dearest!　Take your hat off.

TEDDY.　No!

SCOTTIE.　Please.　I want to see your wonderful hair!
Let me!　[*He takes her hat off and kisses her hair, then her
lips.*]　I adore it, Ted.　Have you ever kissed anybody
that way before?

　　　[*She doesn't answer.*]
You *have!*　Who?

TEDDY.　I can't help it—*how* people kiss me!

SCOTTIE.　But have you kissed too?

TEDDY.　Um . . . I don't remember!

SCOTTIE.　Kiss me, with all your heart now, dear,
please.

　　　[*She leans slowly toward him and kisses his lips.　He
　　　stands up and lifts her in his arms.*]

TEDDY.　Do you know what would make us know
that we loved each other?

SCOTTIE.　What?

TEDDY.　If we hadn't any money at all, just ourselves,
then we'd know.

SCOTTIE [*holding her*].　Couldn't be done.

TEDDY.　But what if I hadn't any money?

SCOTTIE.　But you *have*.　Thank God, there's nothing
like that in ours.

TEDDY [*looking at him keenly and drawing away from*

him a little, realizing that he has had too much to drink].
Scott—does it really mean an awful lot to you—my
money?

SCOTTIE. Kiss me. What does anything else mean?

TEDDY [*holding him off*]. What if you knew this minute
I didn't have a cent? What would you do?

SCOTTIE. Don't say disagreeable things. We're
happy.

TEDDY. Would you want to marry me then?

SCOTTIE. What's the use talking moonshine? We
know each other too well for that, don't we? I couldn't
marry anybody on earth without money.

TEDDY. Is money the most important thing in the
world to you, Scott?

SCOTTIE. Kiss me!

TEDDY. No! No! No! You don't love me. I want
to go. [*Moving away from him*.] Listen. It *is* raining.

[*A slow flash of lightning lights the room and the rain
and wind are heard*.]

SCOTTIE. Nothing but a little spring shower. We'll
have to wait till it's over. Come and sit down again.

TEDDY. No, I don't want to! [*Moving away from
him again to the right*.]

SCOTTIE. Why not? I want to tell you how much I
love you. Kiss me!

TEDDY. No!

SCOTTIE. You've got to!

TEDDY. I won't. Let me go! Scott—*don't*.

[*He draws her onto the bench; she gets to her feet and
pushes him so he falls at length on the bench at the
right*.]

SCOTTIE [*putting his feet upon the bench*]. Oh, this feels
good. Come here, dearie. Where are you? Come here
and sit beside me. Look! see? Here's a nice little place
for you right here.

[*Another flash shows* TEDDY *standing in the middle of
the room, horror-stricken,* SCOTTIE *lying full length
on the bench*.]

TEDDY. Scottie, get up. We must go! I *hate* this!
You're not going to sleep! [*There is a peal of thunder.
The storm increases. She goes to the fireplace*.] Oh, aren't

there any candles here? [*She looks on the table in the alcove and closes the window.*]

    [*And a man opens the door. A flash of lightning shows him young and strong. He wears a rain-soaked top-coat and cap and carries an electric lantern.*]

BILLY. Oh, I hope I didn't frighten you. May I come in? [*Coming in and closing the door.*] I guess you didn't hear me knock and I thought I'd take a chance and walk in.

TEDDY. Where did you come from?

BILLY. Up in the country further. I'm trying to get back to town. Never dreamed this storm was coming. She's a bird. Regular cloudburst. [*Lifting his lantern to see* TEDDY *better.*]

TEDDY. How long is it going to last?

BILLY. Don't know. Looks like an all-nighter. These country roads are going to be in a sweet mess for a car. I skidded at the top of this hill till I thought I was going to glory.

    [*Another blast.*]

Awful—isn't it? [*He turns his flash on* SCOTTIE *and then back at* TEDDY.]

TEDDY. Yes—we—just came in for a few minutes ourselves and got caught. Got caught in the *rain,* I mean. This is my house.

BILLY. Oh, I see. You're not living here?

TEDDY. I've got to get to New York. I've got to. Do you think my car can make it?

BILLY. I'm afraid nothing could do it in this. It's terrific—absolutely terrific! I'm sorry. It's a shame. I wish I could get you in. Can't I make that fire a little better for you? [*He puts his lantern on the mantel-shelf and builds up the fire. The lantern and the fire throw a circle of light over them.*] You're lucky you made this house. At least it's better than lying in the ditch.

TEDDY. [BILLY *glances at* SCOTTIE.] I'm going on the minute it stops a little.

BILLY. She's not going to do that in a hurry. Gee, I'm pretty well soaked. Do you mind if I try to dry out a little?

TEDDY. If you can get anything *dry* to-night, you're welcome.

[*She goes to the armchair.*]

BILLY. It was a great piece of luck for me that you were here, I can tell you.

TEDDY. [SCOTTIE *groans in his sleep.*] He doesn't feel very well.

BILLY. Is he ill? Can I do anything for him?

TEDDY. No—no. He's only dead for sleep. We've been motoring all day.

BILLY. I know. . . . It gets you that way.

[*A pause.*]

Are you warm enough? [*Standing before the fire.*]

TEDDY. Oh, yes—yes. It's all very delightful.

BILLY. It is for me. I must say this is the last thing I expected to happen.

TEDDY. I can't say I exactly planned and schemed for the situation myself.

BILLY. Do you mind my pipe?

TEDDY. Not if you give me one, too.

BILLY. I'm afraid I can't offer you anything but Luckies.

TEDDY. They're all right—if you have enough of them.

[*He lights her cigarette. A crash of thunder.*]

Oh, why did this have to happen? [*Rising and going to the centre.*]

BILLY. The storm?

TEDDY. It's put everything on the blink for me.

BILLY. I s'pose there never was a storm that didn't spill the beans for somebody. But nothing ever seems half as bad in the morning.

TEDDY. This is once when everything's going to seem much worse in the morning. [*Sitting in the armchair.*]

BILLY. But you can make yourself pretty comfortable here for the night.

TEDDY. Oh, yes. I never was so comfortable in my life. Well, it's a delightful evening for a long chat by the fire. I must say I'm glad *you* dropped in. The other member of the party doesn't seem to be adding much to the gaiety of nations.

BILLY. I'm glad to be a better talker than the other fellow is for once.

TEDDY. It certainly is the chance of your life to sparkle. Well, go on—I never was so much in need of entertainment.

BILLY. Well, here's a bright gem. Do you dwell in New York?

TEDDY. Yes. Don't you?

BILLY. Y-e-s—I s'pose I do.

TEDDY. Don't you know whether you do or not?

BILLY. I hardly know whether I'm on earth or not.

TEDDY. What?

BILLY. When you hit the great city for the first time you don't know whether you're living in it or just having a pipe-dream.

TEDDY. The first time in your whole life?

BILLY. Yep.

TEDDY. You don't look it.

BILLY. I s'pose you think I ought to have a ring in my nose.

TEDDY. Go on—sparkle some more.

BILLY. I'm afraid I'm running down.

TEDDY. Oh, don't. If you'll choose a topic of conversation, I'll do my best to keep up.

BILLY. I know a good one.

TEDDY. All right. Fire away.

BILLY. *You.* Who are you? What are you? What do you do with yourself—and what do you like best?

TEDDY. I said a conversation, not a catechism.

BILLY. That's the best I can do.

TEDDY. Well—who am I? Anonymous. What am I? An ordinary girl. What do I do? Amuse myself as much as possible.

BILLY. What do you like best?

TEDDY. To have my own way about everything in the world. Now you. You must be the "dook" in disguise, at least.

BILLY. No—nothing so dressy. I'm an every-day guy —not so long out of the army—who fell into an awfully soft snap in New York.

TEDDY. What sort of a snap?

BILLY. A job somebody got for me through pull—with so much salary to it, it makes me dizzy.

TEDDY. Rather a spiffy dizziness, I should say.

BILLY. Yes, it is. I've been pretty lucky. I've fallen in with some awfully nice people, and I don't mind telling you—I don't know whether I'm coming or going.

TEDDY. I advise you to keep going.

BILLY. You either have to do that or get out. If you stop in the middle, you drown.

[SCOTTIE *groans. They look at him.*]

TEDDY. No—I don't think he's going to contradict you. Go on. What comes next? Oh, yes—how do you like New York? Was it all as wonderful as you thought it would be?

BILLY. Much more wonderful and much more rotten.

TEDDY. What did you like best?

BILLY. The excitement, I s'pose.

TEDDY. What do you hate most?

BILLY. Oh, it would take a week to tell that.

TEDDY. Well, I think we'll be here a week.

BILLY. I hope so.

TEDDY. You say you've met some awfully nice people.

BILLY. I'm just coming from a house-party now—on up further.

TEDDY. Any attractive girls there?

BILLY. Oh, yes. One beauty—one stunner and one peach.

TEDDY. You gobbled the peach, I s'pose.

BILLY. No—the bloom on her cheek kept me guessing.

TEDDY. That's the cleverest thing a cheek can do.

BILLY. Oh, I don't know.

TEDDY. There's nothing so dull as being *sure*. Don't you like something left to the imagination?

BILLY. I *do*. But Lordy! There's precious little a girl leaves to the imagination now.

TEDDY. Oh! That sounds as though you'd been shocked.

BILLY. Shocked? I've been *stunned*. I knew the pace was pretty swift, but—*whew!*

TEDDY. Can't you keep up with it?

BILLY. I'm coming right along. But it knocks the wind out of me sometimes.

TEDDY. If you don't like it—why don't you get out?

BILLY. Oh, I didn't want to go back to the same old thing. I was born on a farm so big you could lose one of these dinky little fellows round here in the fence corners. I wanted to be in New York and see life and it's got me all right. I'm doing just what everybody else is.

TEDDY. You'll get over your provincial ideas. Freedom and frankness and beauty are so misunderstood by the outsider.

BILLY. I'm allowing for all I don't understand, but there's one thing I'm dead sure of.

TEDDY. What?

BILLY. They're making a circus out of some things. The way they get engaged and unengaged makes my hair stand on end. What do they think it is—anyway? A game of tag?

TEDDY. Well . . . why not? What else can it be?

BILLY. The chasing's fun enough—but why get caught till you're sure you want to stay caught forever—till the whole game's over?

TEDDY. How can anybody be sure of that?

BILLY. They could be a darned sight more sure if they went at it as if it was a little something more than a tryout. What on earth do you think being married means?

TEDDY. And what on earth do you think it means?

BILLY. Oh—just the most important thing in the world . . . where everything starts, and where great things come from—if it's right—and where the worst things come from if it's wrong. What on earth do you think it means?

TEDDY. Nobody ever finds what he wants, anyway. And I think it's better to keep our dreams shut up tight and never let 'em out—so we won't be disappointed.

BILLY. I don't. I think it's better to let 'em out and make 'em come true.

TEDDY. Can't be done.

BILLY. Oh, yes, it can.

TEDDY. How?

BILLY. By wishing and wishing—and never taking anything but the best wish.

TEDDY. I wish——

BILLY. What?

TEDDY [*rising*]. Nothing. I wish the storm would stop.

BILLY. I wish I could stop it for you. Let's see how it looks. [*Opening the door and shutting it quickly.*] It's getting worse. You might as well try to swim across the ocean as get to town in this.

TEDDY [*after a pause*]. You must wonder why I'm here. It isn't very easy to explain.

BILLY. Don't try. Why should you?

TEDDY. I came out—because somebody told me not to. And you see I'm having the time of my life.

BILLY. Well, a—a—a . . .

TEDDY. Exactly. Nobody may ever *quite* understand —but I hope *you* do.

BILLY. I understand it's tough luck and I wish to Heaven I could get you back. But it *can't be done*. This is your house—and you go up-stairs and make yourself as comfortable as you can. It's the best thing to do—for a fact. I'll sit here—in this chair by the fire—and everything's all right. You'll have to be game. And you *will* be.

TEDDY. Oh, yes—I'm very game.

BILLY. That's right. You take the light.

[*They go to the door at left.*]

I'll get you back to town in the morning—at daylight.

TEDDY. Oh, no. I'd rather you'd go before—I'd rather you'd be gone when I come down in the morning. It would be easier.

BILLY. Then I'll never see you again. But I'll never forget you. My name's Wade—Billy Wade. Do you want to tell me yours?

TEDDY. I'd rather not.

BILLY. And don't be afraid of anything to-night—will you?

TEDDY. Of course not with you here. You've helped me through an awfully hard place—and you're splendid to understand.

BILLY.   Why shouldn't I understand?   You were held
up by the storm and so was I.   Why should I misunder-
stand you any more than you did me?   You didn't seem
to think I was a highway robber or anything when I
banged through the door.

TEDDY.   Perhaps you are.   Good night.

BILLY.   Good-by.

TEDDY.   Good-by.   A—good-by.   [*She goes out.*]

> [BILLY *watches her off, closes the door, puts some wood
> on the fire, takes the blanket from the table in alcove,
> starts to sit and wrap himself in it—remembers*
> SCOTTIE—*goes to him and puts* SCOTTIE'S *coat over
> him, goes back to the armchair, wraps himself in the
> blanket, and prepares to sleep for the night.   The
> storm rages all through this and during the moment
> the curtain is lowered to denote the passing of the
> night.*]

SCENE II

Daylight comes in at the windows.   BILLY *is asleep in the
armchair, wrapped in a blanket.*   SCOTTIE *is still asleep
on the bench.   A blanket is over him.*   BILLY *awakens,
rouses himself, looks at* SCOTTIE *curiously.   Listens a
moment, puts more wood on the fire, puts on his cap
and coat, takes the lantern, and goes out through the
outer door, leaving it open.   The morning is fresh; the
sun streams in.*   MR. HEYFER *comes into the doorway.*
MR. HEYFER *is seventy, the typical product of a life-
time of hard work in the New England hills.*

HEYFER [*shouting at* SCOTTIE].   Hey, there, what you
doin' in this house?   Hey! Who are you?   [*He goes to*
SCOTTIE *and shakes him.*]

SCOTTIE [*very sleepy*].   What?   What's the matter?
What?   [*Half seeing* HEYFER.]

HEYFER.   I say, what you doing on this property?
How'd you get in?   There's a heavy fine for trespassin',
don't you know that?

SCOTTIE [*getting up*].   Who are you?

HEYFER.   None of your business who I am.   Git out o'
this house!

SCOTTIE.   I will not!

HEYFER.   Well, I guess you will.   I got strict orders
not to let nobody in never—fer nothin'.

SCOTTIE.   Hold on till you know what you're talking
about.

HEYFER.   Don't give me no back talk or I'll——

[TEDDY *comes in from the left.*]
Who a'r *you?*

TEDDY.   Who are *you?*

HEYFER.   This is private property.

TEDDY.   Oh, you're old Mr. Heyfer.

HEYFER.   Law—air you Miss Gloucester?   Where in
the name o' goshum did you come from this time o' day?

TEDDY.   We were driving by last night and got caught
in the storm and came in here.

HEYFER [*looking at* SCOTTIE].   You don't say?   Is he
your husband?

TEDDY.   He is not.

SCOTTIE.   Lucky we got here, wasn't it?

HEYFER.   Was you here all night?

TEDDY.   We were!

HEYFER.   Both of you?

SCOTTIE.   Certainly we were.   What did you expect
us to do, sit out in the rain all night?

HEYFER [*staring in open-mouthed amazement from one to
the other*].   I'd know but what that might a been better.

SCOTTIE.   I'm afraid I don't agree with your point of
view.   Quite a shower, wasn't it?   But a *very* delightful
morning, isn't it?   [*Going to the open door.*]

HEYFER.   How'd you git in?

TEDDY.   We busted in.   Mend things, will you, please,
and shut things up again?   We're going on now.   [*Putting
on her hat.*]

HEYFER.   It certain is peculiar actions.   Does your
pa know you're out here?

TEDDY.   Not at all.   I don't see anything peculiar
about coming into my own house.

HEYFER.   Well, that's as maybe.   I'd know as I jest
quite understand.   [*He goes out at outer door.*]

SCOTTIE. I'm too horribly sorry. I wouldn't have had this happen for anything.

TEDDY. That's all right. It's not your fault.

SCOTTIE. Don't mind it, dear. What difference does it make, after all?

TEDDY [getting her coat]. None whatsoever. Let's get home as fast as we can.

SCOTTIE. But, Ted, it's going to be all right. You don't blame me, do you?

TEDDY. Not the least little bit.

SCOTTIE. It might have happened to anybody. Lots of people are caught in storms.

TEDDY. We certainly were caught.

SCOTTIE. I'll do anything on earth to make it right.

TEDDY. There isn't anything you can do to change it one way or the other. Get your coat and let's go.

MARGARET [calling from outside]. Theodora!

TEDDY. Aunt Margaret!

MARGARET. Theodora—are you there? [MARGARET rushes in. She and TEDDY start toward each other as GLOUCESTER follows MARGARET in. There is a pause. GLOUCESTER and TEDDY look steadily at each other.]

TEDDY. Now, father, I've done nothing on earth I'm ashamed of in the slightest degree.

SCOTTIE. Mr. Gloucester——

GLOUCESTER. Were you here all night?

TEDDY. Yes, we were. And I've done nothing that I'm ashamed of, I tell you.

MARGARET. You believe her, Hubert?

GLOUCESTER. Believe her? Why should I?

SCOTTIE. Mr. Gloucester, this thing isn't at all the way it looks.

GLOUCESTER. Damn you! You . . .

TEDDY. Oh, don't, please. Do you believe I've done a rotten low-down thing, or don't you?

GLOUCESTER. My God! How do I know?

MARGARET. Hubert!

SCOTTIE. Mr. Gloucester, you must——

GLOUCESTER. If you haven't, why are you here?

TEDDY. If you don't know that I'm not lying, I don't care what you think.

MARGARET. Theodora, *explain* it all to him. Hubert, listen.

GLOUCESTER. What is there to listen to? What is there to explain?

TEDDY. Nothing. I wouldn't try to explain for anything on earth.

SCOTTIE. You've got to listen, Mr. Gloucester. The others were all with us that first night and Ted and I motored all day yesterday—and came here last evening just to have a look at the place—and expected to be back in town by ten o'clock. The storm was terrific and we had to stay. We simply *had* to.

GLOUCESTER. That's a *fine* story! By God, it's just as bad to throw your reputation away as it is—to—to—to——

MARGARET. Hubert!

GLOUCESTER. It *is*. What in the name of Heaven do you *mean*—acting like the commonest, lowest kind of a thing? Does *nothing* mean anything to you but this brazen, disreputable, loose conduct? Where do you get it? Where does it come from? What have you done with your bringing-up? How do you expect me to believe—anything but the—what *am* I to believe?

MARGARET. That she's *your daughter*. That all the other things you've let her do—have done this. That she needs your help now as she never needed it before. Theodora—you are going to *marry* this boy, aren't you?

SCOTTIE. Of course she is, we're engaged.

TEDDY. Oh, no, we're not.

GLOUCESTER. What? What do you say?

TEDDY. I'm not engaged to him.

SCOTTIE. Ted!

MARGARET. But didn't you expect to be?

TEDDY. Perhaps. Probably. I don't know. I was considering.

GLOUCESTER. Oh, you were. There'll be no more of that. You'll announce your engagement at once.

TEDDY. Why should I? What good will that do? How can that change anything?

GLOUCESTER. *What?* At least, it's some *faint* hope of persuading people that you haven't quite gone to the dogs. That you wouldn't have been quite so wild as to go off with him if you weren't going to marry him. It's a very little thing, I admit. But at least it's the only thing we *can* do.

SCOTTIE. Ted—listen! Come and marry me now—quick. We'll go on to another town and telephone back to your father that we've eloped.

TEDDY. What?

MARGARET. That's a very good idea, Theodora—really it is. The best possible thing you could do.

GLOUCESTER. Yes, it is. Do it! Do it—and get at it now.

TEDDY. I don't want to.

GLOUCESTER. What?

TEDDY. I don't want to.

GLOUCESTER. It isn't a question of what you want—but a question of saving yourself.

TEDDY. Saving myself from what? I can take care of myself.

GLOUCESTER. So you've thought. And this is what you've got yourself into. You need *me* now. Why do you refuse to do the one thing there is to do? Why do you refuse to do this for my sake?

TEDDY. I'd do a good deal for your sake, dad, but I can't *marry* somebody I don't want to—for your sake.

GLOUCESTER. And why don't you *want* to marry him?

TEDDY. Because I don't love him—like that.

GLOUCESTER. You probably love him as much as you're capable of loving anybody.

TEDDY. You must let me be the judge of that. I can't marry you, Scott—I know now . . . I'm sorry.

[SCOTTIE *turns away.*]

MARGARET. Be careful, dear. Don't make another mistake with this serious thing.

TEDDY [*almost breaking at* MARGARET'S *tenderness, but controlling herself*]. I'm trying not to. Why do you ask me to marry him when I tell you I don't want to? *I don't love him that way*—I tell you. What has anything else got to do with it? How can you be so stupid and old-fashioned and afraid? Of course I've done a perfectly idiotic thing and I'm just as sorry as I can be. But what has that to do with the rest of my life? What if people *do* talk and tell a few lies about me? I'm not going to sneak and do a trumped-up thing as though I *were* guilty. If you can't take me home now, dad, and hold up your head and say, "This is my daughter, and I trust her and know she hasn't done anything wrong," then I never want to go home at all.

GLOUCESTER. And if you don't obey me—if you don't do this little thing for my sake, I don't *want* you to come home.

MARGARET. Hubert!

GLOUCESTER. Are you going to do it?

TEDDY. No!

[GLOUCESTER *goes out quickly.*]

MARGARET. Teddy!

TEDDY. No!

SCOTTIE. Ted?

TEDDY. *No*——

THE CURTAIN FALLS AND REMAINS DOWN ONE MOMENT.
THIRTY-SIX HOURS PASS

SCENE III

The following morning. MARGARET *comes in from the left. She opens the two windows and goes into alcove, where she examines and sorts several pairs of net curtains which are on the table.*

HEYFER [*coming in after passing the window of the alcove*]. Good mornin'. [*He carries a basket covered with a towel.*]

MARGARET. Good morning.

HEYFER. Here's your dinner. Do you want your supper brought over too?

MARGARET. Yes—I think so. I'm not sure yet. And isn't there a woman near here who would like to come in and clean up a little and wash those dishes?

HEYFER. I ain't heerd o' none wantin' to do anything like that for some time. [*Crossing to the door at the left.*] How long do you calkalate stayin'?

MARGARET. I don't know exactly. Does it matter?

HEYFER. Wall, no—in one way it don't, but the folks round here keep askin' me, and they think it's kind o' funny I don't know.

MARGARET. I'm sorry not to be able to keep them informed.

HEYFER. I s'pose you think it ain't none o' their business, but some things is enough to make the dead say a little something.

MARGARET. And may I say a little something? This whole place must be cleaned inside and out. Get a strong young man at it right away.

HEYFER. I guess I'm about the youngest round here, an' I'm pretty busy. I guess maybe some time during the summer I might git round to doin' a little somethin' fer you.

MARGARET. Where are they all? There used to be plenty of people about here to do things.

HEYFER. They're all riding round in their Ford automobiles. We live in a infernal age. Why, my granddaughter Mamie ain't worth the powder'd blow 'er up—running into them ungodly movie shows every night of 'er life—gettin' home long after ten o'clock—first with one feller an' then with another, till nobody ain't got no notion nohow which one she's goin' to marry—if any. The ungodly lawlessness that young folks is growin' up with nowadays is a disgrace to their day an' generation.

[MARGARET *laughs.*]
You think it's funny?

MARGARET. Oh, no—I just seem to have heard that some place before.

HEYFER. Somethin' had ought to be done about it. Somethin' had ought. We're bringin' up a reckless daredevil, good-fer-nothin'——

TEDDY [*coming in from outside, wearing old khaki riding clothes and a brown sweater*]. It's perfectly glorious outside. Why don't you go out and run round a little, Aunt Margaret? It would make you feel like a roaring charger. Little spring things are coming up all over, and, oh, Mr. Heyfer, a little rabbit that looked just like you sat on the wall and said: "Git off this property—who the hell are you?"

HEYFER [*suddenly seeing* THEODORA'S *riding trousers*]. Law—you been out ridin' already this mornin'—what on?

TEDDY. No—I bin waitin'. This is my waiting costume. Don't you like it?

HEYFER. I can't say thet I do. I been kind o' broke in to seein' 'em on a hoss—but not walkin' round on the carpet.

TEDDY. Oh, I'm sorry. I was afraid I'd look too much like the idle rich if I stayed much longer in the other one.

HEYFER. Wall, as ma says, there ain't no use tryin' to understand city ways. There ain't nothin' to hitch to or git hold on one way or t'other—nohow . . . [*He goes out at the left, leaving the door open.*]

TEDDY. Inspiring creature. Oh—what is dad going to do? He's had a day and a night to change. I don't believe he is ever going to.

MARGARET. Are you?

TEDDY. Never. Isn't it a joke? Just because I'm a girl. Scottie's strutting about in town of course, as usual —while I'm waiting here for my father to forgive me. Isn't it priceless! A girl can be alone all day with a man and nobody says a word—but one night in the most innocent accident and she's damned. Lord, the things I could tell that have happened in the daytime! [*Going to* MARGARET *and putting out her hand.*] Aunt Margaret, you've been awfully good. You haven't once said I told you so. I know I've done a damn fool thing and I know I deserve all that's comin' to me—and I think you know what it means to me for you to stick by me. [*She turns away quickly to hide her tears.*]

MARGARET. Teddy, I want to ask you one question.

TEDDY. Yes.

MARGARET. Are you sure you aren't coquetting with Scottie Wilbur now? Are you sure you don't intend to marry him after you've kept him dangling a little longer and make your father suffer a little longer? Uh?

TEDDY. No. I give you my word, I'm not. If I loved Scott, I'd marry him like a shot. But I don't. Of course that's a pretty weak argument coming from me

—I admit—I don't know much about the divine passion, but at least I know it hasn't hit me yet—and I'll never marry anybody till it does.

MARGARET.   But the pity of it is you'll play with it so much you won't know when it comes.

TEDDY.   Oh, yes, I will.   I saw a boy once who was so sure he'd know that if he had said he loved me I would have known he did.   I would have known he would have taken care of me all my life and it was only up to me to be worth it.

MARGARET.   Who is he?

TEDDY.   You wouldn't know.

HEYFER [*coming back from the left with his basket empty*]. She says there ain't much to do to your dinner but to put it on the stove an' take it off agin, but she lowed she didn't know as you could even do that. [*He goes to the outer door*—TEDDY *follows him, imitating his walk.*]   If you belonged to me I know what I'd do to you. [*He goes out and to the left—passing the window.*]

TEDDY.   If you belonged to me I'd have your hair bobbed.

MARGARET.   Well—if you won't give in—the only thing I can think of for you to do—is to share my little income with me and live in an economy you've never even heard of.

TEDDY.   Oh, you're awfully good, Aunt Margaret. But I couldn't do that.   I couldn't.

MARGARET.   Then what *are* you going to do?

EILEEN [*coming in quickly from outside at right—followed by* OLIVER].   Ted!

TEDDY.   Oh, Eileen!

[EILEEN *throws her arms about* TEDDY.]

Hello, Oliver! [*Putting out a hand to* OLIVER *as she still holds* EILEEN.]

OLIVER.   Hello, Ted! [OLIVER *goes to shake hands with* MARGARET.]

TEDDY [*to* EILEEN].   Well, you look like a funeral! Let's hear the worst!   Everybody's very *busy*, I s'pose. I haven't got a rag of character left to my back by this time.   Have I?   Don't look so stunned, Eileen.   What's the matter?   Let's have it?

EILEEN. It's beastly—a beastly rotten shame—the whole darned thing! [*She goes to give her hand to* MARGARET.]

MARGARET. Have you seen Mr. Gloucester?

EILEEN. No. I tried to but he won't let me.

OLIVER. So did I. He won't see any of us. Scott has told us the whole business, Ted.

EILEEN. We might have kept it quiet if it hadn't been for Hallie. Mrs. Rainsford, did she phone you that Ted had said she and Scott might motor out here?

MARGARET. Yes—but she didn't do that till two o'clock that night.

TEDDY. She waited till then so if we were here dad couldn't get here till morning. Nicely planned—wasn't it? Well—what are people saying?

EILEEN. Well, I went out to tea yesterday and to dinner—and to a dance afterward, and by the time I got home the story was you'd done this several times before. They say that's what you keep this place for.

MARGARET. Oh, how can they be so cruel!

OLIVER. Don't, Eileen. What difference does it make what they say?

TEDDY. Oh, I want to know. Don't be delicate. I love the details. I s'pose dad's hearing it all too?

EILEEN. Mrs. Allister's rubbing it in. She's not missing this chance of getting back for all the snubs you've given her.

TEDDY. Mrs. Allister must be really and truly and deeply shocked. She is such a pure and holy lily herself.

OLIVER. What *are* you going to do, Ted? You've got to do *something!*

EILEEN. You can't stay *here!*

TEDDY. Oh, yes, I can—till I *rot.* Dad's *got* to give in. He's got to. He's wrong—just as wrong as he can be!

SCOTTIE [*coming in quickly*]. Hello!

[*They all turn—a pause.*]

TEDDY. Hello!

SCOTTIE. May I see you alone, Ted?

EILEEN. Of course!

MARGARET. Come into the dining-room. Or would you rather go outside?

EILEEN. It doesn't matter. [EILEEN *and* OLIVER *follow* MARGARET *into the dining-room.*]

SCOTTIE. I've been with your father most of the time trying to get him to come and take you home without any question of marrying me one way or the other.

TEDDY. Thanks, old man!

SCOTTIE. But I haven't made the slightest dent in him. I've never seen any one so angry in my life. He's like a raging bull. Horribly cut up too, Ted, gone to pieces. I'm sorry for him—I actually am!

TEDDY. So am I. But *his* way's not the way out.

SCOTTIE. It's the only one under heaven I see. He'll never give in. If *you* do—he's going to be awfully wonderful and generous to you, Ted. But if you don't—he's going to do as he threatened—you know.

TEDDY. Threatened?

SCOTTIE. Money and stuff.

TEDDY. Cut me off?

[*He nods.*]

Oh, that's divine! That's the last touch! You go straight back to him and tell him I don't care whether I ever have a cent of his money or not!

SCOTTIE. Oh, Ted, don't! Don't lose your head! You can't live without your father. Now see here, *tell* him you'll marry me—announce the engagement and break it afterward. I give you my word, Ted. I won't try to make you stick—if you don't want to.

TEDDY. You're a brick, boy, you are. But don't you see I can't do that sort of stuff? It's getting awfully, *awfully* serious with me, Scott. I meant what I said to dad with everything in me, and if I go back on it—I go back on myself! It doesn't hurt *you* a bit—or your reputation. I never promised to marry you. If I had, I'd come through. You know that—don't you? And I'm sorry, Scott, I don't love you that way—but I don't.

SCOTTIE. I'm so sorry about the whole rotten business I could kill myself.

TEDDY [*taking his hand*]. Don't worry. It'll all come out in the wash. If we loved each other well enough we could snap our fingers and tell the whole lot to go sit on a tack. But we don't care—like that, do we?

SCOTTIE [*evading her eyes*]. Why I—you—I do.

TEDDY. Don't try to make a brave speech!

SCOTTIE. If I only had money, Ted.

TEDDY. Yes, I know, I know. It's quite all right.

SCOTTIE. But, Ted, dear—what *are* you going to do?

HALLIE [*coming in from the outer door, followed by* TREVOR]. Oh, Teddy, dearest!

TREVOR. Hello, Ted!

TEDDY. Hello, Trevor. Did you come out to see the show? Tell the others to come back, Scottie.

TREVOR [*taking her hand in both of his*]. This is rotten luck, old girl, isn't it? But we're all in it, you know. We're all red devils by this time.   •

HALLIE. Oh, yes—we're *all* in it. Eileen and I, too. And I'm taking all on my shoulders I possibly can, and telling everybody it was just the merest chance that we didn't *all* come out here.

EILEEN. Hello, hello. [*Coming back from dining-room.*]

HALLIE. Oh, hello.

EILEEN. I say we stop talking and go back to town and let Ted alone!

TEDDY. Oh, no, I don't. I think it's charming of you to come out and bring me the latest bulletins. Have you any choice tid-bits, Trevor?

TREVOR. Plenty. The things I've heard about *myself* since this thing began would fill a book. I wonder I'm not kicked out of every club in town.

TEDDY. You devil! Girls will chase you more than ever, Trevor.

TREVOR. And as for Ollie, well—they haven't done a thing to him. No girl's safe with you after dark, old man. But *Scottie*—oh, I say . . .

[*They all laugh.*]

OLIVER. Oh, shut up, Trevor. Drop it.

TEDDY. No—don't. What do they say about Scottie?

TREVOR. Scottie has a wife and child or two in every town in the States—more or less.

[*They laugh.*]

TEDDY. I'm so relieved. I was afraid they had said *I*

led Scottie into temptation. As a matter of fact I did, of course.

HALLIE. But the worst thing they say about Scottie is that he only wants Ted's money, and compromised her so she'd have to marry him. That's what *I* resent more than anything. That's what *I* get perfectly purple in the face about.

TEDDY. You still look a little pink—dear.

OLIVER. You know *one* man who wants to marry you on any terms at any time. The sooner the better. You know that, Ted.

HALLIE. Gracious! Are you offering yourself publicly, Ollie? How touching.

OLIVER. Why not? I've done it often enough in private. Everybody knows that. If I could marry you this minute, Ted, it would be the greatest thing that could happen to me.

TEDDY. Oliver, you're the most adorable thing that ever lived.

TREVOR. Adorable—*but*—Ollie——

OLIVER. Oh, this isn't a joke—you know.

TREVOR. I'm not so emotional as Ollie, Ted—but I'm absolutely at your service. Will you take me?

HALLIE. Another great moment in a great man's life.

SCOTTIE. I don't see anything so damned funny about it.

OLIVER. I don't, either. It's up to us to kill this stuff and carry Ted through. If we *can't*, we're no good.

EILEEN. That's what I say.

TREVOR. Now, I've been thinking. Couldn't we start something like this—that you stayed at a neighbor's house —and had just come over here in the morning when your father arrived, Ted?

TEDDY. Yes, I think that would be very convincing. Say I came out to spend the night with old Mr. Heyfer. He's attractive enough to account for *anything*.

OLIVER. Ted, you're a scream. Thank God you've got a sense of humor. About the best thing we can do is to treat it as a huge joke.

TREVOR. It *is* a rummy little joke. Isn't it, Scott?

HALLIE. Let's make it as absurd as possible. Scottie

can describe the storm out here, and when people say, "How funny! It didn't rain a *drop* in town," he can make the storm worse and worse. Can't you, Scott? *Was* there really a storm?

SCOTTIE. Oh, no; it was a *beautiful* night. We stayed to see the moon come up.

TEDDY. All the fish stories you can possibly dig up won't be half as fishy as the truth. Scott and I weren't alone here that night.

[*They all look at her quickly.*]

I haven't even told Aunt Margaret this part of it. It's too much to expect even her generosity to believe. Scottie did have a drink or two and went to sleep—over there; and the storm raged—and the door opened—and a young man walked in—out of the nowhere—into the here— and we sat by the fire and talked—and talked—and talked——

[*They laugh.*]

You see—nobody *could* believe it.

EILEEN. And what was Scottie doing all this time?

TEDDY. Scottie was sleeping.

TREVOR. Oh. That was very careless of you, Scottie.

TEDDY [*going to lean on the open door*]. Not so good as the truth. The strange young man said he lived in New York and thought some of the nice people he had met did rather asinine things. And then he said the storm was going to last all night and that I'd better go to bed. And I said I thought I *would*. And I took the young man's light and opened that door, and he said there was nothing to be afraid of—that he would take care of me—and that his name was Billy Wade and that he would never see me again. But he would never forget me. And then he said good-by, and I went up-stairs, and when I came down in the morning—the door was open and the young man was gone—and——

[TEDDY *is standing in the doorway—she stops suddenly.*
After a slight pause, BILLY WADE *comes into sight.*]

Oh—how do you do?

BILLY. Good morning.

TEDDY. I—I—I—I—was just talking about you. [*To the others.*] This is the strange man.

BILLY. I came back to see if by any chance you were still here. I was afraid you had some difficulty getting away. I hoped you had got back to town all right—and yet I hoped by some fluke I'd find you again. That's the only excuse I have for coming back.

[TEDDY *and* BILLY *laugh.*]

TEDDY. I think that's excuse enough—to come back to find a really old friend like me. But they don't believe the story I was telling them—how you blew in.

BILLY. I can scarcely believe it myself.

TEDDY. If he knows which one is Scottie—will you believe it ?

[BILLY *stands smiling and wondering—looking from one to the other.*]

OLIVER. Try it.

TEDDY. Which is the one who was asleep on the sofa that night ?

BILLY [*nodding to* SCOTTIE]. This one, of course.

TREVOR. How do you do it, Ted ?

TEDDY. You never saw *him*—did you, Scott ?

SCOTTIE. What in the world are you trying to do, Ted ?

TEDDY. Mr. Wade—this is Mr. Wilbur.

BILLY. How do you do ?

SCOTTIE. How do you do ?

HALLIE. How very amusing you are, Ted. You always have something up your sleeve. What *is* this ?

TEDDY. They don't believe you were here at all. Can't you say something to convince them ?

BILLY. Nothing but just the truth.

TEDDY. But that's the last thing in the world they can possibly believe.

BILLY. The whole thing was sort of funny, wasn't it ?

TREVOR. Quite funny. But we don't see the point yet.

TEDDY. I *am* telling the truth. I'm not fooling—really. You believe me. Don't you ?

EILEEN. Are you kidding us, Ted ?

HALLIE. It's a priceless story. You're as clever as the deuce. And we've actually *seen* the strange man with our own eyes. And what shall we say when people say: "But *would* she have been alone all night with Scott Wilbur if the young man hadn't fallen from the skies ?"

TEDDY. How *dare* you say that to me, Hallie Livingston! How dare you! I've been the biggest fool in the world—I know. I was stubborn and bull-headed and I thought I could get away with anything—and I've walked right into a beautiful mess with my eyes wide open. I don't want anybody to be sorry for me. It's absolutely my own fault. But I do expect *you* Eileen and *you* Ollie not to think I'm telling a ridiculous lie and trying to put something over on you.

EILEEN. But we don't understand.

TEDDY. What if you don't understand? What difference does that make? And what difference does it make *how* it all looks? I've asked you to believe me—in spite of everything. A perfect stranger came in when things looked just as rotten as they possibly could—but he was big enough and kind enough to—to—to—trust me. And now he sees you don't— You can go back to town and say I've told the most impossible lie anybody ever heard of. You can also say I'm not going to marry Scottie, and nobody knows *what* I'm going to do next, and I don't give a damn what *any* of you think. [TEDDY *breaks for the first time and hurries out. There is a pause.*]

BILLY. Do you mean you really don't believe I was here last night?

[*No answer.*]

I told you I was, you know. I sat here in that chair—till morning—while she was up-stairs and he was asleep there. If it makes any difference one way or the other whether I was here or not—I'll do anything on earth to prove it.

TREVOR. But there isn't anything you can do to prove it, old man. You just ask us to take your word for it—and that's all there is to it.

BILLY. And you do take my word—of course? [*Looking from* TREVOR *to* OLIVER.]

OLIVER. We take Miss Gloucester's word. It isn't necessary to discuss it further.

BILLY. Yes—I see you believe everything she says. Of course you're her friends and know her well—so you couldn't possibly be rotten enough to doubt her in any way. She's lucky to have such good friends to stand by and fight for her. I think I'll wait outside in case she needs somebody who knows she isn't lying. [BILLY *goes outside*.]

TREVOR.   Charming person! Where did Ted dig him up?

HALLIE.   Somebody who lives around here and Ted's making it worth while for him to——

EILEEN *and* TREVOR.   No!

EILEEN.   *Hallie—how could* you?

HALLIE.   Now don't take that tone of voice to me.   I'm just as sorry as *you* are that Ted told such a cock-and-bull story.   But I'm not going to be fool enough to pretend to believe it.   Why, in the name of Heaven, couldn't she have told Scott—if it's true?

OLIVER.   It is true.   But don't tell anybody else—for God's sake.   Let's shut up about the whole infernal business.

EILEEN.   I'd believe Ted Gloucester above everybody else on earth.   But it would be the *worst possible* thing we could do for her to try to make anybody else believe this story, and you've all got to promise that you'll never breathe it to a living soul. [*She looks at the two men. They nod seriously.*]   Hallie?

HALLIE.   I scarcely think you have to say that to *me*.

EILEEN.   And I'm going to make Ted swear she'll never tell it again. [*She goes into the dining-room, closing the door.*]

OLIVER [*after a long look at* HALLIE].   That's a dead serious thing we've sworn to.

HALLIE.   Yes—not to tell anybody there were two men here instead of one.   You look so tragic, Ollie.

OLIVER.   Ted's up against it.   We all think we can get away with anything.   Here's one time we didn't. We all think we're the whole cheese. [*He goes outside.*]

TREVOR [*going out after him*].   Well—we *are*.

[SCOTTIE *starts to follow him.*]

HALLIE.   Scott, don't go. [*He stops—turning slowly toward door.*]   Isn't it awful!   I'm so sorry for Ted.   I don't know what to do.

SCOTTIE.   It's the rottenest deal a girl ever got.

HALLIE.   And isn't it marvellous the way she takes it? I'm so sensitive if it had happened to me it would have killed me. You've been marvellous about the whole thing, Scott. I'm awfully sorry for *you*—too.

SCOTTIE. You needn't be.

HALLIE. But I am. You've done everything under the shining heaven *you* can be expected to do. Don't sacrifice yourself, old dear.

SCOTTIE. Sacrifice myself?

HALLIE. What's this tale Mrs. Allister's telling about her father cutting Ted off if she doesn't marry you?

SCOTTIE. That damned Allister woman ought to have her throat cut.

HALLIE. Oh! It's true, then? You wouldn't be fool enough to be caught like *that*?

SCOTTIE [*evasively*]. Oh!

HALLIE. Or even *with* the money you really don't have to marry her. You don't have to be quixotic about it. Ted's no ingénue—she knew what she was doing, all right.

SCOTTIE. She was only in a daredevil mood. She didn't mean any more harm than a baby.

HALLIE. *Didn't* she? You *are* wonderful about it, dear. I'm crazy about the way you're taking it. So awfully generous. She's such a ninny not to grab you—now that she's got you.

SCOTTIE. Grab me, nothing! She doesn't want me.

HALLIE. Oh, I can't believe that . . .

SCOTTIE. It's so, all right.

HALLIE. Poor boy! I can't bear to see you so unhappy. I wish there was something I could do to buck you up. When you're so lonely, come and play with me. I understand you so well.

SCOTTIE. Do you, Hallie?

HALLIE. All you need is money to make you perfect. I think it would be awful to have your personality hurt by anything as disgusting as no money.

SCOTTIE. But I'll never make any.

HALLIE. Oh, cheer up. God knows the men a girl can love are scarce enough. You ought to have a very large income settled on you for merely being one of those. And Ted's wasn't all the money there is in the world— you know. Do you think my lips are just exactly right?

SCOTTIE. Perfect.

HALLIE. Are they, really ? You're a love. [*Rising and putting her hands on his shoulders.*]

EILEEN [*coming in quickly from the house and stopping as she sees* HALLIE *and* SCOTTIE]. Well—I don't think this is a particularly good time for that sort of thing.

HALLIE. It's a good time for you to mind your own business.

EILEEN. This is my business. Ted's come to her senses and is going to do the only sane thing there *is* to do.

[TEDDY *enters. There is a pause as they turn to her.*]

TEDDY. May I speak to Scottie—alone—please?

HALLIE. Of course, dear—of course. And, Ted, don't go to pieces again. You must be awfully brave. I hope it isn't too late to save yourself—I suppose all you can do is to live it down—the way most people do. And you can count on me to do anything in my power to help you.

TEDDY. I don't intend to lie down and die.

HALLIE. No matter how ghastly people are to you, or how many drop you and cut you completely, you just mustn't mind.

TEDDY. The cutting and dropping will be all on my side.

HALLIE. Oh, very well—if you don't want my help —we'll *see*. Good-by, Scott. See you very soon, old man. [*She goes outside.*]

TEDDY. I'm not going to be insulted the rest of my life for this.

EILEEN. That's right, Ted. Hold your head so high no one can touch you. Shall I tell the others what you're going to do ?

TEDDY. Yes—please.

EILEEN. And I'll tell them not to come back to speak to you now. Buck up, Ted; I'll settle Hallie.

TEDDY. Scott—I was a fool to think I could beat the game. I've got myself where people won't believe me and where my friends can't help me. If you still want me, I'll marry you.

SCOTTIE. Ted !

TEDDY. Go in town and tell dad I'll marry you—that

we'll blaze and have the most gorgeous wedding anybody ever had.

SCOTTIE. Now—you're yourself again—I adore you.

TEDDY. Oh, no, you don't.

SCOTTIE. I do——

TEDDY. Let's be honest! It's a jolly good arrangement for us both—and we'll probably get on as well as most people do who pretend to be in love.

SCOTTIE. But I *do* love you, Ted.

TEDDY. Yes—with all my accessories. Now let's play fair and make the best of it.

SCOTTIE. Dear old girl, I'll try to make you happy.

TEDDY. Well, everybody's going to *think* I'm happy, I can promise you that—and if we don't make a go of it— we'll get our divorce right off the bat.

SCOTTIE. Oh, Ted, don't go into it that way.

TEDDY. Why not? Lord knows it's better to go into it prepared to have a divorce than to suddenly be hit in the head with it later.

SCOTTIE. I can't stand it—to have you take it this way.

TEDDY. I'm only being sensible. I'll make a settlement on you now, Scott, and the whole transaction will be very neat.

SCOTTIE. That's horrible!!!

TEDDY. Slush—I'm only calling things by their own names. What right have we to expect anything else? We've set our own tune—now we'll have to dance to it— and for Heaven's sake let's dance *well*.

SCOTTIE. But——

BILLY [*coming into the outer doorway*]. Pardon me—I don't want to butt in. But I would like to talk to you a minute before I go back—if I may.

TEDDY. Of course you may.

SCOTTIE. But, Ted, you must hurry back to town now.

TEDDY. I have to change. You must hurry in yourself.

BILLY. I'll take you in.

TEDDY. Oh—can you? Go on then, Scott—and Aunt Margaret and I will come with Mr. Wade.

SCOTTIE. Not at all. I can't let anybody else take you.

BILLY. Oh, I think you can trust me to get Miss Gloucester in safely.

SCOTTIE. I'll take her in myself.

BILLY [to TEDDY]. Do you want me to go—or to wait to take you in?

TEDDY. I want you to wait.

BILLY [looking at SCOTTIE]. I'll wait.

SCOTTIE [looking at TEDDY]. How soon will you get in?

BILLY. Just as soon as Miss Gloucester wants to go.

SCOTTIE [starting to the door and stopping to speak to BILLY]. You seem to be rather interested in the situation.

BILLY. You can't blame me for that? Can you?

SCOTTIE. You must realize it doesn't matter in the least whether you were here or not last night. [He goes out.]

BILLY. It matters a good deal—to me. I suppose you're disgusted with me for coming back; I s'pose I said all the wrong things and made everything a thousand times worse than if I'd stayed away. I'm sorry.

TEDDY. Nothing could make it any worse. I gummed it up as much as I possibly could.

BILLY. I was a fool not to have stayed right through —with you—to have told it all myself to everybody.

TEDDY. I didn't want you to. And it wouldn't have done any good. As Hallie says, people will still say: "And would she have been alone all night with Scott if the strange man hadn't fallen from the skies?" You see, it's a hopeless mess—any way you look at it. And I was stupid to have told anybody about you. But it seems rather ridiculous not to be able to tell the most beautiful thing that ever happened to me.

BILLY. They're blockheads.

TEDDY. Oh, no. They're just my friends. Why should I expect anybody to believe me?

BILLY. I'd believe anything you told me.

TEDDY [looking at him for the first time]. But you don't know me.

BILLY. Oh, yes, I do. I know you better than I ever knew anybody. I've thought about you every minute since I saw you and I came back hoping to find you again.

TEDDY. And you found me in a worse fix than when
you went away. But I've taken the only way out there
is. I'm going to marry Mr. Wilbur, and I won't lose my
father's money—and I'm not going under.

BILLY. Marry him? Are you only doing it because
—of this thing that happened?

TEDDY. He's marrying me for my money and I'm
marrying him to save my reputation.

BILLY. That's hell!

TEDDY. Is it? It's often done, you know.

BILLY. You don't have to do that?

TEDDY. My father has a right to force me into it, I
suppose.

BILLY. He has *not*.

TEDDY. What did you think when you found me here?

BILLY. I knew when I saw your eyes that you didn't
have anything to hide.

TEDDY. But you think I did a deadly common, stupid
thing coming out here just to be reckless—by way of
amusing myself?

BILLY. Yes, I do. But why in the name of Christopher
should that put a crimp in your whole life and make you
do a much worse thing now—marry a man you don't love?

TEDDY. It's the only way out.

BILLY. Oh, no. You're in bad—but you could come
out big.

TEDDY. How?

BILLY. By turning this into something big.

TEDDY. It's easy enough for you to talk. You're a
man. Men can do anything.

BILLY. If they *will*. So can a girl.

TEDDY. Oh, no; one party like this for a girl—and she's
done for if she hasn't any money.

BILLY. How much money do you need to live?

TEDDY. I don't know. I don't know. Dad gives me
twenty-five thousand a year and then pays all my debts.
I have three thousand a year of my very own from my
mother and this little place . . . That doesn't leave
much if I throw dad over, does it?

BILLY. Well, I've just thrown up a job of ten thousand
a year which seemed like a million to me.

TEDDY.   Given it up?

BILLY.   Yes.   I got just what was coming to me.   I knew it was crooked when I went into it.   I knew the man stole from the government, and called it big business, but I fell for it . . . and I stuck because of what it could do for me.   But it was eating into me all the time good and hard.   And do you know what happened to me?   After I saw you the other night, I hated it so, I went back and chucked it.   I haven't got a job and it won't be so easy to get another one—but I can look myself in the face—and I'm free.   And I don't see why you can't be the same way.

TEDDY.   You don't know what you're talking about.

BILLY.   The whole point is this.   Do you *want* what you're going back to or don't you?

TEDDY.   It doesn't matter whether I want it or not. It's what I've got to do.

BILLY.   Are you going to let it get you so you'll be just like the rest of them?

TEDDY.   I am just like them.   I'm one of them.   What else can I be?   I thought for a few minutes I could defy it and run away from it.   I thought I'd give up my *soul* not to have to go back.   It all seemed so horrible all of a sudden.   I thought I never could face it and bluff and fight and pretend that I didn't care.

BILLY.   You *do* care—you do hate it.

TEDDY.   I don't dare to let myself hate it—or I never could go through.   I don't dare *think* what I'm going to do—but I know—oh, I *know*.   [*She puts her head forward on the table and with a sob.*]

BILLY.   Then why in the name of God do you do it? How can you—*you*—do anything you're ashamed of?

TEDDY [*lifting her head and going to the outer door*].   But I can't live without my father.

BILLY [*following her*].   With this little place?   What's the reason you can't?   You can take care of yourself.   I'll help you.   That's where I belong—outdoors.   I could make this little farm *sit up*—if you'll help me.

TEDDY.   How can I help?

BILLY.   Work—with your own hands.

TEDDY.   I can't.   I don't know how.

BILLY. Learn. I'll help you. I'll go halves. I'll put what I've got into it.

TEDDY. If I try, with all I've got in me—if I work with my own hands—if I'm not a fool—do you think I can take care of myself?

BILLY. I *know* you can.

TEDDY. How wonderful of you to believe in me. I don't see how you can.

BILLY. I do. Believe in yourself.

TEDDY. But it's all so strange. I've never done anything like this in my life.

BILLY. Don't be afraid. You're stronger now than you ever were in your life.

TEDDY. No, I'm not. I'm awfully weak. I may fail.

BILLY. You can't. You've got hold of something to fight for.

TEDDY. Oh—I'm afraid I'm doing something wild again.

BILLY. No, you're not.

TEDDY. I'll fall down.

BILLY. No, you won't. Pull yourself up. Pull yourself up high.

TEDDY. I'll try. I'll try.

BILLY. No, you'll *do* it.

TEDDY. I will. I will. I *will*.

THE CURTAIN FALLS

ACT III

SCENE: *The lawn before the cottage, with the small white house at the left—the single door opening on the lawn. It is three months later—early in the afternoon.*

The house is a story and a half high, with small windows and solid wooden shutters—faded to a dull green. The ground slopes up at back to an old stone wall. At the centre three stone steps lead up to the little country road. At the right the lawn extends off stage to a group of trees.

Low hills are in the distance. A rustic table stands at the left of the stage—an armchair below it turned in to the table. Up stage there is a similar chair and at the right a garden-bench. These are all of the same rustic style. The scene is simple in the extreme and full of brightness.

At the rise of the curtain, EILEEN, *wearing sport clothes, is selecting a golf club from her bag. She draws an iron out and practises a stroke.* MRS. RAINSFORD *sits at the table sewing.*

EILEEN. I'm off my feed entirely. Playing a wretched game lately.

MARGARET. It always sort of comes and goes, doesn't it?

EILEEN. Yes—especially goes.

MARGARET. Is anybody coming out to play with you?

EILEEN. Ted says Trevor and Ollie are coming. Mrs. Rainsford, [*going to* MARGARET] Ted never speaks of her father to me—would you think me awfully impertinent if I asked if she ever hears from him?

MARGARET. She never has—not a word. It's been three months.

EILEEN. Awful, isn't it?

MARGARET. *Yes*—and yet it has *made* Theodora.

EILEEN. But the future, Mrs. Rainsford. It will be horrible if they never make up.

MARGARET. I used to think so—but— [MARGARET *shakes her head.*]

EILEEN. You don't mean you'd like her to marry Billy?

MARGARET. Why not?

EILEEN. It would be the awfulest thing I ever— I think perhaps I ought to tell you. You know we all promised never to tell anybody that Billy was here that night. We knew it would do Ted more harm than good. But Hallie has told—and it's started everybody's tongue off again.

MARGARET. Oh! Why did she do it?

EILEEN. She did it to stir Mr. Gloucester up and widen the breach between him and Ted. She's afraid Scott may get Ted with her father's money—after all.

MARGARET. It's hideous.

EILEEN. Isn't there something you can do to make Ted go to her father? I've heard that Mr. Gloucester is beginning to melt. Can't you do something?

MARGARET. I don't know that I want to.

EILEEN. Don't you want them to be reconciled?

[MARGARET, *thinking, does not answer.*] When the boys come, tell them to shout to me.

[EILEEN *goes to the cottage. After a moment* GLOUCES-TER *comes quickly and excitedly from the right.*]

MARGARET. Hubert!

GLOUCESTER [*taking her hand*]. Where's Theodora?

MARGARET. Out—somewhere about.

GLOUCESTER. Margaret, if you've let something go on out here and haven't told me, I'll never forgive you. Never!

MARGARET. What?

GLOUCESTER. If you've let Ted get mixed up in an-other affair and haven't warned me——

MARGARET. What do you mean?

GLOUCESTER. Why haven't you told me? Why haven't you kept me informed about everything that she was doing?

MARGARET. Why should I have told you anything about Theodora? Didn't you give her up? Just when she needed you most?

GLOUCESTER. What *is* this thing out here?

MARGARET.   You'll have to tell me what you mean.

GLOUCESTER.   The story is all over town that *another* boy was here with her that night while Scott was drunk and asleep.   That *this* boy was the reason she so suddenly refused to marry Scott.   That he gave up a ten-thousand-dollar job in New York to come here and work for Ted—that he wants her money—and is making love to her.   Is it true ?   Is it true ?

MARGARET.   No—no—yes—some of it.

GLOUCESTER.   How much ?

MARGARET.   Some of the bare facts.   The boy was here that night—yes—Billy Wade.   He came in out of the storm—and stayed with her—and kept her from being terrified.

GLOUCESTER.   And *did* he come back ?

MARGARET.   Yes—but not because he wants her money.

GLOUCESTER.   But he *did* give up his job ?

MARGARET.   Yes.   But——

GLOUCESTER.   But not because he wants her money ? Good heavens, Margaret, have you been taken in like that ?   Why, the fellow's a bounder—an adventurer.

MARGARET.   Oh, Hubert !

GLOUCESTER.   How could you be so gullible ?   I let Ted stay here with you because I thought it would be the best thing on earth for her when she defied me and refused to marry Scott.   And now this thing hits me in the head.

MARGARET.   But it isn't true.

GLOUCESTER.   Oh, yes, it is.   Eileen tells me they had all sworn to keep still—never to tell it—but it seems Hallie wants Scott Wilbur and hasn't got him yet—and in desperation broke her word and told this to keep Scott away from Ted.   It's as plain as the nose on your face.

MARGARET.   Oh, yes.   It's *very* plain.   Of course Hallie told it—and it's all colored and——

GLOUCESTER.   They say they were all drinking that night—and there's no telling what happened to make Ted give up Scott.

MARGARET.   Hubert ! Hubert ! You don't believe any such stuff as that ?

GLOUCESTER [*sitting*]. Oh, I'm in despair, Margaret. I don't know *what* to think or what to do.

MARGARET. Poor Teddy certainly has paid for that one foolish, headstrong thing. And now *this*—a really good and beautiful thing has been distorted and turned against her.

GLOUCESTER. You've been taken in, Margaret.

MARGARET. Oh, no, I haven't. I happen to know the truth. It does sound like a fairy-story to sordid ears that can't believe in anything unselfish and disinterested.

GLOUCESTER [*rising*]. God! And you've let Ted be fed up on that. *Is* this fellow making love to her?

MARGARET. You'll have to ask her that.

GLOUCESTER. You've made a hero of him, evidently. Who is he? What is he?

MARGARET. You'll have to judge for yourself.

GLOUCESTER. Is she going to marry him?

MARGARET. I don't know. Hubert, I've been absolutely quiet in this whole thing—merely watching Theodora work out her own salvation—but I won't be now. If you try to kill what has begun to come to her—I'll fight for her. And I'll fight you.

GLOUCESTER. Do you promise you won't tell her I'm here? Not say one *word* of all this till I see her?

MARGARET. Yes—I promise that.

GLOUCESTER. Which way am I likely to find her?

MARGARET. I actually don't know. Perhaps in the lower garden.

> [GLOUCESTER *goes up the steps and off along the road to left.* MARGARET *sits at the table, taking her sewing.* BILLY *whistles off the stage, and comes swinging along the road from the right. He wears blue overalls and carries a scythe.*]

BILLY [*stopping by the steps to put the scythe over the wall*]. You can see through to the other side of the brook now. About two or more days and I'll have all this side cleared.

MARGARET. How splendid!

BILLY. Has Ted come in yet?

MARGARET. Not yet.

BILLY. I struck another berry-patch all choked up.

Find something new on this little old place every day. Gosh, it's fun!

TEDDY [*coming in through the trees at the right*]. Billy, the black hen has twenty-seven chickens and one duck.

BILLY. Ye gods! The first scandal on the farm.

> [TEDDY *is wearing blue overalls and a large straw hat.*
> *She carries an old market-basket, with some working*
> *tools in it.*]

MARGARET. I speak for the duck. You *must* let me have *something*.

TEDDY. Well—we'll see what kind of a disposition he has. If he's a grouch, you can roast him. What's the matter?

> [*As* MARGARET *wipes her eyes.*]

Have you been crying?

MARGARET. No—of course not.

TEDDY. No tears around here, young woman, or you'll have to pay a fine. [*Going to* MARGARET *and kissing her.*] You blessed thing!

MARGARET [*rising and leaving her sewing*]. I promised to call Eileen. Don't you think she's napped long enough?

TEDDY. I should hope so.

MARGARET [*turning at the door of the house*]. Oh, my dear children——

BILLY [*going to her*]. *Is* anything the matter?

MARGARET. No—only I'm afraid for you somehow.

BILLY. Why?

MARGARET [*putting a hand on* BILLY'S *shoulder*]. Be strong and *sure*—won't you?

BILLY [*putting a hand over hers*]. What about?

MARGARET. About everything. [*She goes in.*]

> [BILLY *stands looking after her.*]

TEDDY. Aunt Margaret's got the gloom. Don't you know it's Saturday afternoon? You ought to have your Sunday clothes.

BILLY [*throwing himself down beside her*]. Well—have you done everything to-day you *thought* you were going to do—when you went to sleep last night?

TEDDY [*beginning to wind the string which is dangling*

from her pocket]. Just about. I got a new chicken-coop made—a tiny, weeny one for the débutantes.

BILLY. They're having a big season, aren't they?

TEDDY. And I got two roosters to stop fighting.

BILLY. How?

TEDDY. Sat on one of them and fought the other one myself.

[BILLY *throws himself on the grass and roars with laughter.*]

And I moved the pigs over into their new quarters and began painting the old ones.

BILLY. Painting the old pigs?

TEDDY. Their *quarters*.

BILLY. Their hind quarters?

TEDDY. You know I'm not going in for snappy dialogue. I'm working.

BILLY. I'm not—go on.

TEDDY. And I got up on the kitchen roof to see if I could find that leak—and coming down I got that place in the stairs mended. Then I had to go and show Heyfer how to dig a ditch. He wasn't doing it my way at all.

BILLY. I'm sorry I missed that conversation.

TEDDY. Then I had to get a board nailed on.

BILLY. Good.

TEDDY. And then I got that. [*Sitting beside* BILLY *and showing him her thumb, which is tied up in a rag.*]

BILLY. *Bad!* But you've still got both arms and legs. I think you've pulled through remarkably well so far, considering the enterprises you've had your hands in—to say nothing of your feet. Where's the other one? [*Looking for the foot she is sitting on.*]

[*They both laugh and lean toward each other impulsively, and, becoming conscious, move away.*]

You've got two more freckles on your nose.

TEDDY. You've got a button off your shirt. I'll sew it on for you. Wasn't I pretty magnificent to darn those socks for you last night?

BILLY. Oh! [*Looking at his feet.*] I've been wondering all day what was the matter with my feet.

TEDDY. I thought it would be a good idea to do it at *once*—so I'd never be requested to do it again.

[*They laugh.*]

BILLY.   Is anybody coming out for tea?

TEDDY.   I hope so.

BILLY.   It amuses 'em to come out and see the flowers bloom, but they haven't the dimmest idea what you've gone through to make them.

TEDDY.   That doesn't matter.   It's been the most beautiful summer of my whole life.

BILLY.   Would you want another one just like it?

TEDDY.   Of course, if it were necessary, but it won't be.   And it's the climbing along making things better that's the fun.

BILLY.   This little farm is just a spring-board—to jump from—to something else.   I'm not afraid of money, Ted, good work will always make it.   But, gosh—aren't you sick of measuring everything with money?   I want to do some things that are *worth* doing whether they ever make a damned cent or not—some things that are worth losing money on—just because you want to try.   And some that are worth spending all you can get on—just because they *ought* to be done.

TEDDY.   Of course, things for other people, Billy.

BILLY.   Yes.

TEDDY.   I never used to think of that at all—but, oh, I've found out so much myself—since I've known you—I want everybody else to know too.

BILLY.   Me, too—I've got some great schemes to tell you about.   I'm awfully ambitious, Ted.   But I have to work like the devil to make the money first to tackle the big things.

TEDDY.   Oh, I like that.   I'll help.

BILLY.   But there are things ahead we've got to look square in the face.   Winter's coming and it will be harder than the summer—lonelier for you.   No friends to count on coming out—and you'll be bored.

TEDDY.   Will you be bored?

BILLY.   It doesn't matter to me.

TEDDY.   And how about you *and* me?

BILLY.   That's it.   That's the thing I've got to face. How can there be any you and me?

TEDDY.   How can there be anything else?   Aren't we going to be together forever?

BILLY. Are we?

TEDDY. I can't imagine anything else—unless the world comes to an end, and then we'd be together anyway.

BILLY. Do you mean you could—marry me?

TEDDY. Why, I've always taken that for granted, Billy. I can't tell when it began—any more than I can think of it ending.

[BILLY *puts his face down in the grass before her— grasping her hands.*]

Billy Boy—look at me. What *is* it? You didn't think it was ever any other way—did you? Look at me. [*She lifts his head and holds it in her arms.*] Isn't that the way you've always thought it was?

BILLY. Oh, Ted, I didn't dare. I don't know whether you realize yet—what it would really mean to give up all you have had—forever. To begin all over again—at the bottom. What if you find you just *can't* get on without it? You'd hate me then.

TEDDY. Why do you think about what I've *had?* It's what we'll *do* that matters. And we'll never stop doing. The end is in us, not in anything else. We may be two great birds—you and I. We may see things no one has ever seen before. It's all in *us*—the magic is.

BILLY. It's in you. If you love me, I'm not afraid of anything. [*He kisses her lips in a long kiss. A whistle is heard off right. He springs up.*] Some one's coming.

TEDDY. I thought you said you weren't afraid of anything?

BILLY. I'm not.

[TEDDY *runs to the door into the house.*]

OLIVER [*coming in followed by* TREVOR]. Hello, there, you look as though somebody had given you a gold-mine.

BILLY. Somebody has. Hello.

TREVOR. How are you?

[*Both* TREVOR *and* OLIVER *wear golf clothes.*]

OLIVER. Where's Ted? Aren't we going to have some golf?

BILLY. Eileen is. I don't know about Ted. I'll tell her you're here.

OLIVER. Eileen here?

BILLY. Yes! She came out yesterday.

EILEEN [*coming out from the house*]. Hello, hello. It's a wonder you wouldn't get here sooner.

OLIVER. Hello, Eileen.

TREVOR. Greetings!

EILEEN. Aren't you going to play, Billy?

BILLY. I'm afraid I can't, thanks. [*Getting the scythe.*] Me for the tub.

TREVOR. I say, old man—have you heard the rumor that Gloucester is coming out to snatch Ted out of this? Kill the fatted calf in a blaze of glory and all that sort of thing?

BILLY [*looking from one to the other*]. No . . . I haven't.

TREVOR. I thought you'd be glad to know it. It would let you out of a nasty situation.

BILLY. What?

TREVOR. You won't relish the story. I'm sure that you're after Ted's money—and if you gracefully retire that will kill it pretty quickly.

BILLY [*after a pause*]. I thought Ted's money was a thing of the past. Out of the running entirely.

TREVOR. Oh, *did* you? I wouldn't have supposed you were so unsophisticated. That's just a little temporary chastisement on father's part, of course. Ted Gloucester's going to be one of the richest girls in the country, some day. That's why I say I know you'll be glad to clear out—so you won't be accused of making a grand-stand play for her money under rather disagreeable circumstances.

BILLY. What circumstances, for instance?

TREVOR. Such as chucking your job—rushing out here to Ted and persuading her to stay out here—after she'd just decided to marry Wilbur.

BILLY. Oh, yes. I *have* been a nut. Of course that's what you think I'm doing. All of you, I suppose?

TREVOR. We're merely checking up the details as other people see them.

BILLY. Circumstantial evidence.

TREVOR. We're only telling you that now is the psychological time for you to step out—as it's in the air that father's going to make a move.

OLIVER. We merely mean that we know you wouldn't want to stand in Ted's way if this *is* going to happen.

BILLY. Oh, yes. I see it all very clearly from your standpoint.

TREVOR. There isn't much of any other standpoint to see it from—is there?

BILLY. None—except *mine*—which cuts no ice whatsoever with *you*—but a good deal with *me*. You couldn't possibly get it through you that Ted Gloucester means a damned sight more to me without her money than she does *with* it. Could you? That would be a little too much to expect you to believe.

TREVOR. Right you are—a little too much.

BILLY. In other words, you think I'm a skunk.

TREVOR. Oh, no—just human.

BILLY. Damn your filthy, low-down——

EILEEN. Please, please.

OLIVER. Well, that's the way things look, Wade. And it's easy enough for you to show that there's nothing in it.

TREVOR. Perfectly easy—by merely retiring.

[EILEEN, *standing back of* BILLY, *motions for* OLIVER *and* TREVOR *to leave her alone with* BILLY. OLIVER *goes out first.*]

A magnificent opportunity to prove that you believe the moon is made of green cheese. But don't expect other people to believe it, dear boy. [*He goes out after* OLIVER.]

BILLY. Do you think what they do?

EILEEN. No—I don't. But the case is too strong against you to try to convince them.

BILLY. Damn their souls!

EILEEN. No use damning them; they're only saying what other people think. But something else does matter.

BILLY. Well?

EILEEN. Ted's going to get so tired and sick of this when the novelty wears off, she'll die. She couldn't any more live without what she used to have than she could fly.

BILLY. How do you know what she can live without?

EILEEN. I know her like a book. And I like you too well, Billy Wade, to see her make a fool of you.

BILLY. Don't worry about me.

EILEEN. It's the new thing that gets her and interests her. I know how many fellows she's been *about* to marry and didn't. She likes new excitement. That's why she's been so amazing about all she's done out here. It was a novelty and *you* were new to her, Billy. Something she'd never come in contact with before. And she's flirted with you from a new standpoint altogether.

BILLY. Eileen, why are you telling me this? You say you're her best friend.

EILEEN. I am—and I'm telling you because I honestly think if she married you it would be the worst possible thing that could happen to you both. You don't realize you're only a new experience to her.

BILLY. I can take care of myself, I think.

EILEEN. I've seen a good many other people who thought that, too. Poor old Ollie hasn't given up hope yet.

BILLY. Oliver Comstock?

EILEEN. Of course. You don't think you're going to fare any better than he has—with all his charm and all his money—do you? It's because I like you so much, Billy, I'm saying this. And, by Jove, I know you're too decent to hang on to her and try to keep her from going back to all the wonderful things that are waiting for her.

[BILLY *looks at* EILEEN *in a long, searching look, and goes off slowly below the house.*]

TEDDY. Hello, everybody, where are the boys? [*Coming out from the house, carrying a tray, with glasses, spoons, and paper napkins.*]

[TREVOR *and* OLIVER *come back from the right.*]

TREVOR. What ho!

TEDDY. What ho! yourself.

OLIVER. Hello, Ted.

TEDDY. Oh, Ollie, you must come and see my chickens. They know me now, every one of them.

OLIVER. Oh, come!

TEDDY. They *do*. They run like mad when I open the gate.

OLIVER. They'd be damn fools if they didn't.

TEDDY. That's the most impassioned thing you've

said to me in ages. Keep it up. I've got eight hundred and eighty-eight. What do you think of that?

OLIVER. I think it's a whopper.

EILEEN. Oh, look at Mrs. Rainsford. She looks good enough to eat. I'm starving.

[MARGARET *comes from the house with a pitcher of iced tea and a basket of gingerbread.*]

OLIVER. How are you, Mrs. Rainsford?

MARGARET. How are you, Oliver? Are you thirsty?

OLIVER. All the way down.

TREVOR. Hello, Mrs. Rainsford. What's in the pitcher? It has a nice color.

TEDDY [*pouring the tea*]. Iced tea. Nothing stronger on the place—unless you'd like a glass of milk?

OLIVER [*taking a bite of gingerbread*]. Lordy, this gingerbread's good!

MARGARET. Give Eileen some. It's Theodora's first attempt.

TREVOR [*choking*]. Ye gods! Why didn't you say so before?

OLIVER. Ted, I brought you some cocktails. Right here. [*Getting a thermos bottle from his golf-bag.*]

TEDDY. I'd rather you didn't, really.

OLIVER. What?

TEDDY. I don't like it.

EILEEN. Well, I do. Give me one, Oliver.

OLIVER. You mean you don't want me to open it?

TEDDY. Yes, please. I hate it.

TREVOR. Hate what?

TEDDY. Thinking you have to have a drink on all occasions.

TREVOR. It's the pleasantest thought I have.

OLIVER. That's all right, Ted. I'm sorry.

TREVOR. Do you mean to say I don't get any?

OLIVER [*putting the bottle back in the bag*]. I guess you can wait.

TREVOR. The country certainly does peculiar things to people. Awfully upsetting—don't you think, Mrs. Rainsford?

MARGARET. Yes, it certainly upsets some things and sets *up* others. All the important things get more im-

portant, and the worthless ones more and more worthless.
Don't they?

TREVOR.   I have a horrible suspicion from the gleam in
your eye that I come under the more and more worthless.

TEDDY.   You come under the head of nothing at all,
Trevor.

OLIVER.   What are you going to do this winter, Ted?

TEDDY.   Stay right here.

OLIVER.   That's impossible.

TEDDY.   The joke of it is you're all sorry for me—and
I'm having the time of my life.   I've discovered that too
much money cheats people out of half the thrilling things
in the world.

EILEEN.   You sound like—who was it said it's easier
for something to go through a camel—than for something
or other to something.

TREVOR.   You mean it's easier for a camel than a rich
man to cross the desert without a drink.

TEDDY.   I had my first lesson in milking this morning,
Trevor.   What would you do if you had to milk a cow?

TREVOR.   I should ask the beast to excuse me.

TEDDY.   She probably would, too.

OLIVER.   Ted, you never looked so well in your life.

TEDDY.   Of course I'm husky.   No more smokes—no
more nerves.   I sleep all night and am interested all day.
It's great to feel this way, Trevor.   Even you would get
so you'd like to wake up feeling like an ox instead of a
shoe-string.

TREVOR.   I don't know that I'm so keen about the ox
effect.

OLIVER [to TEDDY].   Well, I think it's a miracle—nothing less—what you've done.

TEDDY.   Any of you could do it if you had to.

MARGARET.   Of course you have more daring and
cleverness and intelligence than any set of people in the
world.

TREVOR.   Mrs. Rainsford, I suspect you.

MARGARET.   It's true—in spite of appearances.   You
have it all and you're throwing most of it away—just
now.

TREVOR.   Am I included in this?

MARGARET. You haven't the faintest idea of your importance.

TEDDY. You're not included in that, Trevor.

MARGARET. You're an institution—envied and imitated—dreamed of and read about in every city—in every little town all the way down there's a set of you—and you might be an absolutely dynamic power for good.

OLIVER. Might be—what are we?

MARGARET. An equally great one for harm. You don't mind my saying so—quite honestly—do you? [*She goes out at right.*]

TREVOR. Neat little parting shot.

TEDDY. What do *you* think we are—quite honestly?

TREVOR [*rising*]. I think I'm a very charming person with a great many friends almost as charming as I am.

TEDDY. Trevor, I love you fondly, but I can't quite keep up with the way you love yourself. Come and see the chickens—they'll appreciate you.

TREVOR. Yes, I know a great many who do.

EILEEN. Don't look at *me*.

[TEDDY *starts off with* EILEEN *and* TREVOR.]

OLIVER [*calling her back*]. Ted—I'm awfully unhappy about you. You're just fooling yourself thinking you can go on like this. What on earth have you got to look forward to? What are you going to do when it settles down to beastly monotony?

TEDDY. Why, I never was so happy in my life.

OLIVER. But the future, Ted. Have you thought of it?

TEDDY. No . . . the present's more than I can take care of.

OLIVER. I could make you awfully happy.

TEDDY. Oh, Ollie, you say it so well—but you've said it so often.

OLIVER. I could, dear, if you'd only let me.

TEDDY. Don't, please, Oliver—I used to adore having people propose to me—the more the better. But I've had enough to last me the rest of my life.

[BILLY *comes out from the house, he and* OLIVER *look at each other,* OLIVER *goes off at right.*]

Billy, I've been thinking, I want money more now than I ever did in my life.

BILLY. What?

TEDDY. Dad has an awful lot. I want it for you. So you can go on with your dreams and schemes.

BILLY. My schemes will take care of themselves.

TEDDY. No, they can't. And do you know what I'm going to do? I'm going to dad, and tell him my pride's all gone.

BILLY. What?

TEDDY. I'm going to tell him how wonderful you are.

BILLY. You'll do nothing of the . . .

TEDDY. He'll be so proud of you. I'm going to him . . . to-morrow.

BILLY. Not to tell him anything about *me*.

TEDDY. Of course I will.

BILLY. They think I want your money. They wouldn't think anything else.

TEDDY. Who does? No, they don't. Why shouldn't you want it? It's mine. It will be yours.

BILLY. It won't.

TEDDY. Now, Billy, don't be stupid. I want you to have what everybody else has. I want you to have what Oliver has. I want everybody to respect you and feel your power.

BILLY. You want it yourself . . . you mean.

TEDDY. But for *you*.

BILLY. Of course you're tired of this. . .why shouldn't you be? It's pretty dull . . . and pretty grubby . . .

TEDDY. Billy, don't be nasty.

BILLY. I've been up in the clouds, all right. I don't blame you a bit, Ted. It couldn't have been any other way.

TEDDY. What are you talking about?

BILLY. I was even stupid enough to actually think perhaps you'd be willing to give up the whole bloomin' business . . . after a while. I'm awfully glad you've said this *now*. Of course you want your money. Why on earth shouldn't you? Don't think I'm hanging around your feet. You're just as free as the first minute I saw you. Nothing that's happened out here is going to keep you away from what you want . . . not for a second.

TEDDY. From what I *want*?

BILLY. You want everything you've given up, don't you?

TEDDY. Yes. Why not? What's wrong with that?

BILLY. I was an idiot to think I meant any more to you than any of the others.

TEDDY. Than any of the others? . . . Do you think I've ever, anybody else has ever . . .

BILLY. I was a novelty, I suppose. Something different that happened along at a convenient time.

TEDDY. Billy! I hate you! How contemptible of you to say that.

BILLY. Isn't it true?

[TEDDY *takes up a cigarette and throws it down again.*]

TEDDY. Are you saying this because of Oliver?

BILLY. He's only one of a good many, isn't he?

TEDDY. Oh.

BILLY. They've always been throwing it into me that I was only something new . . . and I wouldn't believe it. But what you've just said to me now . . . yourself . . . has opened my eyes. Fool? I should say I *have* been.

TEDDY. Somebody's kindly told you how many times I've supposed to have been in love. I've done a very great many things which were pretty silly. I didn't think it was necessary to review my whole life for you. I certainly didn't expect you to do that for me. But I thought you *did* understand, the new part of me . . . and that nothing on earth could shake your faith in it . . . or make you doubt what I've given to you.

BILLY. You'll want the old excitement, so you can't stand it.

TEDDY. Are you asking me to give up everything . . . all my friends . . . forever?

BILLY. I'm not asking you to give up anything.

TEDDY. I . . . can't make myself over . . . entirely. I can't change all my old habits and feelings and point of view. I *can't*. I'm just like my friends. I'm one of them. After all, how can you expect me to change?

BILLY. My God! I'm not asking you to change. I

love you . . . but I know now I can't take the place of all you've had . . . and you *want* it, Ted . . . you want it.

TEDDY. Of course I do—and I want it for you. Why shouldn't you come into my world and be somebody in it?

BILLY. Because I despise it . . . but I want you to be happy, Ted, and get what you want and what you think worth while in the whole game. And I'm going to clear out so you'll get it quick.

TEDDY. Billy!

[*He goes off below the house.* TEDDY *stands alone a moment.*]

MARGARET [*coming on quickly from the right*]. Has anything happened, Ted? Has your father——

TEDDY. Yes. [*She goes slowly to* MARGARET, *who puts her arm about her.*] Billy says he won't have my money and he won't marry me.

MARGARET. How much do you love him?

TEDDY. More than I ever thought anybody could love anything.

MARGARET. Billy's a big person. It would take a big person to hold him and live up to his ideals.

TEDDY [*moving back in amazement*]. Don't you think *I* could?

MARGARET. You're just a little spoiled girl, dear— who's had her own way all her life, and expected every man she took the trouble to flirt with to be her slave. Billy isn't anybody's slave, you know. If you've burned your fingers on him, I'm sorry. Has he found you out? Is it all over?

TEDDY. It certainly is, so far as I'm concerned. If he's so darned big, I don't want him stooping to me. I may be very small potatoes to some people, but—I know dad will—— If you and Billy are living on such a lofty plane that you can't commune with me, I think I'll clear out and go where——

[GLOUCESTER *comes from the road. After a moment* TEDDY *goes to him with a sob, putting her arms about his neck.* MARGARET *turns away.*]

Father!

GLOUCESTER [*scarcely able to speak*]. There's never been a day or an hour that I haven't wanted you back.

TEDDY. There's never been a day or an hour when I haven't wanted *you*.

GLOUCESTER. Why didn't you come, dear?

TEDDY. How could I?

GLOUCESTER. My little girl! I'll make it up to you.

TEDDY [*putting her arms about his neck again*]. Take me home.

[MARGARET *comes forward again*.]

GLOUCESTER. Margaret, she wants to go home.

TEDDY. Do you want me?

GLOUCESTER. Ted, we'll shut up this house and leave it. Let's get off.

TEDDY. Oh—not just this minute.

GLOUCESTER. Well—pretty quickly. Why not? I hate this place. I'm going to sell it. I want all association with it wiped out.

TEDDY. It's mine, dad. You can't do that.

GLOUCESTER. Why can't I?

TEDDY. I love it; I've been more happy here than I ever . . .

GLOUCESTER. Tut—I'm going to make you happier than you ever have been in your whole life.

TEDDY. How?

GLOUCESTER. By giving you everything you want.

TEDDY. You can't do that.

GLOUCESTER. What? What is there you want—I can't give you?

[TEDDY *moves away*. GLOUCESTER *looks at* MARGARET.]

MARGARET [*coming forward*]. Teddy's had a great disappointment.

TEDDY. Oh, don't tell father that.

GLOUCESTER. Now don't keep things from me that——

MARGARET. He'll have to know, dear. Everybody will know it.

TEDDY. What?

MARGARET. Billy Wade—who has been so splendid this summer—well—Teddy and he—thought they were in love with each other——

TEDDY. Oh, I'll tell it. He—he— That's all there is to it.

MARGARET.   I think you'd better get her away at once.
Billy's changed his mind.   He doesn't want to marry her.

GLOUCESTER.   What do you say?

TEDDY.   Pretty hard for you to get that—isn't it, dad?

GLOUCESTER.   He must be insane.   But it's a blessing,
of course—the best possible way out of any complication
you may have got yourself into . . .   What do you want to
do, Ted?   And we'll do it.   Go round the world?

TEDDY [*sitting on the bench*].   No, thank you.

GLOUCESTER.   Go to live in London?

TEDDY.   No, thank you.

GLOUCESTER.   What do you suggest, Margaret?   Build
a house in town of your own?

TEDDY.   No.

GLOUCESTER.   Want a yacht and a cruise?

TEDDY.   Oh, you always want to *buy* something, dad.

GLOUCESTER.   Well, I don't know many things that
can't be bought.

TEDDY.   I know *one* thing that can't be—and it's the
only thing I want.

GLOUCESTER.   Now see here, Ted.   If you want this
fellow—I'll buy him for you.

TEDDY.   Don't try to dispose of me.   Let me do it
myself.   First of all I want to be let alone—and *think*.
Men aren't everything on earth.   I won't leave my chickens.   I love them, and there's money in them.   Oh, not
what you call money—but what *I* do.   The kind that
you have the fun of getting *one little thing* with to-day—
and you know if you do the right thing you'll get a
little more to-morrow.   *You* don't know anything about
that kind of exhilaration, dad.

GLOUCESTER [*frankly puzzled and helpless, but doing the
best he can*].   Well, you don't intend spending the rest of
your life sitting here with the chickens, do you?

TEDDY.   I may.   I don't know at all.   Regardless of
you—or any other man in the world—I'm going to take
care of myself.

MARGARET.   You must expect her to feel this way,
Hubert.   As I told you, she's had a great disappointment.   Billy Wade is—well, you can't blame her for fall-

ing head over heels in love with him—if I were her age I'd do the same thing.

GLOUCESTER. Well, let's have a look at the paragon. He must be a rather world-shaking character. At least, I'll pay him back for his work out here.

TEDDY. I'd like to see you try it.

GLOUCESTER. Get him, get him. Where is he?

MARGARET. I'll see if he will come and see you.

[MARGARET *goes into the house.*]

GLOUCESTER. My dear child, I want to make you forget all this and make you happy.

TEDDY. That's what several people have said this afternoon. But I seem to have my own ideas of being happy. Do you want me to go straight back into the same things that made me the selfish, absolutely useless thing that I was?

GLOUCESTER. Don't put it on too thick, Ted. After all, you were one of the most successful girls in New York.

TEDDY. Yes, of course—all those things helped to make me a success. To say nothing of what you did for me. Don't you think I don't want all you can do for me now, dad. One side of me wants it awfully.

GLOUCESTER. And you're going to have it.

TEDDY. But another side has found more precious things than that—not only things that have made me happy—but things that are worth being unhappy for. Why, dad, there's something in the world that you and I never knew anything about—things that never touched you and me at all. It's——

MARGARET [*coming out of the house with* BILLY]. Billy, this is Mr. Gloucester.

BILLY. How do you do?

GLOUCESTER [*after a long, steady look at* BILLY]. It seems my daughter is under very heavy obligations to you for what you've done here this summer. I'd like to express my appreciation in a practical way. It will be quite possible to put you in the way of something good in New York.

BILLY. Thank you; I don't care for it.

GLOUCESTER. Oh! I understand you gave up something pretty fair once before in New York. What was that?

BILLY. I was with Alfred Tate.

GLOUCESTER. I've had a good many deals with Tate. And why did you give it up, may I ask?

BILLY. If you insist, because the business is crooked.

TEDDY. Well, father, what have *you* been doing?

GLOUCESTER. Um! And you gave it up to make a living on this scrubby little place instead?

BILLY. It is pretty poverty-stricken living out here.

GLOUCESTER. And yet you persuaded my daughter it was a good thing for *her* to do.

TEDDY. Father!

BILLY. And it was—wasn't it? Better than the other things that were offered her just then?

GLOUCESTER. And you've had the audacity to say anything about marriage to her—with just *this* to take care of you both? And you weren't counting on her money.

BILLY. Oh, there are other places in the world besides New York. And there's a place where I ought to be—doing things I *know* I could do. But I wanted to see the finest life in America. I've had a look. I'm through. I know what I want.

GLOUCESTER. But you don't want my daughter, I understand.

BILLY. Is it necessary to discuss that?

TEDDY. Buy him, dad, buy him!

GLOUCESTER. Have you made love to her—asked her to marry you, and then changed your mind? Have you the faintest idea of the insufferable impertinence of that?

BILLY. Theodora has decided she wants money, and I can't marry her with that, Mr. Gloucester.

GLOUCESTER. What?

TEDDY. Billy, when you thought I didn't have any—you loved me and I know you love me now. It's the money, dad. He won't take me with it, so I give it up—absolutely—everything you could possibly give me.

GLOUCESTER. Steady, Ted. You're talking very big.

TEDDY [*crossing to* BILLY]. Billy, I'm just the way I was an hour ago—and I love you better than anything in the world. Will you marry me?

GLOUCESTER. My God!

BILLY. *Ted!*

MARGARET. You ask him, too, Hubert. Do all you can to hold him.

GLOUCESTER. I suppose I'm turned out—am I—with all my money? Is there anything I could do—give it away—or anything to induce you to accept me as a father-in-law?

TEDDY. You leave me alone with him a minute, dad, and I'll see what I can do for you.

[GLOUCESTER *goes out after* MARGARET.]

Billy—will you marry me?

BILLY. Ted—I know you've flirted an awful lot, but you're the only girl in my life—and if you're fooling me, I'll kill you!

TEDDY [*putting her arms around his neck*]. Go on, dear. I love that.

THE CURTAIN FALLS

THE HERO

A PLAY IN THREE ACTS

BY

GILBERT EMERY

"I'm just old Andy, I am. But Os—Os was a hero."—*Act Third.*

The Hero is printed for the first time by special permission of the author. Applications for permission to perform this play should be addressed to the author in care of Charles Scribner's Sons.

THE HERO

Gilbert Emery, who wrote formerly under the name of Emery Pottle, was born in Naples, New York, of New England stock. After graduating from Amherst College he became successively a reporter, a magazine editor, and a writer of short stories and of a novel, *Handicapped*. He lived abroad for a number of years, publishing in London, during this period, a book of *Poems* and three small volumes, *The Little Village*, *The Little House*, and *My Friend Is Dead*. Mr. Emery held a commission as first lieutenant in the United States Army during the Great War. He is engaged in the theatrical profession, appearing recently as A. L. Royce in Mr. A. A. Milne's comedy, *The Truth About Blayds*.

The Hero is Mr. Emery's first play. It was written in 1920, shortly after his return from France. In a letter to the editor he says, "My idea in writing it was not so much the effect of the war on Oswald, as its reactions on Hester and Andrew. Oswald's character was set, and I am inclined to think his war experience, in the long run, did not greatly modify it. The real problem of the play is Hester." The editor has analyzed the play in the General Introduction.

The Hero was first put on at a series of matinées at the Longacre Theatre, New York, beginning March 14, 1921. So real was the interest displayed by the discriminating critics that it was withdrawn in order to present it under more favorable theatrical circumstances later. It opened a regular engagement at the Belmont Theatre in the fall of 1921 with a somewhat different cast. Eighty performances were given, when despite the continued critical approval it succumbed to the unfavorable theatrical conditions of the season.

The Hero is published for the first time through the courtesy of the author.

CAST OF CHARACTERS

	Longacre Theatre March, 1921	Belmont Theatre September, 1921
ANDREW LANE	Grant Mitchell.	Richard Bennett.
HESTER LANE (*his wife*)	Kathlene McDonnel.	Alma Belwin.
SARAH LANE (*his mother*)	Blanche Friderici.	Blanche Friderici.
ANDREW LANE, JR. (*his son*)	Graham Lucas.	Joseph Depew.
OSWALD LANE (*his brother*)	Robert Ames.	Robert Ames.
MARTHE ROCHE (*a Belgian*)	Jetta Goudal.	Fania Marinoff.

TIME: 1919.

The scenes are laid in the home of the Lanes in a small suburban town near New York City.

ACT I.   The dining-room.
ACT II.   The sitting-room.   Sunday night three months
        later.
ACT III.   The following morning.

THE HERO*

ACT I

SCENE: *The dining-room of a small rented, jerry-built house. The walls are papered with a bright rosy pattern. The woodwork is of a cold, shabby white. Cheap engravings and sentimental colored lithographs hang upon the walls, relics of the eighties and nineties.*

The furniture consists of a "set" of light oak; there is also a sewing-machine in a corner by a window, and a canary-bird in a cage. To the right are two windows, curtained in light, washable material. On the opposite side of the room is a meretricious fireplace, above it an entrance to a kitchen. At centre is an entrance to the hall, a curtained archway.

The rising curtain presents the room in the growing dusk of an October afternoon. By the window at the right sits SARAH LANE *in an old-fashioned wooden rocking-chair, making the most of the light for her darning. She is a dark, spare, dry, country-bred woman of some sixty years of age, with thin, grizzled hair—restless, querulous, suspicious, lonely, critical of but intensely loyal to her own. Her dress is of black and white print and she wears an apron. By the dining-table, the cloth of which has been replaced by a shabby cover of green, coloring some soldiers which he has drawn on bits of paper, is* LITTLE ANDY, *an attractive, intelligent lad of six or seven, rather delicate in looks. He is happy and absorbed, chanting softly an impromptu sing-song of "See the brown soldier! See the blue soldier! See the red soldier!" over and over.*

SARAH LANE [*irritably*]. For mercy's sake, Andy! You make me as nervous as a cat with that rigamarole of yours.
ANDY. What's nerves-as-a-cat, granny?

SARAH [*darning*]. When you get's old as I am you'll know what nervous is all right I guess. I didn't hardly sleep a wink all last night with the teethache, an' I couldn't find nothing to put on it. It's my belief that that Marthy hides things—jest to pester folks.

ANDY. Marthe's *nice*.

SARAH. Oh! She is—is she?

ANDY. Uh huh!

SARAH. Nicer'n your gran'ma, I s'pose you mean. That's a pretty way to talk. When I was a little girl I was taught to love my own folks best. [*She resumes her darning and begins to sing a hymn in a cracked old voice.*]

"There is a fountain filled with blood . . ."

[ANDY *sings also an improvised tune to the words of* "*Nerves-as-a-cat . . . nerves . . . as-a-cat . . .*"]

SARAH [*singing*].

"Drawn from Emmanuel's veins . . .
And sinners plunged . . ."

ANDY [*interrupting*]. Granny!

SARAH [*still singing*].

"Beneath that flood . . ."

ANDY [*louder, more insistent*]. Granny!

SARAH. What?

ANDY [*rising in his chair and kneeling on the big book on which he is sitting, he talks over the back of the chair*]. Miss Fenton in my kindergarten says you ought to love everybody, 'cause we're all God's li'l' fr'en's.

SARAH [*severely*]. "God's little friends!" Andy Lane, don't you ever let me hear you making free like that again with your Blessed Redeemer!

[*Enter* MARTHE ROCHE *through the kitchen door. She is a young, dark, pretty Belgian girl, plainly but neatly dressed.*]

MARTHE [*as she is passing from the kitchen to the hall*]. I go up-stairs to my room, little man, if you want me——

[*As* MARTHE *comes into the room* ANDY *greets her with a* "*Hello, Marty!*"]

ANDY. Marthe . . . I'm paintin' soldiers!

MARTHE [*glances at the soldiers and smiles approvingly*]. Nice! *Chic—mon petit!* [*She goes out through the door.*]

ANDY [*scrambling down from his chair and crossing to* SARAH *with one of his soldiers*]. Lookit, granny! [*Holds the soldier out to her.*] Soldier!

SARAH [*taking the picture mechanically*]. Soldier! Yer uncle Oswald's a soldier too! [*Suddenly overcome by an emotion that bewilders the child.*] Oh, Ossie! Why don't ye come home! Why don't ye come home! [*She sobs dryly, crumpling the paper soldier unconsciously in her hand.*]

ANDY [*in distress, rescuing his soldier from* SARAH'S *grasp*]. Why, granny! You spoiled my soldier, . . . an' you're cryin'!

SARAH [*recovering sharply and pushing the lad away from her, she goes up to the sideboard to take a dose of patent medicine from a large bottle there; she talks as she goes*]. Where'd Marthy say she was goin'?

ANDY [*returning to his painting*]. Up-stairs.

SARAH [*with bottle and spoon in hand*]. She's always a-settin' in her room, that girl. Ain't worth her keep.

ANDY. What's a keep, granny?

SARAH. None o' yer business. [*Puts bottle and spoon back on the sideboard.*] Yer ma'll be gettin' home pretty soon, and Marthy ought to be settin' the table fer supper.

[ANDY *singing his improvised tune to the words, "What's a keep . . . none o' yer business," repeating it over and over through* SARAH'S *speech.*]

SARAH. You better put yer things away, Andy.

ANDY. Won't Uncle Oswald ever come home, granny?

SARAH [*challengingly, as she comes down to her chair*]. Certainly he'll come home! Who said he wouldn't? [*She sits.*] I guess he'll come home to see his mother! Andy Lane—don't you never believe nothin' anybody ever tells you about your uncle Oswald—never!

ANDY. When Uncle Oswal' comes home, granny—do you think he could teach me how to build a camp-fire?

SARAH [*absently darning again*]. Camp-fire?

ANDY. Yes.

SARAH. Good land! Where'd you ever hear o' that?

ANDY. To the kindergarten. Could he?

SARAH. Could he? I guess so. [*Absently.*] Campfire? Land, yes.

ANDY. Where's Uncle Oswal' live?

SARAH. I dunno! [*Retrospectively, regretfully.*] I dunno! Nobody knows. I ain't seen him for more'n twelve years. He was to the war in France—last we heard. He's ben a hero!

> [*Enter* MARTHE *from the hall. She goes straight to the table and looks at the soldiers that* ANDY *is painting.*]

MARTHE [*approvingly, to* ANDY]. Ah!

SARAH [*startled*]. Mercy!

MARTHE [*continuing to* ANDY]. What a fine painter man!

SARAH. Marthy, how you scared me! I wisht you wouldn't act like a ghost 'round the home.

MARTHE [*quietly*]. The world is full of ghosts since the war. [*Sits at the table and begins to study; for when she came in from the hall she brought with her a text-book on shorthand, a stenographer's note-book, and a pencil.*]

SARAH. You talk like them spiritualists. Gives me the creeps.

ANDY [*speaking in a combination of French and English. He has picked up the French from* MARTHE. *Showing her a soldier*]. Marthe . . . see . . . [*Gets out of chair and comes to* MARTHE.] *Ray-gard-ay! Mes soldats. Ray-gard-ay!*

MARTHE [*her arms about him*]. *Mon petit!* They are beautiful! *Tu es artiste toi!*

SARAH. Marthe, I don't want you should teach that child anything in that language that ain't fit for his gran'ma to hear!

ANDY [*singing*].

> "Au clair de la lune
>   Mon ami, Pierrot,
> Prêtes-moi ta plume
>   Pour ecrire un mot . . ."

SARAH [*rubbing her ear*]. We're goin' to get news o' somethin'! My left ear has itched me all day—an' I never knew it to fail. [*Looks over at* MARTHE, *who is studying.*] Marthy!

[MARTHE, *absorbed, does not hear her.*]
Marthy!

MARTHE. Yes, madame?

SARAH. You better begin to clear up and get ready for supper.

MARTHE. [*rises and goes to* ANDY, *behind the table*]. Come, then, my little cabbage, pack up the paint-box.

ANDY. I don't want to . . .

MARTHE [*reprovingly*]. The soldiers must obey orders!

SARAH. I do' know what's keeping Andy's mother. She was a-goin' to get me a little mite of assafetty . . . to the drug-store—an' Andrew ought to be gettin' home soon, too. [To ANDY.] Come, now . . . clear up your things and get ready for supper.

> [*The outer door is heard to shut off left, in the hall. Enter* HESTER *in street dress. She carries a hand-bag, two library books, and a periodical, the "Christian Advocate."*]

ANDY [*rushing to her and seizing her arm*]. It's mummy! It's mummy! What'd you bring me, mummy? What'd you bring me? [*Pulls her down stage to left of table.*]

> [HESTER *is a young woman about twenty-six. Neither pretty nor beautiful, she has yet attributes of both states. She has freshness, frankness, and a good deal of charm. Her expression seems to indicate some inner dissatisfaction. Her garments, quite in keeping with her modest circumstances, show good taste in their becoming lines, and she wears them with a certain distinction.*]

HESTER. Yes, dear—mummy's home. Why—you're all half in the dark! [*She lights the electric drop-light, a hideous thing of varicolored glass over the dining-table.*] There! [*She pushes a button at the left of the door at centre, and illuminates the room.*] You'll ruin your eyes, mother . . . sewing like that.

ANDY [*insistently*]. What'd you bring me, mummy?

HESTER. I've brought two new books from the library —and your *Christian Advocate*, mother—and I shouldn't be surprised if there were some "Life-Savers" in my bag for a little boy named . . .

> [ANDY *seizes her hand-bag and opens it.*]

Dearie! Don't grab! And don't spill everything out!
[*As he takes the candies out of the bag.*]   You may have
just two.   [*She crosses back of the table.*]

SARAH [*rising, going to the window and pulling down the
shades*].   Lucky somebody saves 'lectricity in this family
—er that there's any *to* save.

[MARTHE *is carrying* ANDY's *playthings, that litter the
     floor, over to the serving-table, and placing them on
     the bottom shelf.*]

You're allus complainin' these days, Hester, for somethin'
you haven't got.   What's got into you? 'S a bad sign.

ANDY [*running to* SARAH *with the candies*].   Granny . . .
you can have two—too.

SARAH.   Do' want 'em—spoil my supper!   [*To* HES-
TER.]   Did you get me that assafetty?

HESTER.   Oh, mother—I——

SARAH [*in lofty resignation*].   Forgot it!   I expected as
much.   [*Sits again in the rocker.*]   Well . . . I can pass
another sleepless night.

HESTER.   I . . . Just let me get my things off and
I'll . . .

[MARTHE *takes her hat and coat as she removes them.*]
Oh, thank you, Martha.   Did you get some studying
done?

MARTHE.   It is very hard.   I try my most best—but I
get discouraged often.   [*She goes out into the hall with*
HESTER's *wraps.*]

HESTER.   I don't wonder.   Everything seems all wrong
nowadays.   But don't worry.   It'll come all right, I
guess.   [*Turns to* ANDY.]   Darling—have you been a good
boy?

ANDY [*showing his painted soldiers*].   I been paintin'.
See my soldiers, mummy?   I love soldiers.

SARAH.   He's set there the hull livelong afternoon,
Hester.   They ain't a thing the matter with him.   I can
tell you my boys wasn't coddled like that.

HESTER [*looking at the soldiers*].   Yes, dear, they're
beautiful.   [*As she sees* SARAH *looking at her reprovingly.*]
I know, mother—I know.   [*She evidently has something on
her mind that absorbs her.*]   Martha!

Marthe [*appearing in the hall*]. Yes, Mrs. Lane. [*Comes in at centre.*]

Hester. I wish you'd run down to Simpson's drugstore and get a little assafœtida for . . .

Marthe [*puzzled over the word*]. Fettit . . . ?

[Andy, *sitting on the arm of an old leather chair by the fireplace, is so amused at this that he falls over backward into the chair, mimicking* Marthe's *attempt at pronouncing the word.*]

Hester. Here! I'll write the name on this piece of paper. For mother, it is.

Andy. Take me?

Hester. Yes, you can take Andy.

Andy [*clapping his hands*]. Oh, goody, goody!

Hester. Only wrap his throat well . . . [*Giving* Marthe *the piece of paper with the word written on it.*] Twenty-five cents' worth. [*Gets a coin out of her hand-bag.*] Here it is. [*Gives coin to* Andy.] And don't lose it. Run along now. [*She follows them to the hall as* Andy *and* Marthe *exit.*]

Sarah [*in the rocking-chair*]. An' I dunno's assafetty's what I need, anyway. Guess a dose of Rochelle salts'd be better. I et somethin' that kinda laid on my stomick. [*Suddenly becomes aware that* Hester *is looking at her with a curious expression.*] What?

Hester [*coming down toward* Sarah, *her eyes shining with excitement*]. Mother! I've got something to tell you. While I was out I met Hilda Pierce at the library. She's just back from France. You remember her. She went with the Red Cross. Oh, she had such a wonderful experience!

Sarah. Women better stay to home where they belong. If the men want to fight, let 'em.

Hester. Hilda was in a sort of group—I don't know —that visited hospitals and things—wrote letters for the men—and talked to them.

Sarah. I guess she talked to 'em, all right.

Hester. Mother—she saw—Oswald!

Sarah [*rises and comes to her in agitation*]. Oswal'! *Tell* it—can't you? Can't you talk? [*In sudden fear.*] He ain't . . . dead . . . is he?

HESTER [*patting her hand soothingly*]. No . . . he isn't dead. Or, at least, I don't think so. It was in a hospital —I can't remember the place—and this man was wounded —it was toward the end of the war it happened. Hilda got acquainted with this man. His name was Lane, he said. Then—one day it all came out that he was Andrew's brother.

SARAH [*with almost a sob*]. Oh, my Lord! Was he real sick, did she say?

HESTER. His leg was bad, but the doctors said he'd get well. He didn't know anything about Andrew being married to me, or you being with us, or anything. Hilda was going to write a letter to you for him, but before she got to it they moved him off to another hospital—somewhere— and she never saw him again.

SARAH [*anxiously*]. And she do' know where he is now?

HESTER. No. But, mother, he was with the French Army, not with ours. In a thing they call the "Foreign Legion." And he was all decorated. He'd been perfectly splendid, she said. Just a regular hero. Oh, mother, I think it's just fine—after everything that . . . that . . .

SARAH [*abruptly and suspiciously*]. Everything? What'd Andrew ever tell you about Oswal', I'd like to know?

HESTER [*getting her work-basket from the machine*]. Why—nothing so very much, except that he was—well, pretty wild when he was a boy, and ran away and all that. Why?

SARAH [*only half assured that* HESTER *is speaking the truth*]. Nothin'! That's why. An' if you ever hear anything real bad about my Oswal,' t'ain't true! An' don't you believe it is. He wa'n't such a good son as Andrew, but he wa'n't bad. He wa'n't bad, I tell you!

HESTER [*sitting at the table and mending one of her gloves*]. Andrew never said he was.

SARAH. How'd she say he looked?

HESTER. Hilda said he was handsome. Handsome, in spite of being sick. Oh, I'd have given—I don't know what, for her experience.

SARAH. I guess Oswald's 'bout as good-lookin' as the
Lord intended men-folks should be, though that ain't
nothin' for a man to boast of. She said he wa'n't wounded
bad?

HESTER. No. His foot or his leg, I think.

SARAH [*meditatively*]. Oh, dear—if I could only see 'im!
Hester, you ain't suffered. You ain't suffered. I tell
you women has to *suffer*. Then they *know*.

HESTER [*not bitterly, but regretfully*]. Oh, it's hard
enough this is, when you're never sure from one week's
end to another where the money's coming from to pay
the bills. It seems to me that lately, everywhere I go,
everything I do, I just find pretty things thrown in my
face . . . Only, I can't have them. It isn't that it's
always *pretty* things, though I do like what's nice, but *interesting* things. Things that give women a chance to look
outside their own little dooryards—I don't know—to *be*
something. Something that counts more in the world—I
can't express it and I don't suppose you'd understand.
But it's always been like that—just scraping along,
mamma and I, in that boarding-house in Brooklyn.

SARAH [*who has listened to these words with sniffs of
disdain*]. Well, Hester Lane! Of all the speeches I
ever heard! *Pretty* things! *Interestin'* things! I never!
I dunno what women's comin' to nowadays! Votin'!
I s'pose you'll want to be votin' too—an' dancin'! Women's old's I be hoppin' 'round like monkeys on a hot
stove-lid; and a smokin' of them nasty cigarettes! Their
legs a-showin' at one end, and their backs and bosoms at
'tother! You, a married woman with a child, an' 's good
a husband's a girl should want. Talkin' like that! I'm
ashamed of you! Hester! *A chance!* Chance, fiddlesticks!

HESTER [*out of patience*]. You don't understand! I
can't tell you! I can't ever tell you. You always scold
me like this.

SARAH [*with sarcasm*]. Next thing you'll want to get a
divorce, I s'pose—like all the rest of 'em.

HESTER [*amused*]. Divorce? You don't think I'm
going to run away, do you?

SARAH [*horrifiedly*]. Hester—for the Lord's sake! You ain't thinkin' of runnin' away?

HESTER [*clearing the toys from table and getting ready for the evening meal. The toys she puts on the bottom shelf of the serving-table*]. I've never thought of such a thing. Run! Run where? What for? With a husband and baby who need me? [*More softly as she goes to the right of the rocking-chair.*] Mother—didn't you feel—sometimes, on that awful farm—that you'd give anything to have a chance? Didn't you?

SARAH [*in an embarrassed voice and with a note of confession*]. They was allus a dress I wanted. I see it once in the city when I was a young gal. White muslin with flounces and lace and a green ribbon edge to 'em. [*Dryly, coming out of her mood.*] But I never got it.

HESTER. Poor mother!

[*The two women busy themselves in getting the room ready for supper, clearing the things from the dining-table, changing the table-cloth, and setting out dishes. The following conversation takes place while they are thus occupied.*]

SARAH. Hester, I do' want you should get no foolish notions in your head about bein' too good for your home. Andrew's a good man, Hester, a good man.

HESTER [*mechanically, busy with her own thoughts*]. Oh, yes, Andrew's a good man.

SARAH [*eying her keenly*]. He's better'n you think.

HESTER. Than I think?

SARAH. Maybe you'll have to git your nose right down to the grindstone, young lady, before you know as much as you think you do now.

HESTER. I've suffered enough. There are different ways of suffering.

SARAH [*taking the white table-cloth from the drawer in the sideboard and dropping it on the table before* HESTER]. Pooh! You! You're like all the women nowadays—wantin' somethin' you haven't got an' callin' that sufferin'. [*She goes out to the kitchen. The front door-bell rings.* HESTER *answers it. A man's voice—*OSWALD'S—*is heard in the hall.*]

OSWALD [*off stage*]. Does Andrew Lane live here?

Hester. Yes. But he isn't home yet. Did you wish to see him about something?

Oswald. Well, I kinda wanted to . . .

Hester. Won't you step in? [Hester *appears at the doorway with* Oswald. *He is a young man about twenty-eight, of more than ordinary good looks, somewhat marred by dissipation, rough living, and vagabond wanderings. Despite his battered past, he has kept a certain appealing young charm, a combination of boyishness, impudence, high spirits, recklessness, virility, and moral weakness. The sort of man likely to be rashly loved and rashly forgiven by most women, many men, children, and dogs. He is dressed very shabbily in cheap garments of various colors and qualities. In his buttonhole are tiny ribbons indicative of military decorations. He is slightly lame and carries a stick. On a lead he has a wretched little yellow dog.*] My husband ought to be here very soon. [*Glancing at the clock on the mantel.*] He's generally on the 5.45. If you care to wait——

Oswald [*gazing about the room with interest*]. Why—no —I guess I'll . . . maybe I'll go back toward the station, I might run across him.

Hester [*eying him curiously*]. Yes, you might. Who shall I tell him called—if you shouldn't happen to . . .?

Oswald. Why . . . I used to know 'im—a good while ago. I was from the same hick town as he was, and I happened to hear he lived here. I guess you're his wife, ain't you?

Hester. Yes, I am. [*Smiling.*] Andrew would be so pleased, I'm sure, to see anybody who—— His mother, Mrs. Lane, is living with us. You very likely remember her. If you'd care to see her, she . . .

Oswald [*turns away embarrassed*]. Don't trouble now . . . no . . . I . . . How is the old lady?

Hester. Oh . . . Mother Lane's pretty well, thank you. She . . .

Oswald [*grins as he sees a patent-medicine bottle on sideboard*]. Still taking patent medicine, is she?

Hester [*with an amused little laugh*]. Oh! You do know her, don't you?

Oswald [*dryly*]. Used to. [*Awkwardly.*] Well . . .

guess I'll be pushin' along. Pleased to have met you, Mrs. Lane. [*Sees a match-safe on the mantel.*] Say . . . could I have one of those matches? [*He has an unlighted cigarette in his fingers.*] I'm all out.

HESTER [*amused and amazed*]. Oh, yes.

OSWALD [*goes to the mantel to get a match. He catches sight of a photograph of* LITTLE ANDY *on the mantel and looks at it admiringly*]. Say . . . excuse *me* . . . but that's a fine little kid there. Geez—he's a peach!

HESTER [*flattered*]. Well—we think so. That's our little boy. Little Andrew.

OSWALD. You don't say so? Guess Andrew's pretty well fixed, ain't he? Looks pretty nice here. You and the kid—and all. [*Smiles impudently and charmingly.*]

HESTER [*flushing*]. Well—we of course—it's our home —and we . . .

OSWALD. Some fellows are lucky. Now look at me! You wouldn't think I owned part of the Waldorf-Astoria and two cars, and had champagne for breakfast, would you?

HESTER [*catching the spirit of his jesting*]. Well—of course . . . [*She smiles.* OSWALD *grins with her boyishly.*]

OSWALD. Well—I'll prob'ly see Andrew at the station. Glad to have met you.—Good night to you, Mrs. Lane.

HESTER. What name shall I say if . . .

OSWALD. Little Willie—little Willie Smart! G'night! [*He goes out into the hall. A door is heard to shut.* HESTER *has followed him up to the door. She glances into the hall in amusement and astonishment at the odd visitor.*]

SARAH [*entering from the kitchen, a shawl over her shoulders and a cup in her hand*]. I run over to them Conleys to borrow a little mite o' m'lasses for my gingerbread. Who was that you was talkin' to just now?

HESTER [*crosses to the sideboard, takes an apron from the upper drawer, and puts it on*]. Why—he was the funniest man! You couldn't help but like him. He was just as fresh as he could be. Came to see Andrew. Said he knew him as a boy. And he knows you, too, mother.

SARAH. Land sakes! Who was he?

HESTER [*setting the table*]. He said his name was Willie Smart.

SARAH. Smart? Smart? Wa'n't no Smarts in Fisherville that I ever heard of. What'd he look like?

HESTER. Poor and sickly, but sort of nice—sort of—I don't know. He had a little dog, and he was lame.

SARAH. There wa'n't no Smarts there, never! Hester, you mark my words, he's a burglar, sure as you live and breathe.

HESTER. Nonsense, mother. I'd have trusted him.

SARAH. You're a fool. You're too tender-hearted.

HESTER. Suppose somebody turned your son Oswald out—if he was poor and sick. I guess you'd resent that.

SARAH. I tell you there wa'n't no Smarts there. You get that Pierce girl here to-morrow. I want to talk to her 'bout Oswal'.

HESTER [*stops setting the table—abruptly*]. What made Oswald run—really? What made him run away?

SARAH [*letting the more human side of her nature show for a moment*]. Hester—they's things between a woman and her husband, an' between a woman and her son—no matter what deviltry he gets into—that no man can make head nor tail of. But a woman knows. [*Recovering her usual manner and starting for the kitchen door.*] You better fix your table—an' I'm goin' to make my gingerbread. [*The telephone-bell rings.*] Ain't that that old telephone ringin'?

HESTER. It's the coal man, I guess. He said he'd telephone to-day the best he could do about our bill. [*She goes out into the hall to answer the telephone, talking as she goes.*] I don't know how we're going to get along. It's all so high.

SARAH. My mouth tastes like a copper kittle. Bile, I guess. [*She goes into the kitchen.*]

HESTER [*out in the hall, at the telephone*]. Yes—yes— [*More excited.*] No!—Now—Oh! [*Runs excitedly into the room and to the swing door of the kitchen.*] Mother— Mother Lane!

SARAH [*as she enters*]. What? What is it?

HESTER. He—he's here!

SARAH. Who?

HESTER. Your Oswald!

SARAH. Oswal'! I don't believe it!

HESTER. Andrew! He's telephoned! To prepare us! From the station. He's found him! They're coming! He and Oswald. *Now!* In a minute!

SARAH. Oh, my good Lord!

[*The two women stare at each other, bewildered.*]

HESTER [*with a sudden thought*]. I wonder if . . . if it could be . . .? Why . . . yes! *Willie Smart!*

SARAH. [*She sinks into a chair by the table.*] My boy—Oswal'!—Comin' home!—Are you sure?—They ain't no mistake? Twelve years!—My boy!

[HESTER *soothes her with exclamations of sympathy.*] Oh, my Lord! He's comin' home! [*Bustling about.*] Well—he'll want his supper! We better git the table set right off! [*As she stands by the table she takes a fork in her hand and holds it out.*] What'd I tell you this mornin'—when I dropped that fork and it stuck right up in the floor? Visitor comin'! Is they any sour milk in the house? If there is I'll mix up a pancake-batter fer supper. Oswal' allus loved pancakes. Hester, don't stand there's if you was moonstruck! Do somethin'! My land! My land! [SARAH *rushes off into the kitchen.*]

[HESTER *has paused in the act of setting the table, a dish in her hand, as one gazing on some inner vision.*]

HESTER [*back of the table, half to herself*]. It's so—so strange—coming—like this—just after Hilda's telling us. It makes me feel . . .

[SARAH *rushes in from the kitchen.*]

SARAH. Where's he goin' to sleep, I'd like to know?

HESTER. Oh, dear! Well—he'll have to have Martha's bed—that's all. He's been a soldier and deserves the best we can do. And Martha will have to sleep on that cot in the attic.

SARAH. And plenty good enough for her, I say. I ain't a-goin' to have her tryin' none of her monkey-shines on my Oswal'! [*She hurries back into the kitchen.*]

HESTER. [*She crosses left to the mirror; half to herself.*] Oh, somebody—somebody who'd understand what I . . .

[*She is at the centre of the stage when the door is heard to slam. There is the sound of feet and voices.*]

ANDREW LANE [*calling from the hall*]. Ma! Hester!
Hey there! We got 'im! By gosh! We caught a hero!

[ANDREW *and* OSWALD *enter at the arch.* OSWALD *still
has the dog on the lead and is carrying a battered old
suitcase.*

[ANDREW LANE *is a man about forty, growing fattish
and bald. He is dressed in worn but very neat clothes.
His face shows unmistakably his simplicity of nature,
his indefatigable good humor, his affectionate heart,
his lack of mental capacity to carry him further than
he is to-day—a faithful and honest insurance clerk—
and his reliability as a husband, a son, and a citizen.
His fixed belief that everything is going to turn out
right helps him cheerfully to face the financial worries
from which he has never in his life had a respite.
He has an irritating trick of snapping his fingers as
he talks, which is particularly distasteful to* HESTER.
He carries in his hands two packages from the grocer's.]

HESTER [*running to the door*]. Mother . . . come . . .!
[*Catches sight of* OSWALD.] Willie Smart *is* Oswald!

[SARAH *rushes in from the kitchen and into* OSWALD'S
arms, who is in the centre of the stage, where ANDREW
has shoved him, good-naturedly. ANDREW *is laughing in boisterous good humor.*]

OSWALD [*while* ANDREW *and* HESTER *look on delightedly*].
Ma!

[SARAH *sobs the inarticulate motherings of a woman to
whom the prodigal son is still a boy of sixteen, the
age at which she last saw him.*]

Why, ma! Don't take on so. Ma! . . . Smile for the
gentleman! [*Holds her off at arms' length.*] Ain't a day
older, is she, Andy?

ANDREW. Should say not! Regular chicken!

SARAH [*who, unused to displaying emotion, has recovered
her poise*]. Well—so you've got here at last. Took you
long enough. You got here for your birthday. Lemme
look at you.

ANDREW [*hilariously*]. Well, ma, what do you think of
what the cat dragged in? [*Kisses* HESTER, *who is in front
of the table.*] Hey there, old son—this is your sister, Hester—guess she'll give you a kiss, too. Go to it, Bo!

OSWALD. I never had a sister . . .

ANDREW [*laughing*]. He's bashful!

OSWALD [*with his most disarming smile, looks straight into* HESTER'S *eyes, then goes to her and kisses her on the lips*]. Gee—I'm glad it's you!

HESTER [*rather confused*]. And I never had a brother— Oh . . . why didn't you tell me it was you just now? I almost guessed it . . . I . . .

OSWALD. Well—what do you know about that? Say, sister, we've got to make up for lost time.

ANDREW [*laughing*]. No time like the present!

OSWALD. I wanted to see Andy first. I didn't know whether he'd want a poor nut like me to come in here and muss up his front parlor.

ANDREW. Aw, shut up! Ain't he the card? Comes walking right up to me when I got out of the train, he did. [*Seeing* OSWALD *with his hat in his hand, he crosses up to him and takes the hat.*] Here—gimme that! Just landed this morning, he did! And he says "Hello, And'!" natural's if he'd been walking in for the last ten years. I darn near thought I'd gone nuts when he says "Hello, And'!" Just like . . . [*He goes out to the hall with* OSWALD'S *hat, chattering on to himself.*]

SARAH [*seeing the dog*]. My Lord o' love! For mercy's sake, where'd you get that dog?

OSWALD. She's a war dog. Ain't you, Cafard? Cafard's her name. French. Means "the blues." I collected her in Belgium, or she collected me.

HESTER [*on her knees and petting the dog*]. Old sweetie! [*To* OSWALD, *beside her.*] We'd never have forgiven you, if you hadn't come straight to us!

OSWALD. Honest!

SARAH. I dunno what we'll do with a dog—dirtyin' the house all up. I guess Little Andy'll like 'im.

ANDREW [*entering*]. Oh—he'll be tickled pink. Where is Little Andy?

HESTER. He's gone to the drug-store with Martha.

ANDREW. We got a great kid, Os . . . wait till you see 'im. He's sharper'n a tack.

OSWALD [*looking admiringly at* HESTER]. Looks to me

as if you'd got pretty near everything a fellow needs, Andy, to keep comfortable.

ANDREW [*arms about* HESTER]. Oh—we kinda manage to trail 'long by the band-wagon, don't we, Hester?

[HESTER *nods a tolerant smile*—ANDREW *looks at the dog again.*]

Say . . . speaking of dogs, I heard a good one to-day!

HESTER. Now, Andrew . . .

ANDREW. Honest I did, Hess. "If I cut that dog open what would I find?" [*Thinks for a second.*] No . . . that ain't it. Here it is—"If I cut that dog's lungs open —what would I find?" [*He grins happily as he answers the riddle.*] Why—*the seat of his pants!*

HESTER. Oh, Andrew! You ought to be ashamed.

OSWALD. Gosh! And'! [*He is now sitting in the rocking-chair, and* SARAH *is hovering around him.*] Are you still at them old gags? First time I heard that I kicked the slats out of my cradle, didn't I, ma? You ought to muzzle him, Hester.

HESTER [*laughingly*]. I will.

ANDREW [*still laughing*]. Well—we can't all be born with a funny-bone.

[HESTER *starts for the kitchen.* ANDREW *picks up the two packages which he laid on the table at the beginning of the scene.*]

Here's your coffee, Hess . . . [*Following her toward the kitchen.*] And your prunes. Cost just double now.

HESTER [*at the door up left*]. And the——?

ANDREW [*snapping his fingers*]. Gosh! I forgot the soap!

[HESTER *goes into the kitchen, followed by* ANDREW. *They are heard off stage talking about* OSWALD'S *unexpected return.*]

SARAH. You look kinda peaked, Oswal'. Ain't you well? Does your foot hurt you? You ain't had nothin' to eat, I bet, since you joined that ol' war— The idee! Comin' and pretendin' to be Willie Smart! If I'd a-seen you I'd a Willie Smarted you!

OSWALD. Sure! I'm well, ma.

[HESTER *and* ANDREW *enter again from the kitchen.*]

Don't you fret! We et the Germans!

ANDREW.   Sausages!

[*There is a general laugh.*]

OSWALD.   I was afraid you'd spank me, like you used to!

ANDREW.   And she *did*, too!

SARAH.   Guess you want a good tonic.   That's what!

OSWALD.   Guess I want some of ma's cooking—to take the taste o' Huns out o' my mouth.

[*General laughter.*]

SARAH.   My soul and body!   Guess folks better eat first and visit afterwards.   And that Marthy gone out— [*Crosses over to the kitchen.*]   Come, Hester— [*Exits into kitchen.*]

OSWALD [*rising*].   Who's Martha?   Got two kids, Andy?

ANDREW.   Aw—quit yer kiddin'!

HESTER.   I don't know whether you'll understand about Martha—you see——

[HESTER *and* ANDREW *come close to* OSWALD *to tell him about* MARTHE.]

ANDREW.   Martha's a girl Hess took— I call her Mattie for short—makes her feel more at home.

HESTER.   Yes . . .

ANDREW.   Oh—Hess got all het up about the war. You see, Mattie's a Belgian.   Some folks brought her over here in 1915——

HESTER.   The second year of the war——

ANDREW.   She's an orphan.   Folks killed in the war— right in front of her.   She kinda helps Hester.   She'll go 'way pretty soon, I guess.   Studyin' to be a stenographer . . .

HESTER.   Of course, being a foreigner it's hard for her and . . .

ANDREW.   We give her what we can—and—it's an expense housing her.   But the missis was all for it.   I dunno as . . . [*He walks out to the hall, talking to himself as he goes about* MATTIE.   *He changes to his house-coat—an antiquated jacket.   The gist of his mutterings is as follows:*] Mattie's all right, I s'pose— 'Course she can't help what happened in the war—etc.

HESTER.   I wanted to do something.   Andrew thought

we couldn't. We—oh—it seemed so dreadful not to help poor little Belgium! It wasn't much—but it was our little bit. I—I wanted to do such a lot—you understand? Like you. I—I wanted to— Oh, we've heard—we've heard just to-day about *you!*

ANDREW [*has now changed into his house-coat, and comes out of the hall with a pair of gaily embroidered slippers in his hand. He goes down by the big chair*]. She ain't a bad little girl—Mattie ain't.

OSWALD [*to* HESTER, *flattered*]. Me? Aw—who's been handin' you the bunk about me? Don't you . . .

HESTER. You were *splendid!* We know—and you were wounded!

ANDREW. What'd you think he was—a rocking-chair soldier?

HESTER [*her eyes shining with excitement. Turns to* ANDREW]. Andrew—he was just wonderful! Why, Hilda Pierce is back from France, and she says— [*Looking at* OSWALD, *who is facing them.*] And just look at the ribbons in his buttonhole!

ANDREW [*laughing boisterously*]. Thought they was somethin' some girl give him.

[SARAH LANE *enters from the kitchen and starts for the sideboard, just in time to hear the last of this remark.*]

SARAH. Mercy, Oswal'! You ain't *married*, are you?

OSWALD [*front of rocking-chair, grinning*]. Sure, ma! Two twins right outside in the limousine. I call 'em Clemenceau an' Lloyd George for short. Want to see 'em?

[*General laughter, during which* SARAH *goes to the sideboard and gets a dish.*]

SARAH [*as she goes to the kitchen door*]. Smarty! [*At the door up left.*] Well—you needn't bring none of them foreign hussies home to me!

[*As she leaves by the kitchen door the outer door slams. There is a burst of exclamations out of which we hear——*]

HESTER [*running up to door*]. There they are now!

ANDREW [*crossing and taking the dog from* OSWALD]. It's "Little Andy."

HESTER. Andy, hurry——

[LITTLE ANDY and MARTHE *appear in the arch.   During the excitement* MARTHE *disappears.*]

ANDREW.   See who's here!

HESTER [*to* LITTLE ANDY, *who stands gazing in wonder at the stranger*].   Look, darling!   There's Uncle Oswald!

   [*The lad runs straight down the stage and into* OSWALD'S *arms.*]

OSWALD [*sweeping the boy from his feet and holding him high in his arms*].   Hello there, General Pershing! Where'd you leave your staff?

   [ANDREW *is taking the scene in from the centre of the stage, looking on with paternal pride.*]

HESTER [*taking off the boy's hat and coat as she speaks*]. It's Uncle Oswald, darling!   He's come home from France, where he was—oh, just the most wonderful soldier——

ANDY [*fascinated by his new uncle, and quite at his ease*]. Granny says you're a hero!   Can you build a camp-fire?

OSWALD.   Aw—quit your kiddin', general——

   [OSWALD *is quite as pleased with* LITTLE ANDY *as* ANDY *is with him.*]

ANDY [*as he sees the dog, held by* ANDREW *on the leash*]. Lemme down!   I want to pat 'im.   [*He gets down from* OSWALD'S *arms and runs to the dog, going down on his knees to caress the animal.*]   Look, daddy!

ANDREW [*looking critically at the dog*].   What kind is he, Os?

OSWALD.   He's a she!

   [*General laughter.*]

ANDY.   Uncle Os . . . granny says you're a hero!

OSWALD [*on his knees by the dog*].   Ssh!   Don't you tell Cafard I'm a hero.   She might bite me.

ANDY.   What is a hero, Uncle Os?

OSWALD.   Oh—   [*Grins.*]   A hero is a guy that does somethin' he wouldn't a-done, if he'd stopped to think.

   [*General laughter.*]

ANDY.   Show me how to build a camp-fire, Uncle Oswald?

OSWALD.   Sure, I'll teach you how to build a camp-fire!

ANDY [*clapping his hands with joy*].   Oh, goody, goody!

HESTER [*calls*].   Martha!   I guess she's gone up-stairs.

I'll run and tell her to fix the bed for Oswald. Then you can bring him up, Andy, so he can wash for supper if he wants to. [*To* LITTLE ANDY.] Andy—you take doggy . . . [*To* OSWALD *shyly*.] What's his name, Oswald?

OSWALD. Her name is Cafard.

HESTER. Take Cafard—out to granny in the kitchen, and see if she can't find him a nice little dinner. [*Goes out into the hall*.]

ANDREW [*takes* LITTLE ANDY *to kitchen with the dog*]. There you go, Hagenbeck!

> [ANDY *takes the dog out*. ANDREW *and* OSWALD *are left alone. There is a pause. Each is looking at the other, old memories in their minds*. OSWALD *is rather self-conscious*.]

Well, Os?

OSWALD. Well, Andy?

ANDREW [*nodding toward the arch*]. Pretty nice little girl, huh?

OSWALD. Ay—ugh!

ANDREW. Le's sit down. That bum foot of yours—

> [OSWALD *sits in the rocker*, ANDREW *sits at the left of the table*.]

Well—we got our little home. 'Tain't the Waldorf, but I guess we're pretty lucky, all right. Kinda hard to keep things going these days what with old high-cost-of-living and all. But "Don't worry's" my motto——

OSWALD. Mine, too.

ANDREW. When pa died—you knew about his dyin', didn't you, Os?

OSWALD. Um-hum.

ANDREW. Ma come here to live with us. Pa didn't leave a red cent. When everything was settled, and the debts paid, there wasn't a darn thing but just a little furniture ma hung onto.

OSWALD [*with a little embarrassment*]. I was a good deal of a darn fool in those days, Andy—I dunno why I ever got into that mix-up.

ANDREW [*awkwardly*]. I s'pose most every fellow wonders that—when it's over—I don't know—I'm no better than anybody else—don't pretend to be. Only I never had the money—had to work too hard to raise much Cain. And now—with Hess and the kid—I——

OSWALD [*sincerely*]. Well, you can mark it right down in your diary that little old Os is going to play straight from now on. Honest, I am, And'.

ANDREW. I'm glad to hear it, Os . . .

[OSWALD *has a cigarette in his mouth and is searching his pockets for a match.* ANDREW *takes a match from his own pocket, crosses to* OSWALD, *and strikes the match.*]

We're right with you. [*Lights* OSWALD'S *cigarette.*]

OSWALD. Say—was pa ?—When he found out——?

ANDREW [*frankly—but kindly*]. It pretty near killed him. I guess it *did*, anyway. You see—well—the money part of it was awful tough—but when it came out about Millie—he—well, I guess you know how he'd feel. Os— she's *on the streets* now in Rochester, they say.

OSWALD [*comes toward* ANDREW]. Damn it! I'm sorry—but everything wasn't my fault. If pa'd ever treated me like— Oh well—what's the use——

ANDREW. Boy—I don't want you should ever say anything—too—hard against the old man. He come right acrost when it was up to him. And so did ma. And nobody ever knew the worst of it but old Peters in the bank and us. Folks didn't even know about Millie.

OSWALD. Say, Andy— [*Nods toward the arch*, HES-TER *in his mind, embarrassed.*] Does—*she* know ?

ANDREW. Hess ?

OSWALD. Um-hum.

ANDREW. No. I never told Hester a word—beyond— well, that you was a pretty frisky young fellow, and run away from home. Pa and I—you know that part. He worked and paid back the money on that check you— and the bank let it drop. It came hard for us, Os, but if you've learned your lesson—why——

OSWALD [*dropping uneasily back into the rocker*]. Much obliged—Andy.

ANDREW. That's all right. [*Comes over to him.*] And, Os, I appreciate your wantin' to see me first before you told Hess who you were. [*Putting his hand on* OSWALD'S *shoulder affectionately.*] I don't want to pick open any old sores, boy, specially to-night, when you've just come home to us. And I just want to tell you that what's done's done. Nothin's gained by harping on old mistakes. You're back, and I guess you've about wiped out all that tomfoolishness—or worse—by what you've done over there—in the war. I guess they didn't give you those ribbons in your buttonhole for lookin' at the view. But now the old war's over and everybody's glad of it. Boy, I want you should make my home your home till you get a start, till you get a job, gol darn it, till you get a little home and a cutie of your own. See? [*He sings in comic fashion:*]

> "With his baby on his knee,
>   He's as happy as can be—
> For there's no place like Home, Sweet Home!"

OSWALD [*rises and goes to* ANDREW]. You're damn kind, Andy. I—I—appreciate how you all have treated me. Far's the war's concerned, as the Irishman says, "'Twas a hell of a war, but 'twas the only war we had!"

ANDREW. Gee! That's a good one! Have to remember that.

OSWALD. I'm goin' to pull up, Andy, and—well, I got one or two little things in my head. I'm going to pay you back every cent. We'll be rich yet, and then, by God, we'll . . .

[SARAH *appears at the kitchen door.*]

SARAH. Just wanted to see if you was really there, sonny!

ANDREW [*jovially*]. No, ma—he's gone to take his music-lesson!

SARAH. Your ma's making pancakes!

OSWALD. Hurray for ma! *Bocou* pancakes!

SARAH. No! *Sour-milk pancakes!* [*She goes into the kitchen.*]

OSWALD. Look! You got ma pullin' them nifties! Gee, And'! It's *bon* to be back . . . just lemme get started again and . . .

ANDREW [*consulting the book*]. Say—d'j ever hear this one, Os? "If a man ate his mother-in-law, what'd he be?"

OSWALD. No, and I don't want to. All the eats I'm interested in now is ma's pancakes. Say, you ought to have that Joe Miller nerve killed, And'!

ANDREW. No . . . honest . . . this is a good one.

[HESTER *appears in the arch.*]

HESTER. Now you boys have got to stop talking and get right out of the dining-room. We'll never get supper ready. [*Comes down to the table.*]

OSWALD. Gee! Listen to General Joffer! Where's the nearest dugout, And'?

ANDREW [*in great good humor*]. Did I ever tell you this one, Hess?

[OSWALD *whispers laughingly to* HESTER.]

Just telling Os . . . "If a man ate his mother-in-law, what would he be?"

HESTER *and* OSWALD [*hand in hand they shout before* ANDREW *has a chance to speak*]. For Heaven's sake, stop! You give us an awful pain!

ANDREW [*not at all discomfited, determined to get out the joke*]. You think you're funny, don't you? *Glad-i-a-tor!*

HESTER. Help!

OSWALD. Ow!

HESTER. Now, Andy, you go up in the attic and open that trunk and get out another blanket for Oswald's bed, while Martha sets the table. Now march!

ANDREW [*goes to the fireplace and begins to take off his shoes. He sits in the big leather chair*]. All right.

OSWALD. I guess I'll have a look at ma and little old Cafard. [*As he leaves.*] And the kid . . . Say—he's a bird, Hester.

[HESTER *smiles.*]

HESTER [*busy at the table*]. Run along, Andrew. We've lots to do. [*Sees what* ANDREW *is doing.*] Oh, *must* you take your shoes off, Andrew?

ANDREW. Aw—Hess, my feet get so darned tired, tramping around all day tryin' to sell insurance. Great having Os home, eh? What do you think of him?

HESTER [*diffidently*]. He doesn't look very well, does he? I suppose he's suffered dreadfully, over there, in the war. I wonder how he'll like it here? How he'll like us?

ANDREW. How? Gosh, he thinks you're a great little girl. Said so. And, by golly, you *are* too. [*Snaps his fingers.*]

HESTER [*reprovingly but not angrily. She has been saying this for years*]. Stop snapping your fingers. [*She smiles as she thinks of* OSWALD.] Does he? Really?

ANDREW [*seriously*]. Say, Hess, now Os has come back, don't you think we kinda ought to hint to Mattie that she'd better begin to look for a job some place? I guess she's about good enough now to go into somebody's office, somewhere, as a stenographer, ain't she?

HESTER. Oh, Andrew! [*She stops working and looks at him wearily.*] Why do you begin that again? We've gone over that——

[ANDREW *snaps his fingers.*]
Don't snap—a thousand times. I tell you she's not ready. I feel a duty to her. We're all she's got since the war. Why do you say this?

ANDREW [*in embarrassment,* OSWALD'S *past in his mind*]. Well—hang it all—Os being back—and the expense—and —well, you see, Os . . .

HESTER [*cutting him short*]. I just won't have it, Andrew, and that's all. When she's ready to go, she'll go. Now please run up and find the blanket.

[ANDREW *rises and starts for the arch. He shakes his head dubiously.* HESTER *sees this; it irritates her.*]
And don't shake your head like that.

ANDREW. [*At this,* ANDREW *shakes his head affirmatively; at centre he meets* MARTHE, *who enters.*] Hello, Mattie.

MARTHE. Good evening, sir. [*She comes down the stage as* ANDREW *leaves the room.*]

HESTER. Well, Martha, if we can ever get these men out of here, maybe we can get supper ready. [*She looks at the table, trying to think of some way to make it more than ordinarily attractive.*] I'm going up-stairs and get those pretty doilies that you embroidered for me for my birthday. We've never used them. I wish we had some flowers for the table, too—but we haven't. When I'm rich, I'll always have flowers on the table.

MARTHE. My mother loved also flowers. Always the

little bunch of them in a glass. [*She looks over toward the serving-table and sees a potted plant there. Smiles.*] What if I put the pot of red ger-an-i-mums there in the middle?

HESTER. Oh, do! How nice!

MARTHE [*fetching the flowers from the serving-table and placing them in the centre of the dining-room table, which is now all set. Wistfully*]. You are all so happy to-night. Your soldier has come back.

HESTER [*patting her affectionately*]. Martha—don't be sad. You're one of us. You must feel glad, too. I'll get the doilies. [*She leaves through the arch.*]

> [MARTHE *goes over to the sideboard, opens a drawer there and takes out some napkins. As she is arranging them* OSWALD *enters.*]

OSWALD [*seeing* MARTHE]. Hello!

MARTHE [*coming to the table for something*]. Good evening, sir.

OSWALD [*coming nearer the table. Looking at her appraisingly*]. I guess you're Martha.

MARTHE. Yes.

OSWALD. I'm Oswald—the prodigal son—the champion veal-eater.

MARTHE [*puzzled at the words*]. "Veal-eater——?"

[*Between them is the table. Mischievously.*]

I thought you were a hero—M'sieu.

OSWALD. God!—have you got that, too?

[MARTHE *busies herself at the table without replying.*]

[*Familiarly.*]

You're a Belgian.

MARTHE. *Oui.*

OSWALD. I bin up in your country—visitin' King Albert—and Mrs. King.

[MARTHE, *unable to resist his contagious good humor, smiles too.*]

Oh—you *can* smile, can you? [*Getting more familiar.*] Martha—I'm going to call you Martha, and you call me Oswald, see? [*Drops into horrible French.*] Martha—*vous-et tray jollee!*

MARTHE [*with apparent coolness*]. *M'sieu est flatteur.* [*Goes up to the sideboard, her back to him.* OSWALD *takes her measure in amused silence as she stands there arranging*

*the napkins. Then he tiptoes up behind her and attempts to
kiss her.]* Ah—no!
[*With his arm about her, the two struggle and come down
stage,* OSWALD *laughing and still attempting to kiss
her. She strikes at him, and tries to get away.*]

OSWALD [*holding her laughingly, despite her struggles*].
Aw—say, Martha! Hit a poor soldier? Why, say, I bin
fightin' for your country— Got wounded up there—see
that lame foot? [*Releases the girl.*] *Vous et* naughty
girl!

MARTHE [*in a tone of reverence*]. Fighting—for my
country!
[OSWALD, *taking advantage of her mood, tries again to
kiss her. She holds him off.*]
Ah, no! Please! [*She looks him piteously in the face,
overcome by a sudden emotion. In a low tone, as it were almost sacramental.*] It is *I* who kiss you—for my country!
[*She kisses him on the forehead and then, embarrassed at her
act, she quickly crosses and goes out to the kitchen.*]

OSWALD [*gazing after her*]. You're a funny kid! [*Left
alone, he takes from his pocket a soiled letter which he glances
at with a grunt of satisfaction and pleasure. He puts the
letter away.*]
[*Enter* HESTER *with the doilies in her hand.*]

HESTER [*coming down to the table*]. Oh! There you
are! Oh—you've made Andrew and your mother so
happy, coming home like this. Why, only this afternoon,
before Andy telephoned—we'd heard about Hilda's seeing
you and all. And your mother just cried—and cried.
Oh! It's just wonderful! And how you fooled me—at
first! Once or twice it crossed my mind, when you looked
at the baby's picture—oh—how could you?

OSWALD. I don't suppose it makes much difference to
you, my coming back, does it?

HESTER. Do you want me to say I'm sorry you came?

OSWALD [*approaching the table. Ingratiatingly*]. You're
awful good to—to your little brother.

HESTER. You're the first *hero* we've ever had.

OSWALD. Aw—cut that hero stuff out—Hester.

HESTER. I can hardly wait for you to tell me all about
your experiences in the war. They've laughed at me so

here—because I cared about the war so—oh, I did care!
Awfully! Like you!

OSWALD [*amused*]. Like me?

HESTER. But you *must have*. If you went there.

OSWALD. Oh! [*With an amused little whistle on two
notes*.]

HESTER. And now you're coming back—one of us—
from the war! It makes it more—*ours*. Don't you see?
Gives *us* a share in it.

OSWALD [*admiringly*]. Say, you're a regular little pa-
triot, eh? Hip-hip stuff! [*Maliciously*.] Brother Andy
didn't go to war—did he?

HESTER [*behind table, flushing*]. No. He couldn't—
he—you see, with us women, and baby—and——

OSWALD [*insinuatingly*]. Did he want to go?

HESTER [*evadingly*]. How could he? [*Defiantly*.] If it
hadn't been for baby, *I'd* have gone. I'd have loved
going! And doing anything. Washing dishes, scrubbing
floors! Washing the boys' clothes. Anybody who's been
there is just wonderful to me!

OSWALD [*with satisfaction*]. Oh! I guess I'm in the
right pew here, all right, all right.

HESTER. I suppose you think I'm—[*laughing in embarrassment*] awfully foolish—like everybody else does.

OSWALD. Who does?

HESTER. Oh—I don't know. Do *you?*

OSWALD [*leaning over the table*]. You want to know what
I think? Well, I think you're just about the sweetest
little bit of . . .

ANDREW [*up-stairs*]. Hess! Hess! Where is that
darned trunk?

HESTER [*blushing in embarrassment and pleasure, drops
her eyes and smiles*]. I think you're just the—biggest
little jollier that— [ANDREW *calls again*.] I'll come up,
Andy, I'll come up! *Willie Smart!*

  [OSWALD *gives an impudently familiar gesture of adieu
      to her as she goes through the arch, and drops with the
      air of a conqueror into a chair by the table*.]

OSWALD. All right . . . Sister!

THE CURTAIN FALLS.

ACT II

SCENE: *The curtain rises on the sitting-room of the Lanes,
lighted at the moment only by the scanty illumination
from the electric light in the hallway. On the left the
room opens into the dining-room; on the right are a
window curtained in cheap cretonne and a fireplace;
at the back, on the left, another archway opens into the
little entrance-hall, whose stairway and hat-rack are
plainly visible beyond the "chenille" hangings of the
archway. The woodwork is spurious light oak, the wall-
paper a faded semblance of dull-green burlap. There
is a central electric chandelier, with pink porcelain candles, and there are also two side-brackets. The furniture
and ornaments of the place are a mixture of pieces from
old* MRS. LANE's *"front parlor," transported thither
from western New York after her husband's death—
black-walnut atrocities; and some, of the* 1890 *variety,
from* HESTER's *girlhood home, a Brooklyn boarding-
house. A couch is near the fireplace (a gas-log), and
behind it is a large table, with a shaded lamp and books.
An "ottoman" stands in front of the couch. At one
side, to the right of the entrance to the dining-room,
stands an old "secretary," a combination of desk and
bookcase. The well-worn furnishings, from the kindly
action of time, a not untasteful arrangement, and an
unpretentious attempt at mitigation of their crudities,
somehow render the room neither unfriendly nor uncomfortable.*

*It is about half past nine of a December evening, three months
after Act I. The door-bell is heard violently ringing.*
MARTHE *presently is seen running down the stairway,
visible through the undrawn curtains of the archway.
A* VOICE *is heard—that of a messenger delivering a
telegram.*

VOICE.   Oswald Lane . . . Cablegram!
MARTHE.   For Mr. *Oswald* Lane?

VOICE. Yes'm . . . cablegram. Sign here.

[*There is a short pause, the outer door is heard to close, and presently* MARTHE *enters from the hall. She turns up the lamp on the table, looks over in the direction of the clock on the mantel, and then illuminates the room fully by lighting the chandelier and side-brackets. She stands there with the cablegram in her hand, looking at it reflectively. A pipe of* OSWALD'S *at the table attracts her attention. She goes to it, picks it up, and presses it to her lips. She puts the pipe down and slips the cablegram into her pocket. She is evidently a prey to very disquieting thoughts. Suddenly she runs into the dining-room, calling to the dog, which she hears whining.*]

MARTHE. Cafard! Cafard! [*She returns with the dog in her arms. She dumps the dog onto the big footstool in front of the rocking-chair, and, slipping to the floor, buries her head in the dog's coat, grateful for the animal's passive sympathy.*] Oh! *Ma pauvre Cafard! Ma pauvre Cafard!* . . . *Tu ne peux pas comprendre—que je suis malheureuse.*

[*The outer door slams. Quick steps are heard in the hall. The girl rises swiftly to her feet, runs to the door with the dog, and thrusts her into the other room.* OSWALD *enters at the arch.* MARTHE *throws her arms about his neck, with endearing little French phrases.*]

MARTHE. *Ah! Mon amour!* . . . *Mon p'tit chou!*

OSWALD [*affecting good humor*]. Break away, Carpentier, break away! [*Glances apprehensively toward the window.*] Look out, kid! That shade's not down, is it? [*A little irritably.*] No. Say! I might want to use my neck again some time—if they should ever want to hang me. [*Disengages himself, and gets out of his overcoat—the old horizon-blue of the French Army. Gives his kepi and coat to* MARTHE *to hang up for him in the hall.*] Gee-z—it's a cold night, I'll tell the world. [*Lights a cigarette. Despite his rather elaborate air of disinterestedness, his eye is sharply on* MARTHE.] Well, I been to the church and told 'em how I won the war— I told you I'd come back ahead of them if I could.

[MARTHE *pulls him down into the centre of the stage,*

her face glowing with admiration. OSWALD is dressed in his poilu uniform—worn, ill fitting, blue. He wears it jauntily and has put on his medals—the French Croix-de-Guerre with palms, the Médaille Militaire. On his left shoulder is the red cord—the fouragère—granted to Légionnaires. There are four service stripes and two wounded stripes on his sleeves.]

MARTHE. Let me look at you! Oh, you are so beautiful in your uniform! My soldier!

OSWALD [*flattered and more expansive*]. Feels kinda good to get into the old duds again, Martie. You know, kid, I get kinda fed up sometimes with—with things here. All these damn rich—a fellow like me—what show's he got? They want to make him work for 'em—for the damn capitalists, that's what. 'Tain't fair! I got's good a right to be rich—better, by God, 'n this old uniform's the proof of it! . . . Good's those greasy hogs! [*He crosses to the left.*] Divide up property, Martha, share and share alike, I say!

MARTHE [*follows him, takes his hand and clings to it passionately*]. Oswald—let us go away! Take me away from here. I—I—hate it! Take me to—I don't care where. I'll work for you—I'll——

OSWALD [*on his guard*]. Sure, kitten, sure! Gimme time—gimme time!

MARTHE. Your brother does not want me to stay here any longer.

OSWALD [*suspiciously*]. Why don't he? How do you know?

MARTHE. Your mother, too. She hates me! She is afraid that I should make you with love for me! I know! I see!

OSWALD. Ma! Oh, don't let ma get your goat, Martie! If ma ever felt real good about anything in the world, she'd think she was sick and take something. [*Turns to her.*] But what's this dope about Andy?

[MARTHE *mutely tries to understand him.*]

I mean—what'd you mean about him? Wantin' you to go? Has—has he got on to anything, do you think?

MARTHE. Oh, Oswald—cannot we tell them now? I

do not like this always hiding and concealing.   Let us tell them.   Then we go and . . .

OSWALD [*impatiently interrupting*].   What about Andy? Get down to brass tacks.   Has he said . . . ?

MARTHE.   No.   But I know.   I feel.   I see him *look* . . . look—if we speak or sit together.   Why does he do this?

OSWALD [*somewhat relieved*].   You keep your shirt on, Marty.   Old And' hasn't got anything on you—nor on me.   He couldn't see the hole in a doughnut—not if you took it out and gave it to him.   But 'f you feel like this about it—why don't you beat it?

MARTHE.   You mean . . . go away?   [*Going a little toward him.*]   You know why I stay here.   For you!

OSWALD [*agreeing amiably, and patting her shoulder*]. Yah!   Sure.   I get you.   We're all right.   But now, kid, about this tellin' 'em—why, naturally I'm all for it.   But it's like this.   I ain't just found out what I want to do yet.   I ain't going to get all tied up in bow-knots with some darn thing that—well, that I can't show my ability at and make good money, too.   And you ain't got that stenographer job yet, see?   We'd want to make our get-away from here, if we told.   No, you just trust your uncle Oswald a little longer, girlie, and, by golly, you'll wear diamonds yet.

MARTHE [*sitting on the couch and facing* OSWALD].   I *can* trust you—always . . . can't I?

OSWALD.   Surest thing you know.   Martie, where's Little Andy?   Is he all right now?

MARTHE [*impatiently, trying to tell him something*].   Yes . . . yes . . . it is nothing.   Oswald—listen . . .

OSWALD [*sincerely*].   I love that kid.   Honest, I do, Martie.   And he loves me, too.   Kinda gets Andrew's goat to see it.   Noticed it, Mart?   Wisht he could have come to the show to-night.

MARTHE.   And—what of *me*?

OSWALD.   Say—it was too bad, girlie, havin' to stay at home with the kid.   You should worry, though.   Me! In a church!   Oh, boy!

MARTHE [*jealously—still sitting on the couch*].   You— you love *me*—like you love Little Andy?

OSWALD. Ain't I told you so—mor'n a thousand times? [*Impatiently.*] God Almighty! Do I have to loop the loop every minute?

MARTHE. Oswald?

OSWALD [*changing the subject.*] Say, Mart, you'd oughta heard the spiel I give 'em about the war to-night. Pershing ain't got nothin' on me. Church full, by golly, and little Os right up in the pitcher's box, with the man of God. [*In derisive imitation.*] "Brothers and sisters, we have in store for us this evening a rare treat—our distinguished townsman, Mr. Oswald Lane.—For a cause that lies near to the heart of every mother and father.—The suffering infants of devastated France!" Oh, mister! And brother Andy singin' like a sore foot in the choir. And when the guys passed around the plate you oughta seen 'em give up. Brother Andy's countin' it now. I ducked.

MARTHE. Oswald—you *do* love me? I want so to hear you say it—just once.

OSWALD. Aw—I got a sore throat from singin' hymns. [*Sings:*]

> "Hear the pennies dropping,
> Listen as they fall,
> Every one for Jesus,
> He will get them all"—*I don't think!*

MARTHE [*who has paid little attention to what he has been saying*]. There is no other girl . . .?

OSWALD. What do you mean?

MARTHE. Not over there? Nor here? Not even—her?

OSWALD [*his eyes narrowing as he looks at her, and in a hard tone*]. Who?

MARTHE [*sullenly*]. Hester?

OSWALD. Cut that out! You hear? Can that!

MARTHE [*fiercely, her suspicions growing stronger*]. Oh! She would love you! I have seen that! Fool!

OSWALD [*in a rage*]. Say! Have you gone clean nuts? If I ever hear you say again that— Say! Have you ever let on anything to her . . . about us?

MARTHE. No! What I care what she think?

OSWALD. Well—you beat the devil, I'll say!

MARTHE [*afraid that he will hold this against her*]. Please —forgive me. I am sorry I say it. [*She gives him the telegram.*] Here—this is for you.

[OSWALD *takes the message, and moves a little away from her. He opens it and reads. A smile comes on his face.*]

Good news?

OSWALD [*eagerly*]. When'd it come?

MARTHE. Just now.

OSWALD. Why didn't you give it to me right off?

MARTHE. I don't know. I forget. [*Coming closer to him. They are both at the right centre of the stage.*] What is it that? [*More excitedly.*] Who sends you a message from Europe? *Who?*

OSWALD [*menacingly*]. If you've read that tele——

MARTHE. The boy *said* it was from far away. [*Hysterically.*] From a woman—is it? Oh—I have seen you smile—and smile— From some girl! [*Snatching at the cablegram.*] You *shall* tell me!

OSWALD [*struggles with her and recovers the paper*]. Oh, for God's sake—stop screaming! Stop it! They'll hear you . . . They'll be here any minute. It—it was from a man. From a fellow over there who wants me to come back and take a job. There!

MARTHE [*dropping back on the couch in exhaustion*]. You—go?

OSWALD. I don't know. Maybe.

MARTHE [*desperately*]. Take me with you—oh—don't leave me alone now! Don't leave me alone!

OSWALD. How the hell can we go anywhere without a cent? Don't be foolish!

MARTHE [*in a slow poignant tone*]. We . . . must—do something.

OSWALD [*apprehensive*]. What'd you mean? [*Crosses to* MARTHE.] Shoot! [*He holds up her head. She looks into his eyes, then drops her head.* OSWALD, *in dismay.*] Oh, my God! Are you sure? [*She nods.*] Why didn't you . . . Why . . . Oh, this is a hell of a thing! [*He walks up and down distractedly.* MARTHE *sobs.*]

MARTHE. You see—I must go.

OSWALD [*trying to get control of himself*]. Stop crying, kid—I gotta think—you lemme think——

[*She sobs aloud.*]

Sure, we'll go away—but you gotta lemme fix things. *Don't you tell anybody!* You hear?

[*The outer door slams.*]

Oh, Christ! Here they come! Stop crying!

[*Sounds of the returning family in high good humor are heard in the hall.*]

SARAH [*in the hall*]. Rill good turnout——

ANDREW. Good big collection, too.

HESTER. Hilda Pierce was so excited . . .

OSWALD [*to* MARTHE]. Duck! [*He pushes her into the dark dining-room and begins to whistle nonchalantly and noisily. The family enters, taking off their outer garments.*] Well, folks? [*Sits on rocking-chair at right.*]

ANDREW [*boisterously*]. Well, old son! You went right over the top this time! And, by golly, they was all right with you. I got the collection right here in my little old pocket, too. [*Goes to secretary and puts the collection from the church in the drawer of the secretary, locks it and drops the key into a small upper drawer.*]

OSWALD. Don't tell Billy Sunday 'bout me, And'. He might offer me a job.

SARAH [*carefully putting aside her best hat and gloves at the table*]. Land alive, Oswald! What a time of it you had over there in them creechers!

ANDREW [*taking off his hat and coat*]. Craters, ma!

SARAH. Ten days he said he was in one——

ANDREW. Ten hours, ma!

SARAH. And nothin' to eat or drink but scrapple.

HESTER. Shrapnel!

SARAH. It don't signify. [*She comes toward* OSWALD.] Your pa was a good talker, too. At prayer-meetin' and down to the Grange. I'm glad you done so good, Oswal', jest to show folks in this town that there's other folks as good as they are, and some better. The Laneses can hold their heads up with any of 'em.

ANDREW [*at the large table at the left, he is putting down, in a little account-book in which he keeps his church records, the amount of the collection*]. That's right, ma.

HESTER [*coming down stage a little, as* SARAH *goes up to a chair to the right of the arch and sits*]. Oh, Oswald—it was just perfectly fine! I could just see it all! It made me feel as if I was right there beside you. And every one was so interested—and when you told about——

ANDREW [*sitting behind the table*]. The boss was there! Come over in his car from Montclair. I told him about it yesterday in the office. He give up fifty bucks, too. I saw him drop it in.

OSWALD [*with mock solicitude*]. Gosh! It's awful to think of them poor millionaires deprivin' themselves like that! I betcha he won't be able to afford anything to eat but Rolls-Royces for a week now!

[SARAH *has taken off her rubbers and is now down near the secretary.*]

Say, ma—you might take him over a quart of oysters. Maybe he'll find a pearl in one of 'em.

SARAH. Me? My heavenly king!— Well, if you ask me, we'd all ought to render thanks to the good Lord for his mercy. [*She puts her rubbers out the hall door.*]

ANDREW [*in a reverent tone*]. A-men!

HESTER [*who has been putting her wraps in the hall*]. I can't get it out of my head. All the cold, and mud— and suffering—and disease—and the wounded—and the dying——

ANDREW. And the dead!

HESTER [*as* SARAH *goes back and sits in the chair to the right of the arch*]. Oswald—you really advanced right over the piled-up bodies of your comrades, as they lay there—dead and dying, in the trenches?

OSWALD. Um-hum.

HESTER. Oh, how could you?

ANDREW. Had to be done, dearie.

HESTER. Why, we don't realize over here what you boys went through! [*Looking at* ANDREW, *who is still seated behind the table.*] There isn't anything in the whole world too good for you—not *anything* . . . Oh! Those awful battles—I can just understand how you felt!

OSWALD [*dryly*]. So could Fritz!

[ANDREW *giggles.*]

SARAH [*rising*]. Land, Andrew, how can you laugh?

I do' want to think of it even. [*Goes to the table.*] Gives me the nawshy! [*She opens her bottle of patent medicine and takes a dose.*]

ANDREW [*rising*]. She's right. Forget it! . . . Say, I told the parson a good one . . .

HESTER [*by the window*]. I'll *always* think of it. So'll every American that—that cares.

OSWALD [*stands and salutes mockingly. Sings the first line of the "Star-Spangled Banner."*]

"Oh—say—can you see . . .?"

ANDREW. Say—I told the parson a bird to-night. You ought to have heard him laugh! Know the one about?——

HESTER [*impatiently*]. Oh!——

OSWALD [*to* HESTER]. Say—if you had him X-rayed, maybe you could find the place in his head that's spoiled.

ANDREW. No! This is a good one. "If you wanted——"

HESTER [*crossing him on her way to the centre of the stage*]. Oh, if he would only stop those awful things!

ANDREW. Aw, Hess . . .

HESTER [*at the hall door*]. I wonder if Martha is in bed? [*Coming down to* OSWALD.] Too bad she wasn't there to hear you speak.

OSWALD. Martha? Don't know. Haven't seen her. I just got here.

ANDREW [*happily*]. Honest! I bet you never heard this one. Listen! "If you wanted a preacher to play on the violin, what would you say?"

OSWALD. I'd say "Shut up!"

[HESTER *stops her ears.*]

SARAH. Who ever heard of a minister of the gospel a-playin' on the fiddle? 'Tain't fittin'! Mercy!

ANDREW. You'd say "Fiddle, D. D.," . . . See? Fiddle—dee—dee! See?

[OSWALD *and* HESTER *look at him with cold eyes.*]

SARAH [*laughing*]. Well, of all the poppycock! Andrew, you do beat all for them anagrams! [*She goes into the dining-room with her bottle of medicine.*]

HESTER. Andrew . . . I wish you'd never tell another one of those horrid things as long as you live.

OSWALD. Every blamed one of 'em's a *dud!*

[SARAH *re-enters and sits on the chair to the right of the arch.*]

ANDREW [*very pleased with himself*]. You folks are jealous, that's all— I was going to say, if Mattie was up, a cup of hot coffee wouldn't a-gone so bad, after winnin' the war. I've got to set sail for New Brunswick, you know, by the ten-thirty. Got to see a feller down there about some insurance.

SARAH. How much was the donation, Andrew?

ANDREW [*busy with his account-book*]. What?

SARAH. How much was the donation?

ANDREW. 'Most five hundred dollars. Guess that's goin' some for this burg.

OSWALD [*carelessly, from the rocking-chair*]. You're the holy treasurer of the works, ain't you?

ANDREW [*proudly*]. Yes, sir—been 'er for four years. And never a penny out in my accounts, by gosh! "Old Rock of Giberalter" the parson calls me. I'm kinda proud of that, too.

SARAH [*from her chair*]. You'll be held up and murdered some night.

ANDREW. Lord bless you, ma! For four years I been bringin' home the collection Sunday nights—pants' buttons, dried wasps, brass pennies, and all—and nobody's ever murdered me yet.

[*Off stage and up the stairs are heard the voices of* LITTLE ANDY *and* MARTHE. MARTHE *is trying to catch the child as he runs down the stairs.*]

ANDY [*is heard off the stage*]. Lemme go—I wanna see my uncle Oswald!

MARTHE. *Mauvais garçon!* Come back!

SARAH [*rising*]. My soul and body!

[*Enter* ANDY, *followed by* MARTHE.]
Look there!

[LITTLE ANDY *is in his night-clothes. He makes straight for* OSWALD. *The latter rises to catch him, and as his arms close about the boy he lifts him high into the air. The entire family cluster around the pair, all talking at once.*]

ANDY. Uncle Oswal'! Tell 'bout the war! Tell 'bout the war!

MARTHE. He heard you all and run from his bed. *Mauvais garçon!*

HESTER. Darling! You'll catch cold.

ANDREW [*grinning*]. 'Nother soldier in the family.

OSWALD [*with the boy in his arms*]. Martie, get my overcoat!

> [*These speeches all come together, but* OSWALD'S *last remark dominates the others.* MARTHE *goes to the hall and fetches the military overcoat.*]

SARAH [*disapprovingly*]. Why—Andy Lane!

OSWALD [*takes the overcoat from* MARTHE *and wraps the boy up in it*]. Looks just like Joffer! Eh, marshal? Say, son, you've got your signals mixed. The attack was set for zero hour in the morning. Back to the dugout for yours!

HESTER. I'll take him up.

ANDREW. No. I will.

ANDY. No! Uncle Oswal'. You! An' I want my "Froggie" what Uncle Oswal' gave me.

> [*They all look for "Froggie," which is a doll, dressed completely as a French soldier. It happens to be on the table.*]

ANDREW. Find his "Froggie."

SARAH. Land sakes—where is it?

MARTHE [*as she finds it*]. Here it is.

HESTER. Thank you, Martha!

> [*She hands the child the doll, which the lad presses close to him.*]

OSWALD [*smiling up at him*]. There you are, old dear. Froggie and all!

ANDY. Daddy! Uncle Oswald teached me to build a camp-fire yesterday, he did!

ANDREW. He did, did he? That's fine!

ANDY. Uncle Oswal'! *Tu es un chic type!*

ANDREW. What's that he called you, Os?

ANDY. Uncle Oswal' and I can talk French together.

> [HESTER *kisses the child.*]

OSWALD. Come on now, general! Give the command!

ANDY [*starts to sing "The Marseillaise"*].

"*Marchons . . . Marchon–ons . . .*"

> [OSWALD *joins him, and they sing together. They march off centre and up the stairs.* HESTER'S *satisfaction is very apparent.*]

ANDREW [*stands at centre and waves up the stairs*]. Bon sour! [*Coming back.*] By golly, he'll have me speakin' French next!

HESTER. How he loves Oswald!

ANDREW. Eh-yah. [*To* MARTHE, *who is sitting at the right of the arch.*] Martha—what about a cup o' hot coffee before everybody goes to bed?

MARTHE. I go to make it, Mr. Lane. In five minutes it is ready. [*She crosses to the dining-room.*]

ANDREW [*comes down and sits in the rocking-chair*]. Mattie don't look very well, Hess—seems to me.

HESTER. Oh, I don't know!

SARAH. [*Now that* MARTHE *has vacated her favorite chair, she goes toward it.*] Sets in her room too much. Needs a good dose o' Epsom salts, I guess.

HESTER [*annoyed*]. Oh—mother!

SARAH. [*She is collecting her possessions—her hat, gloves, etc. Testily.*] Mercy on us! Can't a body say *anything*? I'm goin' to bed. I don't feel none too good myself, though I don't suppose that matters none to anybody in this house. 'F that Marty'd enjoyed the poor health I've allus had, I guess she'd look a good deal more pindlin' than she does now. [*Resignedly.*] I hope none o' you ever knows what it is to suffer with a floatin' kidney! [*She is about to go out through the arch.*]

ANDREW [*who has been rocking and whistling softly*]. Ma!

SARAH [*turning*]. What?

ANDREW. Os made a hit with the boss to-night. He wants to give 'im a job, sellin' insurance.

HESTER [*sitting on the sofa*]. Oh! How splendid!

SARAH [*coming down into the room*]. I ain't s'prised. What's he pay?

ANDREW [*rocking*]. Well—it's a good chance, and prob'ly good pay to begin with. [*Hesitatingly.*] You know, Os has been home more'n two months, and——

HESTER. But we've been so glad to have him here.

ANDREW. Sure. That isn't the point, though. Os . . .

HESTER [*petulantly*]. But why do you talk as though we wanted to get rid of him? You know the whole house has been a good deal brighter since he's been here.

SARAH. With his jokes and all.

HESTER. And I don't know *what* baby would do if he went away. And, anyhow, even if we didn't want him —which isn't true—it would be our duty to—to our country to see that a soldier that fought for us so splendidly was helped in every way.

ANDREW [*softly*]. Now, dearie—ain't that just what we are doing, helping him?

HESTER [*hotly*]. Grudging!

ANDREW. It ain't grudging. Hess—you know—ma knows—that I don't grudge him anything. But it's awful hard sleddin' to get along. I don't know how we're goin' to come out clear, what with prices going sky-high all the time.

[*The two women are silent for a moment.* ANDREW *rocks and whistles softly to the tune of "There is a happy land——"*]

I got the coal bill yesterday. [*Thoughtfully.*] Two or three things have come up that Os might have had, but he didn't seem to want 'em. He——

SARAH [*sitting in her chair*]. He ain't rill well. [*On the defense.*] Hester's right in what she says.

ANDREW. And I don't know as he's actually tried very hard to get anything else. I guess he *is* kinda tired out, too. But we're poor folks [*with a laugh as he tries to make a joke*]—and poor folks ain't rich folks—you know. [*Again he whistles his tune.*]

HESTER [*in a weary voice*]. Oh, I'm so tired of being poor.

SARAH [*always ready to come to the defense of her own*]. They's worse things.

ANDREW [*cheerfully*]. Sure . . . bein' in a hospital.

SARAH. If it's a question of goin'—what I want to

know is—why that Marthy's got to be kept here any longer?

[ANDREW *turns helplessly to* HESTER.]

HESTER [*rising*]. She *is* going.

ANDREW [*in astonishment*]. She is?

SARAH. When?

HESTER. Soon. She spoke to me yesterday about it. She wants to go. If she's ready for it, then of course it's the best thing.

ANDREW. Sure!

SARAH [*rising*]. If you ask me—that young lady's mad 'cause Oswald's come back . . . oh, well—let 'er go. Good riddance to bad rubbish. [*Plaintively*.] Oswal' ain't going to be beholden to anybody, as I have to be.

ANDREW [*soothingly*]. Well—ma—we won't worry.

SARAH. Land! I like to forgot my tonic! [*She leaves by the door at the right.*]

HESTER [*coming behind the table on the left*]. Oswald's trying. I know he's trying to get something to do.

ANDREW. Sure. I don't say he isn't—but—darn it all, if I was a rich man I'd let him set here till he got good and ready. [*Whistles a bar or two.*] I bought him a new suit yesterday.

HESTER. You did?

ANDREW. You know, Hess—we've got little Andy to think of. That money we're puttin' by for his college education don't grow very fast.

HESTER [*again going to the chair and sitting. Discouraged*]. Oh, dear! Nothing seems right in this world.

ANDREW [*turning in his chair so that he can look out to the hall and see if anybody is listening*]. What I was going to say was—Hess—that if you could sort of—you know—to Os. He likes you, and if you could maybe suggest that—? This is a good offer of the boss's——

HESTER [*confidently*]. I know Oswald will take it.

ANDREW. Yes. I guess he will. Hess— [*Looking carefully out of the hall door.*] About Mattie's going— [*Confidentially.*] There ain't any—*special* reason for it—is there?

HESTER [*looking at him sharply*]. Special reason? What do you mean?

ANDREW [*weakly*]. Oh—I don't know—but——

HESTER. But what?

ANDREW [*worriedly*]. Well—Os—you know he's always—sort of—joshin'—everybody—and—well, I didn't know but maybe he'd been gettin' fresh with Mattie—maybe . . .

HESTER [*on her feet, horrified*]. Why, Andrew Lane!

ANDREW. I don't suppose . . .

HESTER [*walking to and fro*]. I don't know how you can even think such a thing!

ANDREW [*trying to get out thoughts that are difficult of expression*]. Well—when two young people get together —you see——

HESTER. I don't believe a word of it! [*Her jealousy is evident.*]

ANDREW. Well—Os is a likable fellow—and——

HESTER. Why—if anything, Martha actually rather dislikes him, I sometimes imagine. [*As she crosses the stage.*] Oh, no!

ANDREW [*rises in relief, and crosses toward the fireplace*]. Well—that's all right. I'm glad to hear you think so. [*Whistles his hymn-tune "There is a happy land—"*] I guess so, too. Wouldn't wonder if Os's kinda got his eye on Hilda Pierce, eh?

HESTER. I don't know. In any case I happen to know that Hilda is engaged to a Red Cross man.

[ANDREW *whistles.* HESTER *looks toward the stairs.*] Guess I'll run up and have a look at baby. [*She starts for the stairs and meets* OSWALD, *who is coming down. She smiles brightly at him.*] Coming right back! [*Exit up the stairs through the arch.*]

[OSWALD *goes down to the couch, where he sits.*]

ANDREW [*whistling*]. Guess I'll go and see if Mattie needs any help. [*As he goes out the door he almost bumps into* SARAH, *who is entering with her medicine bottle in hand.*] Guess I'll go and see if Mattie needs any help.

SARAH [*first putting her bottle and spoon on the table*]. Oswal', I wisht you'd sleep down here to-night.

OSWALD. Why?

SARAH. I'd feel safer 'bout that money. Them burglars can git anywheres—church money, and give for them little babies, too.

OSWALD. All right, ma.

SARAH. Oswal'—that Mr. Thornton has told Andrew he'd give you a good job—sellin' insurance. I want you should go right down to the city to-morrow and see 'im.

OSWALD. Me? Sell insurance? Nix!

SARAH. You can't go on livin' on Andrew's shoulders. Andrew says he thinks you ain't tried as hard as you might to git somethin' to do. He says——

OSWALD. Oh! He throws that up at me, does he? 'Course I can go an' fight so's he can live at home on Easy Street! Damn slacker! That's what they call "Keep the world safe for democracy!" Well, you can tell him from me I ain't going to trouble him much longer.

SARAH. What you goin' to do? [*Anxiously.*] You ain't goin' off again, traipsin' around the world, be you?

OSWALD [*sulkily*]. I got plans.

SARAH. Oswal'—you take this job. Everything'll be all right then. [*Wheedlingly.*] I want you should git to earnin'. I guess I ain't any too welcome in this house. Ossie—you take it, and we'll git a little place to ourselves. Me and you. And I guess, if you wanted to, you could git that Pierce gal—from the flirty way she acted to-night, carryin' on so about you— Ravellin' on your sleeve. Sign o' money! [*She picks it off.*]

OSWALD [*to appease her*]. Money?—Oh, well—I'll see —don't you fret, ma——

SARAH [*piteously*]. Don't seem's if I could bear to have you run off again. I ain't one to tell my feelin's, but this bein' away of yours has jest about killed me— 'F you should start off now— [*A sudden thought and she looks at him anxiously.*] Oswal'—you ben a good boy, ain't you, since you ben home? You ain't done nothin' wrong, have you?

OSWALD [*jumps to his feet. Crosses the stage angrily*]. Oh, between you—you and Andy—you'd drive a fellow right into Sing Sing. Harp! Harp! Harp! Every chance you get. Over a mistake I made once. Can't let it drop. Can't lemme forget. Oh—I'm sick to death of the whole show.   I wish I'd never come home! [*Sits in the rocking-chair.*]

SARAH [*crosses to* OSWALD]. 'F you had any respect for my feelin's, you wouldn't talk like that.   Pretty way for a boy to talk, after all your pa and I and Andy have done for you.

OSWALD.   Go on!   Rub it in!   Rub salt on the sores! You're having fun, ain't you?

SARAH [*tearfully*].   I'd cut my hand off for you, Ossie, and well you know it, 'f I thought it'd do you any good.

OSWALD [*relenting.   A little more kindly*].   Oh, well—I know it, ma—I—I'm all tired out to-night.   I'm worried— 'bout things.   We'll talk it over to-morrow.   It'll be all right.

SARAH [*reassured*].   That's a good boy.   [*To* ANDREW, *as he enters with a tray from the dining-room.*]   I told him. I guess he will, all right.

ANDREW [*places the tray with cups and saucers on table*]. Good for you, Os! . . .

SARAH.   I'm goin' to bed.   I'm about beat out.   [*She picks up the last of her belongings.*   ANDREW *crosses from the table to the secretary.*]   Well, I hope we'll all be alive in the mornin'.

OSWALD [*in the rocking-chair*].   You don't ever worry or anything, do you, ma?

SARAH.   Land—what a day we've had of it!   And me gittin' up an' goin' to old Mrs. Trumble's funeral to-morrow mornin'.   I like to forgot it.   Andy?   I see that oldest Trumble boy on the street the other day.   You know, that lean, pimply-faced one.   To my mind he ain't no better'n a loon.   I says, "How's yer ma?" I says. And he says: "She's ben practically unconscious for two days, and she ain't et nothin' fer a week, an' her tongue's black's the bottom of a kittle; an'"— he says—"you can't tell me them are good signs!"   Good signs!   Land! She was deader'n a door-nail inside twenty-four hours.— 'Night! [*Exit up the stairs to the right.*]

OSWALD *and* ANDREW.   'Night, ma——

OSWALD [*crossing, truculently*].   So—you don't want me in your house any longer?

ANDREW.   Now, Os—I——

Oswald. I s'pose you think because you put me under obligations to you once—you think you've bought me—but——

Andrew [*coming toward him pacifically*]. Os—don't talk that way.

Oswald. By God—it makes me sick! I . . .

Andrew. You know how we're fixed here, Os. Just look at it reasonably. There's nothing I wouldn't do to . . .

Oswald. Well—lemme tell you one thing. I'm not going to work for that damn——

Andrew [*mildly*]. Well, you needn't holler the house down, son, whether you take it or not. I dunno's it makes much difference to me, 's long as you freeze onto some job that'll keep you busy and earn your living. 'Member that story 'bout the Irishman who——

Oswald [*interrupting angrily*]. Aw—you'd drive a fellow nuts, you would. Why don't you come right out and say what you mean—that you don't want me here? You're like all the rest of 'em—fight for 'em, get wounded for 'em, croak for 'em, by God! Save their old country for 'em, by God! and then have 'em tell you to go to hell. No, sir! Not any in mine!

Andrew [*becoming impatient*]. Say—what's the matter with you, anyhow? What's the great idea? You talk like one of these here Bolsheviks. For the Lord's sake, Os, keep off that stuff! 'Twon't do you, or anybody else, any good.

Oswald. It would make a man a Bolshevik just to listen to those rotten riddles of yours! I don't see how Hester stands it.

Andrew [*by the door, with an eye on it to see that* Hester *is not about*]. You needn't worry about Hess.

Oswald [*with an open sneer*]. No—nor you.

Andrew [*regaining his good nature with an effort*]. Well —don't let's get to arguing, Os. Sunday night and all. I shouldn't wonder if what you've done over there has kinda tired you out and put you on the blink physically. And you've kinda lost your pep. That's what the doctors say about a lot of the boys— All I wanted to say was that we all love havin' you here with us, but seein' as how Morgan forgot to—[*with an attempt at a joke*] to take me into partnership with him last week——

OSWALD [*ironically*]. Ha—ha!

ANDREW. Well—you know— [*Gets control of himself again and turns to* OSWALD.] Of course—now that Mattie's going away——

OSWALD [*off his guard*]. Who said she was going?

ANDREW [*quickly*]. Why?

OSWALD. Nothing. Driving her out, too?

ANDREW. Say—cut that out, will you? She's going because she wants to. Told Hess so to-day.

OSWALD [*grunting*]. Oh!

ANDREW. Say, Os— [*He comes down to the right of* OSWALD *anxiously.*] There ain't anything—funny—between you and Mattie—is there?

OSWALD [*furiously*]. No, there ain't!

ANDREW. I wouldn't for ten thousand dollars have——

OSWALD [*rises and crosses to the right*]. Is there any other damn thing you can throw up at me? You've done pretty well so far. Piker! Bolshevik! Yellow dog! And now——

ANDREW [*at the hall door, alarmed at* OSWALD'S *loud talk*]. Sh! . . . Here's Hess! [*He goes down, whistling his favorite hymn-tune.*]

HESTER [*enters and comes anxiously down to* OSWALD, *who has reseated himself in the rocking-chair*]. What's the matter?

ANDREW. Oh—nothing.

OSWALD. Just jawing.

[*Enter* MARTHE *from the dining-room. She has a large white-enamelled, steaming coffee-pot in her hand. She crosses to the table and places it there.* ANDREW *goes to the table.*]

HESTER. There's the coffee. [*She goes to the table and pours the coffee,* ANDREW *helping her with sugar and cream. With a cup in her hand she starts to the right.*] Here, Oswald.

[MARTHE *steps down a pace or two, and as though she were trying to help, takes the cup from her and hands it to* OSWALD. HESTER *looks at her curiously for a second, then goes to the table and hands a cup to* ANDREW.]

Andrew, here is yours—don't you want some, Martha, too?

MARTHE. No, thank you.

HESTER. You look tired. You go to bed. I'll clear up.

MARTHE [*slowly and wearily*]. I am—very—very tired. [*Goes to the hall.*] Good night.

ANDREW [*sitting at the table*]. Good night. "Sleep tight."

[MARTHE *goes up the stairs.*]

HESTER [*with her cup of coffee, going down to the couch*]. She *is* tired.

ANDREW [*drinking his coffee*]. Hess—*you* don't seem so very perky. I've noticed it for about a month.

[OSWALD *is drinking his coffee.*]

HESTER. I'm all right, Andrew. Please don't fuss. [*Drinking her coffee.*]

ANDREW [*affectionately*]. Can't have my little honey-bird getting sick on me.

HESTER [*impatiently*]. Don't be silly.

[*There is a long, awkward pause.*]

OSWALD [*insolently*]. Say, And'! What's the difference between a jackass and a lemon?

ANDREW [*thinking hard*]. A jackass and——

OSWALD [*with a broad wink to* HESTER]. A *lemon*.

ANDREW. Why, I don't know.

OSWALD. I'd hate to send you for lemons.

[ANDREW, *as he realizes the insult, smiles a little hurt smile. There is an uncomfortable silence.*]

ANDREW [*with an effort*]. That's—that's a good one— Ossie—I— [*He chokes up and is unable to go on. Rises.*] Well—if your uncle Dudley is going to set sail for New Brunswick on that ten-thirty, it's time to shove off. Can't afford to be the late Mr. Lane just yet. [*Goes up to the hall and gets into his things, talking to* HESTER *as he does so—coat, hat, rubbers, and umbrella.*] Hess, if I don't get back the first thing in the morning, I want you to take that collection 'round to the bank and deposit it for me. See—dearie? It's quite a lot to have 'round loose. See?

HESTER [*busy with her own thoughts, indifferently*].   Yes
—I see, I will.

ANDREW.   Good.   Well—I'll be toddlin' 'long, I guess.
[*Kisses* HESTER.] 'Night, dear. 'Night, Ossie—think
over that job, won't you?

> [OSWALD *does not answer, but stares straight out in
> front of him.*]

I—'night—I—don't be mad, Os—   [*As he gets no response
he stands there awkwardly for a moment, lonely, unwanted
in his own home.*] 'Night. [*He goes out and the outside
door closes.*]

> [*There is a pause.* HESTER *sets her coffee-cup on the
> table behind her.*]

OSWALD.   You better go to bed.   I'm going to sleep
down here.

HESTER.   What for?

OSWALD.   Ma.   Got to watch-dog the damn money.
[*He nods toward the secretary.*]

HESTER.   On the couch?

> [OSWALD *nods affirmatively.* [HESTER *rises and comes
> toward* OSWALD.   *Diffidently.*]

What *was* it?

OSWALD.   What was what?

HESTER.   Between you and Andrew.   Just now?
When I came in?

OSWALD.   Oh—nothing.

HESTER.   I wish you'd feel that you—could—tell me
things—   [*She takes his cup.*]   Like you would a sister?
Why don't you?

> [OSWALD *does not reply, nor does he look toward her.
> She sighs, and goes over to the table, where she leaves
> the coffee-cup on the tray.*]

Are you going to sleep down here?   Really?

OSWALD.   Uh-hum.

HESTER.   You'll be cold.   I'll bring you some blankets
and a pillow.

OSWALD [*laconically*].   Don't want 'em.

HESTER.   You'll be cold.

OSWALD.   There's a cover there.   I'll put my overcoat
over me.

HESTER [*by the arch*].   Shan't I turn out these lights?

[*Without waiting for a reply she presses the button at the left of the arch and puts out the brackets and the chandelier. The only light left burning now is the lamp on the table.*]

OSWALD. Don't fuss.

HESTER [*near him, after a painful silence*]. Oswald!

OSWALD. Huh?

HESTER. You—you aren't offended with me? About anything—are you?

OSWALD. Me? Nope!

HESTER. You'll be cold without a blanket. [*Crosses.*]

OSWALD. I been colder.

HESTER [*sitting on the couch*]. Oh! [*Suddenly bursts into tears.*]

OSWALD. You're tired out. You better go to bed.

HESTER [*hysterically*]. Go to bed! Get up! Go to bed! Get up again—forever and ever. Oh, I'm sick of it! Sick of it!

> [OSWALD *goes behind the table and puts the cups on the tray.* HESTER *makes an attempt to pull herself together; rises.*]

Don't do that. I'll do it! I—I—don't know what's the matter with me to-night.

> [OSWALD *crosses to the fireplace.*]

I wish you'd let me get you a blanket.

OSWALD [*not unkindly. Pushing her down on the couch*]. You sit down there.

HESTER [*whimpering*]. I'm cold.

OSWALD [*by the window*]. You better go to bed.

HESTER [*on the couch*]. Light the grate, will you, Oswald? I don't care if we *can't* afford it.

OSWALD. All right. [OSWALD *gets a match, strikes it, then sitting down on the low bench before the fireplace, he lights the gas-log. His back is to* HESTER.]

HESTER [*looking toward him*]. It's made—all the difference . . . having you here with us.

OSWALD [*abruptly*]. I'm going away.

HESTER. Go . . . going?

OSWALD. Yep.

HESTER. Where?

OSWALD. Oh—I don't know.

HESTER. I suppose—you are sick of us.

OSWALD. You didn't expect to keep me here always under a glass case—stuffed? Or anything like that, did you?

HESTER. But you've only just come.

OSWALD. And' don't seem to feel like that.

HESTER [*fiercely*]. What has Andrew been saying to you?

OSWALD. What difference does that make?

HESTER. Oh . . . he has . . . he has! I'll never forgive him. Oh—he had no right to! His own brother—a soldier—what was it he said?

[OSWALD *doesn't answer.*]

Tell me! You must!

OSWALD [*crosses to the back and then to centre of the stage*]. Oh,—I don't know. Handed me a little bokay or two—about being a yellow dog, and a cheap-skate, and a chippy-chaser—and one thing and another.

HESTER [*horrified*]. Oswald! Oh! [*Tries to control herself, but the tears will come.*] You—you must be mistaken, Oswald— He—he didn't mean it. He couldn't have. Why—it isn't like him—why——

OSWALD. See here, sis. What's the good of all this? You don't want to get hot under the collar against And'. I know you take this war-stuff pretty seriously and all that. I wish to God there was more women like you. I know how you feel. But you just better forget all about it. I'm going away. You'll settle down to your home life with And'. You'll forget me! You'll see.

HESTER [*her face hard and set*]. I'll never forgive him. Never! *Never!*

OSWALD [*with a laugh*]. Never's *some* time.

HESTER [*after a long pause*]. Are you going to take that place Mr. Thornton . . .?

OSWALD. I'll tell the world I'm not.

HESTER. But, Oswald—don't you think——?

OSWALD [*mimicking*]. But, Oswald——

[HESTER *swallows a sob.* OSWALD *comes over to her.*]

Poor old sis! [*He touches her arm.*]

HESTER [*trembling at the physical contact, she pushes him away hysterically*]. Don't!

OSWALD [*strolling down, carelessly humming*]. All right, excuse me.

HESTER [*rising and following him*]. I don't know what's the matter with me to-night.

[OSWALD *turns to her and smiles, over his shoulder.*]
I . . . I . . .

[*They are both in the centre of the stage.*]

OSWALD [*facing her*]. Well . . . anyhow, we're buddies, eh?

HESTER [*taking his hand in hers. She lays her cheek against it*]. Oh! . . . poor hand . . . all scarred . . . fighting—for us.

[OSWALD, *with a half-pitying smile, disengages himself.*]

OSWALD [*to create a diversion*]. Gosh! Rip in my coat-sleeve! [*Looking at the left sleeve of his coat.*]

HESTER. I'll mend it. I . . . I'd love to! [*In a proprietary manner.*] Oswald—take your coat right off now—mind!

OSWALD [*submits to her; she helps him take off the coat*]. You're a good little sis.

[HESTER, *now that she has a definite service to perform, smiles happily. She fetches her work-basket from the table and sits on the ottoman below the couch.*]

HESTER. I love to do things for you—don't you like me to?

OSWALD [*seated on the couch*]. I'll say so.

HESTER [*now sitting facing* OSWALD *with her back to the audience sewing on the sleeve of the coat. The red glow from the fireplace takes in the two of them. Sentimentally*]. Just think of the stories this old coat could tell, if it could talk.

OSWALD [*grinning*]. I'm thinking.

HESTER [*probing for information*]. Didn't anybody do anything nice for you—over there?

OSWALD. Sure. I asked a Y. M. C. A. guy for a shot of hootch once and he gimme a Bible. He was a kind guy.

HESTER. You're always joking me. I mean—women —weren't there any especially nice to you?— After you got out of the hospital?

[OSWALD *seems lost in memories at this question.* HESTER *is insistent.*]
Weren't there?

OSWALD. Eh? Oh . . . Women! Oh, they's women enough everywhere. Too many of 'em. . . . Say!
It's getting warm here.

HESTER. Isn't it nice—being here . . . so warm and
comfy? Do you know it is the first time we have been
really alone?— Tell me more about the war. I love to
hear about it, and you boys that have really done things
. . . won't ever talk . . .

OSWALD [*stretching himself out at ease on the couch, after
a silence*]. So warm . . . and comfy. Sometimes, over
there, when I'd maybe be sittin' up to my waist in ice-
water and just cussin' out the whole damn show—I'd
think of places, warm . . . and comfy. I never had 'em
—but I've seen 'em—and heard about 'em—like this.

[HESTER, *in sympathy, reaches out her hand to touch
his. Carelessly, and as though by accident, he moves
his hand in time to avoid her outreaching one.*]

I'm a poor lot, Hester, I guess. I've hoboed it, and dead-
beat it all over the darned place. Ever since I was a kid
of sixteen. I've seen the worst of everything—women
and men—and God's made some birds, I'll say. I've gone
down the line with 'em. Greasers in Mexico, chinks in
Shanghai, wops in Naples, niggers in Port Said— Oh, God,
I do know. Everything. Every damn thing— If
they'd been a kid like you waitin' for me—maybe . . .
Then comes the war. I goes in along with a guy named
Bill, that I picked up over in Chili—a Swede. We gets
in the Foreign Legion. God, what a swell bunch!—Gee!
Old Bill was a card. He got his, all right. Falls down in
the attack, right by me! "Come on, Bill!" I says, "to
hell with 'em!"—"I got mine!" he says, and he had.
I couldn't stop to do anything. I never saw Bill again.
[*He sits up on the couch.*] They gimme that junk—
[*Pointing to the medals on his coat.*]

HESTER [*reverently*]. War cross and two palms!

OSWALD. For what I done that day.

HESTER. Taking that dreadful machine-gun!

OSWALD. And bringing six Fritzies back by the
tails. . . . And the next day I gets mine. [*Resentfully.*]
Only I don't die. . . . Bum foot. [*He raises his foot in
the built-up shoe and lets it down with a thud. After a short*

pause he rises; HESTER *rises, too, and helps him on with his coat. She slips down to the couch, and as she sits there she lays her cheek against his left arm.* OSWALD *regards her, half in pity and half in amusement. He seems to be working out some plan in his mind. He frowns, his eyes wander to the secretary, speculatively.*]

HESTER. All you've seen and done. And all I haven't. It doesn't seem fair, somehow.

OSWALD [*at the head of the couch*]. You mean you're fed up, sis?

HESTER. I can't explain . . . you wouldn't understand. Something's wrong, somewhere. Life is wrong, I guess. [*Bitterly.*] Oh, what does it all matter?

OSWALD [*sitting beside her. Trying her out*]. Suppose . . . just for instance—suppose I told you that I was fed up—you understand what I mean—and wanted some place, warm and comfy, as you say, and somebody who'd help make it so. Somebody who'd want me there. Some one who'd understand me, and stick to me—through hell. My kind o' girl. Every fellow's got his kind, you know. Suppose I said I'd been homesick for her, just plain nutty—till I got right where I'd got to have her by me—for keeps. *Had* to! Dotty about her.— Suppose I said all that, Hester? What would *you* say, sis?

[*So great is* HESTER'S *emotion that she cannot reply.* OSWALD *eyes her with a certain amusement, a certain contempt. He rises and crosses to the centre of the stage.*]

You'll know—when I'm gone.

HESTER. Oswald! [*Piteously, after a pause.*] Don't go——

OSWALD [*after a pause, in a cold, matter-of-fact voice*]. No. I ain't your kind, sis—do you get me? [*Looks at the clock on the mantel and then crosses to it.*] Gee! It's 'most eleven o'clock. What do you know about that? [*At the fireplace.*] You're all tired out. All in. You'll feel better in the morning. [*He watches* HESTER *cynically for a moment as she sits huddled up on the couch, trying to comprehend where she is being swept. At last he comes behind her and speaks.*] Hess—lemme give you a tip. You stick to your kid—*he's hero enough for you.*

[HESTER, *utterly at sea, hesitates miserably, seeing her poor little dream shattered to bits. At last she rises and without a backward glance drags herself hopelessly out of the room and up-stairs.*]

[OSWALD *coolly watches her go, a little smile of contempt on his face. As she disappears he laughs shortly. He fetches his overcoat from the hall and standing there with it in his hand he thinks for a moment. Then he drops the overcoat on the chair, goes down to the couch and pulls the afghan up so that it covers the couch. He looks at the couch in resentment. He picks up the overcoat and brings it down and lays it over the foot of the couch. Now, standing in front of the couch, he takes the cablegram from his pocket, and by the light on the table behind him he reads the cablegram over with satisfaction. As he finishes he mutters:* "You betcha I will!" *He crosses to the secretary and puts on the little desk-light. He sits at the secretary. Pulling a sheet of paper toward him, he begins to write—apparently in answer to the cablegram. He pauses and falls into thought. His pen taps the desk mechanically as he debates the question within himself as to whether or not he shall take the money that lies in the drawer before him. His eyes fix the drawer, and furtively his hand reaches out toward the drawer and tries it. It is locked. He looks at the other drawer where he knows the key is placed. Suddenly he conquers the temptation. He crosses decisively to the couch; lifts his coat as though to lay it down under it. Again temptation assails him. He hesitates, thinks, then yields. With a quick step he is at the hallway. He looks out to see if the coast is clear. It is. He goes quickly down and extinguishes the lamp at the table. With an unfaltering step he goes to the secretary, takes the key from the upper drawer and opens the lower one. He takes out the bag of money and crowds it into his left coat-pocket.*]

[HESTER, *in her night-dress and wrapper, with a blanket over her arm and a candle lighted in her left hand, enters at the arch from the stairs in time to see him*

steal the money. She stands rigid with horror. A gasp of anguish from her causes OSWALD *to turn. The two stare at one another for a moment of silence.*]
[MARTHE *runs down the stairs and into the room. Her eyes are on* HESTER *with furious accusation. Her gaze travels to* OSWALD *for explanation. With a mutter of rage* OSWALD *rises and, pushing between the two women, goes up-stairs to his room.* MARTHE *regards* HESTER *with loathing and anger for a moment and then with a little cry of "*OSWALD!*" she follows him up the stairs.* HESTER *stands petrified with horror and anguish. The blanket falls from her nerveless arm as she looks straight in front of her and*]

THE CURTAIN FALLS

ACT III

SCENE: *Same as Act II.*
The following morning.
HESTER *is still in her night-dress and wrapper, though she has placed over her shoulders the afghan which was on the couch. Cold with shame and fear, she is discovered at the bottom of the stairway watching. She has been up all night, waiting for* OSWALD *to appear. She comes into the room. As she does so the clock on the mantel strikes eight. She goes to the window and lifts the shade. The morning sun streams in.*
Hearing a step, on the stair, she nervously turns toward it. It is MARTHE, *who enters. Her disordered hair, red eyes, and distraught countenance betray only too well the fact that she too has spent a sleepless night in tears and anguish. She gives* HESTER *a look of fierce contempt, and without speaking goes toward the dining-room.*

HESTER.   Have you seen him?
[*There is no answer.*]
Have you spoken to him?
[MARTHE *sullenly nods a negative.*]
He's still in his room, isn't he? . . . He mustn't leave this house.   He mustn't.   [*She crosses to the left.*]
MARTHE.   [*Half way to the dining-room door, she turns with an hysterical outburst of passion.*]   Why you come here last night?   Why you stay here so?   You are ashamed to tell me.
HESTER.   What is it to you, anyway—what I do—or what he does?   What's he to you, I'd like to know?
MARTHE.   I love him!   Love him!   You hear?   And he loves me.   *Me!*—not you!
HESTER.   Has he told you that?
MARTHE [*triumphantly*].   Yes, madame!
HESTER [*crossing*].   So—you are the one?   "His kind of girl."   [*Laughs a dry, crackling laugh.*]   You don't see anything funny about that—do you?   It's funny.   Almost

279

as funny as one of Andrew's riddles.　[*Turns to the girl.*]
So you are his—sweetheart?

MARTHE [*still triumphant, but bewildered*].　Yes, madame!

HESTER.　He's your—your—?　Oh, you needn't keep
anything back.　'Tisn't worth while—　Is he?

MARTHE [*defiantly but a little frightened*].　*Oui!*　But
he will marry me.　He will take me away.

HESTER.　Oh, so that's it, is it?　Well—it doesn't
matter—*now*—　When did you talk to him last?

MARTHE [*sullenly*].　Last night, before you came back.

HESTER.　And—he said then he'd take you away?

MARTHE.　Y-y-y-es.

HESTER [*resolutely*].　What for?　Can't he marry you
here?

　　　[MARTHE *does not answer.*]
What for?　[*Goes to her and turns the girl so that she has to
look into* HESTER'S *eyes.　In utter disgust.*]　Oh! . . . it's
that . . . is it?　You fool!

MARTHE [*recklessly*].　I am proud . . . proud . . .
proud of it.

HESTER [*with an eye on the arch*].　Don't scream so!

MARTHE.　You hate me because I am happy!

HESTER.　*You*—happy?　Oh, Martha!

MARTHE.　Yes . . . yes . . . yes!

HESTER.　This is a happy house.

　　　[MARTHE *sobs hysterically.*]
Stop crying!　[HESTER *shakes* MARTHE *by the shoulders.*]
Stop!　[HESTER'S *force dominates the girl and makes her
stop crying.　HESTER speaks in a cold, precise voice.*]　I
don't care what he does—or what you do.　He can take
you wherever he pleases—the sooner the better.　After
I've seen him.　Do you understand? . . .　Listen to me.
Are you listening?　I want you to tell me everything you
know about last night.　Don't lie.

MARTHE [*whimpering*].　I hear you talk.　And talk!
Down-stairs.　I wait for you to come up . . .　You take
off your dress—you go down—to him—　[*Losing control
of herself.*]　Oh!　Madame!　*You shall not take him from
me!*

HESTER.　Oh—stop that ridiculous stuff.　There's no

good going on like that. I want to know what you two intend doing with that money.

MARTHE [*all at sea*]. Money?

HESTER. Who planned it? You or he? He did, I suppose— Didn't it mean anything to you that you'd had a home here? Kindness? Friendship? Care? You could calmly plot together, right under this roof? Knowing what it would mean to us? After having sunk as low as you could with him—you could plan that!

MARTHE. *Mon Dieu!* Plan what?

HESTER. That! [*Pointing toward the secretary.*] You know what he was going to do. That's why *you* came down. [*Less convincingly.*] You have said very wicked things of me this morning. You—you had no right to do so. You ran away from me last night. You wouldn't let me explain. I came down here last night to see if he had enough covers on his couch—it was cold—he was going to sleep here on account of the money—it's true! [*As* MARTHE *sneers.*] When I got to that door—he was— I saw him—*stealing that church money from the drawer!*

MARTHE [*dismayed*]. No! No! [*To herself.*] Oh! *Mon amour! Tu as fait ça pour moi!*

HESTER. Stop talking French!— You wicked girl. I want you to understand one thing clearly! Neither you nor he is going to leave this house till every cent of this money is——

MARTHE [*on her knees before* HESTER]. Madame! [*Clutching the little cross that she wears about her neck.*] I swear to you—as God is my witness, I did not know *anything* of this—believe me—not anything. It is for me that he has done this. For me! Madame—he is not bad. No! No! . . . You shall not hurt him. You shall not.

SARAH [*from up-stairs, calling*]. Hester!

HESTER [*puzzled*]. You didn't *know*—you . . . ?

MARTHE. *Non! Non! Non!*

SARAH [*from up-stairs*]. Hester! Hester! You there —Hester?

HESTER [*sharply*]. Ssh . . .! She's coming. I must get my clothes on. Whatever the truth of this thing is, he mustn't leave this house with that money. *He shan't!*

It would be awful for us. For everybody. Can't you
see? The war—and Little Andy—and everything? *You
mustn't let him go till I get back!* [*She grips* MARTHE *by
the arm.*]   You promise?

MARTHE.   Yes! Yes! Yes!

[*They separate as* SARAH *enters from the stairs and hall.
She is dressed in a black-and-white cotton skirt and
wears a gray flannel bed-jacket.   She is carrying her
best skirt and waist, her hat and her coat and her
"false front."   She crosses and puts her things down
by the mantel as* HESTER *crosses the stage.   SARAH
turns and sees her.*]

SARAH.   My Lord above, Hester!   What in the name
o' mercy you doin' down here in your night-dress?

HESTER [*trying to control herself*].   I just ran down to
look for something that I left here.   I . . .

SARAH [*severely*].   You'll catch your death o' cold.   Get
right up-stairs and put on your dress.   You look like
death and destruction. [*Sees* MARTHE, *who is leaning
against the arch looking toward the stairs.*]   Both of ye!
What's the matter?

HESTER.   It's dreadfully cold. . . . Martha's got a
headache.

SARAH.   Huh!   If she'd a had my newralagy!   I never
slep' a wink till five o'clock this mornin'!   That's why I
overslept.

HESTER [*at the arch*].   We all did. [*As* SARAH's *back is
turned she gives* MARTHE *a warning look and then goes up
the stairs.   SARAH arranges the garments she has brought
down, puts the afghan back in place and smooths it down.*]

SARAH [*working as she talks*].   You jest git down,
Mattie?

MARTHE [*on the watch at the arch*].   Yes.

SARAH.   Hum!   You got the fire started?

MARTHE.   Not yet.

SARAH [*carrying* OSWALD's *overcoat, which was on the
couch, to the chair*].   Well, I never!   What you standin'
there for, like a graven image?   Ain't you never heard
that folks eat breakfast?   Git a move on ye, Marthy!

MARTHE [*her eyes on the stairs*].   My head hurts me.

SARAH.   Huh!   Yer head! [*Looking at the couch, her*

mind on something else.] Didn't Oswal' sleep down here last night?

MARTHE. I don't know.

SARAH [*exasperated*]. I dunno what's come over everybody this mornin'. You all act 'bout's lively's a cigarstore Indian. Yer "I'd know this" and "I'd know that"! I s'pose you expect *me* to git the breakfast. 'Course it's nothin' to nobody that I'm going to ol' Mrs. Trumble's funeral this mornin'. [*She is straightening out the pillows on the couch as she talks.*] An' I was intendin' to git there early so's I could see what they laid her out in. I heard 'twas a white satin shroud. The undertaker told me yesterday at meetin' that she'd begun to mortify and that was why they was a-hurryin' to bury her. She wa'n't much to look at when she was livin' an', now if she's a mortifyin'! Mercy! Them Trumbles is tighter'n bark to a birch-tree. I bet you the coffin-handles is nickelplated. [*She goes to the table and gets the coffee-tray, left there from last night.*] Come right along now, Marty, and help git the coffee. Somethin' hot'll do ye good. Come on now. [*Starts for the dining-room.*] I wouldn't a— overslep' to-day for nothin'.

> [*She goes into the dining-room.* MARTHE *hesitates, but seeing* HESTER *coming down the stairs she follows* SARAH *into the kitchen.*]

HESTER [*enters from the arch. She has made the hastiest toilet, a simple house dress. She begins aimlessly to set the room to rights. From time to time she supplicates aloud*]. Oh, God! Please help me!— Oh, God! Please . . . *please* help me!

LITTLE ANDY [*calling down the stairs*]. Mummy! Mummy! I'm up!

HESTER. Yes, dear. Martha'll come and help you get dressed.

ANDY [*from up-stairs*]. Uncle Oswal's up too! [*He sings as he comes down the stairs, the little French song that* MARTHE *has taught him: "Au clair de la lune," etc. Jumps down the stairs two at a time to the bottom and enters.*]

HESTER [*in terror, as she thinks of* OSWALD]. Oh!

ANDY [*runs to the secretary, where he leaves his "Froggie" that he has brought with him*]. Uncle Oswal' buttoned me. . . . Now you be a good froggie—you'll get your breakfast pretty soon. [*Crosses. Calls.*] Uncle Oswal'! Uncle Oswal'! Come on down, I'm down-stairs.

OSWALD [*from up-stairs*]. All right, general.

HESTER [*on couch as* ANDY *runs into her arms and kisses her*]. My darling! My darling! [*She clasps him tightly in her arms.*]

ANDY [*disengaging himself*]. Oh, mummy! You tickle! Can't I have breakfast? I'll be late for school.

HESTER. In a minute, dear.

ANDY [*as* OSWALD *enters calmly from the stairs, neatly dressed in a new brown suit*]. 'Tain't ready yet.

  [OSWALD *nonchalantly seats himself in the rocking-chair.*]

OSWALD. Ain't it? Well, you and me we'll have to play we're in the trenches, waiting for the gazabo that brings the juice in the coffee-pail, eh?

ANDY. What's juice?

OSWALD. French for coffee.

ANDY [*climbing on* OSWALD'S *lap*]. It is awfully nice havin' you here with us, Uncle Oswal'.

OSWALD. Is it?

ANDY. Awful. You won't never go away—will you?

OSWALD. Not if you say so.

ANDY. We don't want him to go ever, do we, mummy? [*Louder as* HESTER *does not answer.*] Mummy? Do we?

HESTER. Perhaps he doesn't want to stay.

ANDY. But he said he'd stay—didn't you, uncle?

OSWALD. Um-hum.

  [HESTER *stares at him dumfounded.*]

SARAH [*entering from the dining-room*]. It's 'bout ready. Come, Andy . . . an' eat yer orange—it's gettin' late. [*To* OSWALD.] Hungry's a bear, ain't ye, Oswal'? [*As she starts for the dining-room the telephone rings.*] Telephone's ringin'. [*Again she starts for the dining-room. Telephone rings again. She turns and sees that neither of them has moved to answer the bell.*] Ain't you goin' to—? [*Another ring. She goes to the hall as she speaks.*] Land! Have I got to answer that awful thing? [*At the telephone in the hall.*] Oh . . . Andy, is that you?— You are?— At the station? Before long? All right. [*Coming back into the room.*] Andrew's back. He'll be here pretty soon, I guess. He says if the boss calls him up to say he'll be into the city on the ten-thirty. [*Crosses to the dining-room.*] Little Andy can walk along to the school with me, Hester, as long as I'm goin' by there on my way to the funeral.

HESTER [*dully*]. All right, mother, if you wish——

ANDY [*from the dining-room*]. Mummy! Come here a minute! I want you!

HESTER. Yes, dear, I'm coming. [*She looks at* OSWALD *for a second, and then goes quickly into the dining-room.*]

SARAH. I had a cup of coffee in the kitchen. [*She crosses to the mantel and begins to get ready for the funeral. She is thus occupied during the following scene. Slipping off her wrapper, she dresses rapidly, pins on her "false front," and adjusts her hat.*] Them stairs 'bout kill me, what with my roomatism and all, so I brought my dress right down here. . . . Mattie's got your breakfast 'bout ready. She ain't no worker, that girl. I pity the man who gits her. . . . You goin' to see that feller, that Thornton, to-day? . . .

OSWALD. Maybe.

SARAH [*looking in the mirror on the mantel as she adjusts her garments*]. Well—you better. The sooner you git to earnin' the better. . . . I put on a red flannel petticoat this mornin'. My legs git so cold. . . . You better think over what I told you 'bout that Pierce gal. Her folks have got money. . . . [*Sotto voce.*] I want to git away from here. You take that job, Oswal'.— [*Looks at the clock.*] My land alive, look at that time! [*Calls as she hurries her dressing.*] Andy! Come right along! Git yer things on!

[LITTLE ANDY *enters, followed by* HESTER, *who gets him into his coat, cap, mittens, muffler, and rubbers.*]

ANDY. Granny, can I go to the funeral with you?

SARAH. No!

ANDY. Aw!——

SARAH [*looking in the mirror again*]. Mercy! I look more'n a hundred years old to-day!— Well, 'twon't be long before they'll be layin' me away too. An' I guess everybody'll be glad. . . . One thing—I don't want no white satin shroud! . . . [*She adjusts the "false front," then her hat.*] My best black dress's good enough fer me . . . [*She faces* OSWALD.] You mark my words— somethin' is goin' to happen! I dreamed twice in the night of fallin' water. Sign o' trouble, sure.

[ANDY, *now nearly dressed, gives a burst of laughter. Severely.*]

'Tain't nothin' to laugh at! My land, I'll be late an' I shan't see a thing! An' I did so want to know 'bout them coffin-handles! [*She comes to the centre of the stage, all excitement.*] Hurry, Andy! Can't you hurry him, Hester?

HESTER.   He's ready, mother.

SARAH [*to herself*].   Mortifyin'! Mercy!

ANDY [*to* OSWALD].   'Bye!—'Bye!

OSWALD.   Give us a kiss, son.

[ANDY *runs to him.* OSWALD *takes the boy in his arms and kisses him.*]

Good-by! [*Hugs him affectionately, and* LITTLE ANDY *runs up to the arch and out.*]

SARAH [*feeling in her pocket*].   Mercy! Forgot my hand-kerchief! [*She goes back to the mantel, gets the handkerchief that she has left there, and then starts for the arch.*]

OSWALD [*intercepting her there*].   'Bye—ma! [*Puts his arm about her and kisses her cheek.* HESTER *watches him in anguish.* SARAH *looks curiously at* OSWALD, *astonished at this unusual display of affection.*]

SARAH.   For mercy sakes! Anybody'd think we was all goin' on a journey! Come, Andy! [*Exit* SARAH *and* ANDY. HESTER *follows them out into the hall to the outer door.*]

MARTHE [*at the dining-room door. She comes a little way into the room*].   Oswald! . . . I——

OSWALD [*in a low voice, nervously*].   In a minute. Wait! Get back there! [*He pushes her back into the dining-room.*]

[HESTER *enters.*]

HESTER [*in a low, tense voice*].   You've got to give back that money, right now.

OSWALD [*coolly*].   That's what *you* say.

HESTER [*desperately*].   Give it back!

[OSWALD *goes to the table and picks up his pipe, putting it in his pocket, preparatory to going.*]

Do you mean you won't?

OSWALD. You've guessed it!

HESTER [*wildly*]. You shan't go out of this room with that money!

OSWALD. Who's going to stop me?

HESTER. I will. [*She faces him resolutely.*]

OSWALD [*crossing the stage in front of her*]. What do you care about it?

HESTER. What do I care? Why—it's terrible! It's awful! It's criminal! We'll be ruined. The disgrace of it to the family! Give it back. Now. This instant.

OSWALD. Well—Andy'll have to pay it.

HESTER. Andy—pay it! Why—we haven't got a penny and you know it.

OSWALD. Oh—he can get it somehow. What's he ever done, anyhow? He didn't go to war, did he? Let him pay, then. I'm a soldier. I'm his brother. Let him pay!

HESTER [*going to him—in a fury of anger*]. Soldier! You! Andrew pay! Why should he pay for you—and your horrid women? Oh! I know the story of that wretched girl, here, in this very house—right under our eyes. Mine! Your mother's! And you'd planned to rob us, in order to run away and cover up the filthy tracks of your nasty—dirty—ugh!— [*Crosses and sits in the chair before the secretary.*]

OSWALD [*insolently*]. Go to it, Phœbe Snow. You're doing fine. *You're* all right! You're pure! God but you're pure! But it's going to cost you money to pay your laundry bill, my little snowflake. But lemme tell you one thing . . . your dope on Martie is all wrong. She didn't know anything about that little sum of money I . . . borrowed, the kid didn't. Not a thing.

HESTER. You expect me to believe that? Do you think that I don't know you have to take her away? And why?

OSWALD [*coolly*]. Do I?

HESTER. It's all plain enough now. What a fool I was not . . .

OSWALD. You were a fool, all right. That ain't the half of it, dearie.

HESTER. Oh, you're the wickedest man!— You—you —*hero!*

OSWALD [*approaching her chair*]. What did you come down here last night for?— Afterward? You think I don't know? You haven't got anything on me, young lady.

HESTER. Oh—you coward! You *coward!*

OSWALD. Oh, can that stuff! 'Tisn't going to help you any. Listen to me.

HESTER [*distractedly*]. Haven't you any pity?

OSWALD. Listen here. You tried to find out last night if there was any other woman. You know why you wanted to know. And then I handed you that "supposing" stuff. Supposing you were the goat? And you were, all right. God, you were easy! When I first came here I thought you were—well, different from the ordinary run of women. You looked like a good girl—married, with one of the finest kids a woman ever had. And then— little by little I began to see how the wind lay. Just like 'em all, you are. I tested you out last night. Just a regular—well, you know. I'm going to tell you something. I'm going back to France. Back to France, see? To my girl. That's where she is. "My kind of girl." She wants me and I want her. And I'm going to take this money to do it with. Oh, I know all the sweet things you'd like to say about me. What the hell do I care? You and Andy have got to pay. That's the price of that little show you tried to pull off last night. Do you get me?

HESTER [*in intense shame*]. Oh!

OSWALD. Sore because you can't eat your cake and have it too, eh? You better make up your mind to take your medicine quietly.

HESTER [*on her feet*]. I don't care *what* happens! What you do! I won't let you take that money.

OSWALD. What'll you do? Call the police? And disgrace the family? What about your nice, pious friends when they hear the police have arrested the church treasurer's brother?

[HESTER, *realizing the force of his argument, sinks back again.*]

Why, you haven't got the nerve to do it! *And you know it!* That money's going to take me back to France.

HESTER. Oh! Oh! And Martha! Martha—what about her? What are you going to do about her? *As she is?*

OSWALD [*casually*]. Martha? Oh—nothing. Leave her, for you and Andy.

HESTER [*again starting to her feet. In horror*]. Do you mean to say you're going to *leave her*—like that? *Leave her . . . like that?*

OSWALD [*regretfully*]. I've got to. Poor kiddie! I've got to. You can help her out, can't you?

HESTER. Oh, my God! . . . Oh, my God!

OSWALD. Well—I've told you. You asked for it and you've got it. I'm going.

HESTER [*as* OSWALD *takes his overcoat from the chair. In a last appeal*]. Oswald! Oswald! Oh . . . for God's sake, Oswald! . . . Don't take that money! Have some pity on us. For your mother's sake—for Little Andy—for Martha!

OSWALD. You weren't thinking of them last night—Cut that sob-stuff out. I've *got* to go. You understand? *Got* to! [*Goes out into the hallway and gets the suitcase which he brought down with him earlier. Appears in the doorway with hat and coat.*] Think over what I've said, sis. You're up against it. You can't do one damn thing but take your medicine.

HESTER [*beaten and hopeless*]. You coward! [*Sinks down on the couch, back to audience, facing the arch where he is standing.*] You coward!

OSWALD. Say—give my dog to Little Andy for me, will you?

[*The outer door slams.*]

MARTHE [*entering at the dining-room door. Agitatedly*]. What is it? . . . I hear you talk—talk—talk! What have you said to him? [*Calls as she goes through the arch, runs up the stairway and back.*] Oswald!— Where is he?

HESTER [*in a dead voice*]. He's—gone.

MARTHE [*anxiously*]. Gone where?

HESTER. He's got the money. He's gone!

MARTHE. Oh! Oh! Madame! [*Earnestly, pathetically*

honest.] He must not do this. I shall not let him do this. He does not know what he does. He is foolish— frightened—because I am—don't you see?—as I am. When I have seen him, I shall make him understand. Have no fear of that. [*She smiles confidently, patronizingly.*]

HESTER [*realizing the terrible blow she must deal to* MARTHE]. You—you poor girl!

MARTHE. I must go to him. Tell me where he is?

HESTER. Martha, you'll have to know—Martha—try —try to be as brave as you can. He—he's—it's not what you think. He—Martha—he's not coming back any more. He—he . . .

MARTHE. Where is he?

HESTER [*as gently as she can*]. He took the money . . . because—he took it to run away with—away from you, all of us. *He has left you.*

MARTHE. That is not true!

HESTER. If it only weren't!

MARTHE. It is not true!

HESTER. It's true enough, Martha. He's going to— another woman—a girl—in France. That's why he stole it. To get him there. He said so. . . . Not you—nor me. *Her!* He's *left you to me!*

MARTHE. *You!* He threw you away! That is why you tell me this. You *lie!*

[*In the distance a heavy deep-toned fire-bell begins to toll with a suggestion of desolation and menace.*]

HESTER [*realizing the hopelessness of attempting to convince her*]. Ask him! Follow him! Run after him! Then you'll know! [*She cries and goes up to the window.*]

MARTHE. If he goes—I go! Good or bad I go with him—out of your horrible house—forever!

ANDREW [*who has just opened the street door as* MARTHA *collides with him in the hall*]. Where you goin'? What is it? Mattie . . .

[*The hall door slams.*]

She darn near knocked me down! [*At the arch, calling up the stairs.*] Hello, everybody! Hoo, hoo!—I'm home. [*Comes into the room, sees* HESTER, *still by the window.*]

Hello, Hess! Where the dickens is Mattie goin' on the hundred-yard dash?

HESTER. Oh—I don't know. She saw somebody.

ANDREW [*taking off his coat*]. Saw somebody! Gosh! She made me see stars, all right. Must-a seen her best beau go by. . . . Gee! It's a cold mornin'. I nearly froze at the station. The house is cold, too.

[*The bell tolls.*]

'S a fire somewhere, though. I heard the engines as I come along. Big smoke, too. [*Takes the coat to the hall, taking out of the pocket a parcel.*] Here's ma's tonic. [*Places the package on the table.*] Stopped into Simpson's drug-store for it as I came along on my way up from the station. Saw Os running by. I hollered at him, but he didn't pay any attention. Wonder if he's still mad at me! Breakfast ready? I's hungry as a dog. Say, Hess, a feller on the train told me a daisy conundrum—about "Why don't the devil skate——"

HESTER [*her nerves racked to the breaking point*]. Stop! Stop! Stop! Or I'll scream the house down. Stop! [*She crosses down to the couch.*]

ANDREW [*mildly disturbed*]. What's the matter, dear?

HESTER. I—I don't know—I don't feel well, I——

ANDREW. You do look about all in. Can't have my little honey-bird gettin' sick on me. I don't know how this house'd get along without you. [*Whistles for a second—"There is a happy land."*] The answer to that one is— Oh! Oh! I forgot. Didn't want to hear that one, did you? [*He goes to the secretary and puts some papers in it.* HESTER *all the while is watching him in deadly fear that he is going to open the drawer and discover the loss of the money.*] Funny thing. Os got the notion in his head last night that I thought he was spongin' on us. [*Ruminatively.*] Funny kid, Os—gettin' into scrapes since the day he was born, and getting out of 'em by the skin of his teeth. But he ain't bad, Hess—he's headstrong—gets an idea into his nut and— [*Shakes his head dubiously.*] You know I wouldn't have him think we didn't want him here, not for a thousand dollars.

HESTER [*resolved to tell him the truth*]. Andrew—I— I . . .

ANDREW [*comes toward her*]. What, dear?

HESTER [*unable to go on*]. Nothing.

ANDREW [*looking at her closely*]. Say! You look awful, Hess! Maybe it's the flu. Want a doctor?

HESTER. No.

ANDREW. You're all tired out. You're tied down here too close. Wish I could take you on a little vacation. Niagara Falls or somewhere. But we're so darn poor and all— [*He has started toward the secretary. Suddenly he turns.*] Did you see him?

HESTER [*started*]. Who?

ANDREW. Os. This mornin'?

[*She nods.*]

What'd he say?

[*She does not answer.*]

How was he? Did you talk to him? What'd he say?

HESTER [*unable to hold out any longer*]. He . . . he . . .

ANDREW. Huh?

HESTER. He—he— Oh! I guess I'll go up and lie down. [*She is near collapse.*]

ANDREW [*coming toward her, solicitously*]. I guess you better had.

HESTER [*weakly*]. Andrew—oh, Andrew! Be good to me.

ANDREW. Why—why, you poor little kid— [*Smiling.*] I'll carry you up-stairs.

HESTER [*as he attempts to take her in his arms*]. No. Please!

ANDREW. I want to.

[HESTER *holds him at arm's length.*]

Well—I—all right.

[*A fire-engine is heard in the street close by.*]

Where's ma?

[*Another engine-bell clangs.*]

HESTER. The funeral.

ANDREW [*as the engines pass the house*]. Hello! [*Goes to the window and looks out.* HESTER *crosses and sits by the secretary.*] Look at the folks runnin' by! Mattie'll get her death of cold without anything on her. Guess I'll go to that fire when I take that money over to the bank. [*He crosses back to the secretary.* HESTER *is now in the*

chair before the drawer in which the money was left. AN-
DREW *takes the key out of the upper drawer and starts to
unlock the lower drawer.*]

HESTER [*in horror as she realizes that this is the end, that
discovery must come*]. Andrew! I . . . I . . . [*She
tries to arrest his hand. There is a sharp knock on the pane
of glass in the window. A man's voice is heard calling.*]

VOICE. Lane! Lane!

ANDREW [*turning*]. What . . .?

VOICE [*off stage*]. For God's sake, quick! You're
wanted! Quick!

ANDREW [*startled*]. Why—what's the matter? I—
[*He runs out of the room toward the outer door. The door
opens and one hears a murmur of excited voices. The words
predominating in the conversation are "Your brother!"
"Don't get excited, Lane!" "Fire!"*]

> [HESTER, *unhearing, relieved at anything that could
> stop the immediate discovery of the theft, lets her head
> drop helplessly on the desk. Suddenly there is a
> cry from* ANDREW *in the hall and the sound of a door
> slamming.*]

> [*Presently* MARTHE *enters at the hall door from the left.
> Her face is ghastly and gray with horror. She comes
> in, as though in a trance. She covers her face with
> her hands as though to shut out some dreadful sight.*]

MARTHE. Oh!

HESTER [*hearing* MARTHE. *Presently she rises, goes to
her*]. What's the matter?

MARTHE [*staring straight out in front of her*]. He . . .
he . . . is . . . dead!

HESTER. Dead? . . . Who?

MARTHE [*her tearless grief choking her words*]. He . . .
he——

HESTER. He?— Who?— Not . . .?

> [MARTHA *nods.*]

Oh . . . what . . . what . . .?

MARTHE. The fire——

HESTER. Fire?

MARTHE. The—the kindergarten—the——

HESTER [*dazed for a moment*]. Fire! Kindergarten!

[*Screams.*] Baby! [*She staggers out of the room and the outer door slams.*]

MARTHE [*like a frightened little child*]. I'm afraid! I want my mother! I . . . want—my mother.

[*Voices are heard in the hall. A door is heard to open and close.* MARTHE, *unable to endure what she supposes to be the sight of* OSWALD'S *dead body, exits moaning,* "OSWALD!"]

ANDREW [*in the hall*]. He ain't hurt, Hess, he ain't hurt!

HESTER [*in the hall*]. Oh, baby, baby!

[ANDREW *and* HESTER *enter, the former carrying* LITTLE ANDY *wrapped in* OSWALD'S *coat, which shows great holes burned by the fire, and streaks of black.* HESTER *sits on the couch and* ANDREW *puts the child in her arms.*]

LITTLE ANDY. I ain't hurted, mummy—not a bit. Uncle Oswal' come and got me. He found me. The fire got ev'rywhere, and Uncle Oswal' come. Where's Uncle Oswal'?

HESTER [*turns her eyes to her husband questioningly. He breaks into a sob*]. Tell me.

ANDREW. He's gone.

HESTER. Tell me.

ANDREW. I do' know. The kindergarten. Andy lit a camp-fire, he says, and it was all afire in no time, they say. Andy was missing and Oswald run in and got him. And then Oswald run back again, after another little boy, that's what they say—and the roof fell in on 'em. Oh, God—it's awful! Burned to death! That's his overcoat there on baby. And he's gone. And I was here a-talking and making jokes. It's awful.

HESTER [*a look of awe on her face*]. Oh, Oswald could do that! Oh, thank God!

LITTLE ANDY [*getting out from the coat and down from his mother's lap*]. Why don't Uncle Oswal' come home? [*Goes to his father and pulls at his hand.*] What you cryin' for, daddy? Where's Uncle Oswal'?

ANDREW [*to spare the boy the scene*]. Listen, Andy. There's that little dog whining for you in the kitchen.

ANDY [*pulling away from his father*]. Lemme go.

Cafard! Cafard! [*He runs to the dining-room door, where one hears him singing " Au clair de la lune," his troubles soon forgotten.*]

ANDREW [*looking after the boy*]. The little fellow don't sense what he's done. [*He sits beside* HESTER.] Oh—I can't bear it, Hess. If Os had only parted friends with me. . . . Why, I wouldn't a-hurt him any mor'n I'd hurt Little Andy. He was just a kid to me—Os was. I couldn't help but forgive him for the things he'd do. He thought I didn't want him here. Why, I . . .

HESTER [*mechanically*]. Don't. You mustn't, Andrew. You mustn't feel that way.

ANDREW. Everybody loved Os. Andy, you, Martha, everybody. But he—he thought I was hard on him—he died—thinking——

HESTER [*gently, out of her own deep pain*]. Andrew—listen, dear. Don't abuse yourself like that—you were good to him. Wonderful—I—I— Oh, Andrew—Andrew, if I'd only been—as good as you.

ANDREW. Didn't he say anything—this morning—when he went—about me?

HESTER [*determining to lie bravely to him to ease his pain*]. He said: "Tell Andy—I'm sorry—about last night. He's—a good old scout."

ANDREW [*smiling through his tears*]. He said—that? Why—that means everything. You don't know what that means to me, Hess. [*Sobs again, but softly now.*] "Good old scout!" That's like him—just like him. Oh, I knew he was all right. Bless him for that.

HESTER. Andrew—poor Andrew! [*Pause.*] Andrew, God'll forgive our mistakes, won't he?

[ANDREW *puts his arm about her and holds her to him.*] Andrew—there is something else—something— [*She draws away from him.*]

ANDREW [*vaguely*]. "Good old scout," he said. . . . [*Turning to her.*] What is it you say, dearie?

HESTER [*making a great decision. With faltering voice*]. Andrew, that money—the collection—the money you——

ANDREW [*as she hesitates*]. Yes?

HESTER. I gave it—to Oswald—to put it in the bank.

ANDREW [*vaguely*]. Now? This morning?

HESTER. Just now.

ANDREW [*slowly, scarcely comprehending*]. Then it's gone. It's burned. With him.

HESTER. He took it—to put it in the bank.

[ANDREW *sighs heavily, then squares himself to meet the blow.*]

ANDREW. Then we'll have to make it up. That's all. We'll have to make it up——

HESTER. Yes. We'll have to pay it. Oh, Andy, if you knew . . .

ANDREW. 'Tain't your fault, Hester. Don't you worry. Natural enough for you to give it to him to put in the bank for you. Don't fret, honey, 'bout that.

HESTER [*in a sudden break*]. Oh, Andy—Andy! Why didn't I understand?

ANDREW. Sh!— It's all right. [*He sighs heavily, wearily.*] Seems sometimes as though everything hits you all in a heap. . . . We'll get out of it somehow. . . . I'm so darn sorry for you, Hess. I know how you miss all the nice things that other girls have——

HESTER. Andrew! Don't!

ANDREW. Well, it's true—an' I don't blame you. [*He sits thinking for a moment.*] Maybe I can borrow a little money somewhere. And there's that money we been savin' for Little Andy's education.

[HESTER *sighs bitterly.*]

Yes. It's tough, but it's got to be done.

HESTER. I don't mind, Andrew. I'll help you. Oh, Andy—I'm so—so sorry.

ANDREW [*drawing her closer and patting her hand*]. Why, of course. There doesn't anything matter much, dear, so long as I got you and the boy. Thank God for that!— Now I must go an' find ma. Poor ma! And then—go back there to—him——

HESTER [*looking into his eyes with a new love born of her suffering and shame*]. You are a good man, Andrew! Now I know! A good, *good* man.

ANDREW [*humbly and simply taking her into his arms*]. Me? I'm just old Andy, I am. But Os—Os was a hero.

THE CURTAIN FALLS

TO THE LADIES!

GEORGE S. KAUFMAN AND MARC CONNELLY

"Nearly all the great men have been married; it can't be merely a coincidence."—*Act Third.*

TO THE LADIES!

To the Ladies! is the joint creation of George S. Kaufman and Marc Connelly. Mr. Kaufman was born in Pittsburgh, Pennsylvania, in 1889. After several ventures, including an effort to study law, for which he found himself unfitted, he settled down to newspaper work about ten years ago. For a while he conducted humorous columns in the Washington *Times* and New York *Evening Mail*, then did general newspaper work on the New York *Tribune*, finally becoming connected with the dramatic department. For the last six years he has been associated with the dramatic department of the New York *Times*. He has also contributed to *Life* and other magazines. His first dramatic effort, *Some One in the House* (1919), was not a success. In 1920 he adapted *Jacques Duval* from the German for Mr. George Arliss.

Mr. Connelly was born in McKeesport, Pennsylvania, and was educated at the public schools in that town and at Trinity Hall, Washington, Pennsylvania. He is now thirty years old. He was a reporter and an assistant dramatic critic and also conducted a column in Pittsburgh newspapers until 1915. In that year he came to New York to see the production of a musical comedy for which he had written the lyrics. This comedy was a financial failure, and the next laconic sentence in the author's letter to the editor tells the story of the beginning of many another successful career. "Lacked money to go home, so stayed in New York." Mr. Connelly has been doing newspaper work in New York City and contributing to *Life* and other magazines since 1915.

Success came first to this dramatic partnership with *Dulcy*, a comedy dealing with the stupid woman and her effect upon her husband's business prospects, inspired by the column of "F. P. A." in the New York *Tribune*. *Dulcy* opened in Indianapolis on February 14, 1921, and has since played for two seasons throughout the country, including a run of thirty-one weeks in New York. A London production is also impending.

To the Ladies! was first produced at the Lyceum Theatre in Rochester on February 13, 1922, and at the Liberty Theatre in New York on February 20. Like *Dulcy*, it has been spending the season of 1922–23 on a tour of the country. These two plays are analyzed in the General Introduction.

A third play by the Messrs. Kaufman and Connelly, a dramatization of Harry Leon Wilson's story, *Merton of the Movies*, is now running at the Cort Theatre, New York. Their fourth play—it is their third in point of time of writing—is a comedy called *West of Pittsburgh*, which, according to the authors, "satirizes the Winchell Smith kind of rural comedy." It was first tried out in the Spring of last year, and will have its New York première in the coming fall.

Dulcy was published in 1921 by G. P. Putnam's Sons, and also in *Longer Plays by Modern Authors*, edited by Miss H. L. Cohen (1922). *To the Ladies!* is published now for the first time through the courtesy of the authors, who have also furnished the information for this introduction.

CAST OF CHARACTERS

Lyceum Theatre, Rochester, February 13, 1922
Liberty Theatre, New York, February 20, 1922

Elsie Beebe.....................Helen Hayes.
Leonard Beebe..................Otto Kruger.
Chester Mullin.................Percy Helton.
John Kincaid...................George Howell.
Myrtle Kincaid................Isabel Irving.
The Toastmaster...............William Seymour.
The Politician................William F. Canfield.
Tom Baker......................Robert Fiske.
A Truckman.....................J. J. Hylan.
Another Truckman..............Albert Cowles.
A Photographer................Albert Cowles.
The Stenographer..............Norma Mitchell.
The Barber.....................John Kennedy.
The Bootblack.................Paolo Grosso.

Guests at the Banquet

SYNOPSIS OF SCENES

Act I. The home of the Beebes in Nutley, New Jersey.
        A Saturday afternoon.

Act II. Scene I.—The same. Two weeks later.
         Scene II.—You are among those present at the
         annual dinner of John Kincaid's Sons, Hotel
         Commodore, New York.

Act III. The office. Six months later.

TO THE LADIES!*

ACT I

The scene is the living-room of LEONARD and ELSIE BEEBE,
on the ground floor of a two-family house in Nutley,
New Jersey. It is a decidedly livable place, and the
reader is hereby encouraged to think of it as a room, not
as a stage. It is neat, and rather new—the former because it is the home of ELSIE BEEBE, and the latter
because it is the home of a newly wedded couple. It is,
however, distinctly and necessarily modest—LEONARD
BEEBE probably earns forty-five dollars a week, and the
monthly rent of his home is not over forty, if that.
There are two doors—one leading into the rest of the
house, and the other to the porch and the street. When
the latter is opened you get a glimpse of a small porch,
and beyond it somebody else's small porch, just like it.
There are a few windows, which afford the customary
suburban view. The Beebes have a small grand
piano—a wedding-gift—and the usual table, desk,
chairs, and divan, just as other people have them.

The time is about three o'clock on a Saturday afternoon in
the fall. The room is empty when you first see it, and
you have time to accustom yourself to it before LEONARD
BEEBE enters. He comes, rather abstractedly, from
what is probably the dining-room. He is a middle-
class youth of about twenty-five, and somewhere in the
country there are ten million just like him. He leaves
the door open behind him, and as he crosses the room he
seems to remember that he was sent on an errand. He
considers for a moment, then goes to the desk and pulls
open one drawer and then another. Finding nothing,
he tries the drawers in the table. Then he calls to an
invisible figure in the next room.

LEONARD. Hey!

ELSIE [*from the next room*]. Yes, dear?

LEONARD. Which drawer did you say it was in?

ELSIE [*calling*]. On top of the mantel!

LEONARD. Oh! [*He goes to the mantel, gives it a quick glance.*] I don't see it. [*There is no answer.*] It isn't here!

ELSIE. On the mantel?

LEONARD. Huh-huh. [*Those peculiar syllables that mean no.*]

ELSIE [*still calling*]. Wait a minute!

[LEONARD, *much relieved, hurries to the window and peers anxiously out of it. ELSIE BEEBE, his bride of six months, enters the room. She wears a simple house dress, covered with an apron, and carries a little pile of spreads, shirts, and collars, newly arrived from the laundry. Observing him at the window.*]
Oh, Leonard, they are not coming yet.

LEONARD. You never can tell.

ELSIE [*goes to the mantel and finds the desired article—a laundry list*]. Leonard! The laundry list!

LEONARD [*inclined to argue it*]. I didn't know it was folded—I was looking for something big.

ELSIE. Well, if you'd just looked where I told you— [*She breaks off—opens the laundry list.*]

LEONARD [*shamed into it; goes to her and reaches for the list*]. Here, I'll help.

ELSIE. No, you don't need to now.

LEONARD [*squaring himself*]. I want to. [*He reaches for the list; she makes a pretense of withholding it. Under the guise of getting the list,* LEONARD *takes* ELSIE *in his arms and kisses her.*] I wanted to do that, too.

ELSIE. Oh, Leonard, you can be so nice sometimes. I wish you weren't so—so aggravating in little ways.

LEONARD. Well, I said I'd help. [*He takes the list.*] I'll read the things off while you compare them. [*He settles himself for a hard day's work.*] "Newark and Nutley Troy Laundry—" Say, it was one of their wagons that ran over that little boy yesterday.

ELSIE [*patiently*]. Yes, Leonard. Please, go on.

LEONARD. Didn't you read about it? Over on Bloom-field Avenue——

ELSIE. *Please*, Leonard.

LEONARD. All right. [*Reads from the list.*] "Gentle-men's List." [*Snaps his fingers.*] Osgood was the name of the driver.

ELSIE. Leonard—*please*.

LEONARD. "Three—shirts—silk." I didn't know I had any silk shirts.

ELSIE [*without looking up*]. You haven't.

LEONARD. Then they've made a mistake! We've got somebody else's . . . [*He reaches for the laundry as though to examine it; she shoos him away.*]

ELSIE. Leonard—read it carefully.

LEONARD [*looking at the list; begins belligerently*]. Three—[*he observes his error; finishes weakly*] collars.

ELSIE. Now you've got it.

LEONARD [*finding an excuse*]. They print them all so close.

ELSIE. Now if you're going to help, Leonard . . . [*She breaks off; inspects the remaining pieces.*] Only one spread—is that right?

LEONARD. Ah—is that under Gentlemen's or Ladies'? Yes! [*Formally reading.*] "Spreads. One."

ELSIE. And a waist—I know that's right. [*She takes the list and looks at it long and seriously.*] Leonard!

LEONARD. Well?

ELSIE. I'm afraid we can't send anything to the laun-dry—any more.

LEONARD. Now I'm not going to have you doing a lot more laundry! [*A pause.*] If we've got to economize—well, for one thing, I'm going to cut down my lunches.

ELSIE. Leonard Beebe! Promise me that you won't!

LEONARD. Why should I be throwing money away like that when *my wife* is at home working like a dog? I've got *some* self-respect!

ELSIE. Of course, honey. But——

LEONARD. Well, I'm not going to have you taking on that extra work. Here I am, probably going to be chief clerk in a month . . .

ELSIE. Leonard! You don't know that you are at all.

LEONARD. Well, I know it's vacant, don't I? And I know Mr. Kincaid is coming all the way out here to see me, don't I? Just the way he always does when he's going to promote somebody.

ELSIE. But, Leonard, he might not . . .

LEONARD. Of course he will. That's always the way it begins. First he and Mrs. Kincaid pay you a visit; then you get invited to the banquet . . .

ELSIE. Oh, Leonard, I hope so! But we must be careful not to count on it. How much did you pay for the peaches? [*Taking up an account-book.*] Thirty-five, wasn't it?

LEONARD [*at window, looking out*]. Yes. No. I don't know. I can't put my mind on little things to-day, when they're coming out here. This may be a big day for me. What time is it now?

ELSIE [*seated at desk*]. Look at your watch, Leonard.

LEONARD. Huh? Oh! [*He takes out his watch.*] Quarter to three. [*Back to the window.*] How long's it take to drive out from town?

ELSIE. Oh, an hour. Perhaps a little longer on a Saturday.

LEONARD. Well, then—don't you think they'll be here soon?

ELSIE [*very calm*]. It all depends, Leonard.

LEONARD [*nervous*]. On what?

ELSIE. When they started. You said they were leaving at two, Leonard.

LEONARD [*blurting it out, after a pause*]. I think you're wrong about not giving them something to eat. They're going to judge us by—by what we do.

ELSIE. And not by a lot of food. Oh, Leonard, I know you're much smarter than those other men in the office. Why, the minute you came down to Mobile, I said to myself, there's a man who is going to get ahead— to make a name for himself. And now that we're married . . . [*she takes his hand*] I'm *sure* of it, Leonard. All that you need is— [*Hesitates.*]

LEONARD. A chance.

ELSIE [*pretending that that would have been her answer*]. Yes.

LEONARD. If I'm the right man, I'll make my own chance. Remember that piece in *The American* last month? [*Looking for magazine on table.*] "Where Will *You* Be Ten Years From Now?" I read it to you. And I *made* my own chance, too, in a way. I mean, when my success does come, I'll have the satisfaction of knowing that I worked for it.

ELSIE. Of course, Leonard.

LEONARD [*the magazine in hand*]. Of course it was a little bit of luck, my discovering the fire. But when he sent for me, and—said all those nice things—why, that's where I got my work in. I mean, my telling him we had a Kincaid piano, and that you sang little songs, and persuading him to drop in. [*He begins to turn the pages of the magazine.*] The power of will!

ELSIE [*going into his arms*]. Oh, yes, Leonard. I can't get over how—how smart you were.

LEONARD. It wasn't anything that anybody wouldn't have thought of.

ELSIE. Yes, it was—and it was wonderful of you to think of it. Are you sure you did it just the way I—suggested?

LEONARD. Well, you hardly gave me more than just the—germ of it. You only said, if I ever *did* get a chance . . .

ELSIE. Oh, Leonard, I know it was you! You've got to take care of me, Leonard.

LEONARD. I will, all right. I'll make a lot of money—you just watch me.

ELSIE. I'm sure you will. You know, Leonard, I believe in you. I know what a brilliant mind you've got, and I know what you can do.

LEONARD. And he only invites about two clerks every year. The rest are all department heads! It's a pretty big honor.

ELSIE [*bringing up a painful subject*]. Leonard . . .

LEONARD [*looks over magazine pages*]. You can't tell me he'd be coming all the way out here if . . .

ELSIE. Leonard!

LEONARD. Well?

ELSIE. We must owe a lot of—money?

LEONARD. Well, not an awful lot. Some.

ELSIE. More than the four hundred dollars?

LEONARD. Ah—no.

ELSIE [*referring to the account-book*]. Well, according to . . .

LEONARD [*quickly*]. Yes—a little.

ELSIE. Oh, dear.

LEONARD. It wouldn't be so bad if it weren't for—paying so much to get the piano back again.

ELSIE. I'm so sorry we had to borrow money on it. [*A pause; she guesses the truth.*] Leonard! You're not—behind—on it, are you?

LEONARD. Just—a week, about.

ELSIE. Oh, Leonard! If Uncle Fred knew that his wedding-gift to us——

LEONARD. I'll take care of it next week, all right. You see, the man came into the office yesterday . . .

ELSIE. Leonard! Mr. Kincaid didn't find out?

LEONARD. I should say not. Nobody knew where he was from but me. I told him I'd fix it up in about two weeks.

ELSIE. What did he say?

LEONARD. He said he'd go back and tell them that. [*A pause.*] Said he thought it would be all right.

ELSIE. Oh, Leonard! It's all that terrible grapefruit farm—that's what you've always been needing money for! If only you hadn't bought it!

LEONARD [*outraged*]. Not bought the grapefruit farm! I'll bet you when it's bringing us in three hundred and fifty dollars a week you won't say that!

ELSIE. But 'way off in Florida! And how do you know it *will* bring in anything?

LEONARD. Haven't they always? I showed you what it said about it in the pamphlet. "Keep a grapefruit farm for four years and it will keep you for life!" Well, this is two years now!

ELSIE. But it *did* take a lot of money . . . [*she goes to the piano*] and I'm sorry about the piano.

LEONARD. Nothing's going to happen to it—it'll just take a little longer to pay it off, that's all.

ELSIE.   But we need so many things.   Did you buy an electric-light globe?

LEONARD.   Well, I only had—about a dollar.

ELSIE.   Oh, Leonard—what *will* we do? [*Looks at the music-rack.*] And you bought another song.   Thirty cents—that's extravagance.

LEONARD.   It's the spiritual you wanted.

ELSIE.   Oh, it's "Happy Day"!

LEONARD.   I thought maybe you could sing it for Mr. Kincaid.   That's really why I bought it—on account of his coming.

ELSIE [*examining it*].   Yes, this is the one! [*Starts it.*] There's the chord I never could remember. [*She goes into the song.*]

> "Happy day, I see de golden mo'nin',
>   Swing de gate, an' let de trav'leh in;
>   Ring de bell, de sinneh am atonin',
>   Down in hell the devil lies a-groanin',
>   Happy day, my troubles die a-bo'nin',
>   Lord!   Where is de crown I win?"

LEONARD [*as the song finishes he puts his arms around her*].   Like it?

ELSIE.   Yes, a lot.

LEONARD.   Then it wasn't extravagant.

ELSIE.   Oh, Leonard! [*She kisses him.*]

LEONARD.   That isn't much—a thirty-cent song.

ELSIE.   But it's your thinking of it, dearest.

LEONARD.   I'd buy you a whole lot of things—if I could.

ELSIE.   I'm sure of it, Leonard.

LEONARD [*the eternal question*].   Glad you married me?

ELSIE.   I'd do it right over again.

LEONARD.   You wouldn't!

ELSIE.   I would!

LEONARD.   Even if you did—have to leave all your friends in Mobile, and live here in Nutley?

ELSIE.   Yes.

LEONARD.   But if we have to be poor always—if my chance *doesn't* ever come . . .

ELSIE.   Even if it doesn't ever come, Leonard, I'll love you always.   You know that, don't you?

LEONARD. I hope so.

ELSIE. But it's going to come! To-day! I feel it! [*She breaks away from him. He follows; both are humming "Happy Day."*] Now put away your shirts. [*She hands them to him, then takes back the top one.*] This is the one that needs to have the sleeves taken in. [*She unfolds it and throws it on the table.*] Now put those in your shirt drawer, *under* the others, so that you don't wear the same ones all the time.

[LEONARD *starts for the door.*]
And bring me my sewing-basket from the top of the dresser.

LEONARD [*at door*]. From where?

ELSIE. From the top of—[*she recalls her other experience*] never mind. [*She goes out, followed immediately by* LEONARD. *For a moment the room is empty, then she re-enters with sewing implements and shirt.* LEONARD *also returns.*] Take off your coat.

LEONARD. Huh?

ELSIE. I want to measure the shirt.

LEONARD. Oh! [*He starts to take off his coat; feels a package in the pocket as he does so.*] Gosh, here are the cigars! I bought three, just as you said. Forty cents a piece!

ELSIE. They're terribly expensive, aren't they?

LEONARD. Well, you told me to find out the kind he smokes!

ELSIE. That was right. I knew his office-boy could tell you.

LEONARD. Ya.

ELSIE. Did you get the coupons?

LEONARD. Yes—double on Saturday.

ELSIE. Put them on the little tray on the piano. The cigars, not the coupons. [*She gives the piano a lingering glance.*] Oh, Leonard, I hate to feel that the piano isn't all ours.

LEONARD. We'll pay it off. [*A pause.*] I tell you, you ought to give 'em food.

ELSIE. No, Leonard. Come here, now.

LEONARD. I know what! The bottle of champagne!

ELSIE [*measuring the sleeve*].   But it's the only one we have left, Leonard—from our wedding.

LEONARD.   Suppose it is!   We'll never get a better chance to use it!   If we get him feeling good, he'll invite me to the banquet sure!

[ELSIE *hesitates*.]

I'll put it on ice!

ELSIE.   No!   [*Reluctantly giving in*.]   I'll do it in a minute.

LEONARD.   Well, if we're going to give him cigars and champagne, we might as well go the limit, and give him something to eat.

ELSIE.   No!   The cigars are—different.

LEONARD [*looking around impatiently, while she measures*].   That's a genuine La Paz, that cigar.   Same kind E. H. Harriman used to smoke.   There was a long piece about famous men and their cigars last Sunday.   Did you read it—in the *World Magazine?*

ELSIE.   No, Leonard.

LEONARD.   Where *is* that magazine?   I haven't finished the puzzle yet.

ELSIE.   It's in the kitchen.

LEONARD.   You always throw things away.

ELSIE.   Stand still, Leonard.

[*There is a thud against the outside door;* LEONARD *bolts immediately*.]

Leonard!

LEONARD [*opening the door and retrieving a much-folded newspaper*].   It's the paper!   I got a surprise for you!

ELSIE.   What?

LEONARD [*excited*].   They called them up and told them about my putting the fire out, and they said they'd print it to-day!

ELSIE.   Honestly?   That's lovely, dear.   Now come and look at it over here.   Read it to me.

LEONARD [*going to her—she resumes her measuring*].   I will in a minute.   [*He scans the front page.*]   It isn't there.

[*She waits patiently, sewing, while he turns the next few pages.*]

Not here, either. Oh! The Earl of Dorchester got his divorce!

ELSIE. Did he?

LEONARD. M'm—they found the chauffeur!

ELSIE. No! I'm glad!

LEONARD. Here it is—no! Three buildings burned at 625 West 46th. I know where that is. Say, this is funny. They said they'd . . . [*He trails off, searching further.*]

ELSIE. Well, of course, it wasn't a big fire, dear.

LEONARD. It would have been in another minute! Why, the stock-room floor . . .

ELSIE. Still, dear . . .

LEONARD. Ooh, they're going to have another Book-lovers' Contest. First grand prize—a Buick!

ELSIE. I don't want you to enter another of those, Leonard. You never won anything yet, and . . .

LEONARD [*with deep disgust*]. Well, for God's sake!

ELSIE. What, dear?

LEONARD. Listen to this. "Fires of a Day." Way in the back, too. "John Kincaid's Sons, Piano Manufacturers, 525 West 35th Street. Third floor. Damage $60." [*Pause.*] That's all.

ELSIE. Oh! That was mean!

LEONARD. Doesn't even say I put it out.

ELSIE. No. [*She strokes his head motheringly.*] Well, *I* know you put it out, and Mr. Kincaid does, too.

LEONARD. Why, if I hadn't discovered it . . .

[*There is a fancy knock on the door at right.* LEONARD, *thinking it the Kincaids, springs up.*]

There they are!

ELSIE. No—it's Chester.

LEONARD. I wish he'd knock plainer.

ELSIE. We mustn't let him stay.

LEONARD. Oh, he'll clear out.

[ELSIE *opens the door, and* CHESTER MULLIN *enters. A neighbor, occupying the top floor of the same house, and also a worker in the Kincaid plant. An extremely commonplace youth.*]

Hello, Ches.

CHESTER. Hello, Len. 'Lo, Elsie.

ELSIE. Hello, Chester. [*She gathers up some loose papers from the table and begins to put together her sewing things.*]

CHESTER. Cleaning up for the great visit, eh?

ELSIE [*stopping and looking at him*]. Do *you* know about it?

CHESTER. Sure. Everybody in the office knew it when I left. Said the boss had his eye on you and was coming out to invite you to the annual banquet. [*He pauses.*] Maybe.

LEONARD [*pleased but casual*]. Funny how things get around.

CHESTER. If I wanted to stick in the piano business all my life, I'd have gone in for it. But you know what I got up my sleeve.

ELSIE [*wearily*]. Yes.

CHESTER [*taking up a magazine from table*]. And I'll put it over, too. [*Pause.*] But it's got to be soon. Papa says I gotta pay a share of the board, beginning the first of the month. [*Drops lazily into a chair.*]

ELSIE. But that's only fair, Chester.

CHESTER. And did you notice commutation going up again? You'll be sorry I got you to move out here.

ELSIE. It isn't your fault, Chester. We couldn't afford to live in New York.

[CHESTER *is half absorbed in the magazine.*]

LEONARD [*to* ELSIE, *guardedly*]. Say, don't you think you'd better put *that*—on ice?

ELSIE. I'm going now, dear.

CHESTER [*interested*]. Something to drink?

ELSIE. Ah—yes.

CHESTER. Fine!

[ELSIE *looks at him, a glance full of meaning, and departs.*]

LEONARD. [*His manner subtly changes with her departure; a certain man-of-the-world manner is assumed.*] Well, any news?

CHESTER. They say Marcus Loew is gonna put up a theatre out here.

LEONARD. I mean at the office. You said they were talking about the boss coming out here.

ELSIE [*calling from the next room*]. Leonard!

LEONARD. Yes, dear.

ELSIE. Put up the card-table.

[LEONARD *rises, getting his coat from the arm of the chair on which* CHESTER *is sitting.*]

LEONARD. Get off of my coat! [LEONARD *then brings a folded table from a corner.*]

CHESTER. There's where the money is—vaudeville.

LEONARD [*mechanically puts a folded piece of paper under one of the table-legs—the inevitable procedure*]. You know, it's sort of funny how a little bit of a thing will bring something about sometimes. I suppose they know how it began? I mean, the boss sending for me when I put out the fire?

CHESTER [*nods*]. Lot of them think it was pretty smart of you to throw that match there, too.

LEONARD. I didn't! Why, if my success grew out of a thing like that, I wouldn't ever be able to forget it!

CHESTER. What I want to know is, how'd you get him to promise to come out here?

LEONARD. Well—[*with an apprehensive glance into the next room*] I'll tell you, if you don't let it go any further. It was just a—a bit of psychology with me.

CHESTER [*doubtfully*]. Yah?

LEONARD. You know how he feels about all of his employees having pianos?

CHESTER. Don't I look at the sign all day long? "A Kincaid Piano is the Heart of the Home!"

LEONARD. Well, I told him we had one, and he wanted to know where we lived, and I said Nutley, and he said he and his wife were driving to Atlantic City on Saturday . . .

CHESTER. She's coming, too?

LEONARD. Of course. Well, when he said that, I got the big idea for getting him to stop off here. I said: "Well, my wife . . ."

[ELSIE *returns, carrying a table-cover.* LEONARD *stops abruptly as she enters. There is a deep silence as* ELSIE *crosses to the table and lays the cover on it.*]

ELSIE. What are you boys talking about?

LEONARD. Oh, just business, dear. You wouldn't understand.

[ELSIE *departs;* LEONARD *immediately continues.*]
It struck me that maybe if I told him about Elsie's songs,
and the—the way she sings them, why, maybe I could get
him out here. You know the way he is about music?

CHESTER. Off his nut.

LEONARD. Well, I sized the man up, that was all.
Character reading. Remember that ad in *McClure's?*
If a man has a long nose, and—and a high forehead— [*He
reaches for the magazine.*]

CHESTER [*at his ease*]. Well, *I'll* be glad to meet him
socially.

LEONARD. What?

CHESTER. Now I'll get a chance to put over *my* idea.

LEONARD. What idea? Not the piano act for vaudeville?

CHESTER. The piano act for vaudeville. Watch me.

LEONARD. Oh, he won't have time to hear about that,
Chester. He's only going to stop in a little while and go
on to Atlantic City.

CHESTER. Wait till you see how I work up to it.

LEONARD. But, gee, Chester—I don't think you ought
to.

CHESTER. Are you my friend?

LEONARD. What?

CHESTER. I'm just *asking* you; are you my friend?

LEONARD. Of course.

CHESTER. Well, this is my chance! I could never
get in to see him at the office—couldn't get past that guy
Sheridan.

LEONARD [*getting an idea*]. I'll tell you, Chester! Why
don't you suggest it in a letter?

CHESTER. And have one of those babies around his
office get it and take the credit and probably do me out
of the act? I should get gypped that way. Here I get
a chance to meet him socially.

LEONARD. All the more reason why you shouldn't
put it up to him.

CHESTER. Don't you think it! Do you know where
some of the biggest business deals in the world are pulled
off? In people's houses. Over the coffee—or whatever
it is.

LEONARD. Well, I wish you wouldn't.

[ELSIE *re-enters, carrying four champagne glasses.*]

CHESTER. Ah! Glasses!

ELSIE. Chester, we're expecting Mr. and Mrs. Kincaid—right away.

CHESTER. I know. [*He returns to his magazine.*]

ELSIE. So if there's anything you want to do, Chester . . .

LEONARD. Yes—if there's anything you want to do, you see—you could go right ahead and do it.

ELSIE. And then you could come back afterward and talk to Leonard.

CHESTER [*not having heard a word of it*]. Here's that character-reading ad.

LEONARD. Where?

CHESTER. Right here.

ELSIE. Leonard! I wish you wouldn't pay so much attention to those advertisements.

LEONARD. Is that so? Well, that's where I learned about the grapefruit farm.

ELSIE. Yes, I know. [*Her glance goes involuntarily to the piano.*]

LEONARD. A lot of fellows have got good tips out of here. Look! "Babson of Idaho made $600 the First Month." [*To* CHESTER.] That's the pop-corn machine.

CHESTER. Sure, I know.

LEONARD. "McCormick of Michigan made $550."

ELSIE. What McCormick?

LEONARD. Huh?

ELSIE. What McCormick?

LEONARD. Michigan.

ELSIE. What's his first name?

LEONARD. What's the difference if he made all that money?

ELSIE. But did he make it?

LEONARD. Of course he made it. Doesn't it say so right here? And I suppose you think thousands of fellows don't make a lot of money with these correspondence courses, too?

ELSIE. Leonard, don't you see that all those things are for people who—who haven't got it *in* them—who have to acquire all of it from the outside? You're different—you *have* the ability—it's just a case of giving it a chance to come out.

CHESTER. There's only one business I was intended for.

ELSIE [*knowing the answer*]. Yes, Chester. Devising novelties for vaudeville.

LEONARD. You couldn't entertain me, Chester.

CHESTER. I could the public.

ELSIE. Well—don't you ever go and practise sometimes?

CHESTER [*near the piano*]. What are these—cigars?

LEONARD [*quickly*]. Hey!

CHESTER. Oh, I wasn't going to take any.

LEONARD [*tapping the magazine*]. It seems a shame to let all this easy money slip away, that's all. [*Turns a page.*] Here's something I'd like to have.

CHESTER. What's that?

LEONARD [*ignoring him*]. Elsie—here's a book I'd like. *Five Hundred Speeches for All Occasions*. Listen: "Suppose, in a gathering of distinguished and brilliant men and women, the host of the occasion suddenly calls upon you to make a speech? Would you stammer and sit down, or would you electrify one and all by your eloquence, fairly swinging them off their feet by the magic of your words? Watson's Manual of Speech-Making shows you how. Five hundred sample addresses. Clip the coupon to-day."

CHESTER. A friend of mine has one. They're good.

LEONARD. "Send $3 for thirty days' trial; your money refunded if—" It'd be sort of nice to have one of those.

ELSIE. But, Leonard, dear, you're never called on to make a speech.

LEONARD. That's so. But only three dollars. Gee! Here's just the thing they need at the office.

CHESTER. What?

LEONARD [*reads*]. "The Simpson Anti-Check-Raising Machine." That office is terrible—I bet you when I'm chief clerk I'll introduce some modern equipment.

[*An automobile is heard off;* LEONARD *flies to the window.*]

ELSIE [*excited*]. Is it?

LEONARD. [*A pause.*] No. [*Turns.*] Is everything ready?

ELSIE [*tidying up*]. Yes, dear.

LEONARD [*looking at his watch*]. They're late now.

CHESTER. Maybe they aren't coming.

[LEONARD, *at this, drops his watch.*]

ELSIE. Oh, Leonard!

LEONARD [*picks it up and inspects it*]. It's all right. [*To* CHESTER.] You nearly made me break it!

CHESTER. I didn't make you do anything!

LEONARD. You did!

CHESTER. I did not!

LEONARD [*as he crosses to* ELSIE]. Get him out of here. [*He gets an idea.*] Listen, Elsie . . .

ELSIE [*comes to him*]. Yes, dear.

LEONARD. When they come—*you* talk to Mrs. Kincaid, and *I'll* talk to Mr. Kincaid.

CHESTER. I suppose I get a deck of cards?

ELSIE. Chester!

CHESTER. Yes?

ELSIE. Is your mother back home?

CHESTER. Huh? Oh, sure. [*But he stays.*]

LEONARD. Honest, Chester, I don't think you ought to do that.

ELSIE. Do what?

LEONARD. Well, Chester's got this idea . . .

CHESTER. I'm not going to hurt anything.

LEONARD. But if you go ahead and . . .

ELSIE. What is it?

[*A horn is heard;* LEONARD *is at the window in an instant.*]

LEONARD. Here they are! It's a Packard '22! Why don't you get things ready?

ELSIE [*calmly*]. Now, Leonard, dear, you must relax.

LEONARD. Yes—relax! You'd think it didn't mean anything—his coming out! [*Looks through window again, pushing* CHESTER *out of the way.*] A chauffeur and everything! He's helping her out of the car! You ought to see her!

[CHESTER, *by this time, is looking over his shoulder.*] And there's the boss! Here they come!

[ELSIE *has laid away her sewing, and awaits the coming
event with a quiet dignity.* LEONARD *is vastly excited and* CHESTER *only less so.*]

Takes an awful long time to come up those steps. Maybe
he fell!

[*There is a ring at the door.* LEONARD *starts to answer
it;* ELSIE *stops him with a gesture.*]

ELSIE. No, Leonard. [*She opens the door, admitting*
MR. *and* MRS. KINCAID. *The latter enters first—a good-
looking woman, approaching middle age, and fashionably
attired.* KINCAID, *also of middle age, is the conventional
type of business man.*] Mrs. Kincaid? I'm Mrs. Beebe.
[*Waits in vain for* LEONARD *to present her.*] I'm Mrs.
Beebe, Mr. Kincaid.

[KINCAID *shakes hands with* ELSIE.]

LEONARD [*coming to, a wave of the hand toward his wife*].
Mrs. Beebe's my wife.

KINCAID. I'm delighted, Mrs. Beebe. Beebe, how are
you?

LEONARD. All right.

[ELSIE *touches him on the arm. He turns and sees*
CHESTER.]

And, of course, you know—ah . . .

ELSIE [*as he pauses*]. Mr. Mullin. Mr. Mullin, Mrs.
Kincaid. And Mr. Kincaid.

KINCAID. Glad to know you, Mr. Mullin.

CHESTER. Same to you!

ELSIE. Won't you sit down, Mrs. Kincaid?

MRS. KINCAID [*her glance going appraisingly over the
room*]. Why, thank you. [*She sits.*]

[*At a glance from* ELSIE, LEONARD *places a chair for*
MR. KINCAID. CHESTER *is about to take it, but*
LEONARD *deftly moves it away in time and* KINCAID
sits.]

ELSIE. Do take off your coat.

MRS. KINCAID. Oh, no, thank you. I'm afraid we
shan't be staying long. We're motoring to Atlantic City,
you know, and just . . . dropped off for a moment.

[ELSIE *signals to* LEONARD.]

LEONARD. Take your—coat off, Mr. Kincaid?

KINCAID. Well—ah—[*half addressing his wife*] I think

I will, Myrtle. Easy to put it on again. [*Gives hat and coat to* LEONARD.]

CHESTER [*getting a word in*]. Yes!

[KINCAID *throws him a puzzled look.*]

KINCAID [*to his wife*]. Take yours off, too.

MRS. KINCAID. Well, I thought perhaps— [*She meets his steady gaze.*] Yes, dear. [*She removes it.* ELSIE *helps her.*]

ELSIE. It's a lovely cape, Mrs. Kincaid. You don't mind if I admire it, do you?

MRS. KINCAID [*already melting a little*]. Oh, you like it?

ELSIE. It's simply beautiful. I don't think I've ever seen one like it.

[*One after another they all sit. There is a pause;* LEONARD *feels vaguely that it is his turn.* KINCAID *first, then* LEONARD, *then* MRS. KINCAID, *and last* ELSIE, *give a sound of embarrassed pleasure.*]

LEONARD [*trying to be perfectly at ease*]. Well, how's business?

KINCAID. Oh, fair . . . fair.

LEONARD [*nervous*]. That's too bad.

CHESTER [*stepping forward*]. It's going to get better from now on, everybody seems to think.

KINCAID. Well, I'll tell you, Mr.—ah—Mr.——

CHESTER. Mullin.

KINCAID. Mr. Mullin. You know, *ours* is a peculiar line—isn't it, Beebe?

LEONARD. Terrible!

KINCAID. For example, we will feel a seasonal depression very sharply—ahead of any other line. And then there are some fields in which—ah—what is your line, Mr. Mullin?

CHESTER. Huh?

KINCAID. I say, you are in some business?

CHESTER. Well—you see . . .

ELSIE. Chester works for the firm, Mr. Kincaid . . . your firm.

KINCAID. Oh, I didn't—ah— [*He is looking* CHESTER *over.*] Oh, yes—I remember—you're one of the technical men.

CHESTER. Filing department.

KINCAID. Oh, to be sure. A new man, aren't you?

CHESTER. Four years ago.

KINCAID. That so? Well, well!

CHESTER. I don't think I'm gonna be with you much longer, however.

KINCAID. That's too bad. Sorry to lose you.

CHESTER. Well, I don't know that you're gonna quite lose me, either; that is, if a little idea I've got appeals to you.

KINCAID [genially]. I'm very fond of ideas if they're good ones.

[LEONARD and ELSIE are greatly worried.]

CHESTER. Mr. Kincaid. [He takes his time.] Do you realize that the firm has passed up one of the best forms of advertising that there is?

[LEONARD pulls CHESTER'S coat.]

KINCAID. No, I can't say I do.

CHESTER. I refer to vaudeville. I've been studying it, Mr. Kincaid, and I think I've evolved a very good plan to advertise Kincaid pianos, and, of course, look out for number one, too. [He laughs and confidentially touches KINCAID'S arm as he says "number one."] Now, my idea is this: that we take six of the new Kincaid Ultra Player Pianos and put them into a vaudeville act.

MRS. KINCAID. A what?

CHESTER. A vaudeville act. The idea being . . .

KINCAID. Well, that seems novel, I'll admit. But I'm afraid . . .

CHESTER. Wait till I tell you. Did you ever patronize vaudeville, Mr. Kincaid—that is, extensively?

KINCAID. Oh, occasionally I've . . .

CHESTER. Good! Did you ever notice the type of act that has been staple for years? The one that's always good for booking, year in and year out?

KINCAID [laughing]. Well, I'm not sure. The trained seals, I suppose.

[ELSIE and LEONARD laugh.]

CHESTER. That's exactly right—the trained seals.

[LEONARD gives a good tug at CHESTER'S coat—

CHESTER *waves him off with backhanded sweep of the arm.*]

Now what I claim is that I can furnish every bit as much fun with half a dozen of your grand pianos as a man can with an equal number of seals.

[LEONARD *has risen and nervously opens and closes the door.*]

KINCAID.   Suppose you drop in and see Mr. Ames in the advertising department, Mr. . . .

CHESTER.   Mullin.

KINCAID.   Mr. Mullin.   It might interest him very much.

CHESTER.   I certainly will.   You think it's O. K. then? You understand the general line?   We'd open with a conversation.   I'd ask the pianos something and they'd reply with various suitable tunes.   I'd come in, very smartly dressed, and I'd say: "How are you, pianos?   How do you feel to-day?"   Click!   [*He sings it.*]   "I've got rings on my fingers and bells on my toes!"   "Why, you must be in love!   How does it feel?"   Click!   [*Sings.*]   "Bluest of the blue, I'm wild about you—"   Six of 'em, and nobody sitting there at all!

KINCAID.   You realize that the player grand pianos are worth about three thousand dollars apiece?

CHESTER.   Of course.   But you've got to *invest* something if you have any kind of an act.   Gertrude Hoffman . . .

KINCAID [*rises and gets rid of him pleasantly*].   Of course. Now you drop in and see Mr. Ames.

CHESTER.   Thanks.

MRS. KINCAID.   I think it's an excellent idea, Jack.

KINCAID.   Please, Myrtle!

MRS. KINCAID.   Yes, John.

KINCAID [*to* ELSIE, *looking about room*].   Well, Mrs. Beebe, you certainly have a charming little home here.

LEONARD [*right out of the phrase-book*].   We like it.   It has all the advantages of the country, and still it's convenient to the city.

ELSIE [*half under her breath*].   Leonard.

[*He looks at her; she motions toward the cigars.*]

LEONARD. Oh! Excuse me! [*Offering the cigars.*] Smoke, Mr. Kincaid?

KINCAID. No, thank you.

LEONARD [*bowled over*]. What?

KINCAID. Giving it up for the present—doctor's orders.

LEONARD [*with one dollar and twenty cents sunk*]. Oh! [*Offering the cigars to* CHESTER *with a man-of-the-world air, but certain he is going to refuse.*] Chester?

CHESTER. Thanks. [*Takes one.*] I'll smoke it when I go home.

ELSIE. Oh, *must* you, Chester? [*She is on her feet.*] Well, tell your mother I'll come up and see her this evening. [*To the others.*] Chester lives just above us—we took the house together.

LEONARD [*has opened the door*]. Good-by, Chester.

CHESTER [*trapped*]. Ah—yes. Well—good-by, Mrs. Kincaid. Mr. Kincaid, see *you* Monday at the office. [*He goes.*]

LEONARD. Chester had to go.

ELSIE. Chester means awfully well. He feels that he isn't sociable if he—doesn't talk. Somehow there are so many people like that.

MRS. KINCAID. Indeed there are. [*A pause.*] You're from the—South. Aren't you?

ELSIE. Mobile.

KINCAID. Mobile? That's so?

LEONARD [*after a moment of embarrassment*]. Ah— Elsie, what do you say to a little bottle of Mumm's Extra Dry, 1903? Suppose I go and get a bottle . . . [*He starts determinedly for the door.*] If you'll excuse me— [*He goes into the next room.*]

MRS. KINCAID. You've not been married very long— have you?

ELSIE. Oh, no. Just six months, about.

MRS. KINCAID. I wonder if you know the Forresters in Mobile?

ELSIE. Indeed I do! Selena Forrester was at our wedding. She's lovely—don't you think?

MRS. KINCAID. Yes. I've only met Selena once. I knew her father and mother quite well—in Pasadena.

ELSIE. Yes. I guess they're going to live out there.

MRS. KINCAID. But Mr. Beebe isn't a Southerner?

ELSIE. Oh, no. You see, Leonard came down to Mobile to attend his aunt's funeral—and I met him at a dance. I was practically engaged to Carter Wainwright . . . [*To* MRS. KINCAID.] I don't suppose you knew him?

[MRS. KINCAID *shakes her head.*]

But, of course, when I met Leonard—well, you know how it is. [*A bit of propaganda.*] When he wants anything, he—goes right for it. You can't stop him. We were engaged in—three weeks. Carter wanted to kill him.

KINCAID. Three weeks! Pretty quick.

ELSIE. Well, we were engaged for over a year. In the meantime Leonard had come North. He said he was going to have something to *offer* his bride, so he got a position with you, and worked his way up to . . . [*she looks at him*] where he is.

MRS. KINCAID. And you didn't see him in all that time?

ELSIE. No, I didn't. He kept right on working.

MRS. KINCAID. He must have written some wonderful letters.

ELSIE. Oh, he did! [*More propaganda.*] He writes the most interesting letters I ever read— [*To* KINCAID.] You know—Mr. Kincaid—all his letters are—so convincing. Poor Carter wasn't anywhere at all—

[*In the next room a cork pops loudly.*]

He began drinking, and . . .

MRS. KINCAID. That was too bad.

ELSIE. Well, he used to drink even before. In fact, I think really that was what originally interested me in him.

[LEONARD *re-enters, carrying a bottle of champagne with a napkin wrapped around it.*]

LEONARD. Well, here it is! [*Shows label on bottle to* MR. KINCAID.]

KINCAID [*mellowing*]. Ah!

ELSIE. Here, Leonard—let me do that! [*She takes the bottle, takes the napkin from it, and begins to pour.*]

KINCAID [*expansively*]. Very fine indeed!

LEONARD. We must lay in some more of this, dear. Our stock is rather low.

ELSIE [*quickly*].   Leonard's such a joker.

[*The Kincaids laugh belatedly.   So does* LEONARD.]
You'll have to wait till Uncle Harry *sends* more.   [*To the
Kincaids.*]   He gave it to us for the wedding.

KINCAID.   Well, it's certainly very kind of you to—
ah . . .

ELSIE [*signalling* LEONARD *to pass the glasses*].   All
right!

LEONARD [*nervously replies*].   All right!   Oh, excuse
me!   [*Handing one to* MRS. KINCAID *and one to* MR. KIN-
CAID.]   Sorry we haven't something better.

KINCAID.   Well, I hardly know what more I could ask.
Mumm's Extra Dry and—a very fine cigar.

ELSIE [*sees that the cigars puzzle him*].   I wondered why
Leonard bought those cigars—he doesn't smoke himself
—but then he told me it was the kind you smoke.

[LEONARD *has lifted his glass; waits for the others to
drink.*]

KINCAID.   That was thoughtful, I must say.   [*Considers.*]   But I don't quite understand—I only see him
about . . . once a month.   How did you know?

[ELSIE *looks at* LEONARD *with understanding.*]

LEONARD.   Oh, well, I—observe things.

KINCAID.   That's a very good trait.

[*There is a pause.*]

LEONARD [*raises his glass—waits for their attention*].
Well—to the ladies!

KINCAID [*rises*].   To the ladies!

[*They all drink.*]

LEONARD.   Guess you don't get much of *this* any more
—except at . . . [*he looks at* KINCAID] banquets and
dinners, and—places where they have it.

[*There is a pause.*]
Have a little more?

KINCAID.   Oh, no, thank you!

MRS. KINCAID [*as* LEONARD *turns to her with the same
question*].   No, thanks.

LEONARD.   Well—Elsie—wouldn't you like to—sing a
little something?

MRS. KINCAID.   Oh, please do.

ELSIE.   Well—if you really want me to.

KINCAID. Yes, indeed. We've been looking forward to it.

[*A general movement toward the piano.*]

ELSIE [*arranging music*]. Leonard really overestimates my voice. It's—pretty average. He forgets sometimes —when he talks about it.

KINCAID [*patronizingly*]. I—noticed you had one of our pianos.

LEONARD. Yes, sir.

KINCAID. Gives satisfaction, does it?

LEONARD. I should say it does!

ELSIE. Oh, yes, indeed. We couldn't afford one that had to be tuned all the time.

KINCAID [*gives it an approving glance*]. Kept very nicely, too. I like to see young people buy pianos— especially *my* young people. They're a real investment. They not only help keep the home together—they are an object lesson in saving.

LEONARD [*dutifully*]. Yes, sir!

KINCAID. I've spent my life with pianos, Mrs. Beebe. I feel toward them almost like a father. There is a great romance in pianos. Some day, perhaps, it will be written.

MRS. KINCAID [*having heard this before*]. Won't you sing *now*, Mrs. Beebe?

ELSIE. Ah—this is one of our old Southern songs. Maybe you know it. [*She sings "Nobody Knows." The Kincaids pay polite attention; LEONARD follows it tensely, his lips moving.*]

LEONARD [*at finish*]. That's the end.

MRS. KINCAID. M'm. Very pretty, indeed.

KINCAID. Why, yes.

LEONARD [*extremely pleased*]. Think so?

MRS. KINCAID. Lovely!

ELSIE. Of course it's only a little spiritual.

MRS. KINCAID. But very nice. Won't you sing another for us, Mrs. Beebe?

LEONARD [*promptly*]. Why, sure! [*He guides ELSIE back to the piano.*]

ELSIE. Well, if you're positive you'd . . .

MRS. KINCAID. Of course we would, wouldn't we, John?

[*He is absorbed in thought.*]

John!

KINCAID. Oh, yes! I'll be delighted!

LEONARD [*to* ELSIE]. Ah—sing "Happy Day."

ELSIE [*to* MRS. KINCAID]. Ever hear that one?

MRS. KINCAID [*encouragingly*]. I don't think so.

ELSIE. I hope I can play it. I just got it.

[*They settle themselves to listen, and* ELSIE *launches forth on "Happy Day."*]

> "Happy day, I see de golden mo'nin',
>   Swing de gate, an' let de trav'leh in;
>   Ring de bell—"

[*The door-bell rings.* ELSIE *falters, throws a quick glance at* LEONARD, *and then continues with the song:*]

> "—de sinneh am atonin',
>   Down in—"

[*The door-bell sounds again, louder this time.* ELSIE *again looks up at* LEONARD *uncertainly.*]

> "—hell—"

I'm afraid you'll have to go, dear. [ELSIE *turns to the Kincaids.*] I'm sorry.

MRS. KINCAID. It's too bad. Very pretty.

[LEONARD *opens the door, and a burly* TRUCKMAN *appears in the doorway.*]

FIRST TRUCKMAN [*reading from a slip*]. "L. H. Beebe?"

LEONARD. Yes.

FIRST TRUCKMAN [*handing over the slip in a matter-of-fact way*]. Piano!

LEONARD [*staggered*]. What?

FIRST TRUCKMAN [*louder*]. Piano! [*Comes into room; locates piano—returns to door.*] Get them rollers, Jim!

ELSIE. Oh, Leonard!

LEONARD. Now—now, wait! This—this can all be fixed up—I think.

[*The Kincaids are exchanging looks.*]

[LEONARD *looks toward the Kincaids, then somewhat expectantly at* ELSIE. ELSIE *inclines her head slightly toward the next room, as though instructing him to take the* TRUCKMAN *away and try to adjust it.*]

FIRST TRUCKMAN. Huh?

LEONARD. Will you please—come in here with me—a minute?

FIRST TRUCKMAN. Sure.

LEONARD [*to the Kincaids as he crosses*]. Ex—cuse me. [*As they near door.*]
I was afraid you weren't coming. [*Departs awkwardly with the* TRUCKMAN.]

[ELSIE *goes on with the song, her heart breaking. She stammers through for six or seven bars. Then the voice of the defeated* LEONARD *calls from the next room.*]

Elsie!

[*She continues singing.*]

Elsie!

[*She stops.*]

ELSIE [*rising*]. Do you mind? I'll be right back.

MRS. KINCAID. Why, of course.

[ELSIE *goes into the other room.*]

KINCAID [*when they are gone*]. Well!

MRS. KINCAID. It's too bad, isn't it?

KINCAID [*nods slowly, as though evolving something in his mind*]. Ah— [*Snaps his fingers.*] You! [*He beckons to the* SECOND TRUCKMAN, *who has entered and is standing rather insolently in the doorway, a drooping cigarette in his mouth, his cap on his head.*]

SECOND TRUCKMAN [*producing a match*]. Speakin' to me?

KINCAID. I am.

SECOND TRUCKMAN [*he strikes the match*]. Spill it!

KINCAID. What is the name of your—company?

SECOND TRUCKMAN. McEvoy Express.

KINCAID. I don't mean that. You were sent here by a—loan company—I imagine?

SECOND TRUCKMAN. "You imagine" is good.

KINCAID [*controlling himself*]. What is the name of the company?

SECOND TRUCKMAN [*smiling*]. I guess you know, all right.

KINCAID [*annoyed*]. I do not!

SECOND TRUCKMAN. That's a hot one! Well, you'll learn.

KINCAID. My good man, we are guests in this house!

MRS. KINCAID. Now, Jack——

[KINCAID *turns to her.*]

SECOND TRUCKMAN. Is that so?

KINCAID [*turning back to* TRUCKMAN]. It certainly is.

SECOND TRUCKMAN. Well, why horn in on other people's troubles? Ain't you got any of your own?

KINCAID. I am Mr. Beebe's employer. I want to know how much he owes you.

SECOND TRUCKMAN. Search me. Have to ask Mr. Carney.

[FIRST TRUCKMAN *re-enters.*]
There he is.

KINCAID. I want to know how much Mr. Beebe owes you.

FIRST TRUCKMAN [*taking time to look* KINCAID *up and down*]. Don't owe us anything. Owes the Diamond Loan Company twenty-two dollars.

KINCAID [*producing the money*]. There you are! Please give me a receipt.

FIRST TRUCKMAN. Sure.

KINCAID [*to* MRS. KINCAID]. It's worth that—to find out these things.

MRS. KINCAID. And yet I'm sorry, somehow.

[LEONARD *and* ELSIE *re-enter with the air of having reached a decision.* LEONARD, *intent on his errand, starts to cross determinedly; then half-way across decides that he should excuse himself to the Kincaids.*]

LEONARD. I'll—be right back. [*He reaches the door, only to find the* SECOND TRUCKMAN *lounging in the middle of the doorway.*] If you don't mind! [*He pushes past him, nearly knocking him over.*]

ELSIE. I'm—sorry——

FIRST TRUCKMAN [*hands the receipt to* KINCAID]. There y'are.

[ELSIE'S *eyes go to it.*]

All right, Jim. [*The* TRUCKMEN *go out.*]

KINCAID [*coldly and formally*]. Mrs. Beebe—ah—here is a receipt—for twenty-two dollars.

ELSIE. Mr. Kincaid! You didn't . . .

KINCAID [*still in even and cold tones*]. I took the liberty —yes. Perhaps, after all, I owed it to your husband, in view of his little service to us the other day.

ELSIE. But, Mr. Kincaid, he'll pay it back to you just as soon as . . .

KINCAID [*far from cordial, despite his words*]. Oh, no— it will hardly be necessary. And now I'm sure you will pardon us—we have quite a distance to go yet. Are you ready, Myrtle?

ELSIE. You're not—going?

KINCAID. I'm afraid that we must. You'll make our excuses to—your husband, won't you?

ELSIE [*on the verge of tears*]. But . . . he'll—be——

KINCAID [*formally, as he prepares to go*]. We enjoyed— the singing—very much——

MRS. KINCAID [*too sweetly*]. Very nice indeed, dear. [*Getting into coat.*]

[KINCAID *clears his throat pompously; gets his hat and overcoat.* MRS. KINCAID *stands ready. The strain is felt by all.*]

KINCAID [*as he advances to the door*]. Well! [*He opens the door; turns back to* ELSIE.] Good day.

ELSIE [*choked up*]. Good—day.

KINCAID [*the door held open for his wife*]. Ready, Myrtle?

ELSIE [*at first hardly able to speak*]. Mr.—Kincaid.

KINCAID [*turning*]. Yes.

ELSIE. Would you mind—closing the door . . .

[*He hesitates.*]

just a minute?

[KINCAID *does so.*]

I know you—think—that Leonard's been extravagant— but he hasn't. I mean, you think he's been spending money foolishly . . .

KINCAID. Oh—no. [*Then again the formal employer.*] Well—I'll admit I'm a little prejudiced, but I don't like to see any of our young men in debt. It indicates—bad management. Especially a married man. He was promoted a short time ago. He should think of his family—his future.

ELSIE [*eagerly, the words tumbling over each other*]. But he *has*, Mr. Kincaid—that's just what he *has* been thinking about. He's been making an investment . . .

KINCAID. Really?

ELSIE. Buying—a farm!

KINCAID. Oh, is that so? [*There is nothing in his manner to indicate a change.*]

ELSIE. A grapefruit farm—in Florida!

KINCAID. Oh!

ELSIE. He's been saving every penny he could, just to pay off what we owed on it. And then, just a few days ago, he had a chance to pay off all the balance at a big reduction. The—the company made him an offer to—so . . . [*she finishes with a rush*] we borrowed four hundred dollars on the piano. But he did buy the farm with it, and, after all, that's saving.

[KINCAID *is silent.*]
Isn't it?

KINCAID [*decidedly unconvinced*]. Oh, indeed, yes. Of course we in the business world have standards of our own, Mrs. Beebe, and I couldn't expect you to be familiar with them. [*He is again in the act of departure.*] You see, we have a rather sentimental feeling about pianos in our place. We feel the piano is the heart of the home, and—but, after all, there is no reason why you should feel called upon to explain to—*me.*

ELSIE. Oh, but there is! If I—if I could only make you understand! But, of course, you've never been poor—either of you— [*She turns to* MRS. KINCAID, *and addresses her from this point on.*] I mean—really poor—so that a few dollars actually mattered, and you had to be awful careful what you did with them. So that you had to plan weeks ahead . . . so much for each little thing, and if something came up that you hadn't counted on, and that just *had* to be paid, why, it meant doing without something that you—almost had to have to live. But you see—we've—done that—ever since we're married. And then, when it looks as though you've almost helped each other out of it—and the chance comes—oh, if I could only make you understand . . . [*She is still talking to* Mrs. Kincaid.]

Kincaid [*almost gently*]. I'm—over here, Mrs. Beebe.

Elsie [*hardly pausing*]. So you understand—that's why I did feel that I had to explain it . . .

> [Leonard *re-enters. There is a pause as he throws open the door and closes it behind him. He gazes from one to the other, trying to grasp the situation; looks at the piano, then at* Elsie.]

Leonard [*speaking as he enters*]. Chester only had three dollars—excuse me— [*To* Elsie.] They're—gone?

Elsie. Yes, dear.

Kincaid [*at door*]. Ready, Myrtle?

Mrs. Kincaid. Ah—yes. Oh! I forgot my bag. [*She indicates it on the table.*]

Kincaid [*surprised*]. You—really?

Mrs. Kincaid [*firmly*]. I forgot my bag.

> Elsie *gets the bag from the table and hands it to him. He gives it to* Mrs. Kincaid.]

Kincaid [*turns to* Leonard]. Oh, Beebe. [*He tries to make it as casual as possible.*] I forgot to mention that we'll expect you at the banquet of the personnel at the Commodore on the 18th. We . . . we like to have one or two of you younger fellows present, you know.

Leonard. Why—why—it would—yes!

Kincaid. That's fine. I intended mentioning it earlier, but—[*looks at* Elsie] I forgot. We want you to come, too, Mrs. Beebe.

Elsie [*again possessed, now that victory is hers*]. Oh, thank you. I'll be delighted.

Mrs. Kincaid. Mr. Kincaid thinks your husband's a very promising young man.

Kincaid. And I want to make him even more so. [*To* Leonard.] By the way, you'll be expected to say a few words—just anything that—strikes you.

Leonard [*trying to hide his nervousness*]. Sure. What'll I—speak about?

Kincaid. Oh, anything at all—of a business nature. [*A pause.*] Well—good day, Mrs. Beebe.

Elsie. Good day. Good day, Mrs. Kincaid.

MRS. KINCAID. Good-by, my dear. [*She takes her hand.*] I hope we can meet again some time.

ELSIE. I hope so.

MRS. KINCAID. Good day, Mr. Beebe.

LEONARD. All right!

KINCAID. Good day.

LEONARD. Good day.

[*All four go out. MRS. KINCAID first—then KINCAID— ELSIE and LEONARD, still exchanging good-bys. There are voices, the sound of a car, and then LEONARD and ELSIE re-enter.*]

ELSIE [*yielding to the excitement*]. Leonard—you got it!

LEONARD. What—what happened?

ELSIE. You heard! Oh, Leonard!

LEONARD. But—the piano!

ELSIE. Mr. Kincaid paid it!

LEONARD [*again the head of the family*]. He did, huh? I don't like that so much.

ELSIE. Oh, Leonard, they nearly took the piano! [*A sentimental impulse carries her over to it; she sits.*]

LEONARD [*following her*]. They couldn't have taken it! [*He is beside her at the piano.*]

ELSIE Leonard, do you realize what's happened? You're going to the banquet! [*She strikes a few gay notes in sheer happiness.*]

LEONARD. Sure! I told you it was coming, didn't I? [*He joins in—they sing a line or two of "Happy Day."*]

ELSIE [*bringing herself up sharp with a chord*]. Leonard, you've got to make a speech!

LEONARD. Gosh! I'd forgotten about that! I know! [*He dashes for the magazine.*] The book! *Five Hundred Speeches for All Occasions.*

ELSIE [*rises, but does not leave the piano*]. Oh, do you think you'll need that, Leonard?

LEONARD. You bet your life!

ELSIE. Well—all right. [*Her uncertainty about the book vanishes in the greater joy of the Kincaid invitation.*] Oh, Leonard! [*She sits again and begins to play "Happy Day." She sings it softly.*]

LEONARD. Where is it? Oh! Here it is! Three dollars! [*Working feverishly, begins to hum the tune.*

Pulls money from his pocket; holds it up for ELSIE *to see.*]
Chester's three dollars! Just pays for the book! [*Works
and hums again.*]

> [*When* ELSIE *reaches the last two lines her voice dies
> down;* LEONARD *takes it up strongly.*]

Kindly send the Man-u-al of Speech-Making! Leon-ard
H. Bee-be! Nutley, New Jersey! [*On the final chord he
is still writing feverishly as*

THE CURTAIN FALLS

ACT II

Scene I

The scene is the same as Act I, the time two weeks later. It is evening—about six o'clock.

As the curtain rises, LEONARD *is seen in evening clothes, but jacketless, declaiming before a mirror. He occasionally consults his notes. On the table is a copy of "Five Hundred Speeches for All Occasions."*

LEONARD [*to an imaginary audience*]. "I am feeling at this minute exactly like the seasick passenger on the ocean liner who was asked by a fellow passenger who was amused by his illness: 'Are you afraid you are going to die?' 'No,' said the sick man, 'I am afraid I'm *not* going to.' As an orator I am *non est*. However, I do have a slight advantage on the man in the story in that I can make my remarks brief. To-night is a big night for me—[*he pounds the table*] in every way. I feel that it is a signal honor that has been accorded me, and I thank you for it. It is indeed an honor to be a member of an organization . . ." [*He pauses to address* ELSIE, *who is in the next room.*] "Member" sounds all right. It's a lot better than "fellow worker." [*He gets no answer. Undismayed, he turns back to the mirror.*] A vast improvement. [*He resumes the speech.*] " . . . A member of an organization that includes two thousand five hundred fellow workers and is doing so much for our community life. As a member of it . . ." [*He drops the orator pose again and calls to* ELSIE.] See, that's got it all over just saying fellow worker. It's . . .

[ELSIE *appears in evening dress, carrying* LEONARD'S *dinner-jacket. She hasn't paid any attention to his remarks.*]

ELSIE. Now wait till it cools before you put it on. You mustn't pack it away like that again, dear. [*She is placing it over a chair.*]

333

LEONARD. It looks all right.

ELSIE. It does *now*. We'll have to start soon, dear.

LEONARD. We've got lots of time. We're going to the station by taxicab.

ELSIE. Leonard Beebe! You didn't order a——

LEONARD. I certainly did. It's only a dollar . . . a Green and White. You don't want to get those slippers all dirty, do you?

ELSIE. It's perfectly dry and I was going to wear my carriage-boots.

LEONARD. Besides, it gives me more time to rehearse.

ELSIE [*uneasy*]. You're not putting anything more in it, are you, dear? It seemed just the right length to me.

LEONARD [*showing her the notes*]. Look, I made another change. Sit there and I'll go through it again.

[*She isn't very enthusiastic.*]
You still don't like it, do you?

ELSIE. I think it's wonderful for what it *is*. I simply still believe you could have written a better one yourself.

LEONARD. Better than one written by experts?

ELSIE. You could have made it less like a regular speech and more like the way people talk.

LEONARD [*positively*]. People don't go to a banquet to hear people talk just—the way they talk. They could hear that at home.

ELSIE. Of course I don't know much about banquets, dear.

LEONARD. Well, I can tell you. Regular speeches— that's the thing. Do you think this fellow—ah—J. Montgomery Watson—would have gone to all the trouble of getting up this book if—if he hadn't learned that people wanted them? Look! [*He reads some of the titles.*] "Speech at the Funeral of a Dear Friend." "At a Ship's Concert, Aboard a Vessel Bound for England." Then— "Aboard a Vessel Bound for America" . . . "For France," and so on.

ELSIE. Yes, darling, I understand, but still . . .

LEONARD. A thing like this—a business dinner—a man knows best about. Of course I'm glad you're going, but still—well, I mean as long as it's just a business organization, why——

ELSIE. You mean you'd rather I wouldn't go, Leonard?

LEONARD. No, I want you to go—-as long as all the other men's wives are going.

[*She turns away.*]

But I've got a chance to be chief clerk of the department, if I do this right. I can't seem to make you understand.

ELSIE. Why, Leonard, I do understand. And I won't discourage you or stand in your way any more. I'll just remember that you're—my champion—and that you're doing it for both of us.

LEONARD [*partly pacified*]. Well, then!

ELSIE. And if you don't think I ought to go to the dinner, Leonard——

LEONARD. Oh, it isn't that. Besides, they expect you, and—I want you to go, all right. [*He embraces her rather awkwardly.*]

ELSIE. Oh, Leonard, I don't know what I'd do without you. And I do so want you to win to-night—you've only that man Baker to beat, and I'm sure his speech can't be half as good as yours.

LEONARD. That's the first good word you've said about it. You never said anything about my discovering that this speech would just fit. You see what it was in the beginning. [*He points to the book.*]

ELSIE. Yes, dear.

LEONARD [*reading the title*]. "Upon Assuming the Presidency of a Club, Society, Turn-Verein, etc." See—No. 47?

ELSIE. Of course, dear. And it was very clever of you to make the changes. I wish that taxi would come.

LEONARD [*getting ready for the speech again*]. Well, are you ready?

ELSIE. For what, dear?

LEONARD. To hear it, of course.

ELSIE. Oh! Again?

LEONARD. Well, you want to help me, don't you? Gee whiz, you ought to do *something*! The least a man's wife can do is to help him when——

ELSIE. Of course, dear. First put on your coat.

LEONARD [*struggling into his coat*]. Ah—here—you hold the notes. [*He hands her several sheets of paper.*] Say, isn't that evening paper here yet? It's supposed to have a list of the guests in it.

ELSIE. It's late to-night. Now hurry, dearest—the cab will be here very soon. Now, I'll sit over here! [*She sits in front of him.*] Now I'm all right. Ready!

LEONARD [*with elaborate preparations*]. "Honored President, Mr. Toastmaster, Ladies and Gentlemen and Guests—" [*Breaks off.*] I wouldn't even have known for sure how to begin if it hadn't been for——

ELSIE [*hastily*]. It's very good.

LEONARD. "I am feeling at this minute exactly like the seasick passenger on the ocean liner—" [*he puts his hand on his stomach*] "who was asked——"

ELSIE. Oh, I wouldn't do that, Leonard.

LEONARD. What?

ELSIE. This. [*She indicates his gesture.*]

LEONARD. Why not?

ELSIE. You see, it's an after-dinner speech.

LEONARD. Well, all right. [*Battling through the first part.*] "Exactly like the seasick passenger on the ocean liner who was asked by a fellow passenger who was amused at his illness—" Are you watching the notes?

ELSIE. Oh, I know that's right.

LEONARD. "—Amused at his illness: 'Are you afraid you're going to die?' 'No,' said the sick man, 'I'm afraid I'm *not* going to.'" Then I wait while they laugh.

ELSIE [*uncertainly*]. Yes.

LEONARD. It's good, don't you think?

ELSIE. Ah—yes—but I thought if you could think of one of your own——

LEONARD. [*His face brightens.*] How about the one about the Irishman and the hotel clerk? And the Irishman came in and said: "Be Jabers——"

ELSIE [*hastily*]. I guess the other one's all right.

LEONARD. The sick one? Well, all right. [*Striking an attitude.*] "As an orator——"

ELSIE. I'd be careful about the way I stood, Leonard.

LEONARD. Well— [*He relaxes a little.*] "—As an orator, I am *non est.*" [*He pauses, well pleased with himself.*]

ELSIE [*prompting*]. "However——"

LEONARD. I know what it is. I was just thinking that *"non est"* is pretty good. It's the sort of thing a man without any background would never get.

ELSIE. You'd better hurry, dear.

LEONARD. "However, I have a slight advantage on the man in the story in that I can make my remarks brief." [*He pauses.*]

ELSIE [*prompting*]. "To-night."

LEONARD. There's a pause there.

ELSIE. I wouldn't make it too long.

LEONARD [*reading from book*]. "You will find that it rests people, particularly if they're worked up at all." Ah—"To-night is a big night to me—" [*pounds table*] "in every way."

ELSIE [*rises*]. Oh, Leonard, it *is*, too. If that other man should get the promotion——

LEONARD. Now, what's the use of worrying——

ELSIE. But I can't help feeling—what would become of us, Leonard? We owe so much money——

LEONARD. Nonsense! I'll get it sure. Watch if I don't. [*Goes back to the speech.*] "I feel that it is a signal honor that has been conferred upon me, and I thank you for it."

[CHESTER'S *peculiar knock is heard on the door.*]

ELSIE. It's Chester. At this hour. [*She opens the door; CHESTER steps into the room, newly attired in a light checked suit. LEONARD never stops talking.*]

CHESTER. Well, how's the speech-making business?

LEONARD [*motioning him to be silent*]. "Hope that with a continuation of the team-work shown in past years it will grow and flower in strength and achievement. I feel very humble and very proud, and I thank you very much, indeed." Hello, Chester. [*This is all in one breath.*]

ELSIE. That's beautiful—now I'll get your things, dear.

CHESTER. Don't go, Elsie! [*He pauses impressively.*] Take a look at your ex-fellow worker!

LEONARD. What!

ELSIE. Chester! You've been discharged!

CHESTER. Discharged? I should say not! I'm quitting!

LEONARD. When?

ELSIE. What are you going to do?

CHESTER. The big time!

LEONARD. Really?

ELSIE. Oh, I'm so glad! Tell us all about it!

CHESTER. Well—nobody knows yet, see? I haven't told them at the office that I'm quitting, because—it isn't quite all settled.

ELSIE. Oh!

CHESTER [quickly]. But it will be. I'll tell you what happened! When the old man didn't have vision enough to see the piano act, I took it right over to the Knabe people the next day, and—[he pronounces it to rhyme with "Abe"] I saw this Mr. Spaeth—he's the head of pretty near the whole thing, he says. And what do you think?

ELSIE. Well?

CHESTER. Well—I'm to have an audition—[he tackles the word very carefully] on Thursday.

ELSIE. But, Chester——

CHESTER. Listen! All the department heads are going to be there—some of them. And if I make a hit with it they'll arrange for me to go right into vaudeville. And say!

LEONARD. Well?

CHESTER [turning to LEONARD]. Maybe I won't make some speech to the old man when that happens. I'm just going to walk right past Sheridan into his office and say, "Look here, J. K. New York ain't big enough to keep you and I in the same business. So here's your old job," I'm going to say, "and if you ever drop in at the Palace, why, look me up."

ELSIE. I'm so glad, Chester. It's time to get ready, Leonard. I'll get your coat. [She goes into the next room.]

CHESTER. I got a route all laid out—the way I'd like to do it. I'll try out at some little place like Mt. Vernon, just to sort of get used to it, you know—then, say, the Royal, Alhambra, Riverside—and I'll keep the Palace for about the fourth week, and say! I may put a couple of girls in the act—you know, sitting on the pianos! Lends class. Then after the Palace—say, do you know that an act can get twenty-four consecutive weeks in New York nowadays? And think of sitting around the N. V. A. club-house and meeting all those vaudeville head-liners! Sophie Tucker, Franklyn Ardell, Valeska Suratt, Eva Tanguay——

LEONARD [*his mind going back*]. "I am feeling at this minute exactly like the seasick passenger on the ocean liner who was asked by a fellow passenger——"

CHESTER. Just what are you doing?

LEONARD. I was running through some of the speech.

CHESTER. Aw, hell!

LEONARD [*half to himself*]. "'Are you afraid you are going to die?' 'No,' said the sick man——"

CHESTER. Are you pulling *that* one?

LEONARD. What's the matter with it?

CHESTER. Fox time!

[ELSIE *returns, wearing her evening cape and carrying* LEONARD'S *overcoat, scarf, etc.*]

ELSIE. Leonard, I'm almost sure I hear the taxicab. I'm sorry, Chester.

LEONARD. Of course that newspaper would be late just to-night. Did yours come, Chester?

CHESTER. I think it's up there. Yes, I remember I was looking up the bill at Moss's Broadway.

ELSIE. Now, Leonard, you don't need to——

LEONARD. Well, if it's got an account of the dinner in it! Chester can get it while I'm putting my things on.

CHESTER [*rises*]. Oh, sure—I didn't understand. That's right, there *is a* piece about the dinner.

LEONARD. See?

CHESTER. I won't be a minute! [*Dashes off.*]

ELSIE [*holding his coat for him*]. Now, Leonard!

LEONARD. I'm getting sort of nervous.

ELSIE. Leonard! There's nothing to be nervous about. You know your speech very well, and, besides, I'm right there beside you——

LEONARD. "As an orator I am *non est*. However, I do have a slight advantage on the man in the story in that I can make my remarks brief. To-night is a big night for me"—[*hits table*] "in every way. I feel that it is a signal honor——"

ELSIE [*suddenly serious*]. Leonard!

LEONARD. "It is indeed an honor to be a member of an organization——"

ELSIE. Leonard!

LEONARD. Well?

ELSIE [*putting her arms around him*]. If you don't get it, you won't worry, will you? I'll love you just the same —always.

LEONARD [*with real tenderness*]. I will you too, Elsie.

ELSIE. And if something *does* go wrong, and you don't get it——

LEONARD. We'll still be all right. We'll go down to Florida, and raise grapefruit, and make a lot of money.

ELSIE. Yes!

[*There is a thud against the door.*]

LEONARD [*breaking away*]. That's the paper! [*He dashes to the door, followed by* ELSIE, *and brings in the folded newspaper.* ELSIE *looks out the window.*]

ELSIE. I don't see the taxi yet.

LEONARD [*feverishly scanning the paper*]. They've *got* to print our names this time!

ELSIE. Yes, dear.

LEONARD. Here it is—right under our advertisement! [*Reads.*] "John Kincaid's Sons"—"97th Anniversary"— "Among those present"—"Mr. and Mrs."—"Mr. and Mrs. George Spelvin"—"Mr. and Mrs. Leonard Hamilton Beebe—" [*This with a triumphant whoop.*]

ELSIE. Let me see!

LEONARD. There you are—Mr. and Mrs. Leonard Hamilton Beebe! What do you think of that?

ELSIE. Oh! I'm so proud of you!

LEONARD. We must get a lot of copies of this! Remember, the Home Edition! Good Old Home Edition! [*A moment's pause while he turns another page.*] Elsie! [*The paper slips from his hands.*]

ELSIE. Yes, dear. [*Observing that he stands transfixed.*] Why, what's the matter?

LEONARD. It's the grapefruit!

ELSIE. The—grapefruit? [*Half understanding.*] Leonard!

LEONARD. It's—no good!

[*She stands looking at him as he raises the paper and falteringly reads the head-lines.*]

"Public Loses Ten Million in Land Swindle. Worthless Florida Farms Sold Through Advertisement as Fertile Soil. Promoters Arrested in New Orleans—" [*The paper slips again from his grasp.*]

ELSIE [*catching it*]. Francis D. Stevens. That *was* the man—wasn't it?

[LEONARD *nods, miserably.*]

[*The couple stand silent for a moment and then the cheery voice of* CHESTER *is heard. He enters.*]

CHESTER. Here we are! Full list of the guests of honor! All the details— Why, what's the matter? [*He gets no answer.*] Huh?

ELSIE. Why—nothing. Just something Leonard was telling me.

CHESTER. Oh! Well, I'll get out then. I see you got *your* paper.

LEONARD. Yes. [*Summons all his strength.*] Good night, Chester.

CHESTER. Good night. 'Night, Elsie.

ELSIE. Good night, Chester.

CHESTER. Here's hoping you put it over at the dinner, Leonard.

LEONARD. Thanks.

CHESTER. Anyhow, you get a swell feed. Wouldn't mind if I was going. Hotel Commodore, isn't it?

LEONARD [*still mechanically*]. Yes.

CHESTER. Be a good dinner, all right. Soup to nuts. [*He goes. There is an appreciable interval, and then the sound of a motor-horn is heard—three sharp and summoning toots.*]

ELSIE [*going to him*]. That's it, Leonard. Leonard. [*He faces her.*] You know I love you and believe in you. Why, this thing doesn't matter. When you have your promotion, and are making a lot of money, why, you won't think anything about it. It's a bit of a disappointment at first, but everybody has them—I don't care who it is. And no matter what happens, we have each other.

[*A pause.*]

Leonard!

LEONARD. Yes.

ELSIE. I want you to take me—in your arms.

    [*He does.*]

That's right. And kiss me.

    [*He does so.*]

Again.

    [*He does so.*]

And remember that no matter *what* happens to-night—whether you win or lose—it makes no *real* difference—to *me.*

 LEONARD. I'll—win!

ELSIE. Of course you will!

    [*Three more sharp toots of the auto-horn.*]

    [ELSIE *dries a tear.*]

My powder-puff. I'll be right back. [*She goes off, then calls from the next room.*] Be sure you have everything, Leonard.

    [LEONARD *begins to feel in his pockets, mechanically at first, then more and more frantically as he fails to find the object of his search. Having searched all his clothes, he begins on the room. He looks under furniture, in drawers, starts throwing everything topsyturvy. He grows more and more wild as he continues. When he has the room in complete disarray,* ELSIE *re-enters.*]

ELSIE. Leonard! What on earth are you doing?

LEONARD [*gasping*]. My—notes! I've lost them!

ELSIE. Good heavens, Leonard, I have them. [*Holding them up in her left hand.*] You didn't think I'd leave them for you, did you?

    [LEONARD *gathers hat from sofa and runs after her. The lights go out, the curtain falls, then rises almost immediately to reveal——*

SCENE II

The annual dinner of John Kincaid's Sons at the Hotel Commodore, New York. The speaker's long table faces the audience; behind it is a large curtain decorated with an American flag. There are all the minutiæ of the formal banquet—the smilax-decorated table, the open

boxes of Pall Mall cigarettes, the demi-tasse cups (the meal itself is over), the souvenir programmes, and the assorted cakes. Several familiar faces can be seen in the places of honor—specifically, MR. KINCAID and his wife, and LEONARD and ELSIE. About fifteen persons in all are seated at the table—the TOASTMASTER centre, with a great floral piece in front of him. The table stretches beyond the stage at both sides—there are dozens of unseen guests.
The voice of a speaker is heard before the curtain rises.

VOICE OF SPEAKER. And so the situation rapidly improved, and again the wiring department is fully up to the standard of the others. [*A pause.*] The twelfth and last problem that faced us—namely, the contract disagreement between the N. A. A. C. A. and the C. N. P. M. League— was also felicitously solved last March—

[The curtain rises. All the diners are gazing to the right, whence comes the voice of the speaker. He is evidently concluding a long and wearisome address, and every one is bored. One man is toying with his water-glass; LEONARD is playing with his menu-card; from which he has bitten several pieces. Some of the men are smoking. The TOASTMASTER is looking at his watch. There is a brief pause after the curtain rises, and then the off-stage voice is heard again.]

the N. A. A. C. A. agreeing that the overtime clauses had been unfair and inequitable, and conceding virtually unanimously to each and every one of the demands of the C. N. P. M. League. [*A pause.*] I'm afraid that I have slightly exceeded the five minutes that was allotted to me—

[Every man at the table looks at his watch.]

but I felt that the problems facing the N. A. A. C. A. and the C. N. P. M. League at the Farmingham plant were in effect a handicap and an enchainment to the trade in general, and for that reason warranted the ample discussion that I have given them before you ladies and gentlemen here to-night.

[LEONARD has been balancing one spoon on top of another; ELSIE quietly removes them; he settles back.]

I want to thank you all for your interest, and to say in conclusion that I am glad to report that the plant is once again running smoothly, and that our troubles have all been settled, at least temporarily, and as Pippa says in the poem—

[*There is a heavy cough from an unseen diner.*]

"Everything is all right with the world." At least, in so far as the N. A. A. C. A.—

[*Another cough.*]

and the C. N. P. M. League are concerned. Ladies and gentlemen, I thank you.

[*There is a polite round of applause. The diners adjust themselves more easily in their chairs; chat with their neighbors for a second.*]

[LEONARD, *constantly expectant that he will be called upon next, produces his notes from his pocket. At the right there is a good deal of clattering of dishes, which continues when the* TOASTMASTER *arises to speak.*]

TOASTMASTER. I am sure that Mr. Moffam's story of the Farmingham strike has been both instructive and interesting to every one here. I think I am safe in saying— [*he breaks off, annoyed at the noise*] will the waiters please not clear the tables while the speeches are going on?

[*The noise stops.*]

It's very annoying. [*He clears his throat and starts again.*] I say—

[*The cougher is heard again.*]

Mr. Moffam need not apologize for the forty-five minutes that he has used. And I am sure that we are very grateful to him for making the trip all the way down from Farmingham—just to be with us to-night. [*A pause; he clears his throat.*] It is with great regret that I announce that one of our foremost speakers cannot be with us this evening. He is a gentleman with whom you are all familiar—namely, Mr. Dudley Field Malone. He has sent me this telegram, however—[*he lifts a telegram from the table*] explaining why he cannot be with us, and—ah—stating how very, very sorry he is. [*Reads.*] "W. J. Henrici, Hotel Commodore, New York. Regret that I cannot be with you. Signed, Malone."

[LEONARD *starts to applaud, but it doesn't take very well.*]

It gives me great pleasure to announce, however, that in his place we have with us to-night—another gentleman, whom many of us have admired in his long and valuable public life. I am sure that he will have a message of importance to deliver to you. I take great pleasure in introducing—[*he consults a card*] former State Senator Martin L. Cassidy.

[*There is a round of applause.*]

CASSIDY [*rises. A machine man, a product of the East Side, and still a bit rough in speech and manner*]. Mr. Toastmaster, ladies and gentlemen of the John Kincaid's Sons' organization, and—guests. I feel very happy to have the honor of addressing such a distinguished and representative gathering as are assembled here to-night. The piano is a great symbol of the great heart of America. We are a music-loving nation, and there is probably no instrument manufactured that is to be found in so many homes, and which brings so much pleasure to hundreds of thousands—nay, millions—as the piano. The piano! The piano calms us when we are sad and inspires us when we are in the mood for art, music, or a little good-natured fun. It is no longer a luxury, it is a necessity—the birthright of American citizenship.

[*Applause.*]

And how about the men who are striving daily throughout the United States to give this great music-loving people a better grade of this great instrument than they have ever had before? Does the country appreciate it? Do certain political parties that can help or hinder the industry appreciate it?

[*The cough comes again.*]

I think I can truthfully say that the Democratic party, which is constantly fighting for the betterment of our national life, has always been aware that the making of pianos is one of the great industries of the country—

[*Applause.*]

and is a lifelong friend of every man, woman, and child in the piano business. The hour is growing late, and I have no doubt there are many interesting speakers still to come, but I hope I will be allowed the privilege—nay, the honor—of paying a slight tribute to a man who is representing you right now in Washington, fighting your battles and trying to keep the Republican party from heaping new taxes upon the piano industry. I refer to that peerless and fearless representative of his constituents' interests in the House of Representatives in the Congress of the United States at Washington, D. C.; that 100 per cent American, and himself a lover of music; that brilliant son of old Father Knickerbocker, the Honorable Simon J. Strausheimer! I happen to know that Congressman Strausheimer not only favors removing the taxes from American piano manufacturers but is particularly anxious that a strong protective tariff on foreign, un-American musical instruments be put through at the earliest possible moment.

[*There is a strong applause, breaking out before he has finished the sentence.*]

In a personal interview that I had with him in Washington a few weeks ago—in the very shade of our dear capitol—

[*His voice breaks a little.*]

I happened to inquire on this particular point. "Congressman Strausheimer," I asked, "do you believe that the Democratic party will be able to do anything in this connection in the near future?" And he answered, in that quiet and simple way that has made him beloved by thousands: "I do! I am going to put up a stiff fight, and will battle tooth and nail to see that the native piano manufacturer gets a chance!"

[*Applause.*]

"In fact," he said, "I have saw the President about it this morning." I only want to say further that Simon J. Strausheimer will be before you for re-election this fall. And you cannot do better, particularly you ladies and gentlemen of the great piano trade, than to send back to Congress a man of the people, for the people, and with the people! I thank you very much for this opportunity to meet you. [*He sits down. The applause dies, and the* TOASTMASTER *is about to rise when* CASSIDY *consults his watch, gets up, shakes hands with the* TOASTMASTER, *and departs—doubtless to a dinner of the Watchmaker's Association, where Congressman Strausheimer will turn out to be the friend of the watchmaker.*]

TOASTMASTER [*when* CASSIDY *is gone*]. I am sure that

Senator Cassidy's report of the work being done at
Washington is encouraging to all of us.

[LEONARD *takes his notes from his pocket, spreads them
out, misses a page. He searches;* ELSIE *helps him.
The search runs through practically all of the* TOAST-
MASTER'S *next introduction.*]

I wonder if I need introduce—the next speaker. I don't
think I need to name him—[*he looks squarely at* KINCAID;
all applaud] but I think I will tell you something about his
ancestors. About a hundred years ago a young fellow
from Boston came down to New York to make some money
for himself and his young bride.

[*Again the clatter of dishes.*]

I must ask the waiters to try and be a little quieter!

[*The noise dies down.*]

An expert in several lines of business, he decided that
making pianos was as promising a line as any then being
offered to young men. He was the first—John Kincaid.

[*Applause.*]

His little factory prospered. Then a son came along to
bless the young couple's home. Then another son—
[*rapidly*] two years later. The boys grew to manhood and
were taken into the firm as partners. To-day the fourth
generation of that family stands in the shoes of his fore-
bears, and has the proud satisfaction of realizing that the
trust left him by his father has been well guarded. Ladies
and gentlemen, I am going to ask for a few words from our
dear Governor.

[*There is enthusiastic applause, which* LEONARD *leads.*
KINCAID *gets up.*]

[*The* TOASTMASTER *signals to all to join in singing
"He's a Jolly Good Fellow." All rise and do so,
very badly.*]

KINCAID [*benevolently*]. Mr. Toastmaster, ladies and
gentlemen of the personnel, and honored guests: I had
hoped Mr. Henrici would not force me to make a speech,
as I am a notoriously bad speechmaker.

[*Somehow this is accepted as humorous and every one
laughs heartily, which pleases* KINCAID.]

I don't believe that an old dog can be taught new tricks—

[*New outburst of laughter.*]

and—as I said—I am greatly surprised to be called upon. [*He takes a few notes from his pocket; looks them over.*] But Mr. Henrici is just as merciless at the banquet-table as when he hands me the monthly statements.

[*Laughter.*]

However—

[*The cougher is heard again;* KINCAID *glares.*]

I just want to say that I am particularly proud to be the head of an organization—[*consults his notes*] that is represented by such a brilliant group of ladies and gentlemen as I see before me here to-night.

[LEONARD *applauds.*]

Our boys may not be beauties to look at—

[*Laughter.*]

but our ladies certainly can take care of that department, and I think we should be proud of them. [*Looks at notes.*] But in all seriousness—I am very proud of being a descendant of the young man who brought his bride from Boston so long ago, and I am sure that he is watching over us here to-night and wishing us success.

[*Another cough.*]

As our advertisements so truly say—[*reads from his notes*] "The Kincaid piano is made by men who put love into their work"—

[*One more cough—the* TOASTMASTER *motions for the cougher to depart.*]

and I am going to ask you to join me in a silent toast to the memory of the founder of this great business. Ladies and gentlemen, a silent toast. [*He bows his head; the others do likewise. The moment is impressive.* KINCAID *indicates with a turn of the head that the silent toast is at an end. Continuing.*] To turn again from the grave to the gay—

[*Loud laugh from* LEONARD.]

I want to tell how happy I am to be with you to-night, just as one of the boys, and how happy Mrs. Kincaid is to be here as just one of the girls.

[*This is accepted as another hot one and gets a round of applause.* MRS. KINCAID *rises and bows.*]

And that reminds me of the colored man who was sitting

alongside a river when along came a man who wanted to be rowed across. "Can you row?" asked the man as he glanced at a skiff near by on the shore. "No, sah, I'm afeerd I cain't," replied the darky, flashing his white teeth in a good-natured smile. "All right," said the traveller. "You get in and watch the boat for me for a minute while I call on a man on the other side of the river." So the darky got in and the man started rowing to the other side. He arrived and attended to his business, and came back to find the darky waiting. Then he rowed him back to the other side again. It was very warm, and when the man got out he wiped his forehead and said: "It's very strange, uncle, that you can't row a little boat." "Row a boat!" cried the darky. "Laws-a-mussy, ah kin row a boat, all right. Ah thought you meant could I ro' like a lion!"

[*A moment's silence—then the* TOASTMASTER *breaks into laughter. All follow his cue.*]

You see, the darky knew how to row, all right, after the journey was ended. [*He gets another laugh of understanding on this.*] That reminds me of another very funny story about a Swede named Yon Johnson——

MRS. KINCAID [*touches him on the arm and whispers*]. John——

KINCAID. Well—we'll let that one pass. The point I wanted to bring out is really a serious one. It is the fellow who rows the boat that really gets something done, and I am very proud to head an organization that contains men who don't think they have "to ro' like a lion," but are willing to help row the boat instead. Some of you gentlemen present have been with the organization ever since I entered it myself, not a few, including Mr. Sanborn and Mr. Downey over there, having been employees long before I showed up. And that leads me to my final little surprise. [*He pauses, impressively.*] It has long been the hope—of the company—to do something for its loyal employees—something in recognition of the services that they have given. I am glad to announce that that moment is now at hand, and that our employees, particularly those who have been with us for some years, are to be rewarded. [*He pauses; every one is paying close atten-*

tion.] Beginning January 1st—[*a pause*] every man who has been with the company five years or more—[*a pause*] will be entitled to wear a button—a solid silver button which is to be known as the Kincaid Service Button. We feel— the directors—that money is but a poor return for loyalty. And so we have devised this little silver button—which will be marked with one gold stripe for each five years of service. To illustrate—a man who has been with us ten years will have two stripes; fifteen years, three stripes, and so on. The expense of the buttons will, of course, be borne entirely by the company. Ladies and gentlemen, I thank you. [*He sits down; there is a fine burst of applause. Everybody talks to his neighbor for a moment.* LEONARD *is becoming more and more nervous, taking a sip of water every moment, loosening his collar, etc. Finally the* TOASTMASTER *rises.*]

TOASTMASTER. As one of the directors I had, of course, known Mr. Kincaid's—little surprise—and, I want to say —because I think you are entitled to know it—and he would never tell you himself—that the idea of the button . . . was originated—by Mr. Kincaid, and that all thanks should go to him personally.

> [*Scattered applause. A* PHOTOGRAPHER *enters, and touches the* TOASTMASTER'S *arm—hands him the photo, whispers the price, etc.*]

I am requested to announce that the flash-light photographs taken at the beginning of the evening have been finished, and may be purchased from Mr.— [*Turns to inquire the name.*]

PHOTOGRAPHER. Pegliovgok!

TOASTMASTER [*giving it up*]. At the door as you go out. The price is one dollar and fifty cents, and I am sure that you will find them worth treasuring in future years. [*Hands photo to* MRS. KINCAID, *who passes it along the table. The* PHOTOGRAPHER *departs.*] And now, as most of you know, it is the custom at each of our organization dinners to invite new blood to be present. To-night we have two new junior members. In fact, I believe I violate no confidence in announcing that the chief clerkship in the retail sales department, now vacant, will be filled by one of these two young men. It is, I am sure, a friendly rivalry.

The first young man is one who has shown more than usual promise in the zeal, intelligence, and loyalty—

> [LEONARD, *who has been growing more and more nervous, now tips over a full glass of water. His neighbors move back quickly to avoid being splashed. There is a halt while a napkin is spread over the wet spot.*]

I take great pleasure in introducing Mr. Thomas Wood Baker.

> [BAKER, *self-possessed and calm, rises.* LEONARD *joins tardily in the applause.*]

BAKER. Honored President, Mr. Toastmaster, ladies and gentlemen and guests: I am feeling at this minute exactly like the seasick passenger on the ocean liner who was asked by a fellow passenger who was amused at his illness: "Are you afraid you're going to die?" "No," said the sick man, "I'm afraid I'm *not* going to."

> [*Laughter.* LEONARD *and* ELSIE, *of course, look at each other in astonishment.* BAKER *continues, vastly at ease.*]

As an orator I am *non est.*

> [LEONARD *and* ELSIE *are paralyzed; it is unquestionably Speech* 47.]

However, I have a slight advantage on the man in the story in that I can make my remarks brief. [*He pauses, just as the book told him to.*] To-night is a big night to me in every way. [*Thumps table.*]

> [LEONARD *is nearly under the table;* ELSIE *is whispering to him.*]

I feel that it is a signal honor that has been accorded me and I thank you for it. It is indeed an honor to be a member of an organization that includes so many thousand fellow workers, and is doing so much good in our community life. As a member of it I shall always try to give the organization the service it expects of a man in my position, and hope that with a continuation of the team-work shown in past years it will grow and flower in strength and achievement. I feel very humble and very proud, and I thank you very much indeed. [*He sits down, to a fine round of applause.* LEONARD, *however, has given up the ghost; he looks at* ELSIE *with death in his eyes.* ELSIE *pats his hand and whispers to him, but he shakes his head; he is not equal to the emergency. The* TOASTMASTER *rises again.*]

TOASTMASTER. I don't think Mr. Baker need have fear of anything. [*A pause.*] And now I am going to ask the second member of the younger generation to say a few words. That he is a young man of promise was evidenced by a recent act of his. What might have been a dangerous fire was rapidly extinguished by his quick action, and the fire confined to a small space with practically no damage— [*then adds, as an afterthought*] and was covered by insurance. Ladies and gentlemen, I take pleasure in introducing—[*he consults a card*] Mr. Leonard Hamilton Beebe, of the cost accounting department.

[*The* TOASTMASTER *sits down; there is a round of welcoming applause;* LEONARD *does not rise. There is a terrible pause, all eyes are turned to him. Then he rises, trembling with fear—attempts to articulate the words of his speech.* ELSIE *pulls him to his chair and gets up in his place.*]

ELSIE [*when the surprised diners have had a chance to adjust themselves*]. Mr. Beebe and I—have prepared a little surprise for you to-night. Just about the middle of the afternoon—this very afternoon—Leonard suddenly got laryngitis—he does once in a while, and it was all he could do to speak above a whisper. He was feeling a little better when we got here, but he was afraid he wouldn't be heard if he spoke himself—so he gave me the gist of what he was going to say. [*Looks at* LEONARD.] Didn't you, dear?

[LEONARD, *helpless, shakes his head.*]

So if you don't mind—this is Mr. Beebe's speech—just as he—fixed it up for me. Do you mind?

[*There is a hearty burst of applause.*]

Well—Mr. Beebe wants me to say that what he was going to talk about was—sanity. [*She laughs nervously;* LEONARD *tugs at her.*] I think I remember, dear. I re-fer—I mean he refers—to a spirit that's coming back into the business world after being gone for a long time—a spirit we've got to recognize and hold on to. I mean—I mean, he means—that after a good many years of dilly-dallying and lecturing and theorizing about how to get a little humanity into business, to-day we're actually going ahead and getting it instead.

[*Applause—she is surprised.* LEONARD *begins to perk up.*]

It seems to me that about everybody in the world has written a book or designed a chart or advertised some kind of university course in the magazines that will show you how to get a personality by mail, make friendships according to science, or strengthen your character by mathematics. A great many people have apparently been trying to find human nature all laid out and classified in text-books and on maps.

[LEONARD *offers the notes.*]

That's all right, dear. Now, Mr. Beebe knows he's pretty young, but he's been able to observe that relief is in sight—at least, in his own business. And he has been able to observe something else—and that is that a business man, a big business man—[*her glance goes to* KINCAID] can be just as simple and human in the way he runs his business and selects his employees as—anybody—and he doesn't lose a thing by it.

[KINCAID *swells with approval.*]

The main trouble with most business men to-day is that they're so busy looking for some kind of a—machine, that will attend to business for them, that they're either too bored or too tired to attend to life. Now, John Kincaid has shown you how to get away from all that. You may not realize it, but he has. He's shown you that there are still such things as—understanding in business, and—that simple, maybe old-fashioned ways of doing things—are just as efficient—and a little more so—than all your psychology and Applied—Morale—what-do-you-call it, and things like that. Now, why don't you follow his example? Go in for business, and go in for it just as much as you want to! But for God's sake try to be a little bit human! [*To* LEONARD.] That's about what you wanted me to say, wasn't it, dear?

LEONARD [*finding his voice*]. Approximately.

[*There is terrific applause.* ELSIE, *nearly in tears,*

starts to rise, but LEONARD *is on his feet ahead of her.
He bows graciously; the applause continues. He
blows a kiss; beams on the crowd. The men crowd
around to congratulate him— Only* MRS. KINCAID
goes to ELSIE.]

THE CURTAIN FALLS

ACT III

The scene is that most sacred of masculine institutions—the office. The time is six months later. There are three doors. One rather forbidding one warns you that it is the private sanctum of John Kincaid*—PRIVATE. One of the others leads to the general office, and the third to the elevator and the street. On the walls are huge maps of South and North America, studded with those mysterious colored thumb-tacks that mean something or other. A prominently placed sign assures you that* THE KINCAID PIANO IS THE HEART OF THE HOME. *There is also the framed original of a drawing used for advertising copy, showing happy men working in a busy factory. Below it are the words* THE KINCAID PIANO IS MADE BY MEN WHO PUT LOVE INTO THEIR WORK. *Over the stenographer's desk is a small sign that says merely* NEATNESS. *There are pictures of famous pianists seated at Kincaid pianos; there are factory photographs and banquet flash-lights. There is a huge and complicated-looking filing cabinet, with a circular index so formidable in appearance that you are certain no one could ever understand it. There is the customary office equipment in the way of desks, chairs, telephones, and time-saving machines of all sorts. And, finally, there is a red glass electric signal at* Mr. Kincaid's *private door. When this is lighted it means that* Mr. Kincaid *must not be disturbed on any account.*

At the rise of the curtain Leonard *sits thoughtfully at a big desk, drumming with a pencil, and dictating to* Miss Fletcher. *With the rise of the curtain the sound of a riveting-machine comes through the open window. There is obviously a building going up just around the corner, but it is old stuff to those in the office, and they pay no attention to it. This noise lasts just a few seconds each time that it is heard.*

LEONARD [*already a regular business man*]. "—so I cannot say just what our attitude in the future will be in regard to the department. Mr. Toohey now has twelve girls in the mailing department, but believes with me that men not only could do the work better but much more quickly than women." Paragraph.

[*The riveting-machine is heard.*]

"As you know, we believe that as a general rule women are not so capable as men in business. The increased staff in the new building will require six more members for the department." Send the same letter to the Acme Agency.

[*The riveting-machine again.*]

MISS FLETCHER. Yes, sir. How about that letter to those business people?

LEONARD. What was that?

MISS FLETCHER. You were going to let them know if you would speak at their meeting.

LEONARD. Speech! Oh! Yes, I'll give you that right now. Elliott, wasn't it?

[*She nods.*]

"James W. Elliott, Business Builders, Knickerbocker Building. Gentlemen:

"In regard to your kind invitation to speak at the weekly meeting at Carnegie Hall next Thursday night on the subject 'Young Men and the Spirit of Modern Business,' I wish to state that a previous engagement will call me out of town on that date. I regret very much not being able to give a little talk to the young men of your organization. And remain yours very truly." Those are very interesting meetings, Miss Fletcher.

MISS FLETCHER. Yes? That's good.

LEONARD [*severely*]. I'm afraid you have missed the spirit of modern business.

MISS FLETCHER. Oh, is *that* what it was? [*She goes to her desk.*]

[HENRICI, *the toastmaster, arrives from the outer office.*]

HENRICI. Mr. Kincaid in there?

LEONARD [*busily working*]. Yes.

HENRICI. All right for me to go in?

LEONARD. Oh, sure!

HENRICI. I want to ask him about the Fernandez appointment.

LEONARD. Oh, *I* can tell you about that!

[HENRICI *halts.*]

Mr. Kincaid and I were just talking it over.

HENRICI. Has he come to a decision?

LEONARD. Well, no, he isn't quite sure yet.

HENRICI. Is that so?

[KINCAID *enters briskly from his office; puts a paper on* LEONARD'S *desk.* LEONARD'S *grand manner changes with* KINCAID'S *entrance. He rises, offering his chair to* MR. KINCAID.]

LEONARD. Sit here, Mr. Kincaid?

KINCAID [*to* HENRICI]. I wanted to see you, Will. [*He sits at the desk.*] Now, exactly what territory would Fernandez look after down there?

[HENRICI *steps up to the map;* KINCAID *is preparing to write.*]

HENRICI [*examining the map*]. Beginning at Rio——

LEONARD [*explaining it*]. Rio Janeiro.

KINCAID [*notices that his pencil needs sharpening*]. Just a minute.

LEONARD [*busily*]. Just a minute.

KINCAID. [*He uses the pencil-sharpening machine, then speaks the next monosyllable as he takes the pencil out of the machine.*] Yes?

HENRICI. Rio Janeiro——

KINCAID [*repeating, as he starts to write*]. Rio Janeiro . . . [*Notices that the pencil point is broken.*] One second. [*He sharpens the pencil again in the machine; as he does so the riveting-machine is heard again.*] All right.

HENRICI. Buenos Ayres——

LEONARD. Buenos Ayres. [*A different pronunciation.*]

KINCAID [*the point broken again*]. Bu-nos Aires! [*A third pronunciation.*] Just a moment! [*He takes out a penknife and begins to sharpen the pencil.*] [*To* HENRICI.] You know, if this is the right man, he can reorganize the entire South American trade.

LEONARD. That's right.

KINCAID. I'll ring for that agreement. Which button is it?

LEONARD. Number four.

KINCAID [*presses one of the row of buttons; listens for the buzz, presses again*]. Try that department phone. Is there something wrong with these, Miss Fletcher?

MISS FLETCHER [*working at her desk*]. Yes, sir. They're out of order.

KINCAID [*to* LEONARD]. That memorandum.

LEONARD [*has taken up one of the telephones, tries to signal; gets no response, puts it down*]. They don't answer.

KINCAID. Miss Fletcher, will you ask—what's his name?—in the contract department——

MISS FLETCHER. Mr. Sherwood.

KINCAID. Mr. Sherwood—to send in that South American memorandum.

[*As* MISS FLETCHER *gets to her feet the riveting is heard again.*]

MISS FLETCHER. That damned thing is going to drive me crazy. [*She departs with emphasis.*]

LEONARD [*to* HENRICI]. Cigar?

[HENRICI *takes it, nodding his thanks.*]

[*To* KINCAID.]

Cigar?

[KINCAID *takes one.* MISS FLETCHER *re-enters.* LEONARD *gives lighted match to* HENRICI *and* KINCAID. *He is a business man for fair, right now.*]

KINCAID [*to* MISS FLETCHER]. Well?

MISS FLETCHER. They're sending it right in.

KINCAID [*as* LEONARD *lights his cigar*]. Ah!

MISS FLETCHER [*sitting at her desk*]. I was to remind you about the barber, Mr. Kincaid.

KINCAID. Oh, yes. If you don't mind running down for him——

MISS FLETCHER [*rising wearily*]. Yes, sir. [*As she nears the door.*] And the manicure?

KINCAID. Not to-day.

[MISS FLETCHER *goes.*]

That manicure! She's a butcher!

[*The three men compare their finger-nails across the desk.*]

LEONARD. Elinor? Look!

[CHESTER, *the same old* CHESTER, *arrives with the de-*

sired document. Seemingly the Palace is getting along without him.]

Here's the boy!

[CHESTER *delivers the paper, waits for a dismissing nod, and goes.*]

[*With a letter picked up from the stenographer's desk.*] That letter to the agencies—about sending women.

KINCAID.   Put it on my desk.

[LEONARD *goes into the private office.*]

HENRICI [*watching* LEONARD *depart*].   Making good in here—young Beebe?

KINCAID.   Very promising.   I was pretty hard up for somebody when Sheridan quit—then I thought I'd give *this* boy a try.   *Now* I think I'll make the job permanent.

[LEONARD *re-enters from* KINCAID's *office.*]

LEONARD [*busily*].   I put it on your desk.

KINCAID.   Very well.

HENRICI [*rising*].   Then as soon as you decide on Fernandez, I'll hear from you?

KINCAID.   That's right.   Very soon, now.

LEONARD.   We'll let you know.

[HENRICI *departs, not without a hard look at* LEONARD. KINCAID *settles himself with the contract, becomes interested in the quality of the paper.   He examines it.*]

KINCAID.   Is this the same paper we've been using?

LEONARD.   No, sir.   It's Haverfield Bond.

KINCAID.   Ah!   I like this paper very much.   I'd like to have them use that in all our documents and correspondence.

LEONARD.   It certainly is a fine paper, but a little more expensive than the others.

KINCAID.   The best is the cheapest when it comes to paper.   Nothing so reveals a man as his stationery.

LEONARD.   "Nothing so reveals"—I read that one.

KINCAID.   Now—let me see.   Have you that Zanesville correspondence?

LEONARD.   No, sir.   It's in the new triplex file.   Triplex simplicity.

KINCAID [*at the file*].   Oh!   How do you work it?

[LEONARD *rises, goes proudly to it, and reads from directions.*]

LEONARD. "Swing major index to desired color—swing back to Index G—then reverse to preceding letter, thereby unlocking the index drawer." [*Pulls index drawer open; a file flies up with a loud noise.*]

KINCAID. Simple, isn't it? [*Looks at the index, then at the indicator, and finally finds the color on the dial.*] Deep scarlet! [KINCAID *opens the bottom drawer, the deep scarlet one, and removes a girl's sweater and a pair of rubbers.*] What the—

[MISS FLETCHER *has re-entered.*]

Miss Fletcher——

MISS FLETCHER. I beg your pardon. [*Takes sweater and rubbers.*]

KINCAID. I've been looking for the Zanesville correspondence. Do you know where it is?

MISS FLETCHER. Yes, sir—I had to put it in the other room. I'll get it.

KINCAID. Well, why didn't you put it in here?

MISS FLETCHER. I can't work that one yet. But I'm taking lessons. [*She departs.*]

[*Telephone-bell on desk rings;* LEONARD *answers.*]

LEONARD. What? . . . Oh! [*To* KINCAID, *who is closing the drawer of the filing cabinet. It flies open again, hitting his arm.*] Ah—Mrs. Beebe is down-stairs. I asked her to come and see the new office. [*There is a question in his voice. He turns back to the phone.*] Just a minute.

KINCAID. Oh, of course.

LEONARD [*into phone*]. It's all right—send her up. [*He hangs up.*] I thought maybe you—wouldn't mind.

KINCAID. Oh, not at all. We haven't seen Mrs. Beebe here for some time.

LEONARD. She takes quite an interest in my work.

[MISS FLETCHER *enters, hands some papers to* KINCAID *and goes to her desk.*]

[*A* BARBER *in white coat, and carrying a small satchel, also enters.*]

BARBER. Ready, Mr. Kincaid?

KINCAID. Oh, yes. I've been waiting for you, Frank.

BARBER [*exchanging nods with* LEONARD; *speaks to* KINCAID]. I shaved a friend of yours this morning.

KINCAID [*as he goes into his office*]. Who was that?

BARBER. Ex-Congressman Strausheimer.

[KINCAID *goes into the private office. The* BARBER *follows. The red light goes up outside* KINCAID'S *office.* LEONARD *sits at the desk, one eye on the outside door, obviously posing himself a bit for* ELSIE'S *entrance. When he gets well settled the door opens and an undersized* BOOTBLACK *enters—a grown man, not a boy.* LEONARD *props up his foot, with a good deal of delight in the operation; the* BOOTBLACK *begins to shine his shoes.* LEONARD *looks over some letters, then at the door again.*]

LEONARD. Oh, Miss Fletcher.

[*She turns.*]

Did all this mail come in at 1.13?

MISS FLETCHER. No, sir. The clock in the stamping-machine is broken.

LEONARD [*puffs his cigar, leans back.* MISS FLETCHER *gives him an observant look.* LEONARD *picks up a letter and pretends to be interested in it. He is posed perfectly. A knock—he speaks casually*]. Come in!

[*Enter* ELSIE. *She, at least, is just the same.*]

Ah, Elsie!

ELSIE [*a little overawed by it all*]. Hello, Leonard.

LEONARD [*with a great air of business*]. I'll be with you in a minute.

ELSIE. Yes, dear.

LEONARD. Just take a seat.

[ELSIE *takes one, against the rear wall.* LEONARD *looks through a few letters, checks them.*]

Now, then!

[MISS FLETCHER *looks at* ELSIE *over her shoulder.*]

ELSIE [*rising*]. Oh, Leonard, it's awfully nice!

LEONARD [*offhand*]. Just an office, just an office.

[MISS FLETCHER *rises, as if about to depart.*]

LEONARD. Miss Fletcher, this is Mrs. Beebe.

[*The two girls nod.*]

[*Ostentatiously.*]

I'll have some more dictation later.

Miss Fletcher.   Thank you very much.

Leonard.   You're welcome.

[Miss Fletcher *goes.*]

Miss Fletcher is my—ah—secretary.

Elsie.   Leonard, it's all just wonderful!

Leonard.   Like it?

Elsie.   And you look too cute for anything.

Leonard [*with look at the* Bootblack].   Hush! I'll show you something.   [*He points to* Kincaid's *office.*]   See that door?

Elsie [*reads*].   "Mr. Kincaid, Private."   Oh, Leonard, is *he* in there?

Leonard.   Sure.   See that red glass?

Elsie.   Yes.

Leonard.   When that's lighted—see, it's lighted now?

Elsie.   Yes.

Leonard.   That means he's in conference, and isn't to be disturbed by anybody.   See?

Elsie [*dutifully*].   Not by anybody.

Leonard.   Not by anybody.   [*He picks up a slip of paper.*]   Now, watch!   [*He goes boldly into* Kincaid's *private office.*]

Elsie [*as he turns the knob*].   Oh!

> [Leonard *disappears within the private sanctum, closing the door behind him.   For a moment* Elsie *stands waiting, then* Leonard *proudly re-enters, again closing the door.*]

Leonard.   Except me.   [*He sits down again; the* Bootblack *resumes.*]

Elsie.   Leonard, what did you say to him?

Leonard.   Just a casual question about business.

Elsie.   Oh, Leonard, I'm so proud of you.

Leonard.   There isn't anybody else in the place that can walk right in like that.

Elsie.   It's just wonderful.

Leonard.   Some of them try it, but they've all got to see *me* first.

> [*The* Bootblack, *finished with* Leonard, *rises and goes into* Kincaid's *private office.*]

Every one has to come in here and see me—   I've had these phones put in—I can communicate with every floor in the building. [*He continues talking until* ELSIE *stops him.*]

ELSIE. Leonard, there's nobody here—we're alone.

LEONARD [*his manner changing*]. Hello, Elsie.

ELSIE. Hello, Leonard!

[*They kiss across the desk.*]

LEONARD [*with a touch of bashfulness*]. It's all mine.

ELSIE. Oh, Leonard! It's wonderful! Just what we used to dream about—when we were first married. Remember?

LEONARD. Uh-huh. Just think of it— I'm his secretary! It's come—success!

ELSIE. I knew you would, dear, and you have!

LEONARD [*going to her*]. *I* didn't do it all. You helped. [*Takes her in his arms.*]

ELSIE. Oh, no, I didn't.

LEONARD. Yes, you did. You helped a lot. I couldn't have done it without you.

ELSIE. Why, yes, you could, dear!

LEONARD. Then let's say *we* did it—together.

ELSIE. Together!

LEONARD. Just you and I. And that we'll always do things together—no matter what happens.

ELSIE. No matter what happens.

LEONARD. Forever and ever!

ELSIE. Forever and ever!

LEONARD. Amen!

ELSIE. Amen!

[*They kiss, sealing a pact.*]

And you'll go on—up and up——

LEONARD. Yep! I'll be a partner soon——

ELSIE. But, Leonard——

LEONARD. Yes?

ELSIE. Don't you think you'd better be a little more careful about your—manner—here in the office?

LEONARD. How do you mean?

ELSIE. Well, I notice just now with Miss—[*hesitates at name.* LEONARD *gives it to her*] Fletcher—you were a little brusque——

LEONARD. Oh, that? I was just being businesslike.

Listen, I know how to behave in business all right. Don't forget I've got a pretty good model in John Kincaid.

[*Enter* CHESTER, *carrying a number of blue slips.*]

CHESTER. Say!—oh, hello, Elsie!

ELSIE. Hello, Chester. Are *you* in here too? Isn't that nice?

LEONARD [*quickly*]. *He* isn't in here.

CHESTER. Say! That new efficiency fellow—what's his name?

LEONARD. Mr. Benchley?

CHESTER. Yeh. Well, he wants everybody to fill out another one of these slips—home address, telephone number, and favorite sport, if any.

LEONARD. Just leave it on the desk!

[CHESTER *puts it down.*]

Not there—over there.

[CHESTER *moves it.*]

Now let me see! [*He begins to sort papers importantly; looks over a document.*] H'm, Elsie, it's going to be about ten minutes before I can go to lunch. Ah—just happened to notice this. Needs attention. [*He taps the paper.*] Would you mind—waiting down-stairs for me? I mean, it'll just be—a few minutes—and—it looks better if——

ELSIE [*rises*]. Why, of course, dear!

LEONARD. I really didn't think you'd be here so early, or——

ELSIE. It's quite all right. I'll see you later, Chester.

CHESTER. That's good.

ELSIE. Leonard is going to show me over the new building after lunch.

CHESTER. Don't forget to come in the filing department. See our Turner Jefferson self-adaptable triplex filing system. Maybe *you* can explain it to me.

ELSIE. I'll come back when you aren't busy, Leonard.

LEONARD [*bent over his desk*]. Uh!

[ELSIE, *getting no further response, departs.*]

CHESTER [*with a move toward* MISS FLETCHER's *desk*]. Where's Miss Fletcher? I gotta give *her* one of these. [*He extends a slip.*]

LEONARD. She'll be right back.

[CHESTER *drops a slip on* MISS FLETCHER's *desk.*]

CHESTER [*sadly by her chair*]. Funny, my doing this work.

LEONARD. Oh, I don't know.

CHESTER. I'm just marking time, that's all. If this weren't a bum theatre season you wouldn't see me here.

[TOM BAKER, *the defeated candidate, enters from the inner office.*]

BAKER. Mr. Kincaid in?

LEONARD. What?

BAKER. Is Mr. Kincaid in?

LEONARD. What do you want to see him about?

BAKER. Is he in?

LEONARD. You've got to tell me your business.

BAKER. Who said so?

LEONARD. I did!

BAKER. There's a fine chance of my doing it.

LEONARD. Then you can't see him.

[BAKER *crosses.* LEONARD *stops him.*] Wait a minute! See that light? He's in conference.

BAKER [*turning to* CHESTER]. I don't believe it! This guy thinks he's got the world by the tail! [*Turns to* LEONARD.] Why, you aren't even his secretary yet! And maybe you won't be!

LEONARD. Now, look here——

BAKER. You think you can get by with murder in here. All because you wrote one little bit of a speech. And *then* had to have your wife say it for you!

LEONARD. That's *your* story!

BAKER. And if you ask me, it wasn't much of a speech, either!

LEONARD. Well, all right, all right!

BAKER [*leaning over the desk*]. No, it isn't all right! I'll say what I think and I think it was a bum speech!

CHESTER [*to the rescue of his friend*]. Now listen here, Baker——

LEONARD. Chester! You keep out of this!

CHESTER. And let him say it was a bum speech! I *will* not!

LEONARD [*comes between* CHESTER *and* BAKER]. Chester —you don't know what you're talking about! Now——

CHESTER. *I* thought it was good! What do you know about that?

LEONARD. Chester!—for God's sake!

BAKER. You didn't even hear it!

[LEONARD *is frantically trying to keep* CHESTER *and* BAKER *from getting together about the speech.*]

CHESTER. Is that so? Well, I heard him rehearsing it!

LEONARD. No, he didn't. I never made that speech! [*To* CHESTER.] You never heard me at all!

CHESTER. I did so.

LEONARD. You did not!

CHESTER. I did so! I remember it myself! About the seasick passenger—the one you got out of the book!

BAKER [*whirling him round*]. What seasick passenger?

LEONARD [*trying to push* CHESTER *out*]. I tell you I threw that speech away!

BAKER [*excited*]. What else did he say? Something about how he was *non est* as a speechmaker?

CHESTER [*trying to wrench himself loose from* LEONARD]. You know darned well he did! What are you trying to do?

LEONARD. I didn't say anything of the kind! That was all thrown away! And if you say it wasn't, I'll— [*He is in fighting temper.*]

BAKER. Oh, I'm on! You had to have your wife *save* you! Went and got promoted on something his *wife* did!

LEONARD. I tell you it's a lie! I never was going to make that speech! I wrote a whole new one!

BAKER. You did *not!*

[KINCAID *enters, attracted by the noise.*]

You were going to make *my* speech, only I made it first! And your wife had to save you! Laryngitis! A yellow streak—that's what it was!

CHESTER [*sees* KINCAID]. Cheese it! Cheese it! [*Goes quickly, snatching up a paper from the desk.*]

KINCAID [*firmly*]. May I inquire what this is all about?

[LEONARD *and* BAKER *turn. There is a pause.*]

Well?

LEONARD. Why—he—he came——

BAKER. I'll tell you! He never wrote that speech his

wife made at the banquet—the one you promoted him for! He didn't have a damned thing to do with it! He wasn't able to make one *himself*, and so he got his *wife* to do it for him!

> [*There is a moment's terrible pause. In the midst of it the* BARBER *and the* BOOTBLACK *emerge from* KINCAID'S *office.*]

BARBER. Good day, Mr. Kincaid.

KINCAID. Good day, Frank.

BARBER. See you to-morrow.

KINCAID. That's right.

> [*The* BARBER *and* BOOTBLACK *go out. There is again a pause as* LEONARD *and* BAKER *wait in silence for* KINCAID'S *verdict.*]

You may go, Baker.

BAKER. I shouldn't have said just what——

KINCAID. You may go.

BAKER. Yes, sir. [*He goes; the telephone rings.* LEONARD *moves as though to answer it;* KINCAID *raises his hand, stopping him.*]

KINCAID [*answering phone*]. Hello! Oh! Henrici. Fernandez? No, I haven't decided yet. I'll let you know. [*Ice in his tones.*] Beebe.

> [LEONARD *comes closer to the desk.*]

It is not my custom to take advantage of information that comes out—like this, but—this is too serious a matter to be ignored. I hope, of course, that—Mr. Baker was mistaken, but—I shall expect you to tell me the truth. You *did* write the speech that Mrs. Beebe delivered at the dinner?

> [LEONARD *is unable to answer.*]

Didn't you?

> [*Still* LEONARD *cannot reply.*]

Beebe, this is a very serious matter. Am I to understand that—you have been deceiving us?

LEONARD [*in a whisper*]. It—wasn't exactly that way. The way it came up——

KINCAID [*insisting*]. Did you or did you not—write that speech?

LEONARD [*after a pause, in a voice hardly audible*]. No, sir.

KINCAID. Your—wife—did it all?

[LEONARD *nods*.]

Great Scott!

[*In undertone*.]

Beebe!

[*After slight pause*.]

LEONARD. Yes, sir?

KINCAID. This is regrettable, but my duty is clear. From the beginning it was that fresh little speech—perhaps I should say the spirit of fellowship—behind it, that interested me. Now I'll admit that you've been very helpful since you came into this office, but my organization must be made up of men of initiative. And for one of my personal staff to be in any sense—well—[*he fishes for the word*] moulded or controlled by—his wife— [*He pauses*.] I can't look upon that with much favor.

LEONARD. But, honestly——

KINCAID. And the fact that you have deceived me— in this matter, must also be taken into consideration. [*There is a pause*.] Beginning to-morrow, you will resume your former position at the old salary.

LEONARD. But, Mr. Kincaid——

KINCAID. That is final, Beebe. [*He goes into his office*.]

[LEONARD, *utterly crushed, takes a despairing look around the office and then drops into a chair. He lifts a few papers listlessly and puts them down again. He is staring into space as* MISS FLETCHER *re-enters*.]

MISS FLETCHER [*breezily*]. Anything more before lunch, Mr. Beebe?

LEONARD [*after a pause*]. Huh?

MISS FLETCHER. I'm going to lunch now, if you don't need me.

LEONARD. No. Yes. It's all right. I—don't need you.

MISS FLETCHER. Isn't anything the matter, is there?

LEONARD. No.

MISS FLETCHER. I'll be back about three. I just want a soda. [*She goes out*.]

[LEONARD *again takes stock of his surroundings; straightens himself in the chair; tries for a minute to be the old* LEONARD, *but it doesn't work. He is again a beaten man when* ELSIE *re-enters*.]

ELSIE [*brightly*].   Ready yet, dear?

LEONARD [*speaking with difficulty*].   Ah—what?

ELSIE.   Ready for lunch?

LEONARD.   Not—right now.

ELSIE [*alarmed*].   Leonard, what's the matter?

LEONARD.   Nothing—that—you can help.

ELSIE [*anxiously coming to him*].   Leonard!   Look at me!

[*He does so, with considerable difficulty.*]
Something has happened!   What is it?

LEONARD.   I'm . . . not his secretary . . . any longer. I'm going back to the old job.

ELSIE.   Leonard!   Not really!

LEONARD.   He—just this minute—this—none of this is my office any more. [*He drags himself up from the chair.*]   I'm going to be a—clerk again.

ELSIE.   But—but—Leonard, what did you do?   What happened?

LEONARD.   He just—[*he takes a moment; flares up for a second*] it was Chester's fault!

ELSIE.   Chester's?

LEONARD.   No, I—guess it wasn't, but—Tom Baker, he came in and began talking—and then in—some way— it came out about the—speech—*you* know——

ELSIE [*hanging on his words*].   Oh!

LEONARD.   And then—before I knew it—Kincaid was standing there, and—he heard it—and—oh, I don't know——

ELSIE.   Oh, Leonard!

LEONARD.   Oh, Elsie!

ELSIE.   Don't *you* care, dear!   You know that I'm standing beside you, don't you?

LEONARD.   Yes.   Beside a clerk.   Kincaid was right. That's all I am.   Even if I had gone right up the ladder— and everybody thought I was a big success, I'd know they were all being fooled.   That underneath it all I'd still be just—an—ordinary every-day clerk.

ELSIE.   Leonard, you mustn't say that.   I'm sure you'll get the job back again.   Now, you are not to worry.

LEONARD.   Not worry?   When he's just——

ELSIE. No! Let me talk to Mr. Kincaid and maybe he'll change his mind.

LEONARD. No—no—you mustn't!

ELSIE. But he might. You can't lose anything by it, Leonard! Now, you wait right here, while I go in and——

[KINCAID *re-enters*.]

KINCAID. Oh! [*He makes a movement as though to turn back*.]

ELSIE [*calm and self-possessed*]. Please don't go, Mr. Kincaid! I was just coming in to talk to you.

KINCAID. Indeed!

ELSIE. You see, Leonard has just told me—what's happened.

LEONARD. Elsie! Mr. Kincaid, she—she doesn't mean to—she doesn't understand—she's just a woman——

ELSIE. Leonard, would you mind waiting out there?— [*points to the outer office*] while Mr. Kincaid and I have a talk?

LEONARD. Well, I——

ELSIE. It'll only be a minute—then you can come back.

LEONARD. Well—oh—yes! [*He makes a departure, somehow.*]

ELSIE. Won't you sit down, Mr. Kincaid?

KINCAID. Mrs. Beebe, I assure you that any discussion would be quite in vain.

ELSIE. I'll only ask you a few questions and—if you can answer them satisfactorily, why, that'll end it!

KINCAID. Satisfactorily? Questions about what?

ELSIE. Just about Leonard—and me.

KINCAID. This is very extraordinary, Mrs. Beebe. I am not required to——

ELSIE. Now, in the first place, you've demoted Leonard because I—well—because I helped him a little bit.

KINCAID. Mrs. Beebe, I pride myself on being something of a judge of men, and—my experience has shown that the man who would be likely to require—ah—such assistance as you gave your husband—

[*She starts to speak; he interposes quickly.*]

even on this one occasion—is not the kind of man whom it is wise to advance to an executive position.

ELSIE. But, Mr. Kincaid, if a wife sees a chance to help her husband, don't you think he'd want her to do it?

KINCAID. Mrs. Beebe, it is one of my characteristics to act promptly and with decision. I have never deviated from that custom and my mind is made up so far as your husband is concerned. He is not the man I thought him and he must return to his original position. And now you will pardon me—there are other matters that I must attend to. [*Turns to go.*]

ELSIE. But, Mr. Kincaid——

[MRS. KINCAID *arrives.*]

MRS. KINCAID. Oh, hello, dear!

KINCAID. Ah, Myrtle!

MRS. KINCAID. And Mrs. Beebe! How do you do?

ELSIE. How do you do? Mr. Kincaid—would you mind repeating to Mrs. Kincaid what you've just been saying to me?

KINCAID. What's that? I'm afraid I have some important work that——

MRS. KINCAID. Just a second, Jack!

KINCAID. Really, Myrtle!

MRS. KINCAID. What is it, Mrs. Beebe?

ELSIE. Mr. Kincaid thinks that if a husband is helped in business by—his wife—that he won't ever amount to anything.

MRS. KINCAID [*mildly yet terribly*]. What!

ELSIE. He's made Leonard a clerk again, on account of the speech.

MRS. KINCAID. Really!

KINCAID. Myrtle, I can't stay here and——

[HENRICI *re-enters.*]

HENRICI. Oh, pardon me! How are you, Mrs. Kincaid?

MRS. KINCAID. How do you do, Mr. Henrici?

HENRICI. There's a man here from the *Piano World*. Have you made up your mind yet about Fernandez?

ELSIE [*uneasily aware that she doesn't belong*]. I think perhaps I'd better . . .

HENRICI [*to* ELSIE ; *thinking he is driving her away*]. Oh, no, no! I'll just be a second. [*To* KINCAID.] I thought perhaps you—might have got the report you were expecting.

[KINCAID, *fencing for a moment's time, observes his wife closely out of the corner of his eye.*]

KINCAID. Well, ah, I haven't quite—if you'll ask him to wait ten minutes——

HENRICI [*looks at watch*]. I'm afraid that'll be too late!

MRS. KINCAID. Oh, while I think of it, dear, I forgot to order that book I wanted—will you do it? Pardon me for interrupting.

[*This last is to both* KINCAID *and* HENRICI.]

HENRICI [*mumbling it*]. Oh, of course.

KINCAID [*with a great show of generosity*]. Why, certainly, my dear. I guess there's no use waiting any further. [*To* HENRICI.] We'll go ahead with the appointment of Fernandez.

HENRICI. I understand. Then I can get ready to ship?

KINCAID [*with great authority*]. Everything is settled.

HENRICI. I'll get right after it! Good day, Mrs. Kincaid.

MRS. KINCAID. Good-by, Mr. Henrici.

[HENRICI, *with a nod to* ELSIE, *goes out.*]

KINCAID [*pompously*]. Well, I'm glad that's off my mind. [*Starts for the door.*]

MRS. KINCAID. Now, Jack—to resume.

KINCAID. What?

MRS. KINCAID. To resume!

KINCAID. We can talk about that later!

MRS. KINCAID. No! Jack!

[*He stops.*]

You've demoted Mr. Beebe because you've learned it was *Mrs.* Beebe's speech?

KINCAID. I certainly have. Have you known it all the time?

MRS. KINCAID. In a way—yes.

KINCAID. Oh, Myrtle—suppose you step in the office with me—there are several things I'd like to talk over!

MRS. KINCAID. You mean about the appointment of Mr. Fernandez?

KINCAID. Myrtle!!!

MRS. KINCAID.   It's all right, dear.   Mrs. Beebe understands.

KINCAID.   How's that?

ELSIE.   Oh, yes.   You see, I've known about Mr. Fernandez all along.

KINCAID.   Is that so?

ELSIE.   So when Mrs. Kincaid said she'd forgotten a book I knew that Mr. Fernandez was—was all right! Just as when she forgot her bag at our house, and you invited Leonard to the banquet, I thought perhaps it was a signal.

KINCAID [*trying to be quite dignified and not succeeding at it*].   Well, this is all quite—beside the point——

MRS. KINCAID [*enjoying herself*].   I should say, Jack, that it were very much *to* the point.

ELSIE.   Oh, I didn't mean to let on that I knew, Mr. Kincaid.   I hoped I could get you to reinstate Leonard without it!

KINCAID.   I—I do not admit that this particularly alters the situation, Mrs. Beebe.   It so happens that Mrs. Kincaid is—ah—rather a good judge of men and women. I sometimes use—her judgment—merely to—ah—supplement my own—you understand.   But ours is—a peculiar case.

ELSIE.   Oh, so's ours!   Oh, Mr. Kincaid, if you only knew it—why, nearly all the men you meet are just like you and Leonard!   They don't let you know it—and I suppose sometimes they don't really know it themselves—always—but somewhere in back there's somebody—a wife or some one—who's helping them all the time—either giving them encouragement—or—perhaps doing real things like Mrs. Kincaid.   Nearly every man that ever got any place, Mr. Kincaid, has been married, and that couldn't be just a coincidence!

KINCAID [*after a slight pause*].   Ah—what do you think of all this, Myrtle?

[CHESTER *enters. *MRS. KINCAID* is about to speak when she sees him, and changes her plan.*]

MRS. KINCAID.   Suppose we have Mr. Beebe come in. I'm sure things could be arranged.

CHESTER.   Oh—excuse me.   [*Takes a quick glance at*

the stenographer's desk; addresses KINCAID.] Ah—you don't happen to know if Miss Fletcher filled out that slip, do you?

KINCAID. If she did what?

CHESTER [*giving him a look*]. Never mind. [*Turns and opens the door again.*]

MRS. KINCAID. Oh, Mr. Mullin!

CHESTER [*stopping*]. Yes.

MRS. KINCAID. If Mr. Beebe is out there, ask him to step in.

CHESTER. Yes, ma'am. [*He thinks he sees the slip on* MISS FLETCHER'S *desk; takes a step toward it.*]

KINCAID [*annoyed*]. What are you looking for?

CHESTER. Nothing! It doesn't matter, anyhow. It's only for the efficiency department. [*He goes out.*]

ELSIE [*taking it for granted that everything is settled*]. Oh, I'm so grateful, Mrs. Kincaid!

KINCAID. Now, just a minute. I'm not bound to abide by Mrs. Kincaid's decisions.

ELSIE. No, but you always do.

KINCAID. On the contrary, I do not—and in this case——

MRS. KINCAID. In this case, dear, Mrs. Beebe might become very valuable to you. And now that Mr. Sheridan has quit——

KINCAID. And *why* did he quit? Only because you made it so—so——

MRS. KINCAID. Oh, he never would have developed, darling. You would have seen. [*To* ELSIE.] Some one Mr. Kincaid picked out while I was away.

ELSIE. Oh!

MRS. KINCAID. You see, my husband may make an error once in a while, but he's always big enough to acknowledge it.

[LEONARD *enters.*]

Aren't you, dear?

KINCAID. Huh?

MRS. KINCAID [*pointedly, as though instructing him to go to* LEONARD]. *Aren't* you, dear?

KINCAID [*looks again at the two women, then goes to* LEONARD]. Beebe!

LEONARD [*not meeting his eye*].   Yes, sir!

KINCAID.   I have felt from the beginning that you were a valuable man.

LEONARD.   Huh!

KINCAID.   This was all just a—test.

LEONARD.   Well—er—well—er—I don't—   [*Looks toward* ELSIE.]

KINCAID.   I have always intended that the job in here should be yours.

LEONARD.   Yes, sir, but—I'm sure that I—   [*To* KINCAID.] Excuse me!   Elsie!

ELSIE [*in a quick whisper to him*].   It's all right!

MRS. KINCAID.   You'll get Sheridan's salary.

KINCAID.   Myrtle!

ELSIE.   Oh, thank you, Mr. Kincaid.

KINCAID.   Ah—suppose you come into my office and talk it over?

LEONARD.   Er—yes. [*Throws* ELSIE *a triumphant look*.]

KINCAID.   There are several things I want to discuss with you.   [KINCAID *goes into his office*.]

LEONARD [*stepping to* ELSIE'S *side*].   The whole thing was a test.

ELSIE.   Yes, dear!

LEONARD [*roguishly*].   You were mixed up in this some way.

ELSIE.   No, I wasn't.

LEONARD.   Oh, yes, you were.   But seriously, he's a wonderful man.

KINCAID [*returning*].   Are you coming, Beebe?

LEONARD.   Yes, sir.   Have a cigar!

KINCAID.   Just wait in there—I'll only be a minute!   [LEONARD *enters the sanctum*.]

Mrs. Beebe.

ELSIE.   Yes, sir?

KINCAID.   I sincerely hope that any information—about things—[*as he sees* MRS. KINCAID'S *eyes on him, draws* ELSIE *aside a bit and lowers tone*] that you may have picked up, will not go any further?

ELSIE.   Oh, no, indeed.

KINCAID.   Thank you.

ELSIE. Not unless——

KINCAID [*quickly*]. I understand! [*He goes.*]

[ELSIE *and* MRS. KINCAID *are left alone.*]

MRS. KINCAID. Now I must be going—Mrs. Fernandez is waiting for me. We've been shopping together all morning—some clothes for South America. You were quite right about her.

ELSIE. I thought you'd like her.

MRS. KINCAID. Yes, I think Mr. Fernandez will be very successful down there. She's *such* an able woman! Won't you have lunch with us?

ELSIE. I can't to-day. I'm lunching with Leonard.

MRS. KINCAID. Very well. I'll see you Tuesday, as usual.

[*They shake hands.*]

[ELSIE *watches her go, then turns to enter* KINCAID'S *office. As she nears the door the warning red light flashes on—*KINCAID *is in conference, and must not be disturbed.* ELSIE *smiles, looks around the office, and drops into a chair to wait for her lord and master.*]

THE CURTAIN FALLS

TOPICS FOR DISCUSSION

WHY MARRY?

1. Has the playwright any doctrine concerning marriage to preach? Does he state a problem or is he simply concerned with painting a picture of life?

2. Which of the characters in *Why Marry?* give the impression of being gentlemen and gentlewomen? How does the author establish the distinction between them and the rest? Is it done by the stage descriptions or by what the characters do and say and leave undone and unsaid?

3. Why does it require more skill to create the proper tone in social comedy in America than in France or England? What is there in the terms used, the names and titles in European countries that acts as an aid to the dramatist in quickly establishing the social values?

4. Compare the criticism of moral standards in *Why Marry?* and in *Nice People*. In which play is the method more artistic? How have the changes in life in America between 1917 and 1921 affected both the point of view of a dramatist in dealing with such questions and the kind of appeal that may be expected from an audience?

5. How is the element of suspense maintained in *Why Marry?* Is the dénouement to be looked upon as a concession to the public opinion that the leading characters have defied, or is it to be justified as a dramatic device to bring the motive of the play to a logical conclusion? (See Mr. Williams's own statement concerning this point.)

THE EMPEROR JONES

1. How does *The Emperor Jones* differ in structure from the usual play?

2. Why is monologue the natural method of dramatic expression in a play with this motive?

3. How does the beating of the tom-tom aid in the establishment of a mood of terror? Does this mood disarm in any way the critical faculties of the audience? If it does, how does this help in the creation of the supernatural effect?

4. Why could not the climax of this play be reached in a briefer time? What part does the physical fatigue play in the mental and spiritual development of Jones?

5. In which of the scenes does Jones most perfectly identify himself with the action of the supernatural characters?

6. What have you to say concerning the suggestion that the climax would have been more effective if Jones had died through an excess of fear rather than through the silver bullet? What change would have to be made to fit such a theory?

NICE PEOPLE

1. What is the dramatic purpose in the first scene? Is it merely background or are the characters distinguished by what they say and do?

2. Is the dissipation represented for satiric purposes only, or does it play an integral part in the drama? What is the limit of drunkenness as a dramatic motive? How far should it be represented on the stage? Does the author make use of it legitimately?

3. Is the attitude of Mr. Gloucester and Mrs. Rainsford consistent in the first and in the second act? How do the other characters reveal themselves in their attitude toward Theodora?

4. What is the real cause of the sudden determination on Theodora's part not to marry Wilbur?

5. Is the conclusion logical or illogical? Would the play have been more true to actual life if Theodora had gone back to the life she knew best? Could there have been an effective dramatic ending if she had done this?

THE HERO

1. How does the author prepare the audience for the final tragedy? When is the first mention of a camp-fire in the play? Is it brought in naturally?

2. How does the playwright introduce the main motive of the play? What is it?

3. Would Oswald's reaction to the situation have been the same if there had been no war, but if he had been absent for a like period and had had some other sobering experience?

4. Compare the attitude of Oswald toward Hester with that of Robert Mayo to his sister-in-law in Eugene O'Neill's *Beyond the Horizon*, and contrast both with a similar relation between Paolo and Francesca in George H. Boker's *Francesca da Rimini* (1855). What is the difference in the modern way of approaching such a situation from that employed in the romantic play of 1855?

5. Explain how the power of circumstances determines:
   (*a*) Andrew's attitude toward Oswald's continued presence in the house.
   (*b*) Hester's rebellion against her lot in life.
   (*c*) Oswald's determination to steal the money.

6. Contrast the different attitudes Oswald takes to the several forms of temptation he encounters.

7. What function does Sarah Lane play in the drama? Is she merely comic relief? (Notice the way in which she enters in the third act when the emotion would otherwise become too tense.) Or does her character show in any way in either of her sons? And does her presence in the house affect the plot in any way?

8. Study the absolute reality of the last scene, the manner in which the events, rapid and tragic, fit into place, and the art with which the dramatist clears the stage so that husband and wife will be left alone together.

9. Does the tragedy leave one with a sense of exaltation, with a feeling that the death of Oswald has made

life better for Hester and Andrew? Note that
Hester has preserved Andrew's illusions with regard to Oswald.

TO THE LADIES!

1. Are the two leading characters consistently drawn?
2. Does Elsie Beebe wish to preserve her illusions concerning her husband? Is it indicated that she
   sees through him as completely as the audience
   does?
3. What elements in the play secure and hold the sympathy of the reader?
4. Why is this play essentially more true to life and more
   worth creating than a novel or play like *Main
   Street?*
5. What is the fallacy in the critical attitude which
   presumes that an unpleasant ending to a play is
   necessarily a strong ending or essentially more
   dramatic than a happy ending?
6. How does this play illustrate the difference between
   comedy, which is based upon character delineation,
   and farce, which is based upon mere mechanical
   situation? Where does it make use of the farcical
   treatment and how is it brought back to real
   comedy?

COLLECTIONS OF AMERICAN PLAYS

IN THE ORDER OF PUBLICATION

REPRESENTATIVE AMERICAN PLAYS. Edited by Arthur Hobson Quinn. The Century Company, 1917. Contains Godfrey's *Prince of Parthia;* Tyler's *The Contrast;* Dunlap's *André;* Barker's *Superstition; Charles the Second*, by Payne and Irving; Smith's *The Triumph at Plattsburg;* Custis's *Pocahontas, or the Settlers of Virginia;* Bird's *The Broker of Bogota;* Willis's *Tortesa the Usurer;* Mrs. Mowatt's *Fashion;* Boker's *Francesca da Rimini;* Mrs. Howe's *Leonora, or the World's Own;* Boucicault's *The Octoroon, or Life in Louisiana; Rip Van Winkle* (as played by Joseph Jefferson); Steele MacKaye's *Hazel Kirke;* Howard's *Shenandoah;* Gillette's *Secret Service; Madame Butterfly*, by Belasco and Long; Fitch's *Her Great Match;* Mitchell's *The New York Idea;* Thomas's *The Witching Hour;* Moody's *The Faith Healer;* Percy Mackaye's *The Scarecrow;* Sheldon's *The Boss;* Miss Crothers's *He and She*.

REPRESENTATIVE PLAYS BY AMERICAN DRAMATISTS. Edited by Montrose J. Moses. E. P. Dutton & Company. Vol. I (1918) contains Godfrey's *Prince of Parthia;* Rogers's *Ponteach;* Mrs. Warren's *The Group;* Brackenridge's *Battle of Bunker Hill;* Leacock's *The Fall of British Tyranny;* Low's *Politician Outwitted;* Tyler's *The Contrast;* Dunlap's *André;* Barker's *Indian Princess;* and Noah's *She Would Be a Soldier*. Vol. II not yet published. Vol. III (1921) contains Burke's *Rip Van Winkle;* Boker's *Francesca da Rimini;* Bunce's *Love in '76;* Mackaye's *Paul Kauvar;* Howard's *Shenandoah;* Thomas's *In Mizzoura;* Fitch's *The Moth and the Flame;* Mitchell's *New York Idea;* Walter's *Easiest Way;* and Belasco's *Return of Peter Grimm*.

REPRESENTATIVE ONE-ACT PLAYS BY AMERICAN AUTHORS.
Edited by Margaret G. Mayorga. Little, Brown &
Company, 1919. Contains twenty-four one-act
plays.

MODERN AMERICAN PLAYS. Edited by George Pierce
Baker. Harcourt, Brace & Howe, 1920. Contains
Thomas's *As a Man Thinks;* Belasco's *Return of
Peter Grimm;* Edward Sheldon's *Romance;* Ans-
pacher's *Unchastened Woman;* and Massey's *Plots
and Playwrights.*

LONGER PLAYS BY MODERN AUTHORS (American).
Edited by Helen L. Cohen. Harcourt & Brace,
1922. Contains Fitch's *Beau Brummel;* Thomas's
Copperhead; Kaufman and Connelly's *Dulcy;* and
Tarkington's *Intimate Strangers.*

See also for amateur and semiprofessional American
plays:

The Provincetown Plays. Volumes appear periodically,
containing the work of Eugene O'Neill, Susan
Glaspell, and others. Frank Shay. Six volumes now
issued (1916–18). *Plays of the Harvard Dramatic
Club.* Edited by George P. Baker. Two volumes
have appeared. Brentanos, 1918–19. *Wisconsin
Plays.* Edited by T. H. Dickinson. First and
Second Series. Huebsch, 1914–18. *Morningside
Plays.* Frank Shay, 1917. *The Grove Plays of the
Bohemian Club.* Edited by Porter Garnett. 3 vols.
San Francisco, 1918.